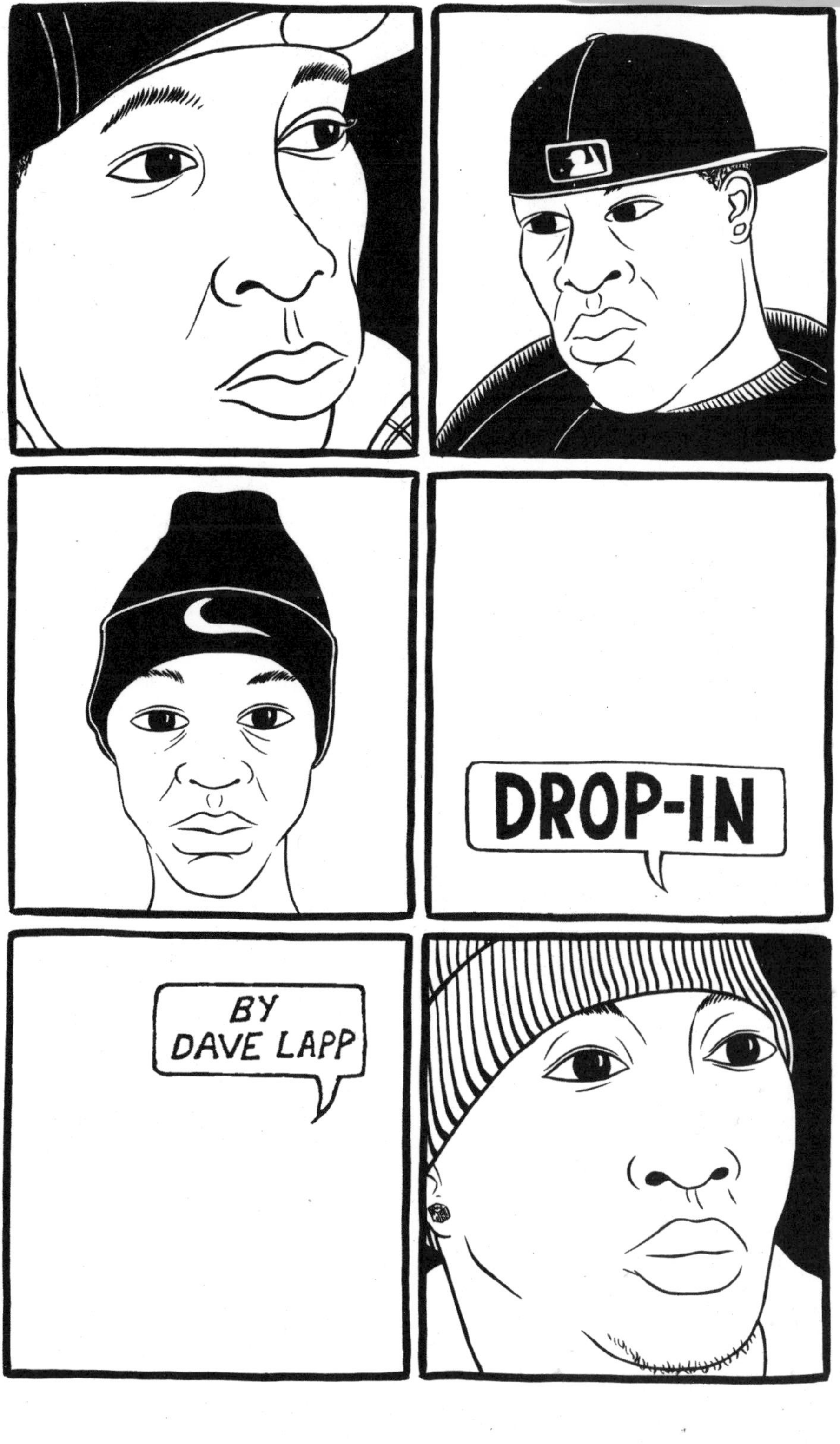
DROP-IN
BY
DAVE LAPP

Library and Archives Canada Cataloguing in Publication

Lapp, Dave, 1965-
        Drop-in / Dave Lapp.

ISBN 978-1-894994-33-0

     I. Title.

PN6733.L36D76 2008   741.5'971   C2008-905845-3

Dépot Legal, Bibliothèque nationale du Québec
Printed and bound in Canada by Gauvin Press.
Distributed by Litdistco: 1-800-591-6250

My many Thank Yous go out to Chester Brown, Joe Ollmann, Andy Brown,
Kerby Waud, Walter Dickinson, Harvey Fong, Fiona Smyth, Dave Howard,
Conan Tobias, Brian Burchell, Seanna Connell, Lola Rasminsky, my family,
and Lydia for putting up with such a kook!

conundrum press
PO Box 55003, CSP Fairmount, Montreal, Quebec, H2T 3E2, Canada
conpress@ican.net   www.conundrumpress.com

conundrum press acknowledges the financial assistance of the Canada Council for the Arts
toward our publishing program.

Canada Council   Conseil des Arts
for the Arts   du Canada

introduction

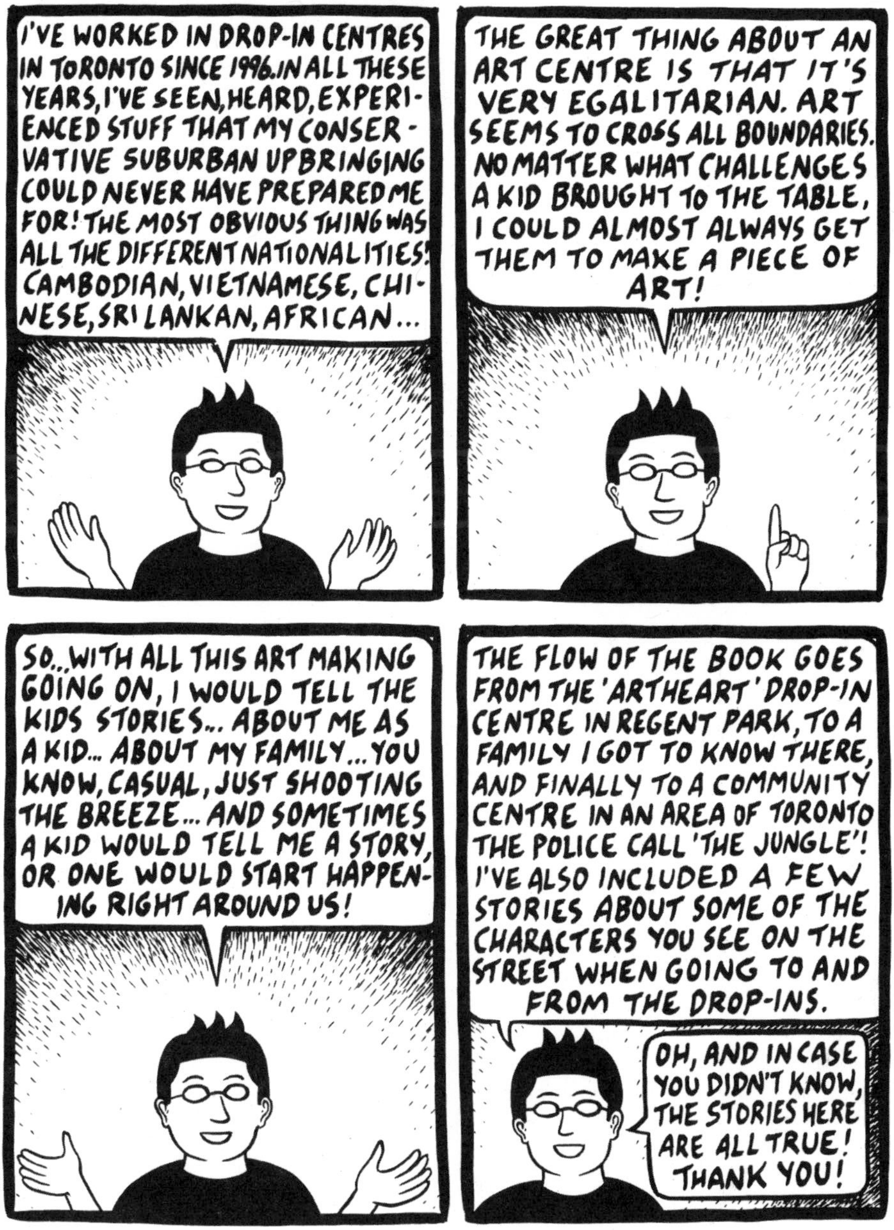

I'VE WORKED IN DROP-IN CENTRES IN TORONTO SINCE 1996. IN ALL THESE YEARS, I'VE SEEN, HEARD, EXPERIENCED STUFF THAT MY CONSERVATIVE SUBURBAN UPBRINGING COULD NEVER HAVE PREPARED ME FOR! THE MOST OBVIOUS THING WAS ALL THE DIFFERENT NATIONALITIES! CAMBODIAN, VIETNAMESE, CHINESE, SRI LANKAN, AFRICAN...
THE GREAT THING ABOUT AN ART CENTRE IS THAT IT'S VERY EGALITARIAN. ART SEEMS TO CROSS ALL BOUNDARIES. NO MATTER WHAT CHALLENGES A KID BROUGHT TO THE TABLE, I COULD ALMOST ALWAYS GET THEM TO MAKE A PIECE OF ART!
SO... WITH ALL THIS ART MAKING GOING ON, I WOULD TELL THE KIDS STORIES... ABOUT ME AS A KID... ABOUT MY FAMILY... YOU KNOW, CASUAL, JUST SHOOTING THE BREEZE... AND SOMETIMES A KID WOULD TELL ME A STORY, OR ONE WOULD START HAPPENING RIGHT AROUND US!
THE FLOW OF THE BOOK GOES FROM THE 'ARTHEART' DROP-IN CENTRE IN REGENT PARK, TO A FAMILY I GOT TO KNOW THERE, AND FINALLY TO A COMMUNITY CENTRE IN AN AREA OF TORONTO THE POLICE CALL 'THE JUNGLE'! I'VE ALSO INCLUDED A FEW STORIES ABOUT SOME OF THE CHARACTERS YOU SEE ON THE STREET WHEN GOING TO AND FROM THE DROP-INS.
OH, AND IN CASE YOU DIDN'T KNOW, THE STORIES HERE ARE ALL TRUE! THANK YOU!

whales

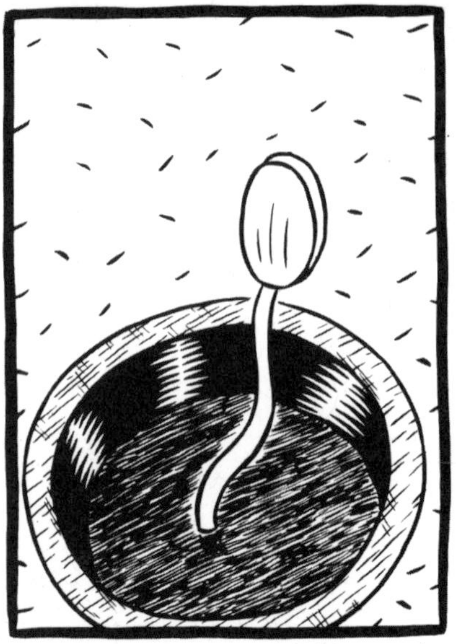

My first day back at the art centre. The kids won't be let in today, we're doing clean up. Looking down I see a little plant growing up from the sludge of the drain hole.

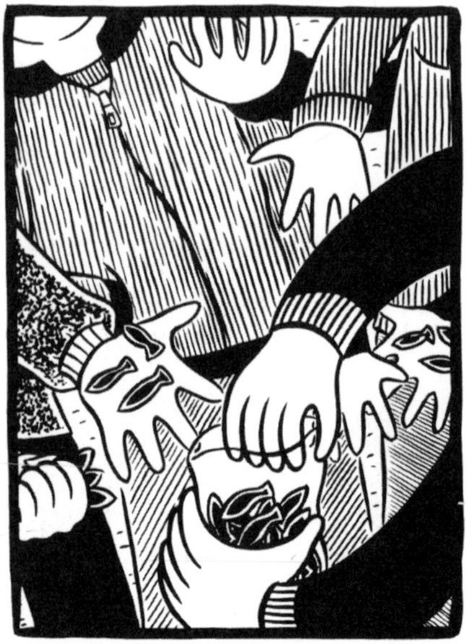

Up above there's a thumping, pounding, booming! I walk up the stairs and hand out little blue gummy whales to the waiting kids. Some of the whales end up in the snow.

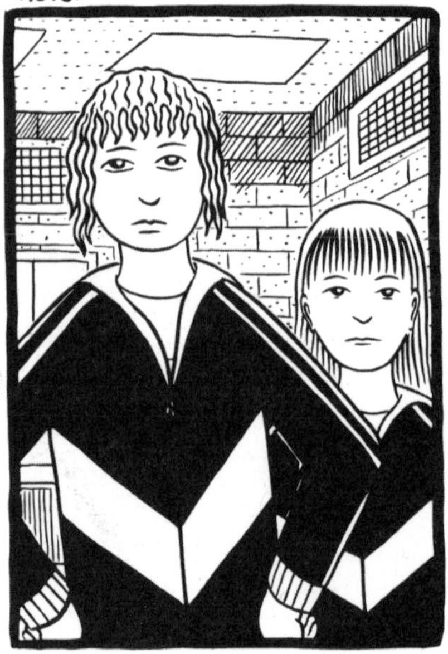

No kids are supposed to come in, but here are two little girls in matching jackets who are going to stay.

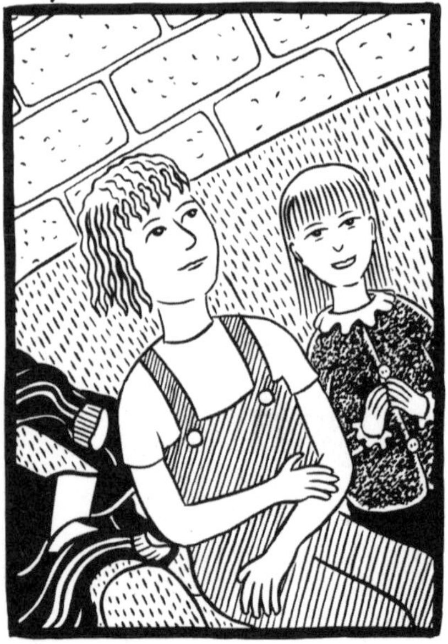

Deanna and Tania. Tania has two brothers, and three dads, and lives with her mom, and her brother, who is ten, tried to jump out of the school window.

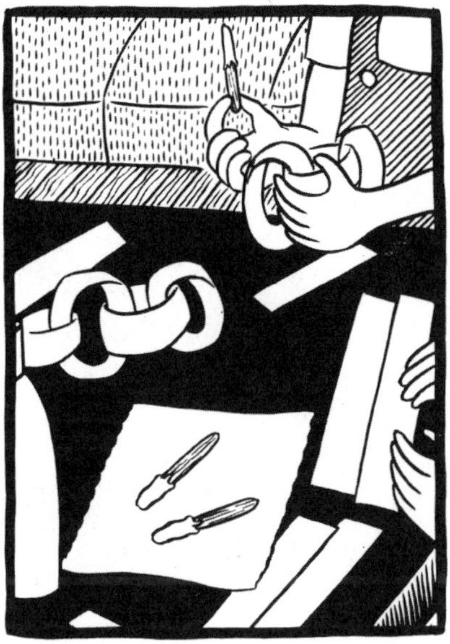

As we cut and paste, Tania tells me of the crazy lady who said 'Am I of this world? My stove is crusty.' We're making paper chains.

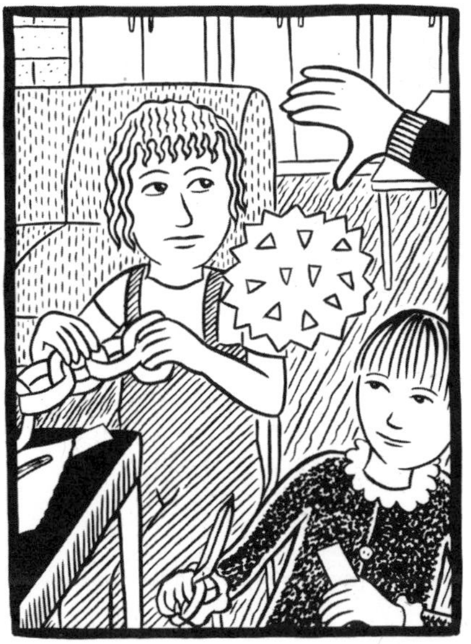

Tania says the crazy lady's kids were taken from her, and that she bangs on her door all hours of the day, and sometimes she gets followed by her. I drop my paper snowflake on Tania.

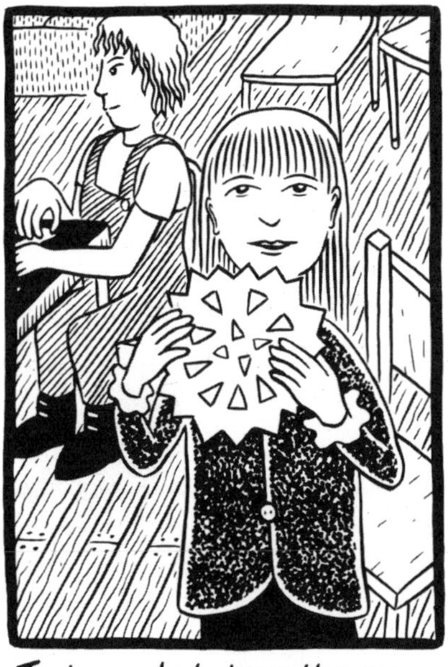

Tania wants to keep the snow-flake. She wants me to keep her story secret. I lock my lips and throw the key away.

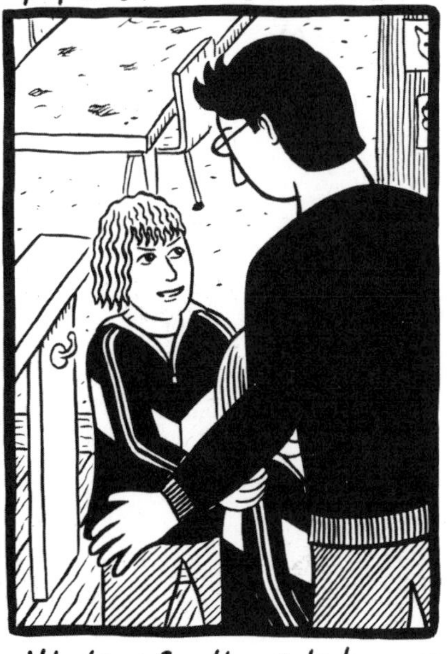

It's time for the girls to go and there's some commotion. Deanna is acting up and running around. Finally she pushes Tania into me saying 'Hug him! You want to hug him!'

path

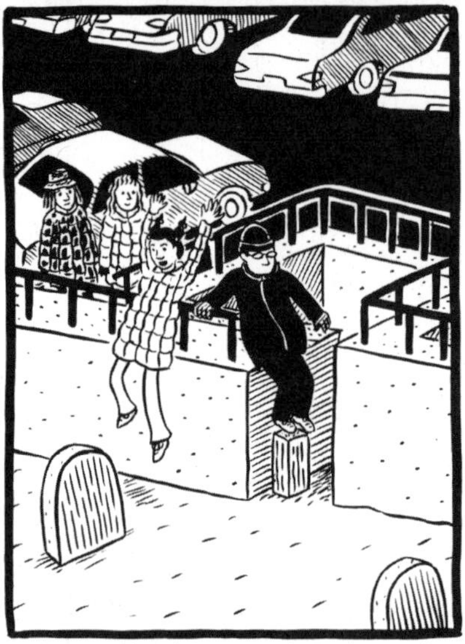

Me and the three girls take the short cut through the graveyard. Samantha says the gravestones look like chess pieces.

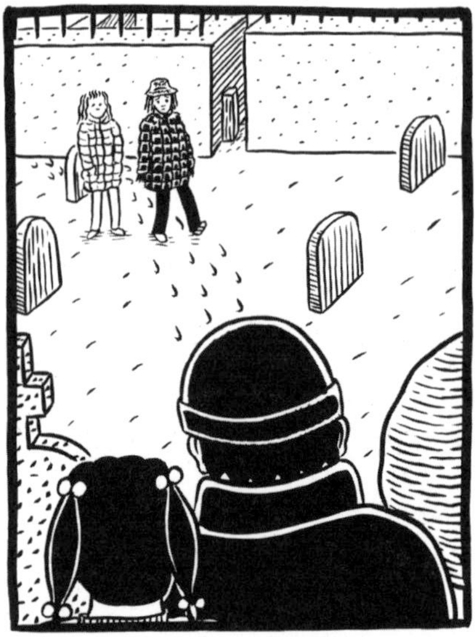

Ashley and Vanitie hang back by the wall... Vanitie is nervous about stepping on the graves. I tell her to follow the path in the snow and she'll be okay.

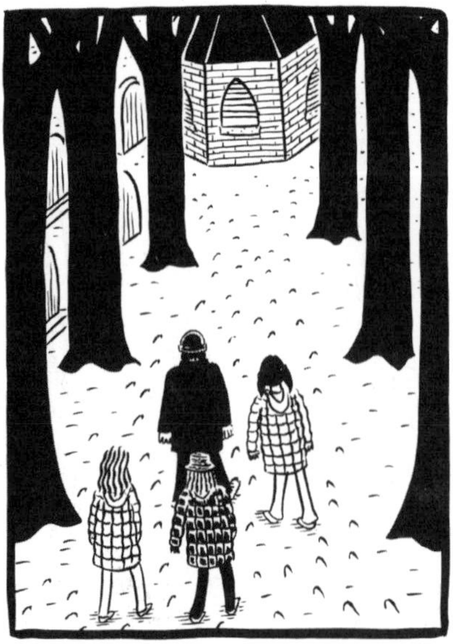

The path here is marked by trees on either side and we all feel safer here!

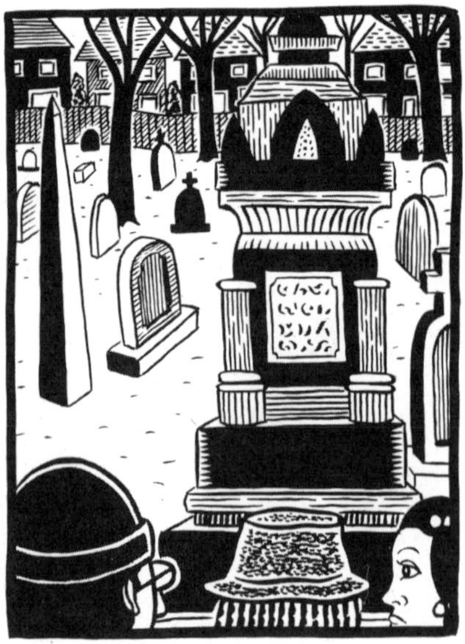

To our right is a huge monument. Vanitie says 'That guy must have been rich!' I tell her 'No, they buried a giant here!'

As we walk along we wonder why you shouldn't walk across graves... I offer it's because their spirit could jump into you...this prompts a discussion about heaven, hell and in between!

One of the girls wants to walk out among the graves. I tell her 'Okay, but if a ghost follows you home, don't blame me!... She stays with us...

Eventually we decide that people didn't walk over graves in the past because improperly dug graves could cave in, and you'd land on the dead body!

On the way out we feel better seeing an angel that we pretend is giving us the 'thumbs up'.

Today there's just two girls who're up ahead clawing, grabbing, and snarling at each other shouting 'Wolverine! Wolverine!'

This is our second time here and we decide to leave the 'safe' tree path and take the narrow path that leads right through the graves...

If the tombstone name isn't facing you, you're safe...if it is, you have to jump over...you can't walk on top of a body!

This path isn't as easy as we thought! We take many giant leaps!

We pause at the little stone angel who's missing a hand...

...I try to creep them out by saying maybe the stone hand is crawling around the graveyard somewhere!

Samantha says 'Maybe the hand has a bracelet with wings on it.'

Vanitie clutches my arm as we pass the long shadow of pine trees...we're almost out...

Today's our last visit to the graveyard and Vanitie won't be join-
ing us on the grave path...'I'm not
jumpin' over no graves today because of what Samantha said
about that baby!'

So we split up...Vanitie going down
the safe path between the trees,
Samantha and I go to walk between the graves...

We can see Vanitie on her path.
Samantha wants to hide on
her!

Samantha leaves the path to
hide between two huge tomb-
stones whispering 'C'mon Dave!
C'mon!'

I tell her 'We don't need to hide, Vanitie's way over there! She can't see us anyway.' I really don't want to get too close to those graves...

Vanitie was so afraid today... but didn't we just see her dancing with a skeleton in the classroom singing ♫What's your flavour? Tell me what's your flavour?♫

We don't want Vanitie to be too scared, so we hurry along the path jumping over graves...The corner tombstone almost fooled us!

Vanitie waits for us outside the cemetery gate...she wouldn't walk with us because 'Samantha said she heard a baby screaming last night and it might have been a ghost!'

sharing

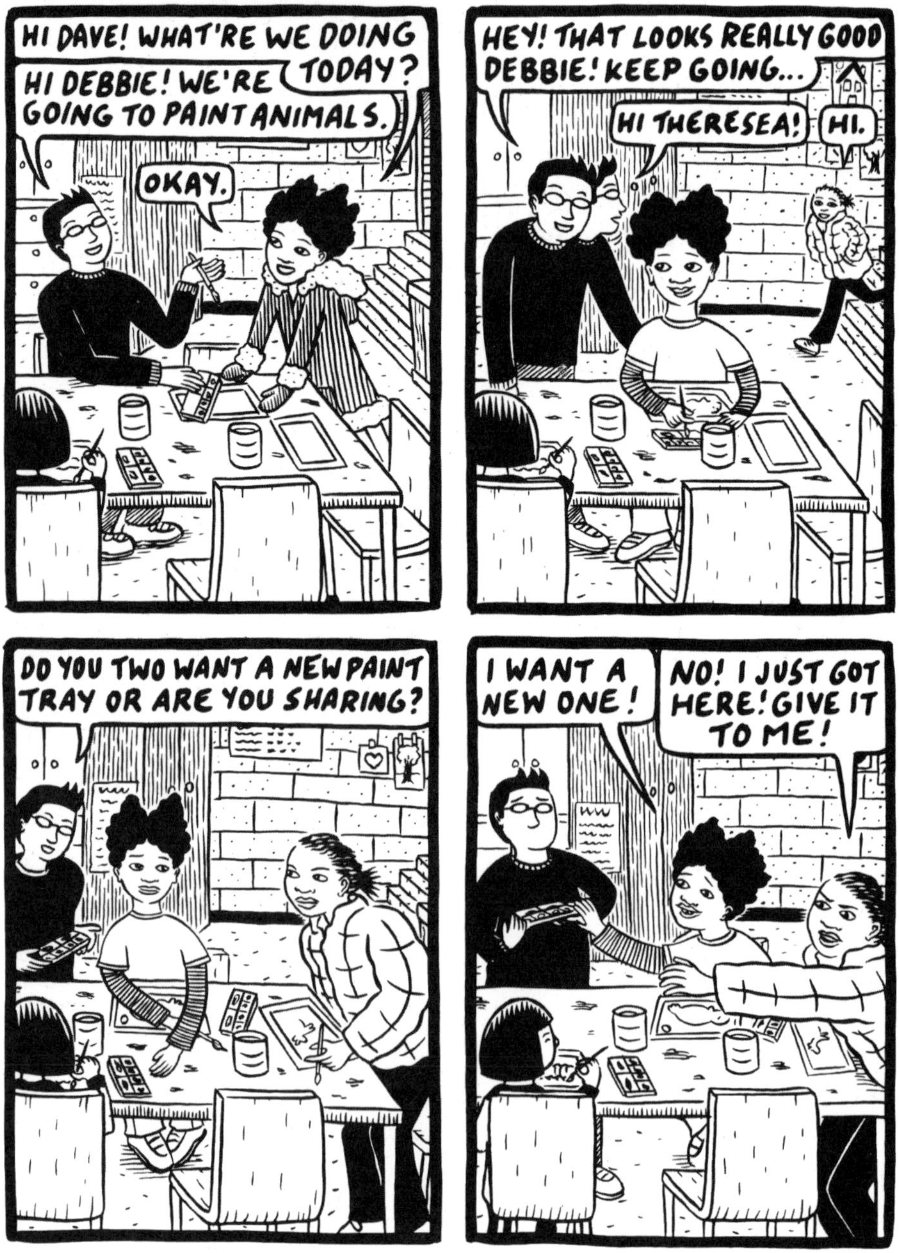
HI DAVE! WHAT'RE WE DOING TODAY?
HI DEBBIE! WE'RE GOING TO PAINT ANIMALS.
OKAY.
HEY! THAT LOOKS REALLY GOOD DEBBIE! KEEP GOING...
HI THERESEA!
HI.
DO YOU TWO WANT A NEW PAINT TRAY OR ARE YOU SHARING?
I WANT A NEW ONE!
NO! I JUST GOT HERE! GIVE IT TO ME!

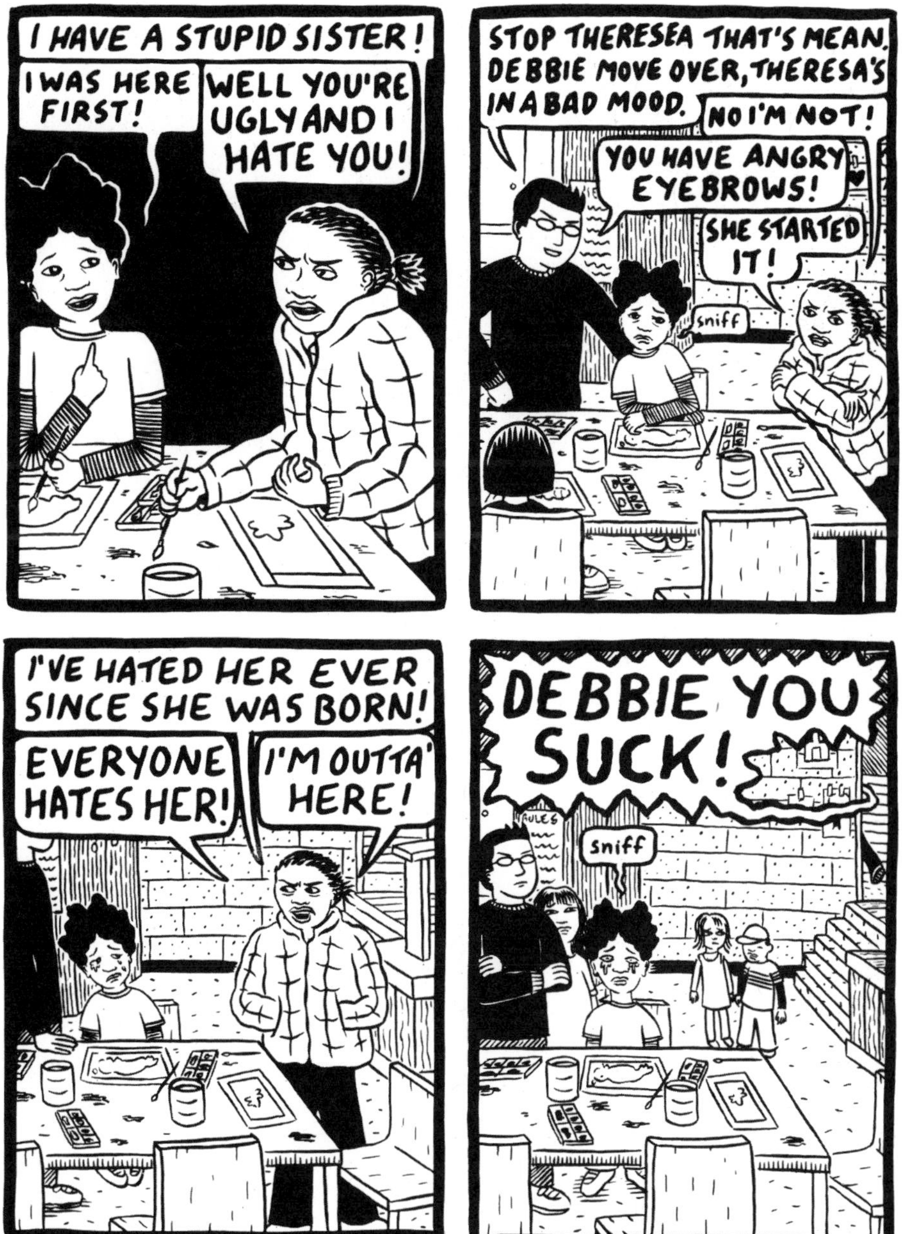
I HAVE A STUPID SISTER!
I WAS HERE FIRST!
WELL YOU'RE UGLY AND I HATE YOU!
STOP THERESEA THAT'S MEAN. DEBBIE MOVE OVER, THERESA'S IN A BAD MOOD.
NO I'M NOT!
YOU HAVE ANGRY EYEBROWS!
SHE STARTED IT!
sniff
I'VE HATED HER EVER SINCE SHE WAS BORN!
EVERYONE HATES HER!
I'M OUTTA' HERE!
DEBBIE YOU SUCK!
sniff

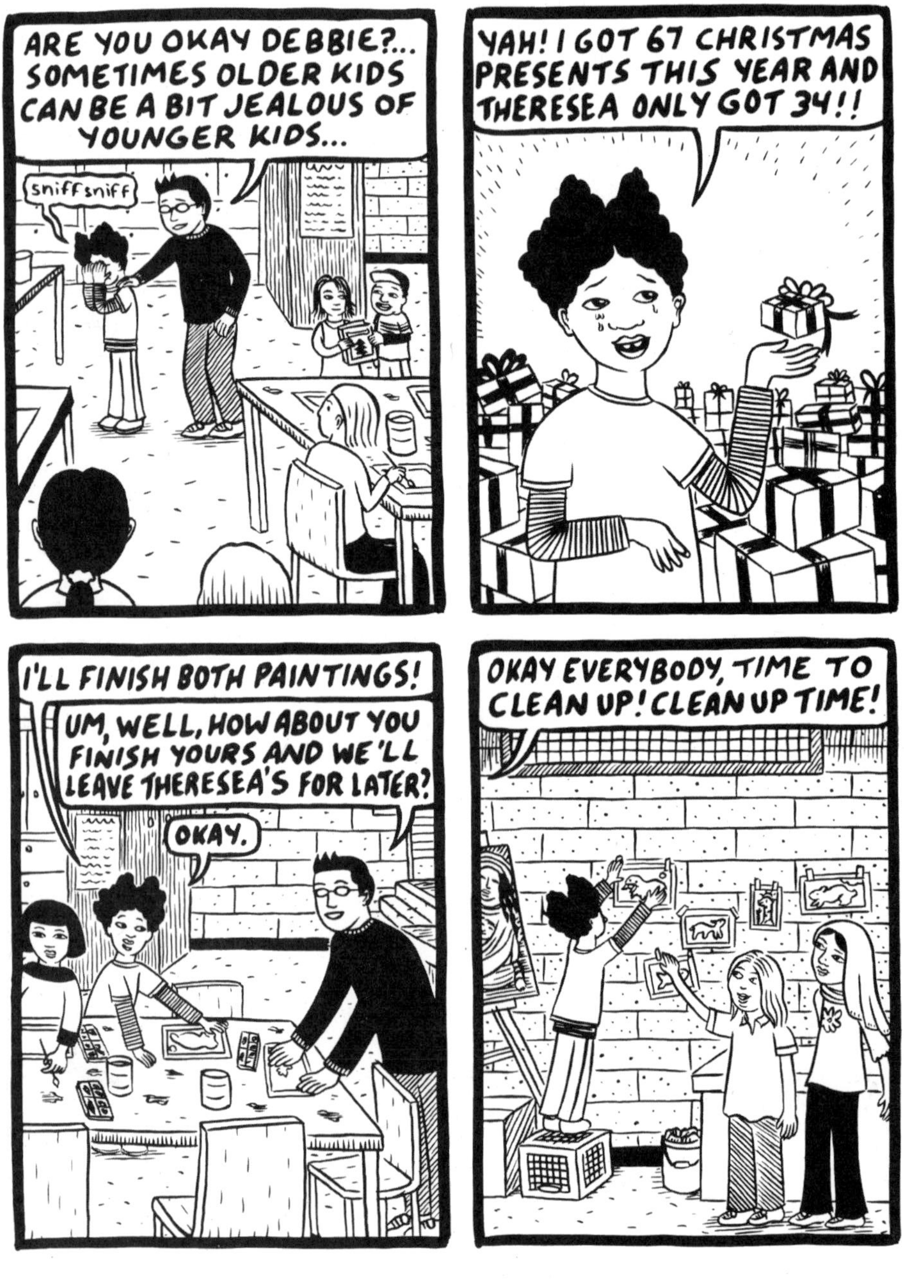
ARE YOU OKAY DEBBIE?... SOMETIMES OLDER KIDS CAN BE A BIT JEALOUS OF YOUNGER KIDS...
sniff sniff
YAH! I GOT 67 CHRISTMAS PRESENTS THIS YEAR AND THERESEA ONLY GOT 34!!
I'LL FINISH BOTH PAINTINGS!
UM, WELL, HOW ABOUT YOU FINISH YOURS AND WE'LL LEAVE THERESEA'S FOR LATER?
OKAY.
OKAY EVERYBODY, TIME TO CLEAN UP! CLEAN UP TIME!

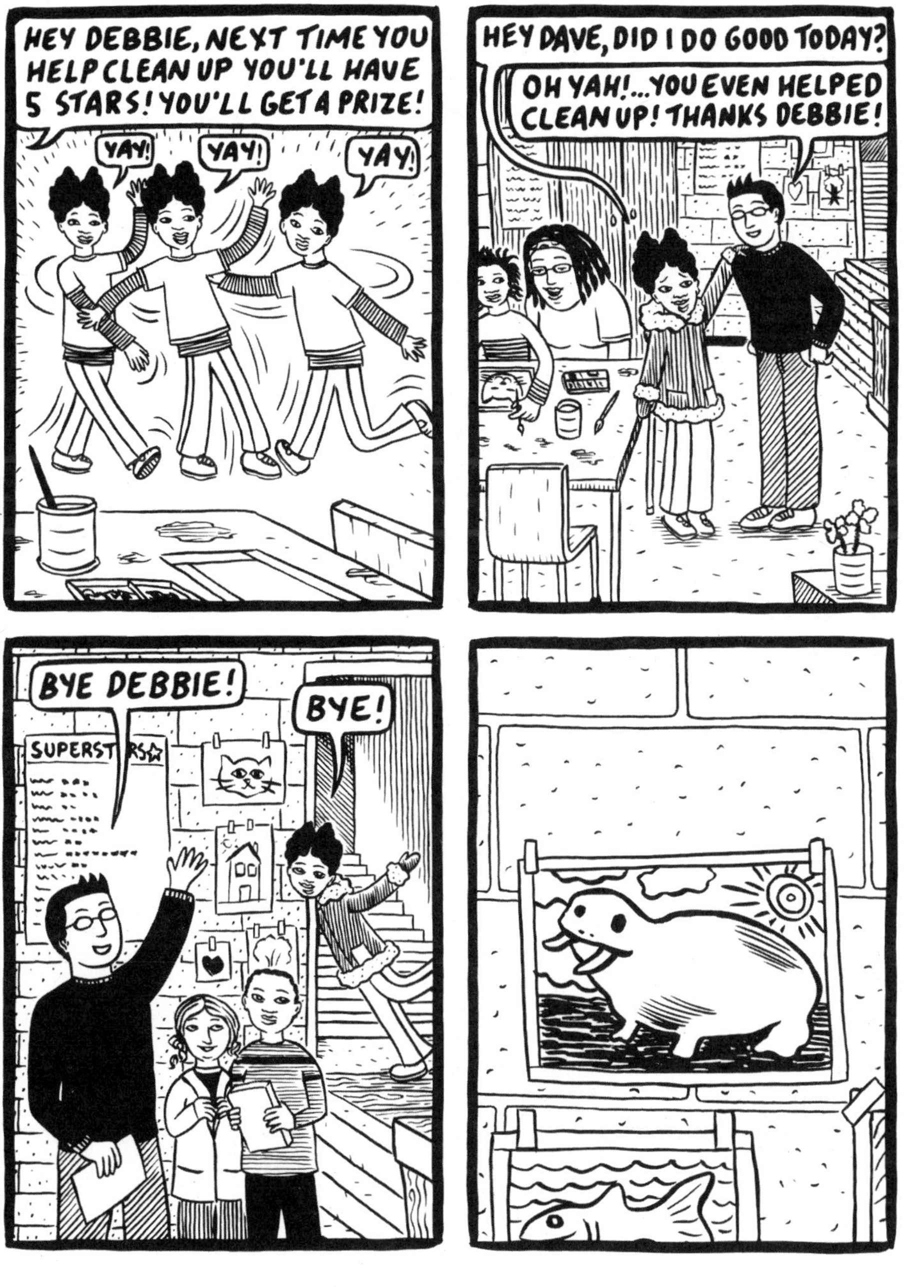
HEY DEBBIE, NEXT TIME YOU HELP CLEAN UP YOU'LL HAVE 5 STARS! YOU'LL GET A PRIZE!
YAY!
YAY!
YAY!
HEY DAVE, DID I DO GOOD TODAY?
OH YAH!...YOU EVEN HELPED CLEAN UP! THANKS DEBBIE!
BYE DEBBIE!
BYE!
SUPERST RS

dora

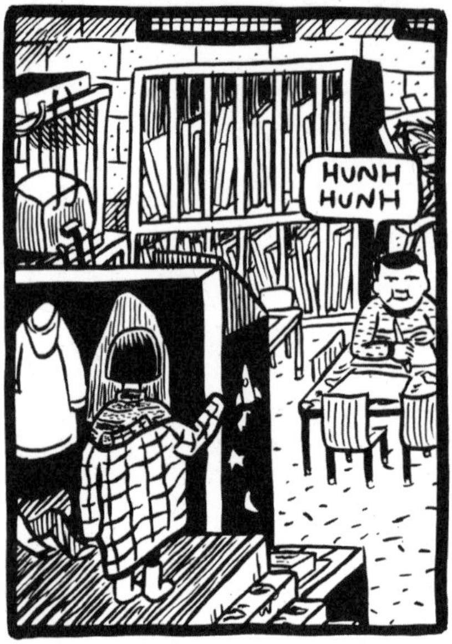
HUNH
HUNH

Henrietta had a bad day at the art centre, and this is how it started... (in her own words) ..."Forti is there looking at me and laughing.

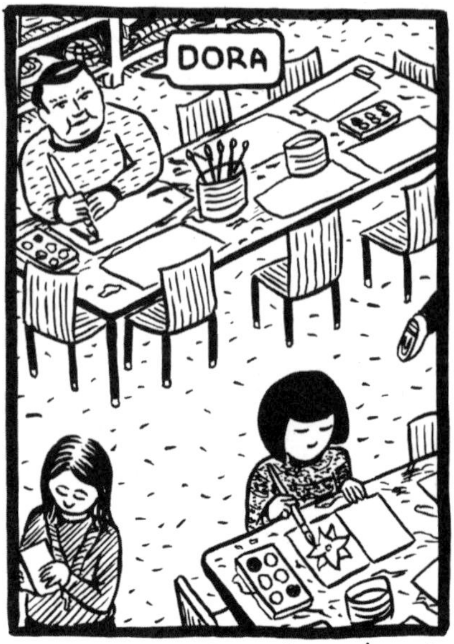
DORA

I went downstairs to paint cards for Paula's wedding...

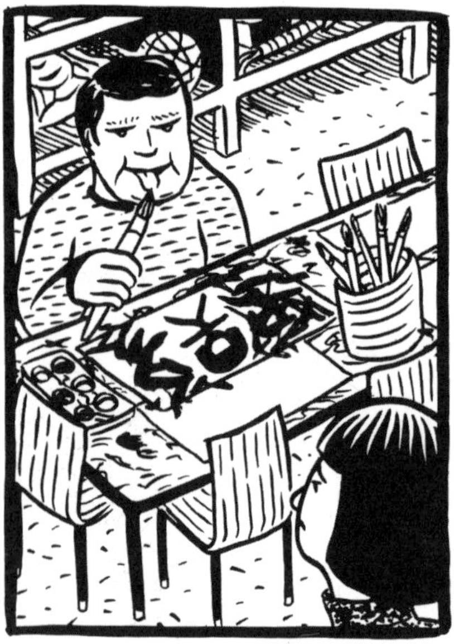

I look behind me and he licks on his paintbrush... that's disgusting! It gave me the goosebumps!

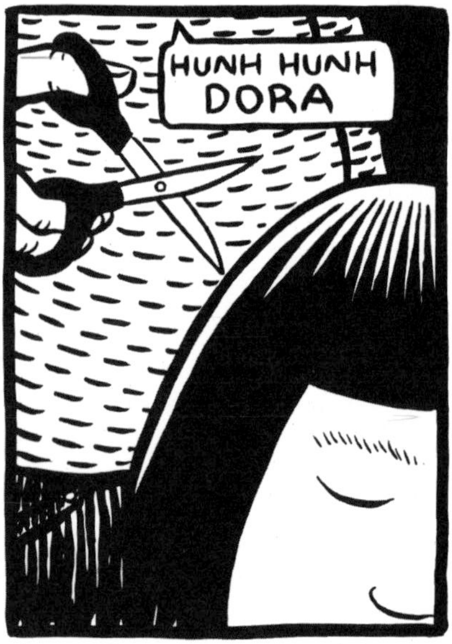
HUNH HUNH
DORA

I was doing my art when he snuck up behind me with a pair of scissors trying to cut off my hair because he thinks my hair is 'Dora the Explorer'!

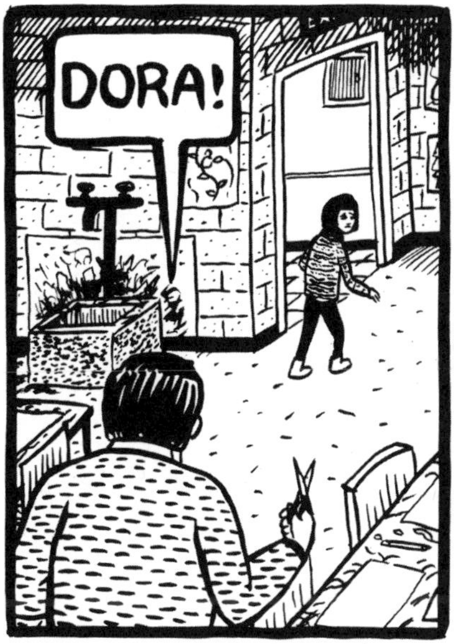
DORA!

I got up and went to the girls' wash-room so he wouldn't follow me there...

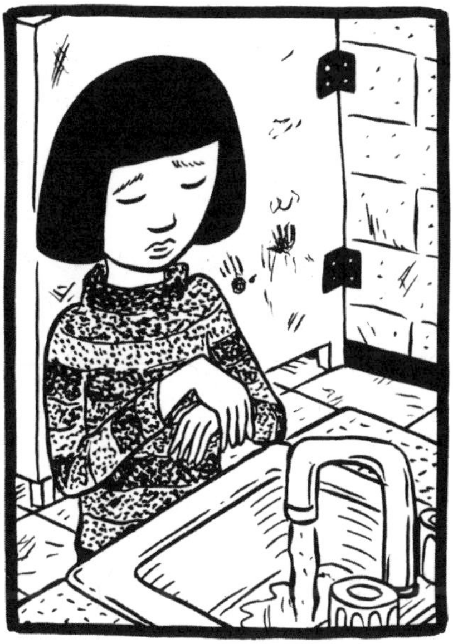

I had to, like, wait there, and I washed my hands because they got a bit dirty...

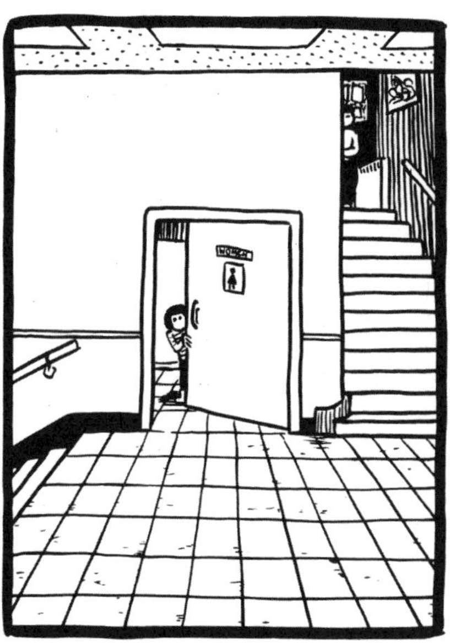

I looked out to see if he was there, but I did not see him...

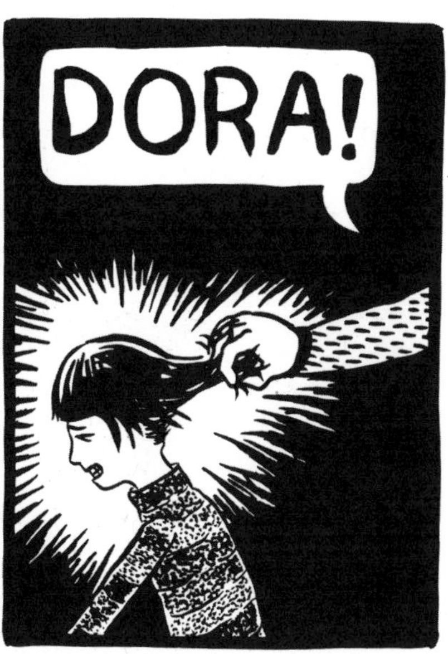
DORA!

I went back to the art centre, but he followed me from down the stairs and he grabbed my hair once, but hard!!

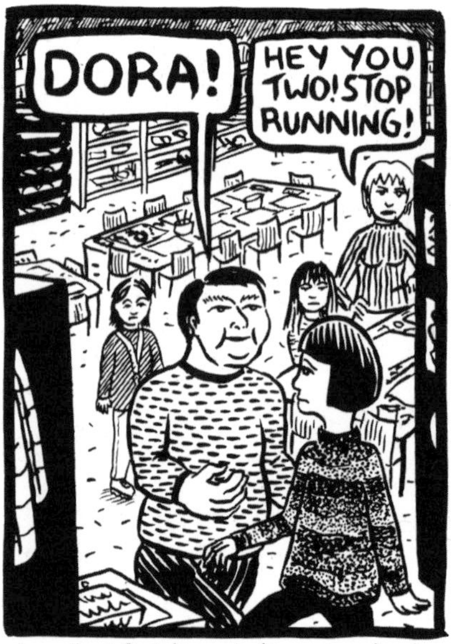
DORA!
HEY YOU TWO! STOP RUNNING!

I walked fast through the art centre to the computer area, but not running because of the rules ... Forti was still following me... (that's the worst thing about life).

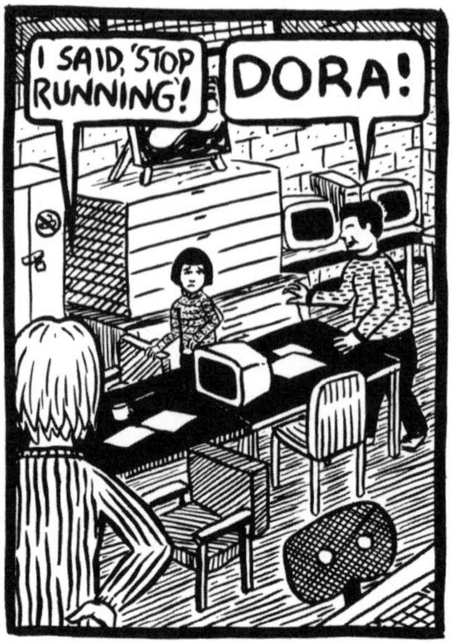
I SAID, 'STOP RUNNING'!
DORA!

Forti runs after me, chasing me around the tables... I really don't want to run 'cause I don't want to get kicked out of the art centre and Deanna says 'Stop Running' ... so I stop.

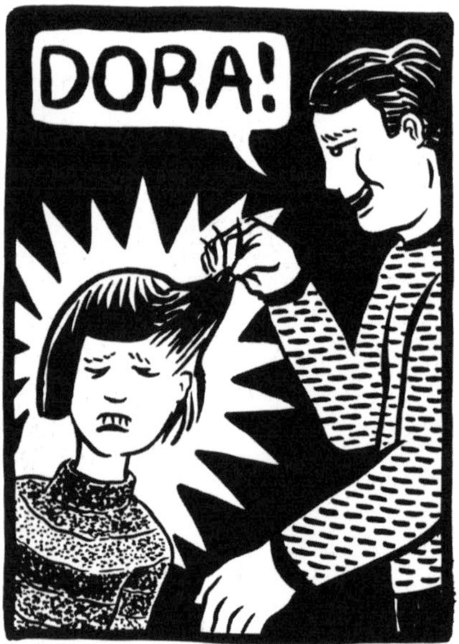
DORA!

... suddenly Forti pulled my hair and I cried...

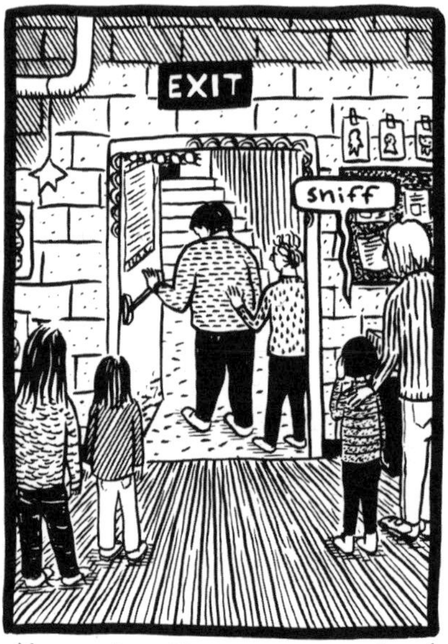
EXIT
sniff

His sister Stella came and tried to make him to stop by putting him outside the door to wait...

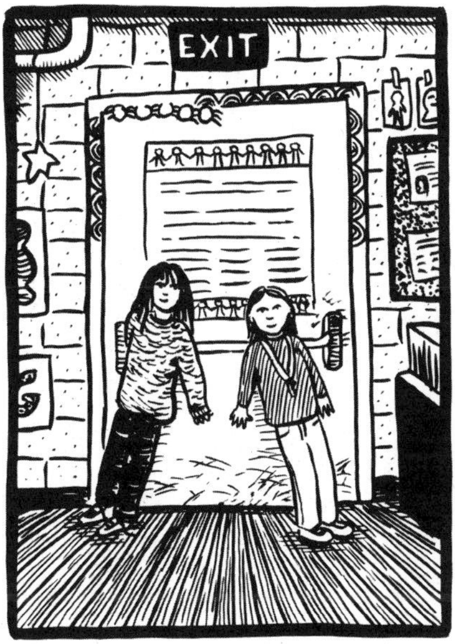
EXIT

Michelle and Diamond guarded the door 'cause he was waiting for me to come out and he was pushing the door and Michelle said 'He's kind of like... strong!'

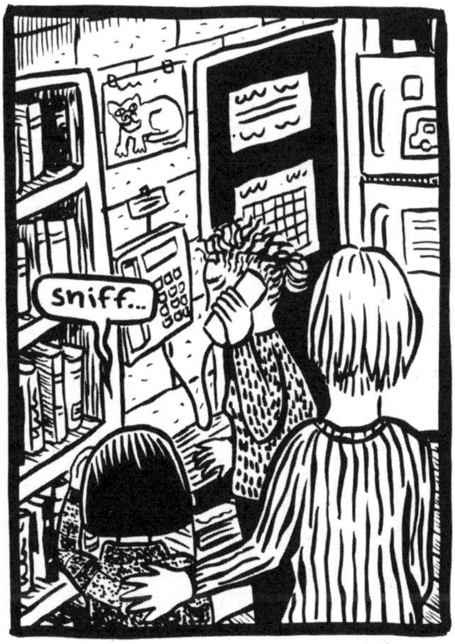
sniff...

Stella called her mom and dad to come to the art centre quickly...

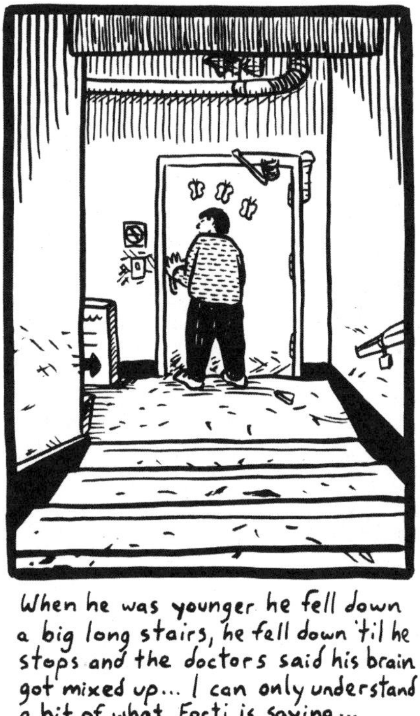

When he was younger he fell down a big long stairs, he fell down 'til he stops and the doctors said his brain got mixed up... I can only understand a bit of what Forti is saying...

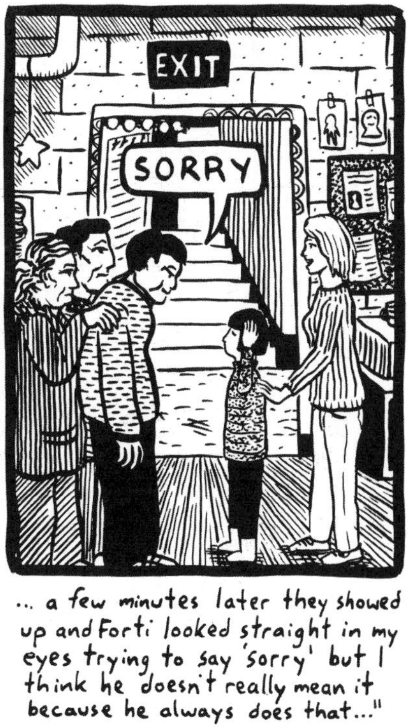
EXIT
SORRY

... a few minutes later they showed up and Forti looked straight in my eyes trying to say 'sorry' but I think he doesn't really mean it because he always does that..."

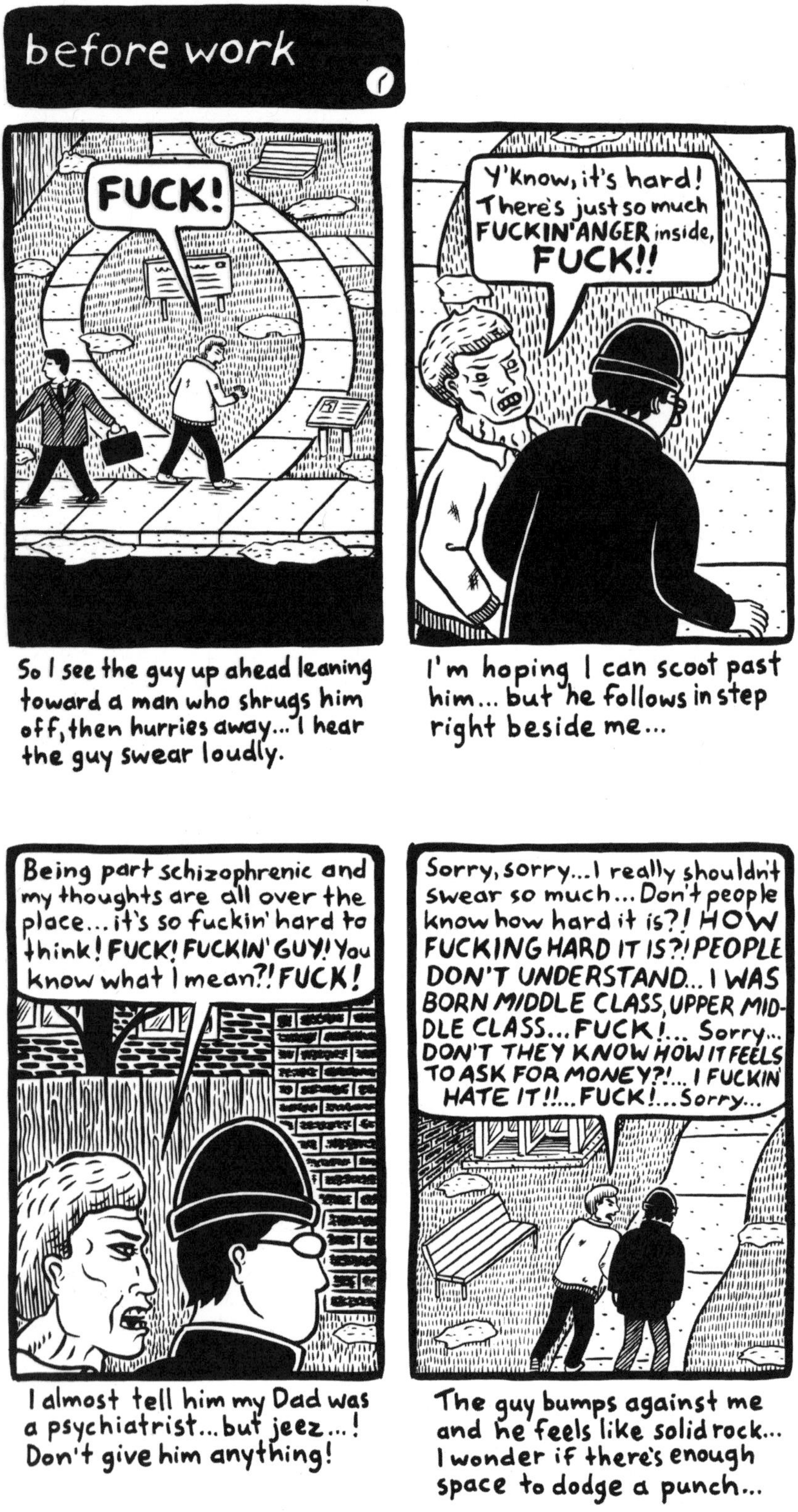
before work
FUCK!
So I see the guy up ahead leaning toward a man who shrugs him off, then hurries away... I hear the guy swear loudly.
Y'know, it's hard! There's just so much FUCKIN' ANGER inside, FUCK!!
I'm hoping I can scoot past him... but he follows in step right beside me...
Being part schizophrenic and my thoughts are all over the place... it's so fuckin' hard to think! FUCK! FUCKIN' GUY! You know what I mean?! FUCK!
I almost tell him my Dad was a psychiatrist... but jeez...! Don't give him anything!
Sorry, sorry... I really shouldn't swear so much... Don't people know how hard it is?! HOW FUCKING HARD IT IS?! PEOPLE DON'T UNDERSTAND... I WAS BORN MIDDLE CLASS, UPPER MIDDLE CLASS... FUCK!... Sorry... DON'T THEY KNOW HOW IT FEELS TO ASK FOR MONEY?!... I FUCKIN' HATE IT!!... FUCK!... Sorry...
The guy bumps against me and he feels like solid rock... I wonder if there's enough space to dodge a punch...

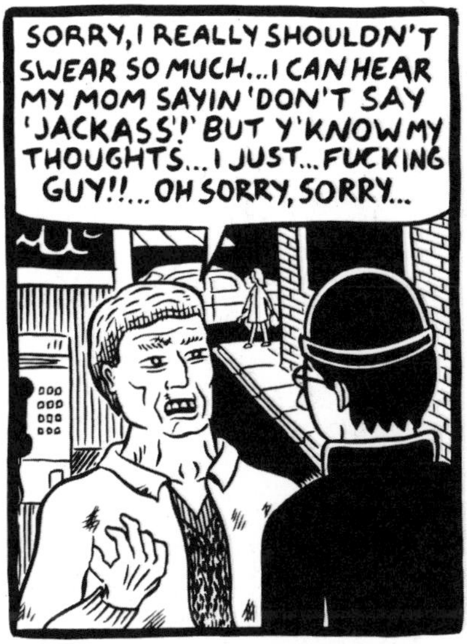
SORRY, I REALLY SHOULDN'T SWEAR SO MUCH... I CAN HEAR MY MOM SAYIN 'DON'T SAY 'JACKASS'!' BUT Y'KNOW MY THOUGHTS... I JUST... FUCKING GUY!!... OH SORRY, SORRY...

To calm him, I want to tell him to look at the birds...! Be careful, don't set him off.

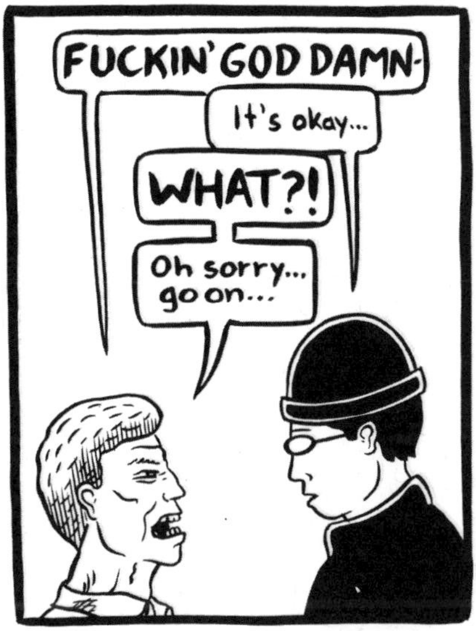
FUCKIN' GOD DAMN-
It's okay...
WHAT?!
Oh sorry... go on...

I cut his roll of words off... I interrupt for a second and he's furious! God, just let him do the talking... be agreeable.

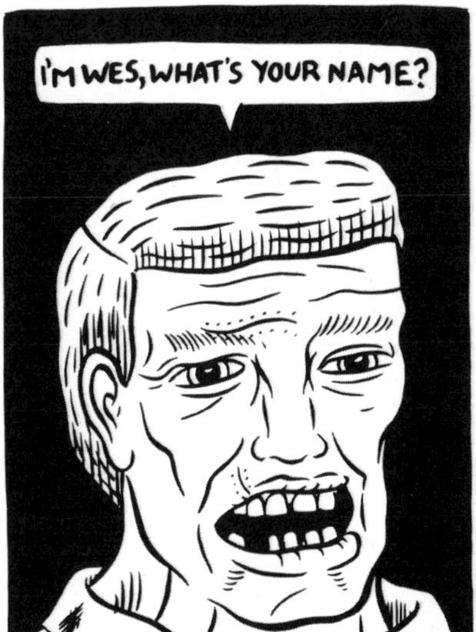
I'M WES, WHAT'S YOUR NAME?

So we stop to cross the road and I get a good look at his face... huge fresh red scar across his brow... scars on his lips, ice blue eyes... I can't lie... I tell him my real name.

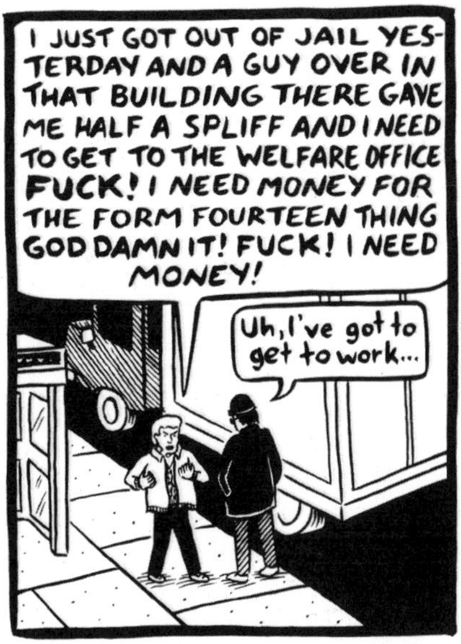
I JUST GOT OUT OF JAIL YESTERDAY AND A GUY OVER IN THAT BUILDING THERE GAVE ME HALF A SPLIFF AND I NEED TO GET TO THE WELFARE OFFICE FUCK! I NEED MONEY FOR THE FORM FOURTEEN THING GOD DAMN IT! FUCK! I NEED MONEY!
Uh, I've got to get to work...

I feel around in my pocket for some change... sheesh... how much to get rid of this guy?!

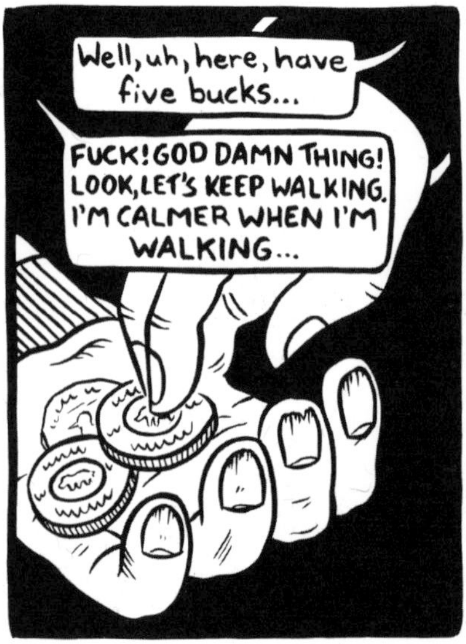
Well, uh, here, have five bucks...
FUCK! GOD DAMN THING! LOOK, LET'S KEEP WALKING. I'M CALMER WHEN I'M WALKING...

I give him five dollars.

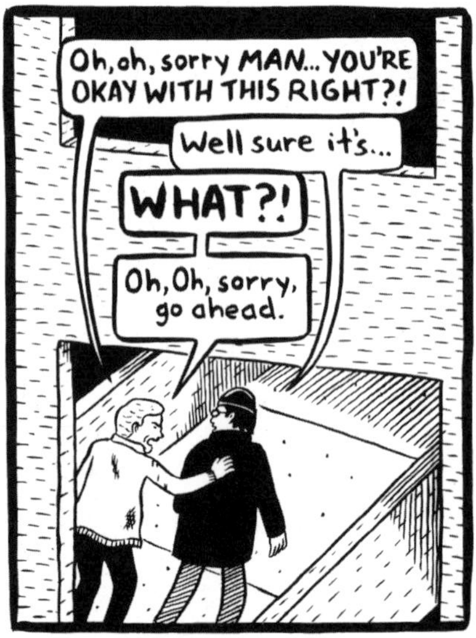
Oh, oh, sorry MAN... YOU'RE OKAY WITH THIS RIGHT?!
Well sure it's...
WHAT?!
Oh, Oh, sorry, go ahead.

We cross over to the parking garage and he pats me on the back.

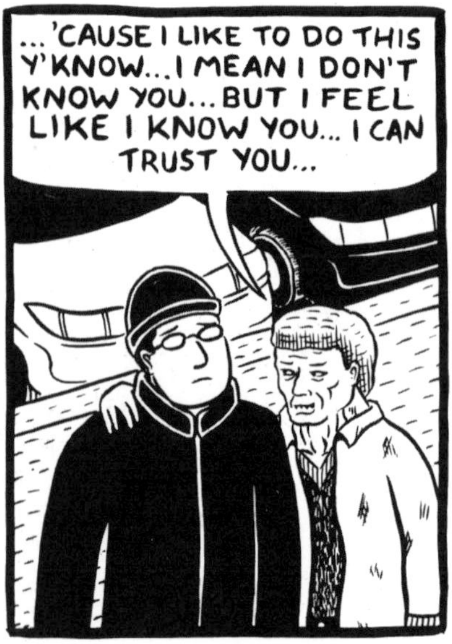
...'CAUSE I LIKE TO DO THIS Y'KNOW... I MEAN I DON'T KNOW YOU... BUT I FEEL LIKE I KNOW YOU... I CAN TRUST YOU...

He pats me on the back more and more and more, then he puts his arm around my shoulder...

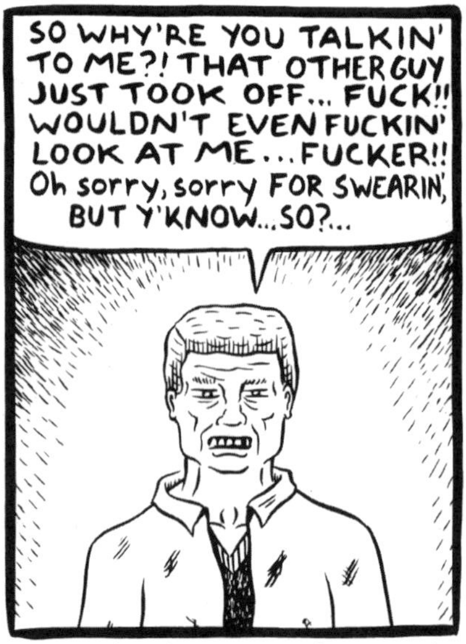
SO WHY'RE YOU TALKIN' TO ME?! THAT OTHER GUY JUST TOOK OFF... FUCK!! WOULDN'T EVEN FUCKIN' LOOK AT ME... FUCKER!! Oh sorry, sorry FOR SWEARIN', BUT Y'KNOW... SO?...

We stop to cross another road and I sure don't want to stop too long...

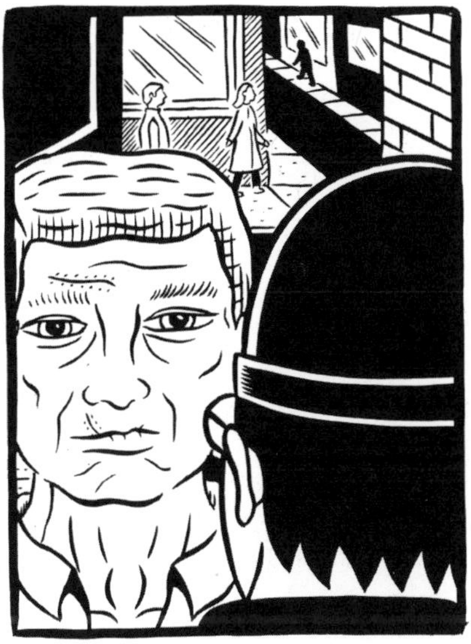

I'm looking him right in the eye... I can see it twitch... FUCK!... What do I say?!

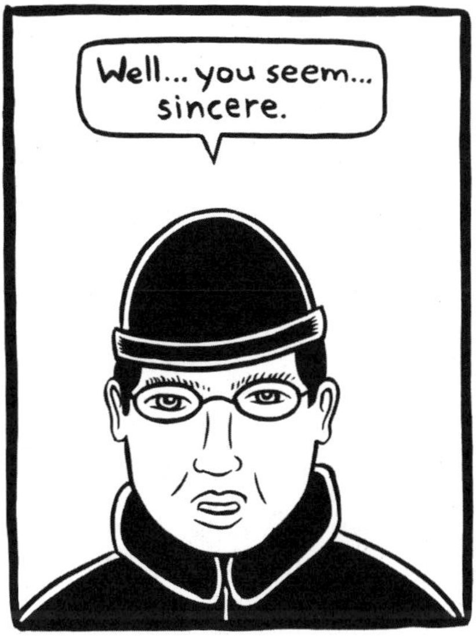
Well... you seem... sincere.

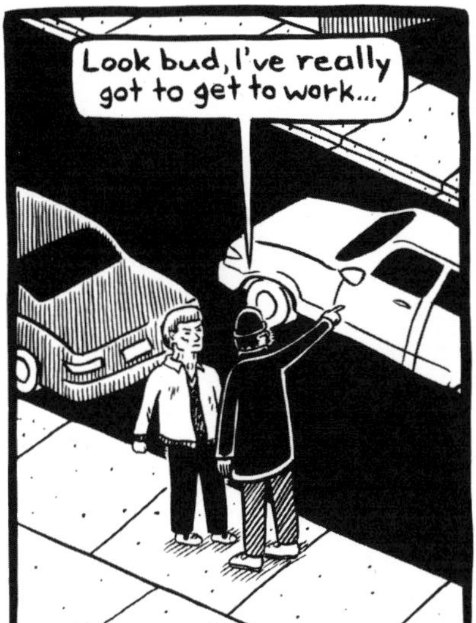
Look bud, I've really got to get to work...

I've got to ditch this guy...

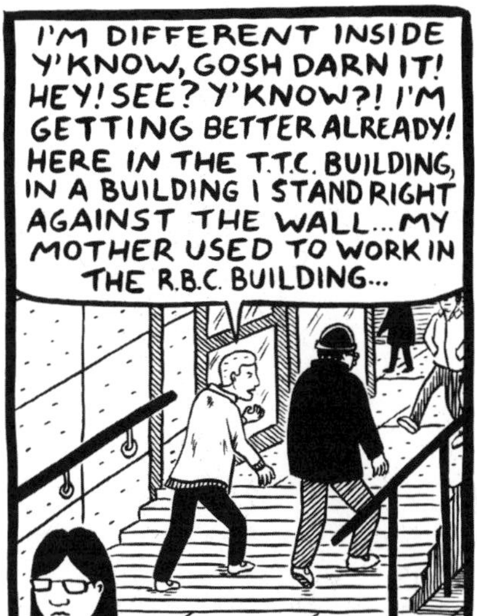
I'M DIFFERENT INSIDE Y'KNOW, GOSH DARN IT! HEY! SEE? Y'KNOW?! I'M GETTING BETTER ALREADY! HERE IN THE T.T.C. BUILDING, IN A BUILDING I STAND RIGHT AGAINST THE WALL... MY MOTHER USED TO WORK IN THE R.B.C. BUILDING...

When he mentions his mother again, I want to tell him he looks like Paul Newman... but don't give him anything...!

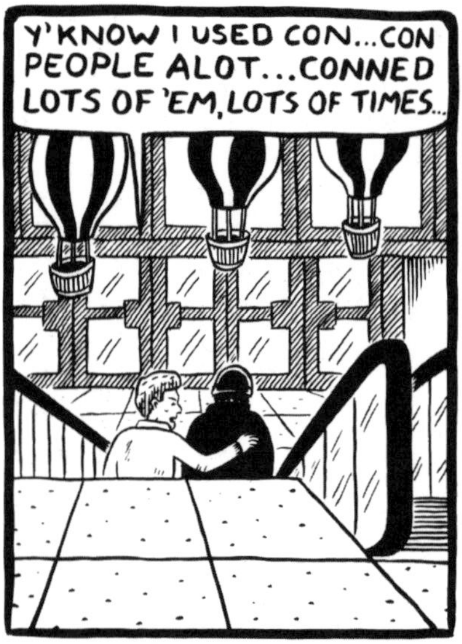
Y'KNOW I USED CON...CON PEOPLE ALOT...CONNED LOTS OF 'EM, LOTS OF TIMES...

So we go down the stairs and I really want to get rid of this guy...he's putting his arm around me again...

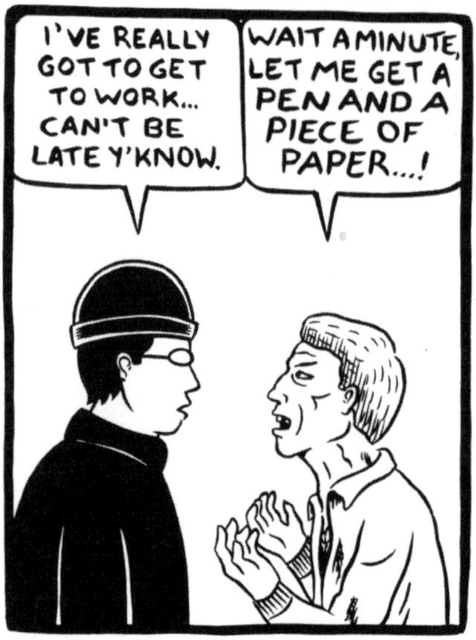
I'VE REALLY GOT TO GET TO WORK... CAN'T BE LATE Y'KNOW.
WAIT A MINUTE, LET ME GET A PEN AND A PIECE OF PAPER...!

We get to the subway entrance and I think I'm free... SHIT! I've got to think of a fake name and address...

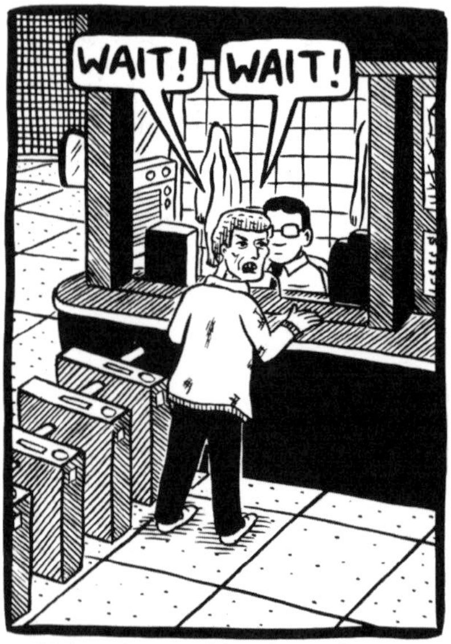
WAIT!
WAIT!

He's asking the ticket guy for a pen and he keeps looking over his shoulder... shouting!

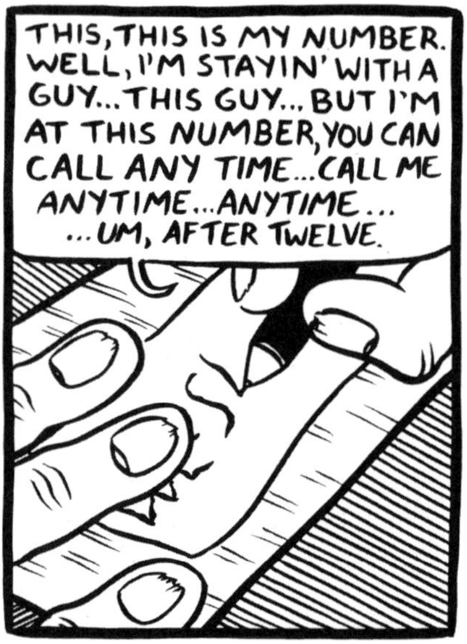
THIS, THIS IS MY NUMBER. WELL, I'M STAYIN' WITH A GUY... THIS GUY... BUT I'M AT THIS NUMBER, YOU CAN CALL ANY TIME...CALL ME ANYTIME...ANYTIME... ...UM, AFTER TWELVE.

He can barely scrawl his name out on the sheet... Thank God he doesn't want any info from me!

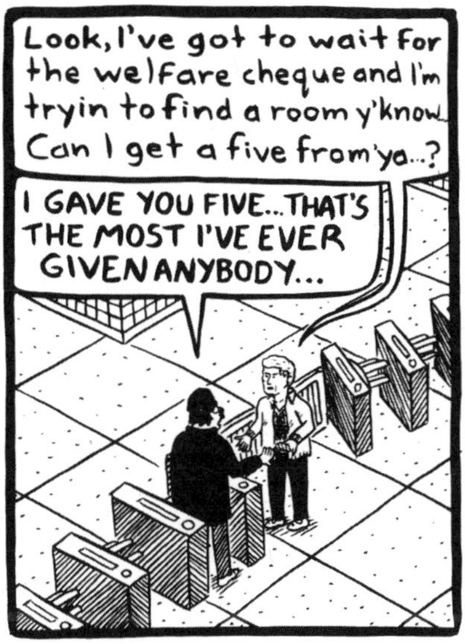
Look, I've got to wait for the welfare cheque and I'm tryin to find a room y'know... Can I get a five from 'ya...?
I GAVE YOU FIVE... THAT'S THE MOST I'VE EVER GIVEN ANYBODY...

I tell him the truth again.

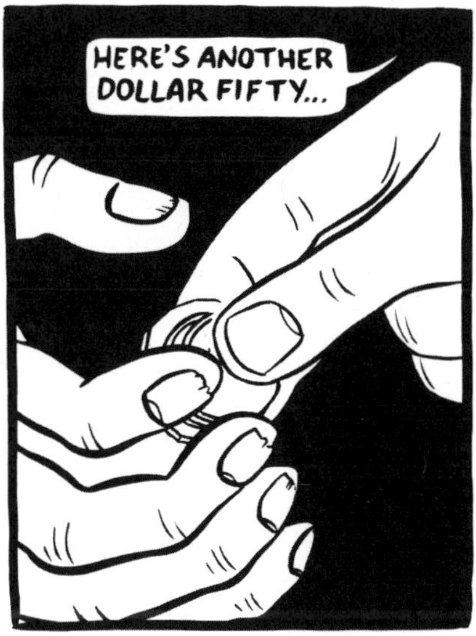
HERE'S ANOTHER DOLLAR FIFTY...

...maybe a bit more money will get rid of him.

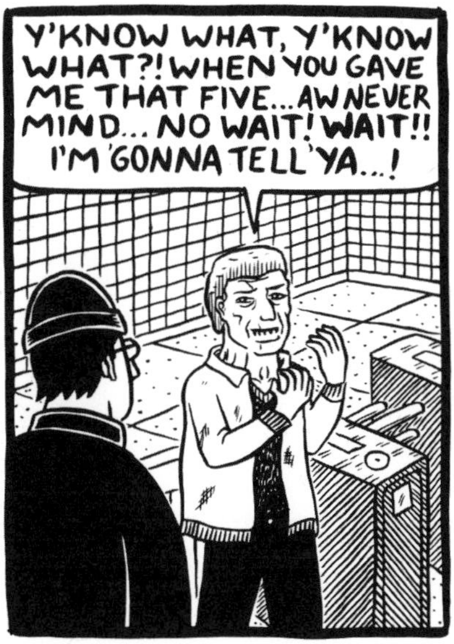
Y'KNOW WHAT, Y'KNOW WHAT?! WHEN YOU GAVE ME THAT FIVE... AW NEVER MIND... NO WAIT! WAIT!! I'M 'GONNA TELL 'YA...!

Aw, what now?... What the hell is he doing now?!...

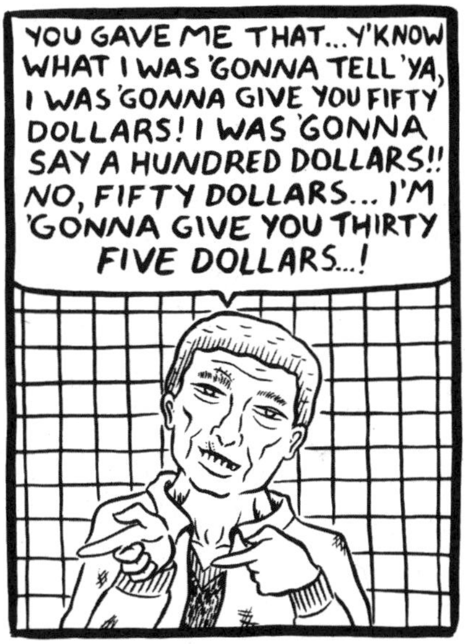
YOU GAVE ME THAT... Y'KNOW WHAT I WAS 'GONNA TELL 'YA, I WAS 'GONNA GIVE YOU FIFTY DOLLARS! I WAS 'GONNA SAY A HUNDRED DOLLARS!! NO, FIFTY DOLLARS... I'M 'GONNA GIVE YOU THIRTY FIVE DOLLARS...!

Aw jeez... it's some pathetic, garbled con attempt... sigh, this is sad.

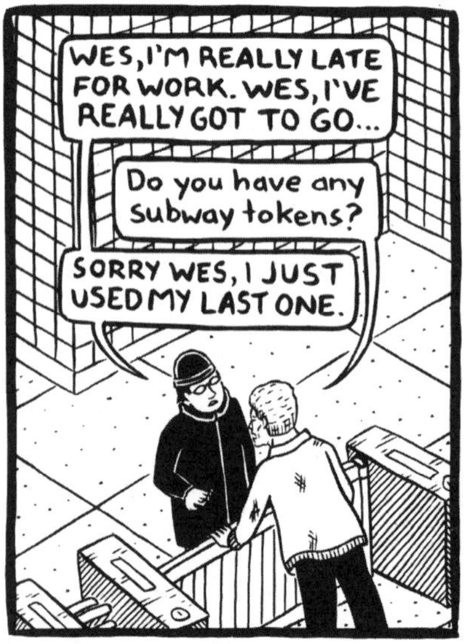
WES, I'M REALLY LATE FOR WORK. WES, I'VE REALLY GOT TO GO...
Do you have any subway tokens?
SORRY WES, I JUST USED MY LAST ONE.

It's not working and he knows it...the truth again, luckily...

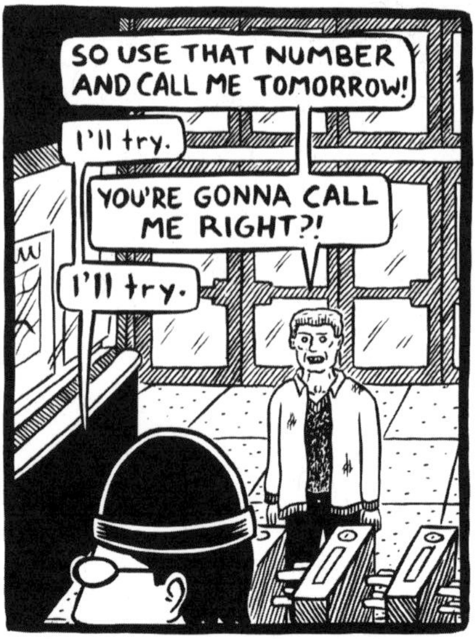
SO USE THAT NUMBER AND CALL ME TOMORROW!
I'll try.
YOU'RE GONNA CALL ME RIGHT?!
I'll try.

Finally on the other side of the turnstyle I feel free! Calling after me I'm feeling sorry for him... <u>now</u> I lie!

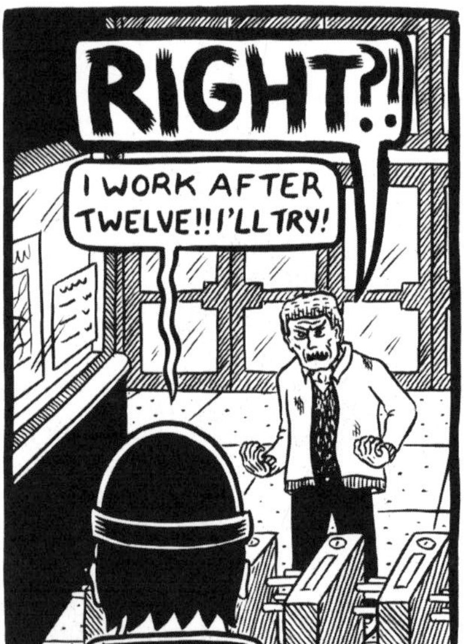
RIGHT?!
I WORK AFTER TWELVE!! I'LL TRY!

He shouts so loud it erases my pity...replaced with fear... I lie again... I almost want to tell *him* I <u>will</u> call ... jeez!

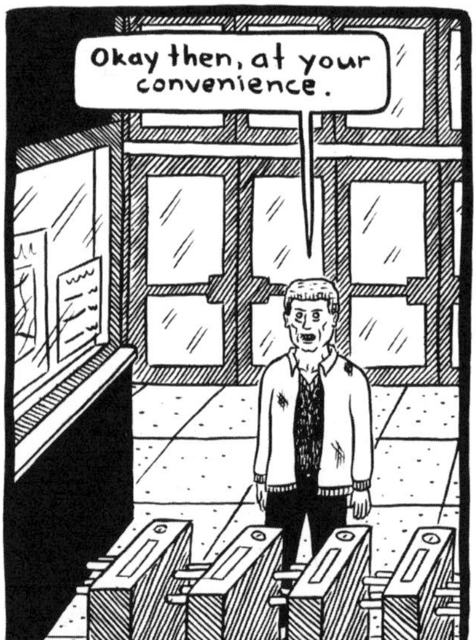
Okay then, at your convenience.

I hurry downstairs hoping, praying he doesn't follow me... Wes doesn't.

button

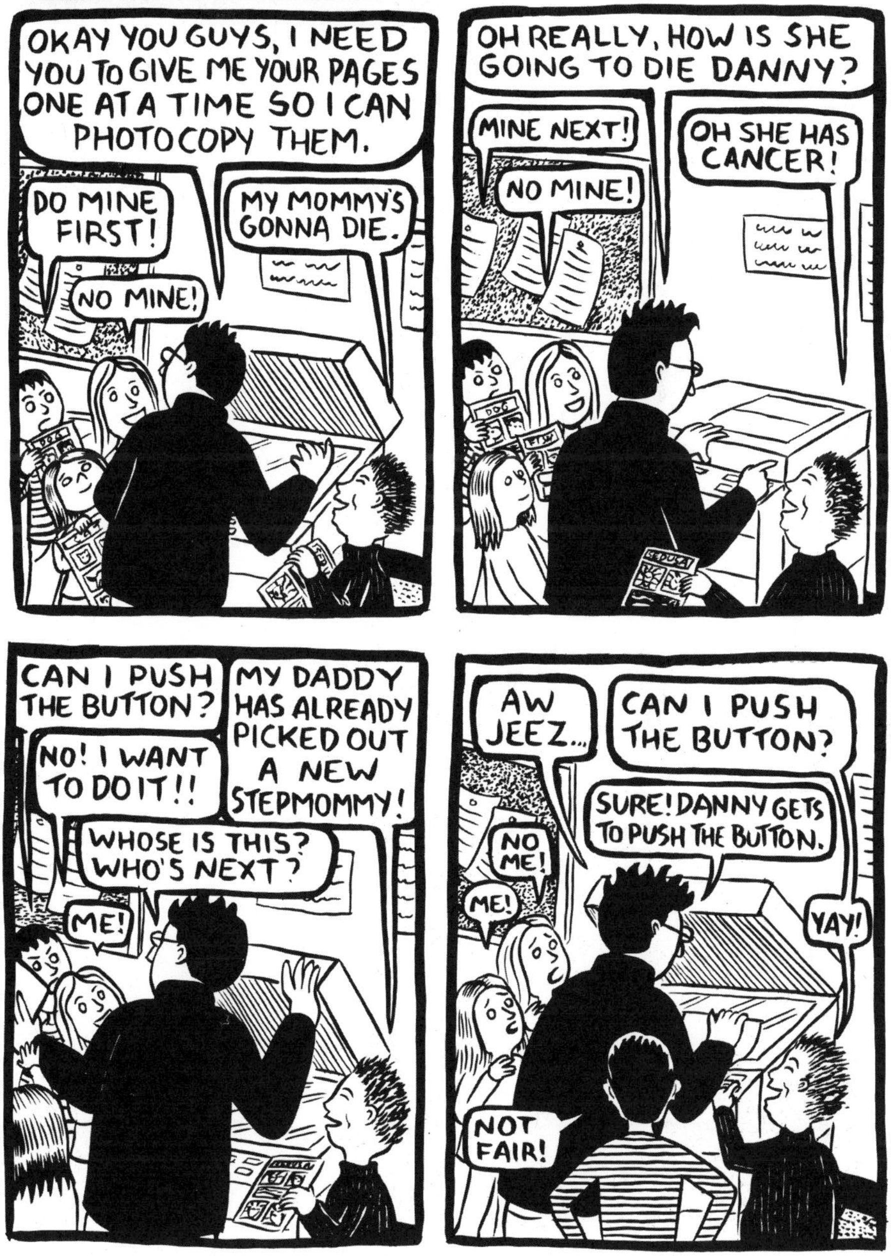
OKAY YOU GUYS, I NEED YOU TO GIVE ME YOUR PAGES ONE AT A TIME SO I CAN PHOTOCOPY THEM.
DO MINE FIRST!
NO MINE!
MY MOMMY'S GONNA DIE.
OH REALLY, HOW IS SHE GOING TO DIE DANNY?
MINE NEXT!
NO MINE!
OH SHE HAS CANCER!
CAN I PUSH THE BUTTON?
NO! I WANT TO DO IT!!
MY DADDY HAS ALREADY PICKED OUT A NEW STEPMOMMY!
WHOSE IS THIS? WHO'S NEXT?
ME!
AW JEEZ...
CAN I PUSH THE BUTTON?
SURE! DANNY GETS TO PUSH THE BUTTON.
NO ME!
ME!
YAY!
NOT FAIR!

knife

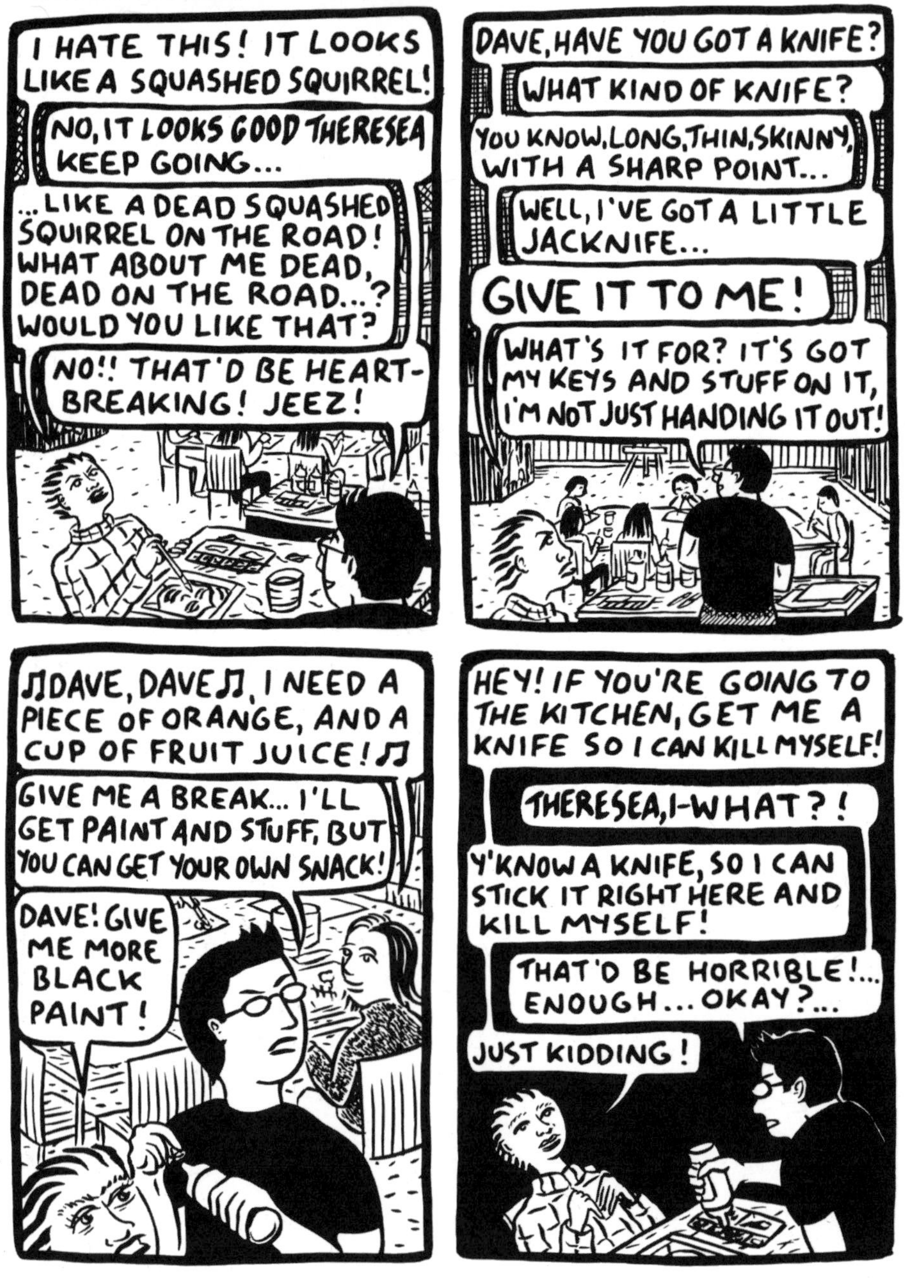
I HATE THIS! IT LOOKS LIKE A SQUASHED SQUIRREL!
NO, IT LOOKS GOOD THERESEA KEEP GOING...
...LIKE A DEAD SQUASHED SQUIRREL ON THE ROAD! WHAT ABOUT ME DEAD, DEAD ON THE ROAD...? WOULD YOU LIKE THAT?
NO!! THAT'D BE HEART-BREAKING! JEEZ!
DAVE, HAVE YOU GOT A KNIFE?
WHAT KIND OF KNIFE?
YOU KNOW, LONG, THIN, SKINNY, WITH A SHARP POINT...
WELL, I'VE GOT A LITTLE JACKNIFE...
GIVE IT TO ME!
WHAT'S IT FOR? IT'S GOT MY KEYS AND STUFF ON IT, I'M NOT JUST HANDING IT OUT!
♫DAVE, DAVE♫, I NEED A PIECE OF ORANGE, AND A CUP OF FRUIT JUICE!♫
GIVE ME A BREAK... I'LL GET PAINT AND STUFF, BUT YOU CAN GET YOUR OWN SNACK!
DAVE! GIVE ME MORE BLACK PAINT!
HEY! IF YOU'RE GOING TO THE KITCHEN, GET ME A KNIFE SO I CAN KILL MYSELF!
THERESEA, I-WHAT?!
Y'KNOW A KNIFE, SO I CAN STICK IT RIGHT HERE AND KILL MYSELF!
THAT'D BE HORRIBLE!... ENOUGH... OKAY?...
JUST KIDDING!

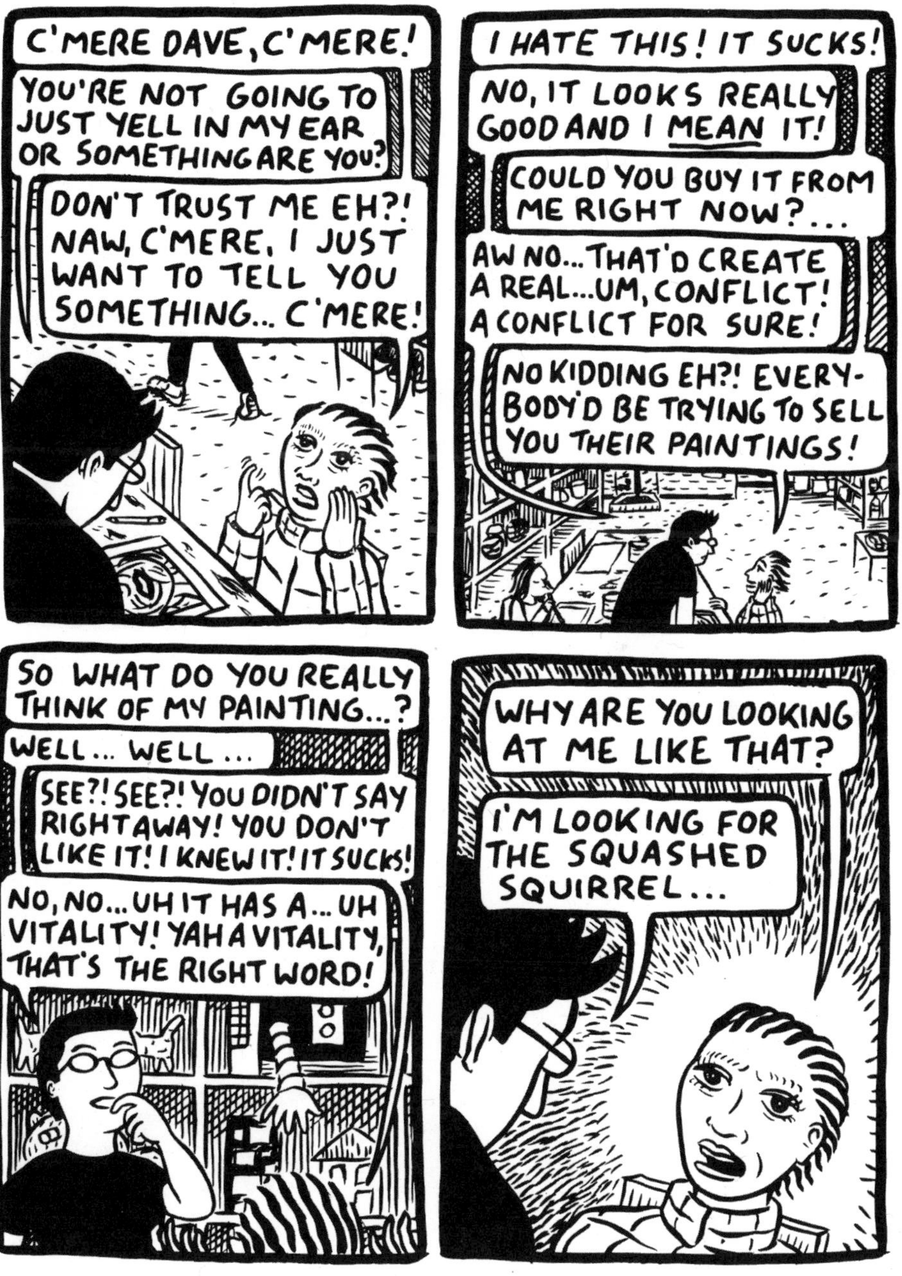
C'MERE DAVE, C'MERE!
YOU'RE NOT GOING TO JUST YELL IN MY EAR OR SOMETHING ARE YOU?
DON'T TRUST ME EH?! NAW, C'MERE, I JUST WANT TO TELL YOU SOMETHING... C'MERE!
I HATE THIS! IT SUCKS!
NO, IT LOOKS REALLY GOOD AND I MEAN IT!
COULD YOU BUY IT FROM ME RIGHT NOW?...
AW NO... THAT'D CREATE A REAL...UM, CONFLICT! A CONFLICT FOR SURE!
NO KIDDING EH?! EVERYBODY'D BE TRYING TO SELL YOU THEIR PAINTINGS!
SO WHAT DO YOU REALLY THINK OF MY PAINTING...?
WELL... WELL...
SEE?! SEE?! YOU DIDN'T SAY RIGHTAWAY! YOU DON'T LIKE IT! I KNEW IT! IT SUCKS!
NO, NO... UH IT HAS A... UH VITALITY! YAH A VITALITY, THAT'S THE RIGHT WORD!
WHY ARE YOU LOOKING AT ME LIKE THAT?
I'M LOOKING FOR THE SQUASHED SQUIRREL...

garden

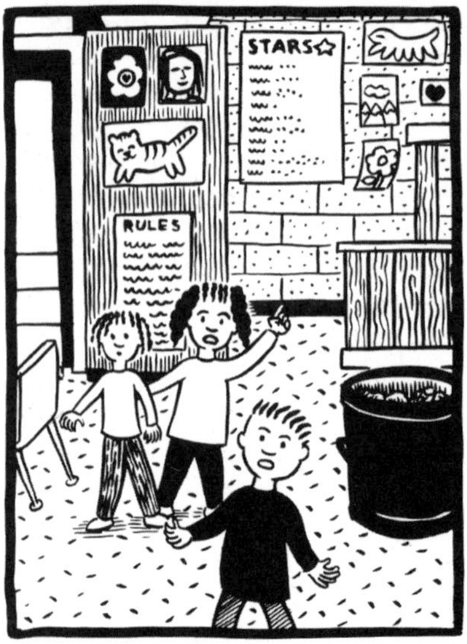
STARS☆
RULES

Several kids keep rushing in and out of the art centre exclaiming 'There's a dead baby squirrel in the garden! There's a dead baby squirrel in the garden!'

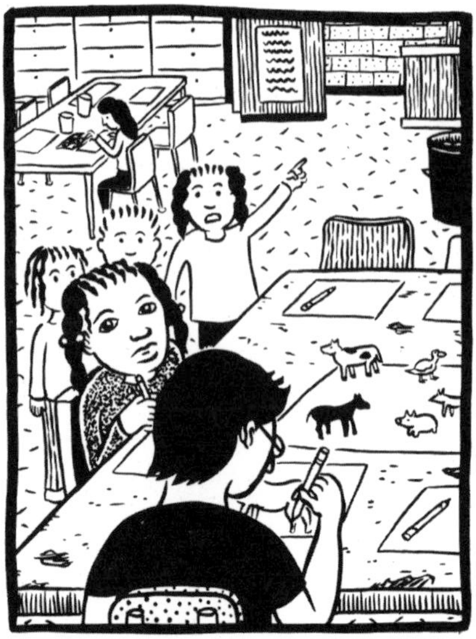

I'm trying to salvage my badly drawn horse... again the kids, 'There's a dead baby squirrel in the garden! There's a dead baby squirrel in the garden!'

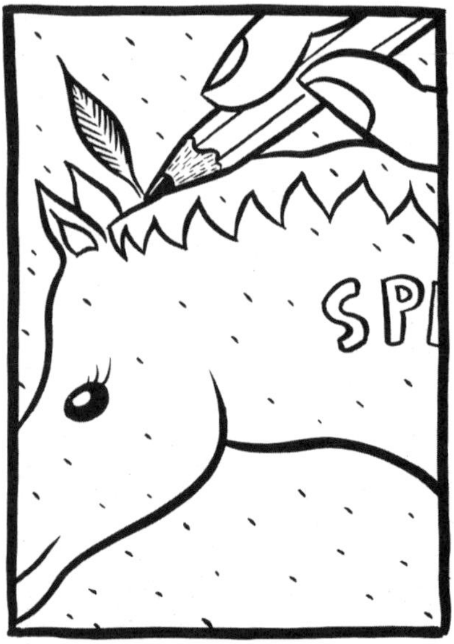
SP

Theresea wants to draw over my horse, adding a feather to its mane and writing 'spirit' on it's side. 'There's a dead baby squirrel in the garden!'

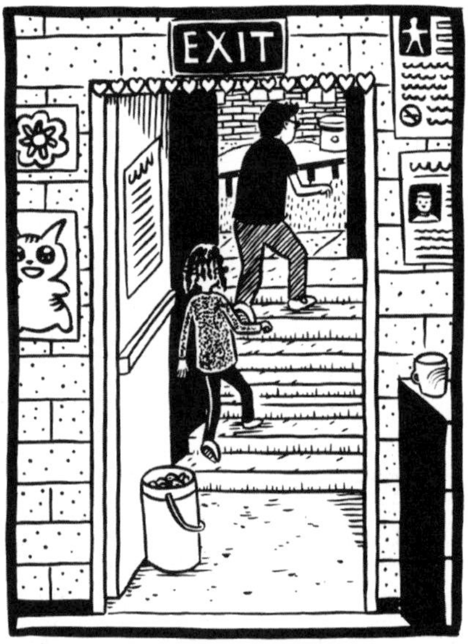
EXIT

It's the third time the kids have come in talking about the dead baby squirrel...! Okay... Theresea and I are going to have a look...

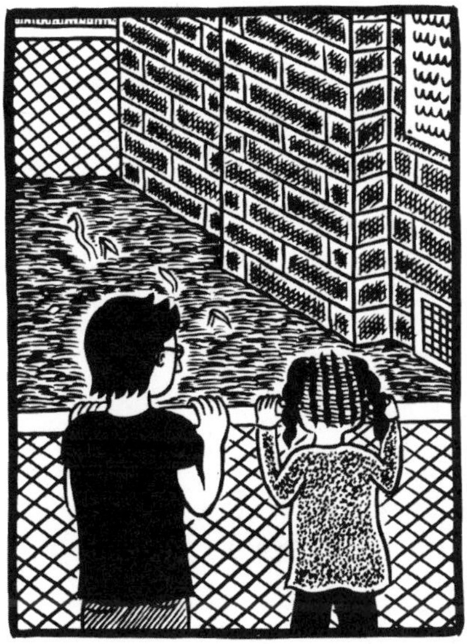

We look at the little pink thing lying in the dirt... Theresea says 'Just hop the fence!'

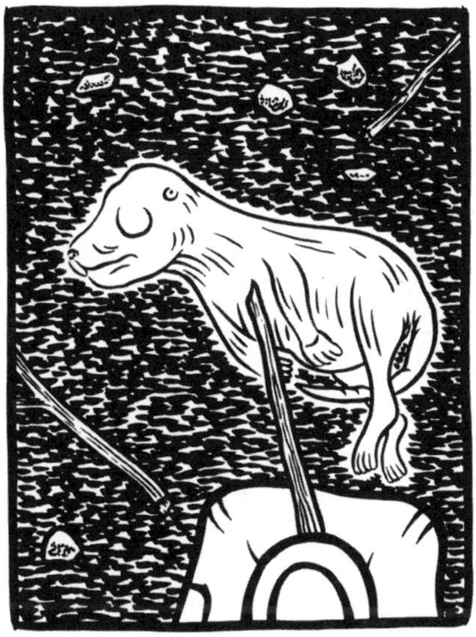

I help Theresea over the fence then poke at the baby squirrel with a stick. Theresea says 'Don't do that!'

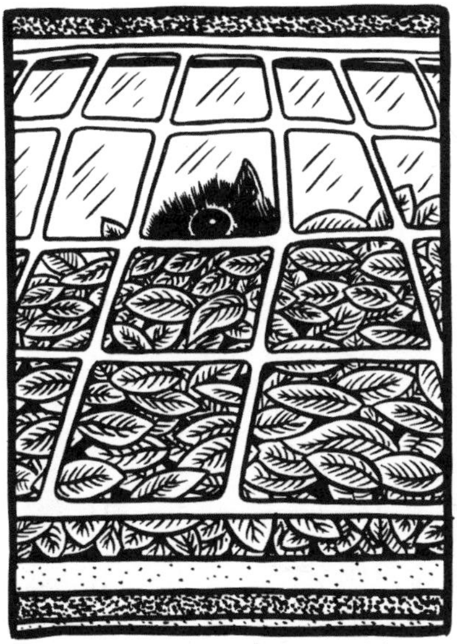

We see the head of the mother squirrel peeking from inside the wire mesh holding her nest... I offer 'She's not moving... maybe she's in shock...'

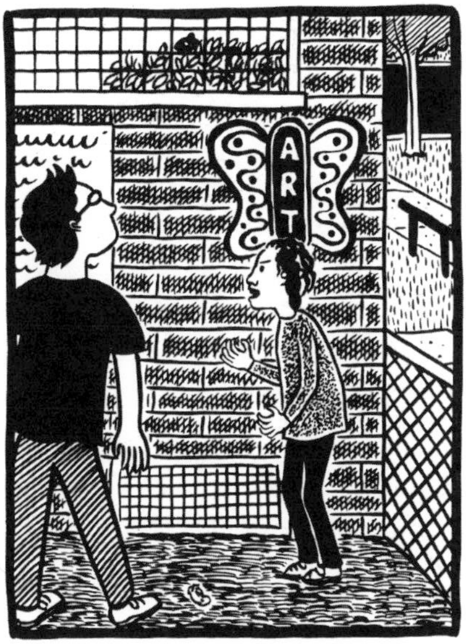
ART

Theresea snaps 'What do you think?! She's terrified!'

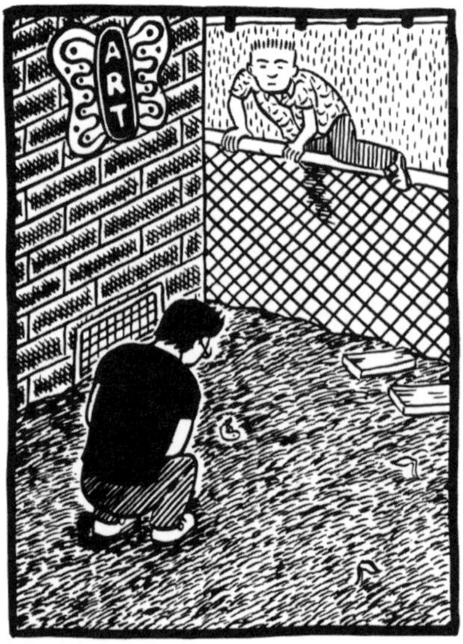
ART

Theresea leaves and Dominic hops the fence to have a look.

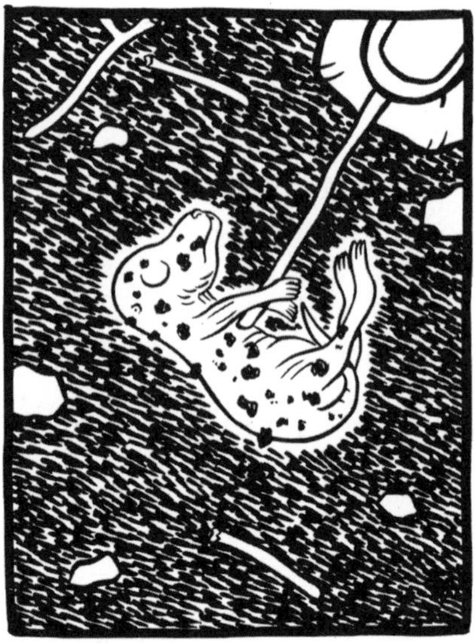

He flips the thing over and I tell him not to...this side is covered with dirt, and I want him to draw the good side.

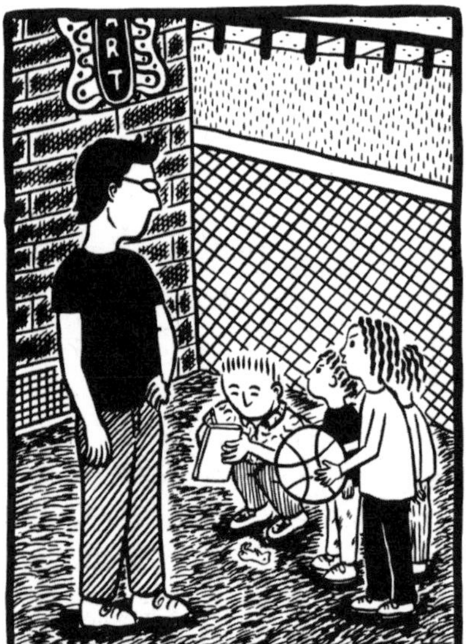
ART

Dominic's drawing and three little kids have come through the garden gate to join us.

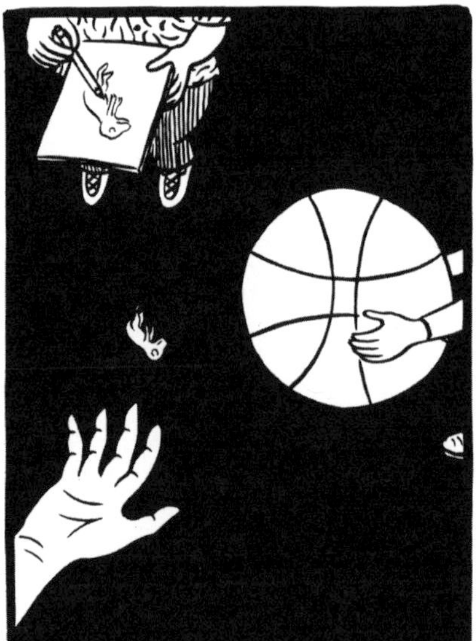

Atisha has a basketball and she wants to drop it on the squirrel... I tell her not to...it has death germs, the very worst germs of all!

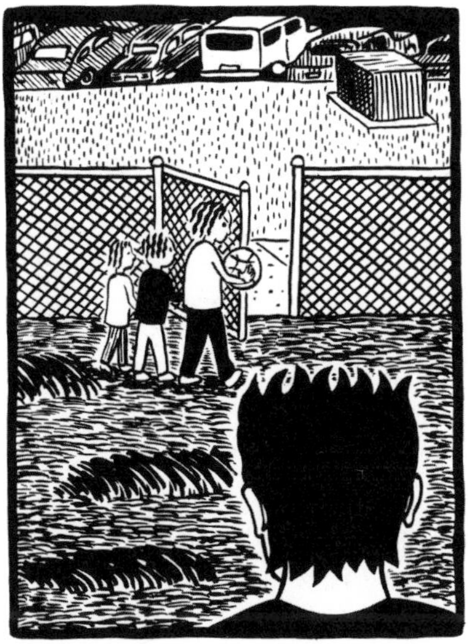

The three of them whisper to each other and wander out of the garden... I suggest to Dominic 'They probably want to come back later and crush it.'

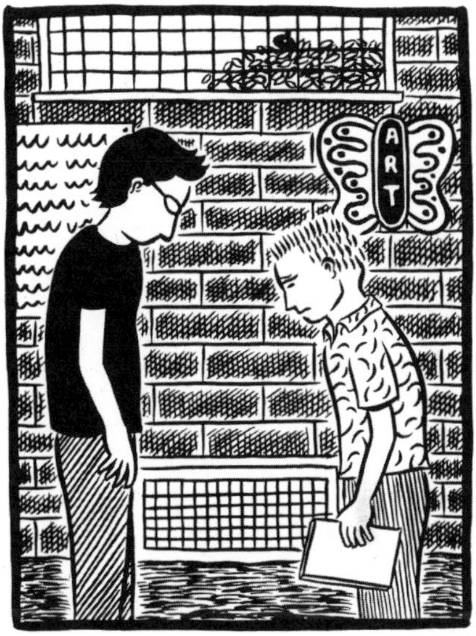
ART

Dominic thinks about it, looks at the dead baby squirrel...'That's not right, we should bury it.'

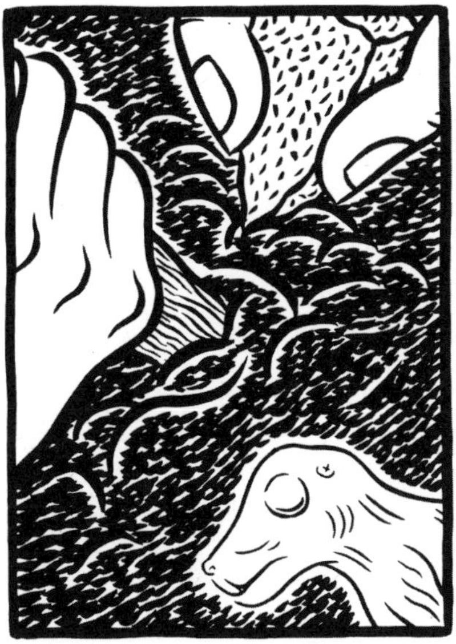

Dominic digs with a stick and I dig with a rock... we dump the little thing in and I wish we could put some seeds in with it...

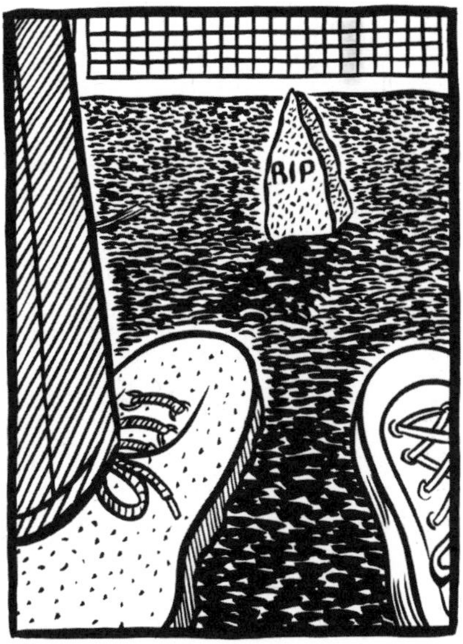
RIP

The rock has a good tombstone shape to it and Dominic says 'Write R.I.P. on it with the pencil!' We both laugh as it looks pretty good!

dogs

Panel 1:
HI SAMANTHA, HI VANITIE! GRAB A SEAT... TODAY WE'RE DRAWING CATS AND DOGS.. USING THESE LITTLE TOYS.... OR YOUR IMAGINATION...OR BOTH.

I WAN'NA USE A TOY!

ME TOO!

Panel 2:
DO ANY OF YOU GUYS ACTUALLY HAVE A CAT OR DOG?

NAW.

SORT OF...

Panel 3:
..WE USED TO HAVE TWO DOGS..

OH YAH...WHAT HAPPENED TO THEM?

WE HAD'DA GIVE THEM AWAY WHEN WE MOVED HERE.

AW, THAT'S TOO BAD...

YAH, BUT NOW I'M GETTING A WOLVERINE!

Panel 4:
GRRR! SNARL WOLVERINE!

GRR! SNARL! WOLVERINE!

SO...DO YOU HAVE ANY PETS HIEN?

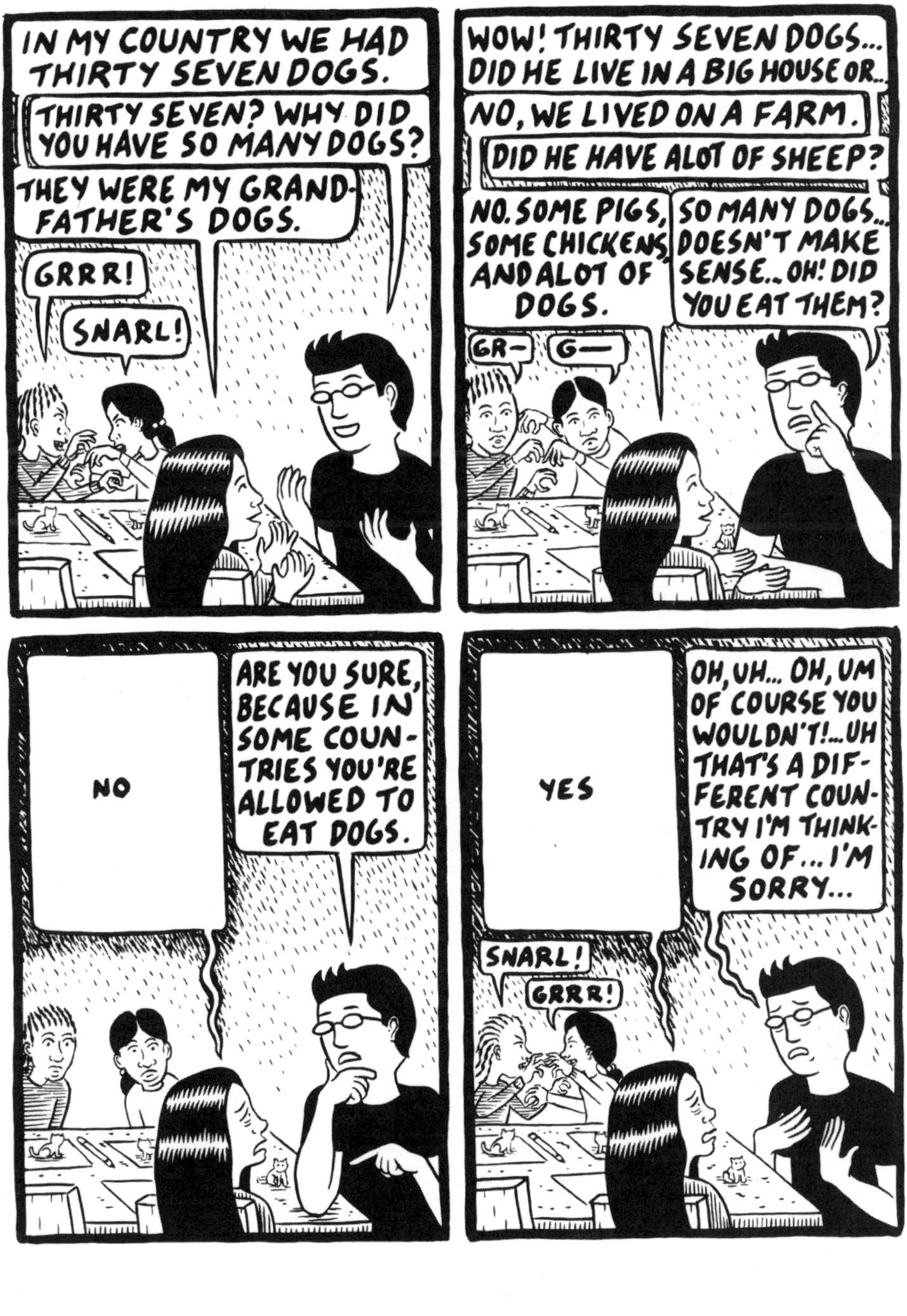
IN MY COUNTRY WE HAD THIRTY SEVEN DOGS.
THIRTY SEVEN? WHY DID YOU HAVE SO MANY DOGS?
THEY WERE MY GRAND-FATHER'S DOGS.
GRRR!
SNARL!
WOW! THIRTY SEVEN DOGS... DID HE LIVE IN A BIG HOUSE OR...
NO, WE LIVED ON A FARM.
DID HE HAVE ALOT OF SHEEP?
NO. SOME PIGS, SOME CHICKENS, AND ALOT OF DOGS.
SO MANY DOGS... DOESN'T MAKE SENSE... OH! DID YOU EAT THEM?
GR—
G—
NO
ARE YOU SURE, BECAUSE IN SOME COUN-TRIES YOU'RE ALLOWED TO EAT DOGS.
YES
OH, UH... OH, UM OF COURSE YOU WOULDN'T!... UH THAT'S A DIF-FERENT COUN-TRY I'M THINK-ING OF... I'M SORRY...
SNARL!
GRRR!

afraid

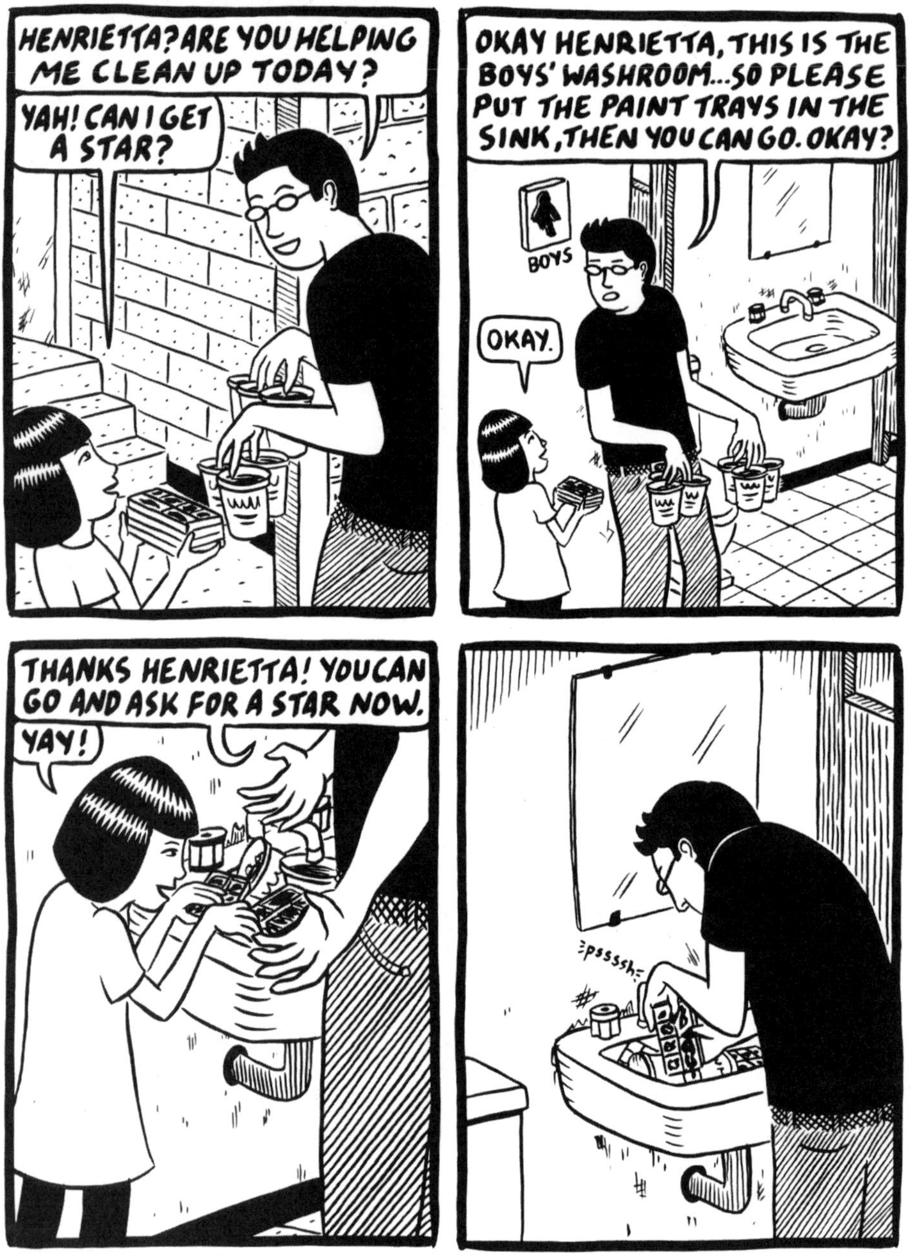
HENRIETTA? ARE YOU HELPING ME CLEAN UP TODAY?
YAH! CAN I GET A STAR?
OKAY HENRIETTA, THIS IS THE BOYS' WASHROOM...SO PLEASE PUT THE PAINT TRAYS IN THE SINK, THEN YOU CAN GO. OKAY?
BOYS
OKAY.
THANKS HENRIETTA! YOU CAN GO AND ASK FOR A STAR NOW.
YAY!
pssssh

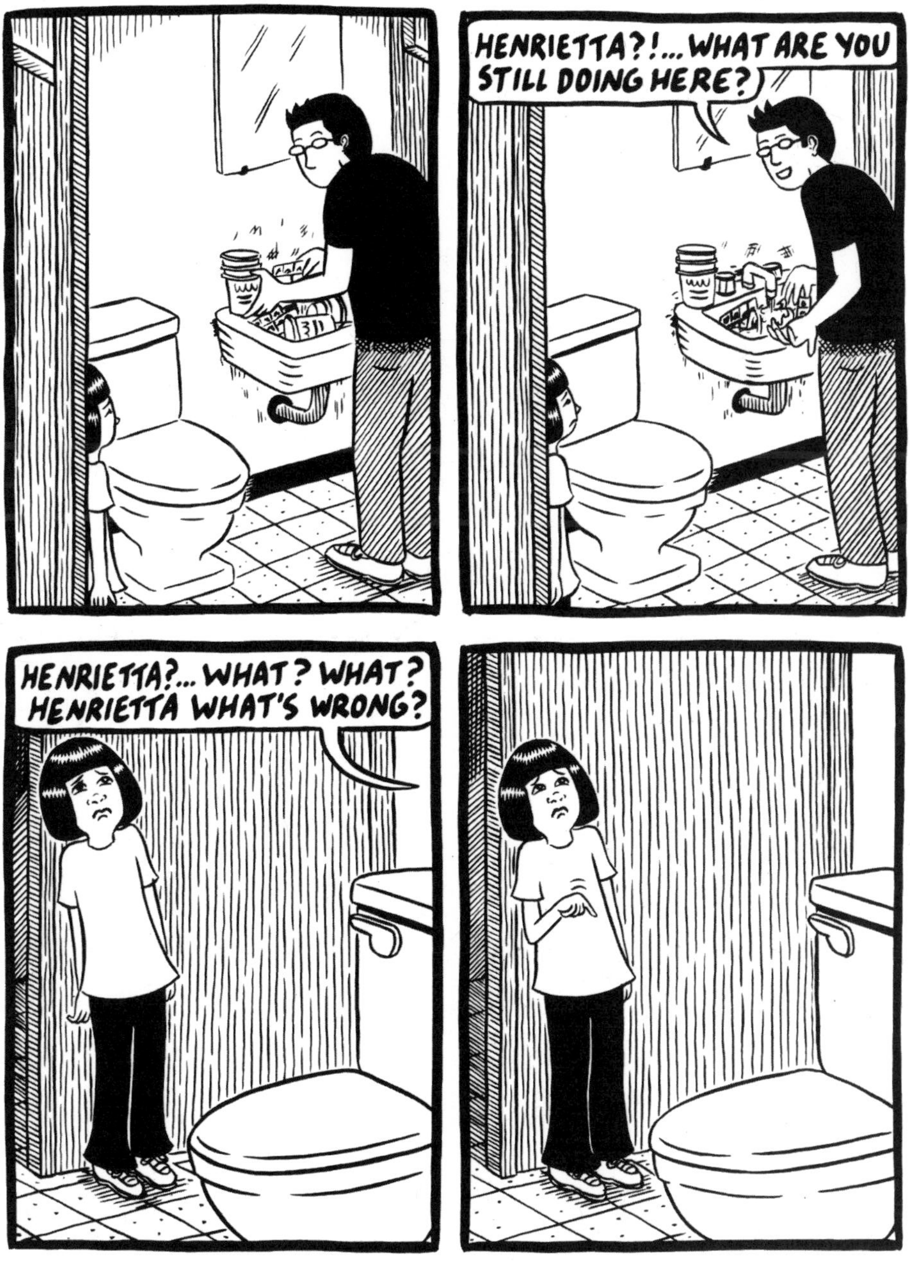
HENRIETTA?!... WHAT ARE YOU STILL DOING HERE?
HENRIETTA?... WHAT? WHAT? HENRIETTA WHAT'S WRONG?

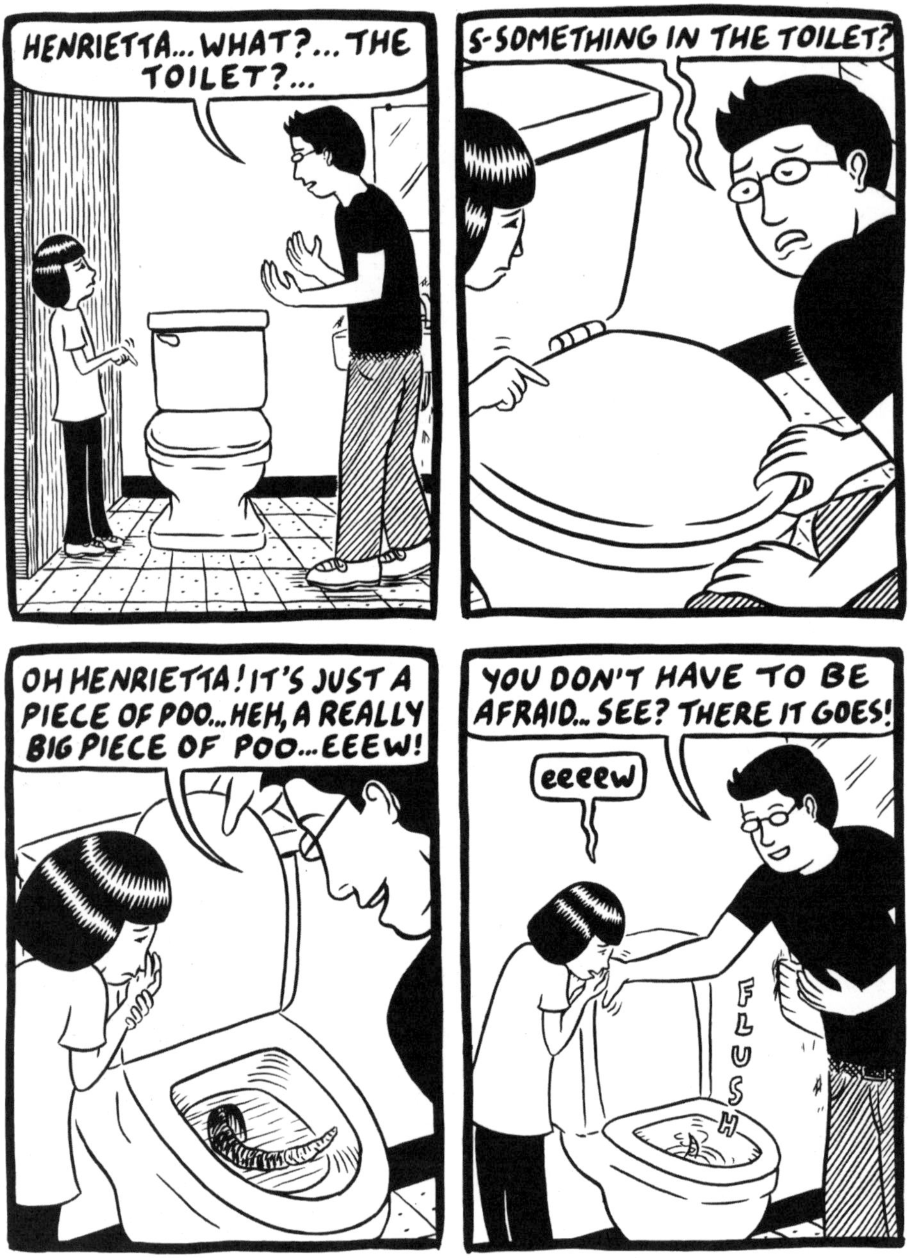
HENRIETTA... WHAT?... THE TOILET?...
S-SOMETHING IN THE TOILET?
OH HENRIETTA! IT'S JUST A PIECE OF POO... HEH, A REALLY BIG PIECE OF POO... EEEW!
YOU DON'T HAVE TO BE AFRAID.. SEE? THERE IT GOES!
eeeew
FLUSH

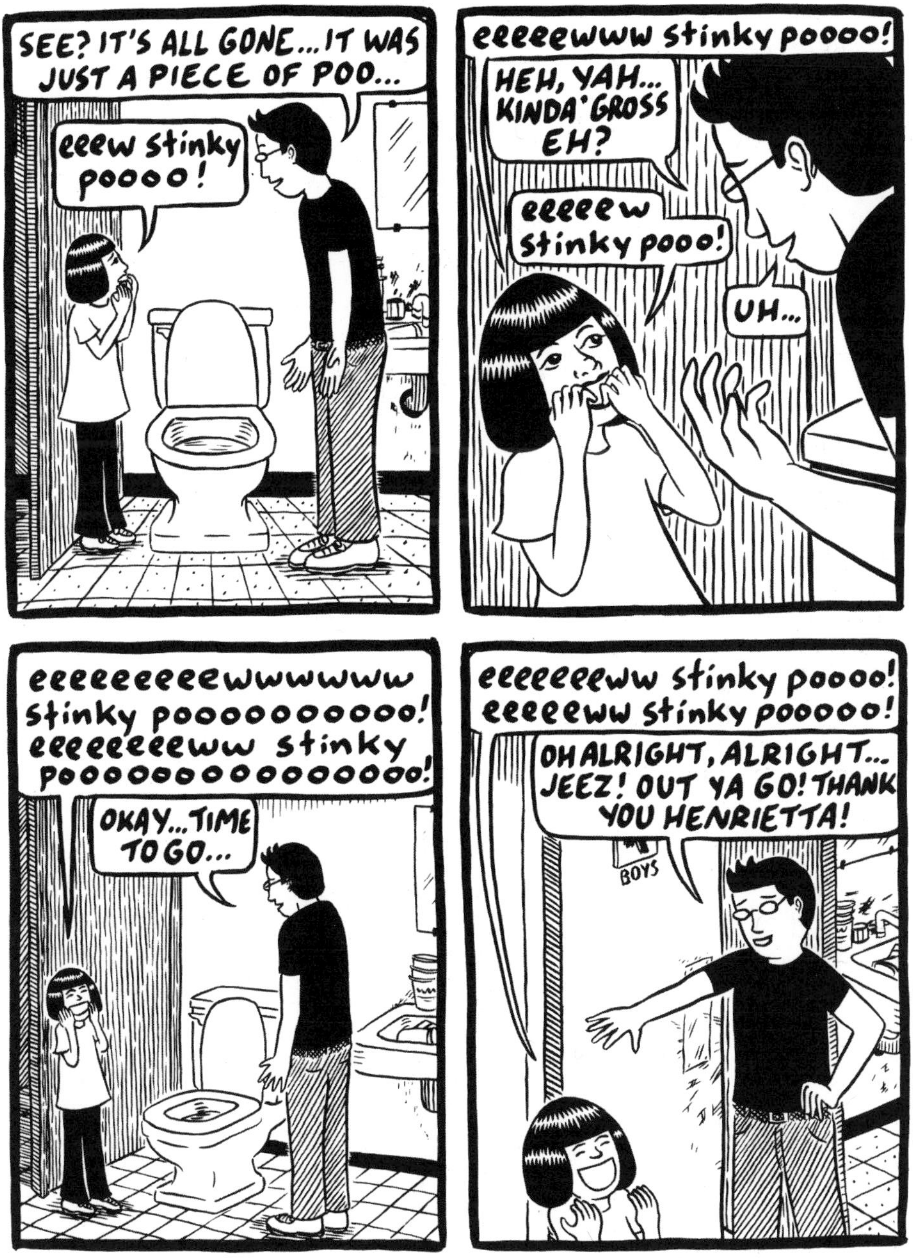
SEE? IT'S ALL GONE...IT WAS JUST A PIECE OF POO...
eeew stinky poooo!
eeeeewww stinky poooo!
HEH, YAH... KINDA' GROSS EH?
eeeee w stinky pooo!
UH...
eeeeeeeeewwwwww stinky poooooooooo! eeeeeeeeww stinky poooooooooooooooo!
OKAY...TIME TO GO...
eeeeeeeww stinky poooo! eeeeeww stinky pooooo!
OH ALRIGHT, ALRIGHT... JEEZ! OUT YA GO! THANK YOU HENRIETTA!
BOYS

doll

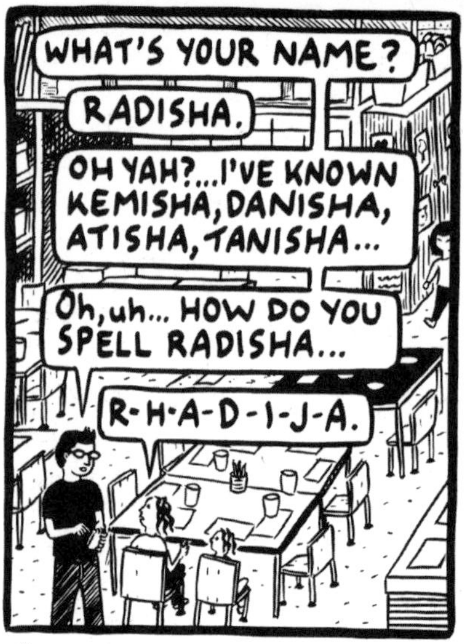

WHAT'S YOUR NAME?
RADISHA.
OH YAH?...I'VE KNOWN KEMISHA, DANISHA, ATISHA, TANISHA...
Oh, uh... HOW DO YOU SPELL RADISHA...
R-H-A-D-I-J-A.

Two new girls have come to the art centre.

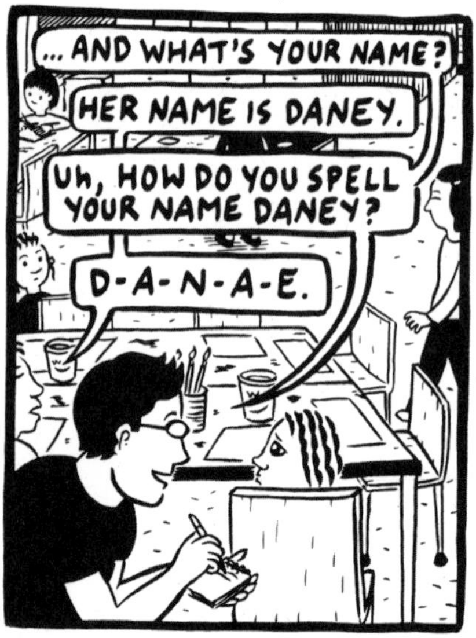

...AND WHAT'S YOUR NAME?
HER NAME IS DANEY.
Uh, HOW DO YOU SPELL YOUR NAME DANEY?
D-A-N-A-E.

I ask the little girl her name and her sister replies...and spells...

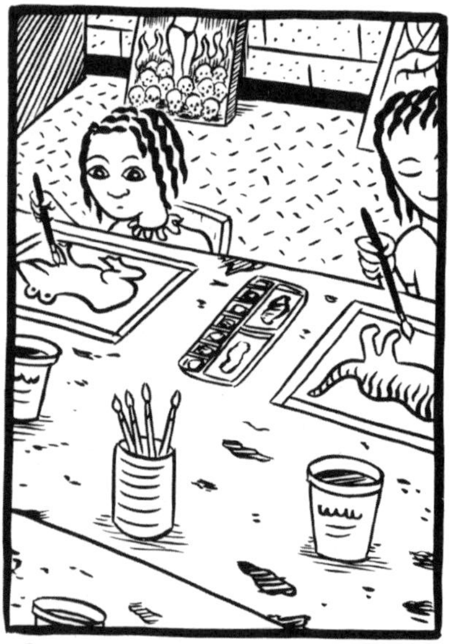

So the girls start painting... a frog and a tiger.

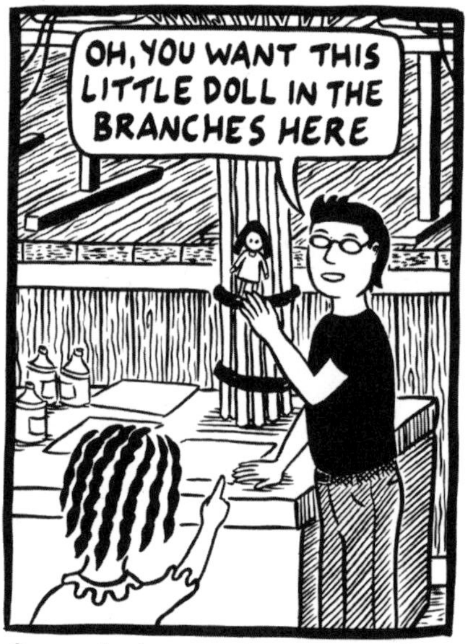

OH, YOU WANT THIS LITTLE DOLL IN THE BRANCHES HERE

Danae's done with her painting and she's pointing, pointing, pointing at something...

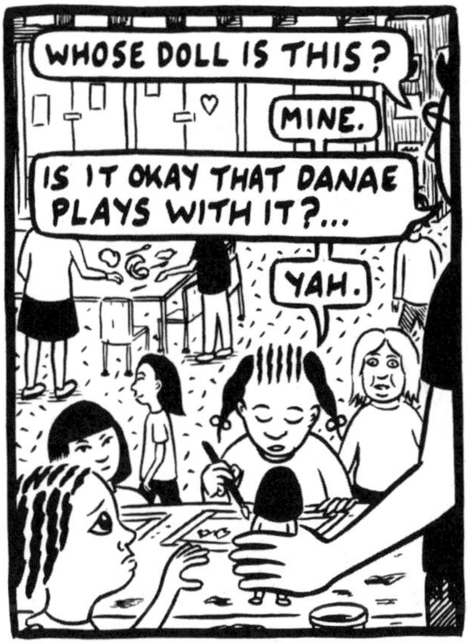
WHOSE DOLL IS THIS?
MINE.
IS IT OKAY THAT DANAE PLAYS WITH IT?...
YAH.

It's always good to ask permission...

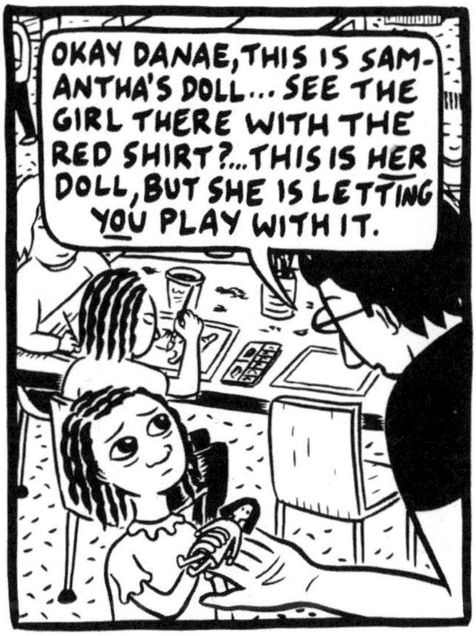
OKAY DANAE, THIS IS SAMANTHA'S DOLL... SEE THE GIRL THERE WITH THE RED SHIRT?... THIS IS HER DOLL, BUT SHE IS LETTING YOU PLAY WITH IT.

...and be clear... and repeat...

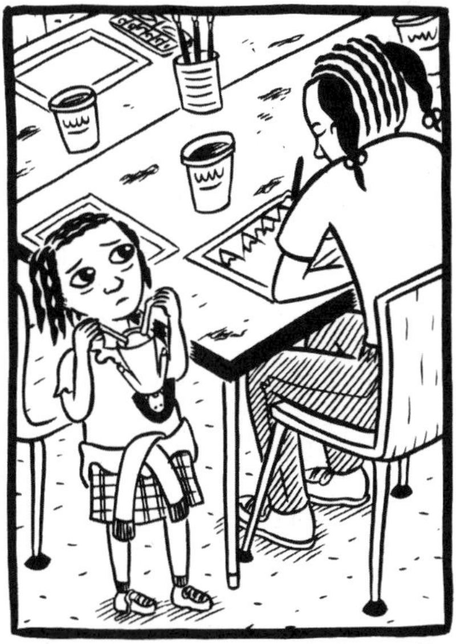

She takes the doll over to Samantha and silently pulls the legs apart, trying to get Samantha's attention...

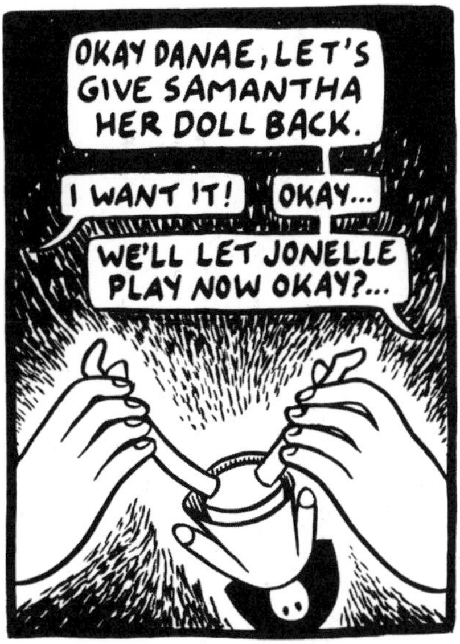
OKAY DANAE, LET'S GIVE SAMANTHA HER DOLL BACK.
I WANT IT!
OKAY...
WE'LL LET JONELLE PLAY NOW OKAY?...

Samantha's not looking and Danae's trying to pull the legs even wider and I suddenly feel protective... what's she trying to show...?!

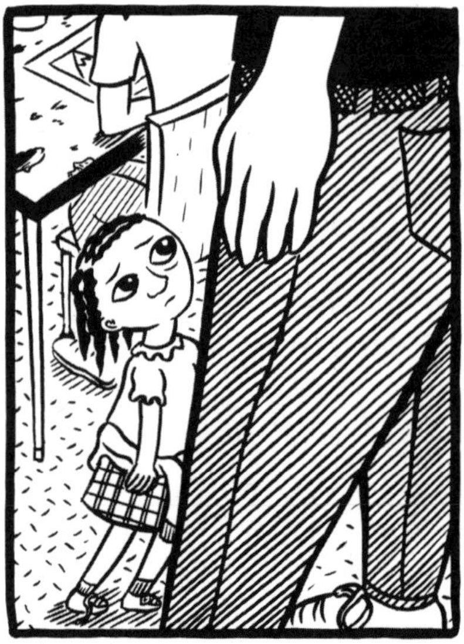

She silently stares up at me... leaning into my leg... she wants something... I pat her on the back...

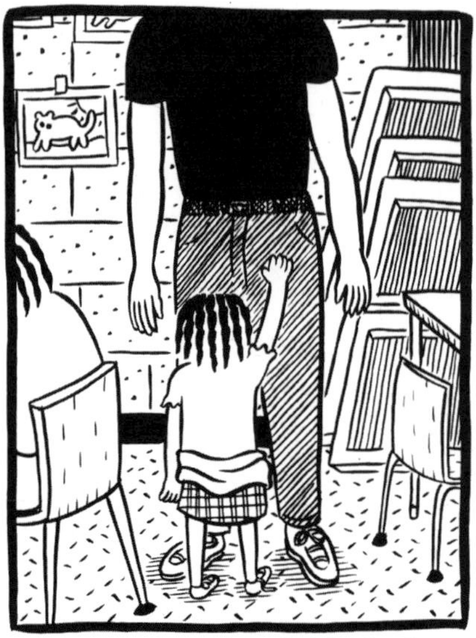

I walk around the table looking at the kids' art. Danae follows me and when I stop, she pushes her hand on the front of my pants.

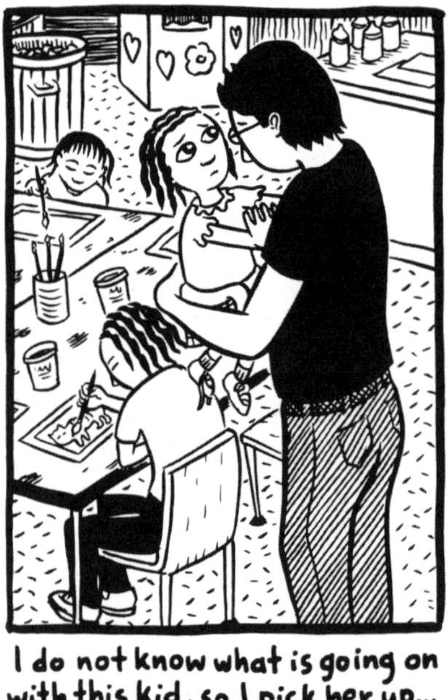

I do not know what is going on with this kid, so I pick her up... she wants up...? I don't know!

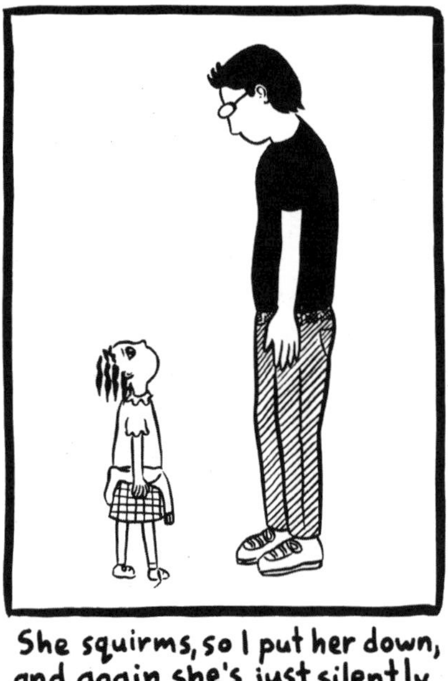

She squirms, so I put her down, and again she's just silently looking up at me...

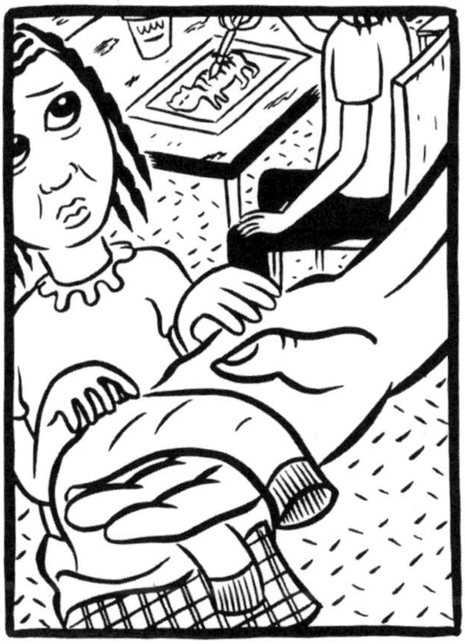

She takes the sleeve of the red sweatshirt tied around her waist and places it in my hand...

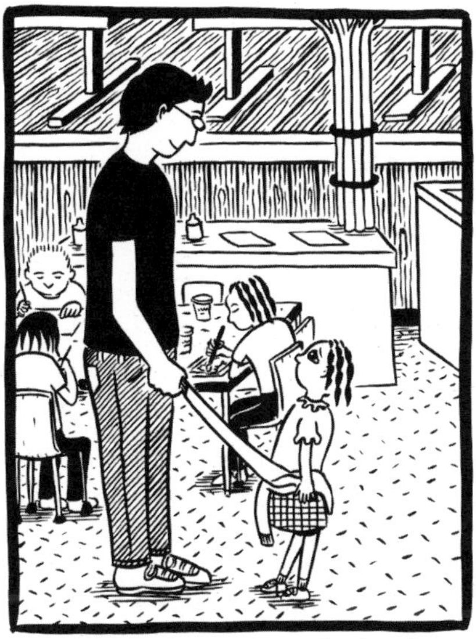

Oh... maybe she wants to play... I tug on the sleeve like a leash and she leans back... staring at me blankly... then her sister speaks...

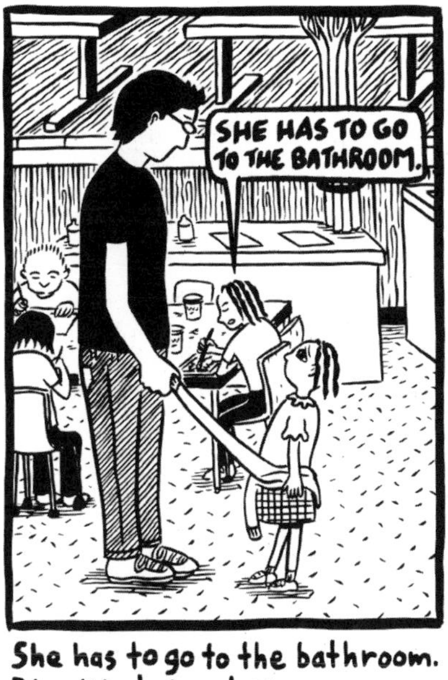
SHE HAS TO GO TO THE BATHROOM.

She has to go to the bathroom. Rhadija takes her.

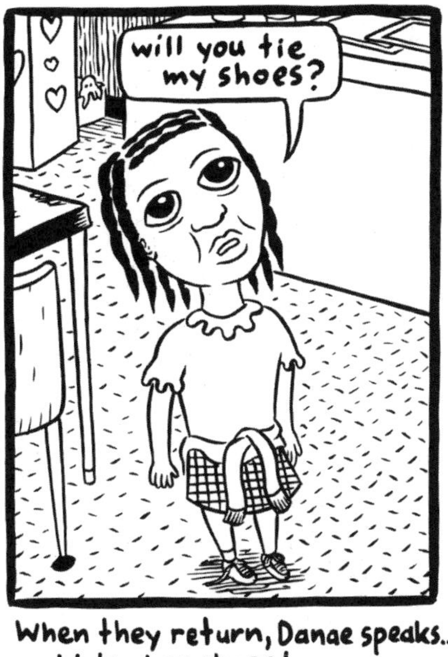
will you tie my shoes?

When they return, Danae speaks... and I tie her shoes!

after work

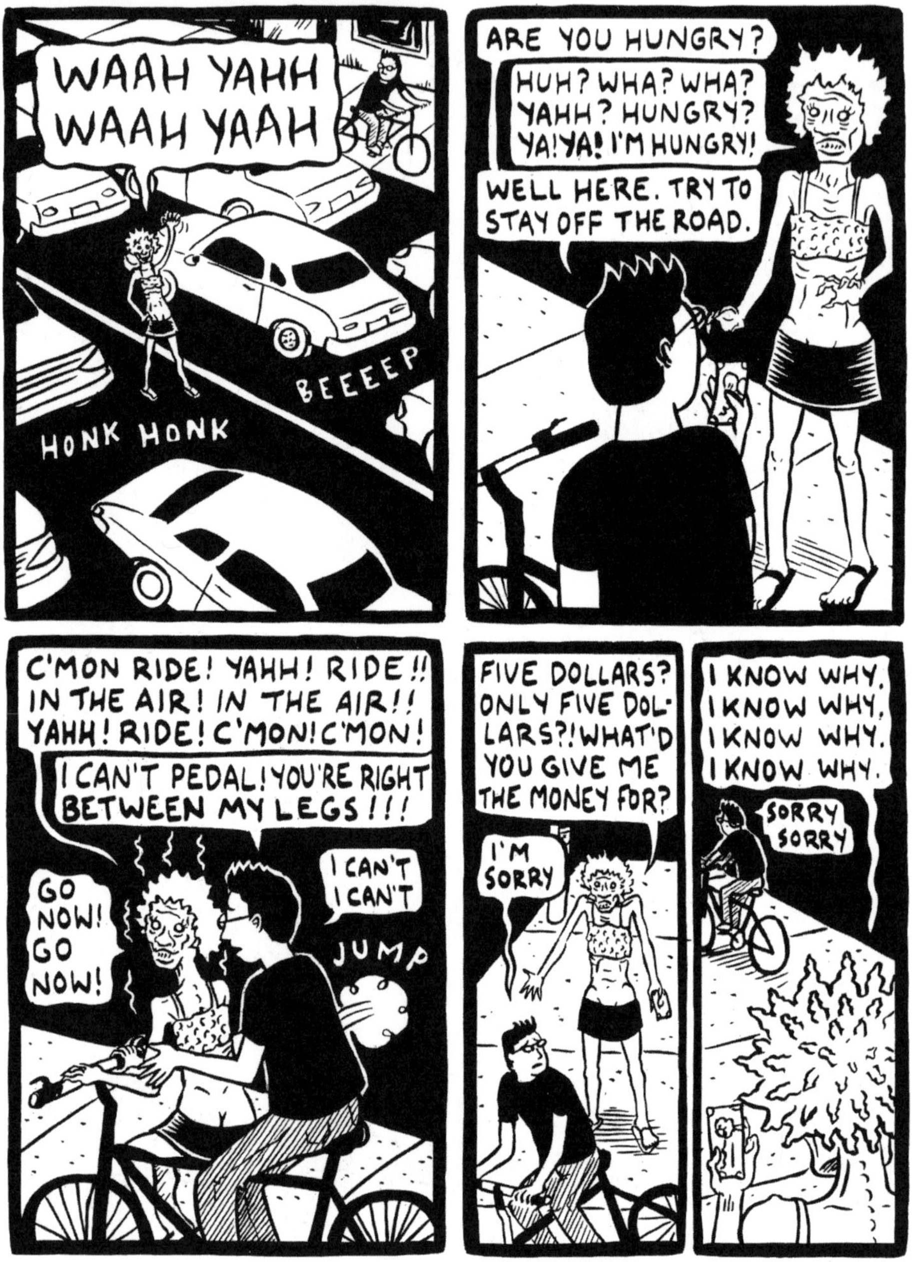
WAAH YAHH WAAH YAAH
BEEEEP
HONK HONK
ARE YOU HUNGRY?
HUH? WHA? WHA? YAHH? HUNGRY? YA! YA! I'M HUNGRY!
WELL HERE. TRY TO STAY OFF THE ROAD.
C'MON RIDE! YAHH! RIDE!! IN THE AIR! IN THE AIR!! YAHH! RIDE! C'MON! C'MON!
I CAN'T PEDAL! YOU'RE RIGHT BETWEEN MY LEGS!!!
GO NOW! GO NOW!
I CAN'T I CAN'T
JUMP
FIVE DOLLARS? ONLY FIVE DOLLARS?! WHAT'D YOU GIVE ME THE MONEY FOR?
I'M SORRY
I KNOW WHY. I KNOW WHY. I KNOW WHY. I KNOW WHY.
SORRY SORRY

fair

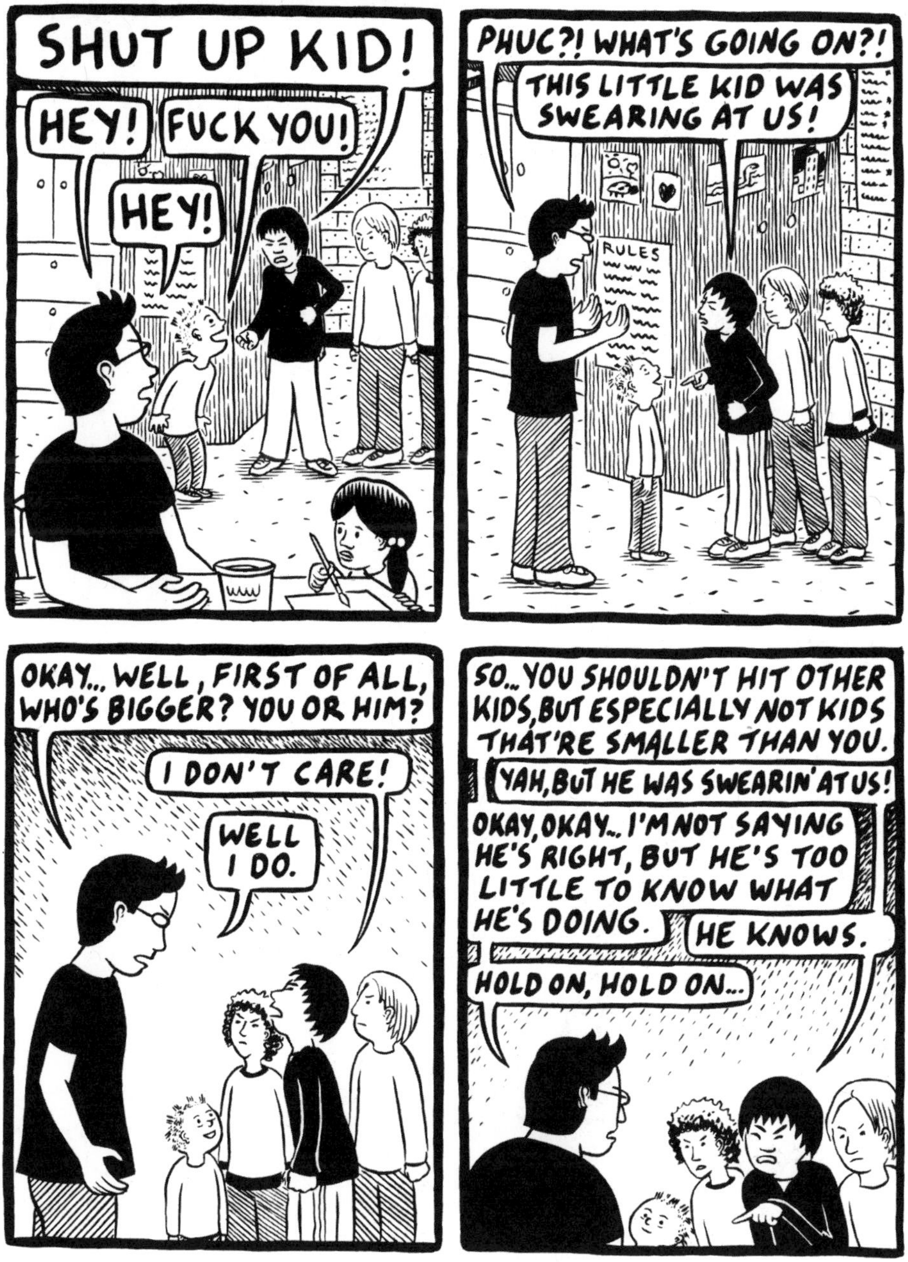
SHUT UP KID!
HEY!
FUCK YOU!
HEY!
PHUC?! WHAT'S GOING ON?!
THIS LITTLE KID WAS SWEARING AT US!
RULES
OKAY... WELL, FIRST OF ALL, WHO'S BIGGER? YOU OR HIM?
I DON'T CARE!
WELL I DO.
SO... YOU SHOULDN'T HIT OTHER KIDS, BUT ESPECIALLY NOT KIDS THAT'RE SMALLER THAN YOU.
YAH, BUT HE WAS SWEARIN' AT US!
OKAY, OKAY... I'M NOT SAYING HE'S RIGHT, BUT HE'S TOO LITTLE TO KNOW WHAT HE'S DOING.
HE KNOWS.
HOLD ON, HOLD ON...

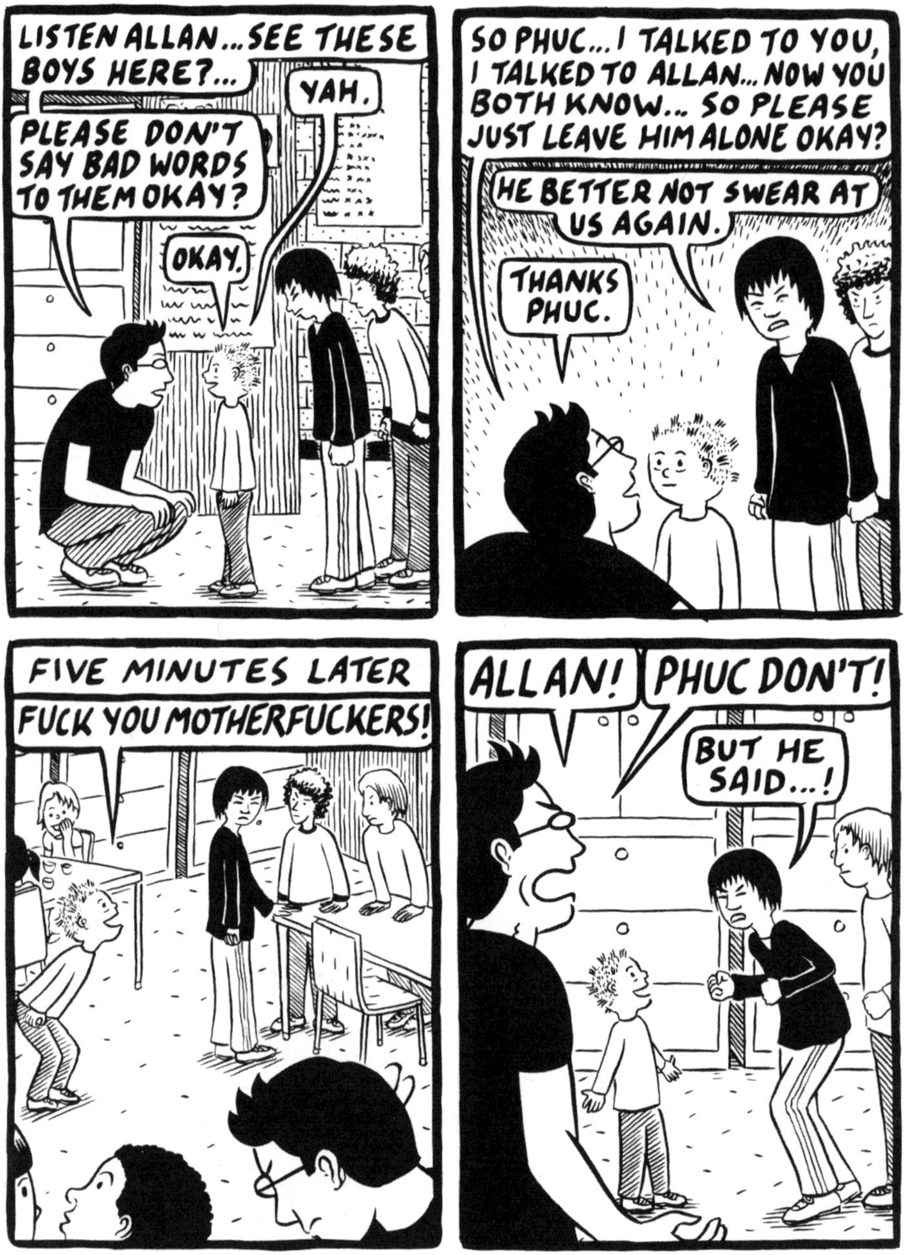
LISTEN ALLAN... SEE THESE BOYS HERE?...
PLEASE DON'T SAY BAD WORDS TO THEM OKAY?
YAH.
OKAY.
SO PHUC... I TALKED TO YOU, I TALKED TO ALLAN... NOW YOU BOTH KNOW... SO PLEASE JUST LEAVE HIM ALONE OKAY?
HE BETTER NOT SWEAR AT US AGAIN.
THANKS PHUC.
FIVE MINUTES LATER
FUCK YOU MOTHERFUCKERS!
ALLAN!
PHUC DON'T!
BUT HE SAID...!

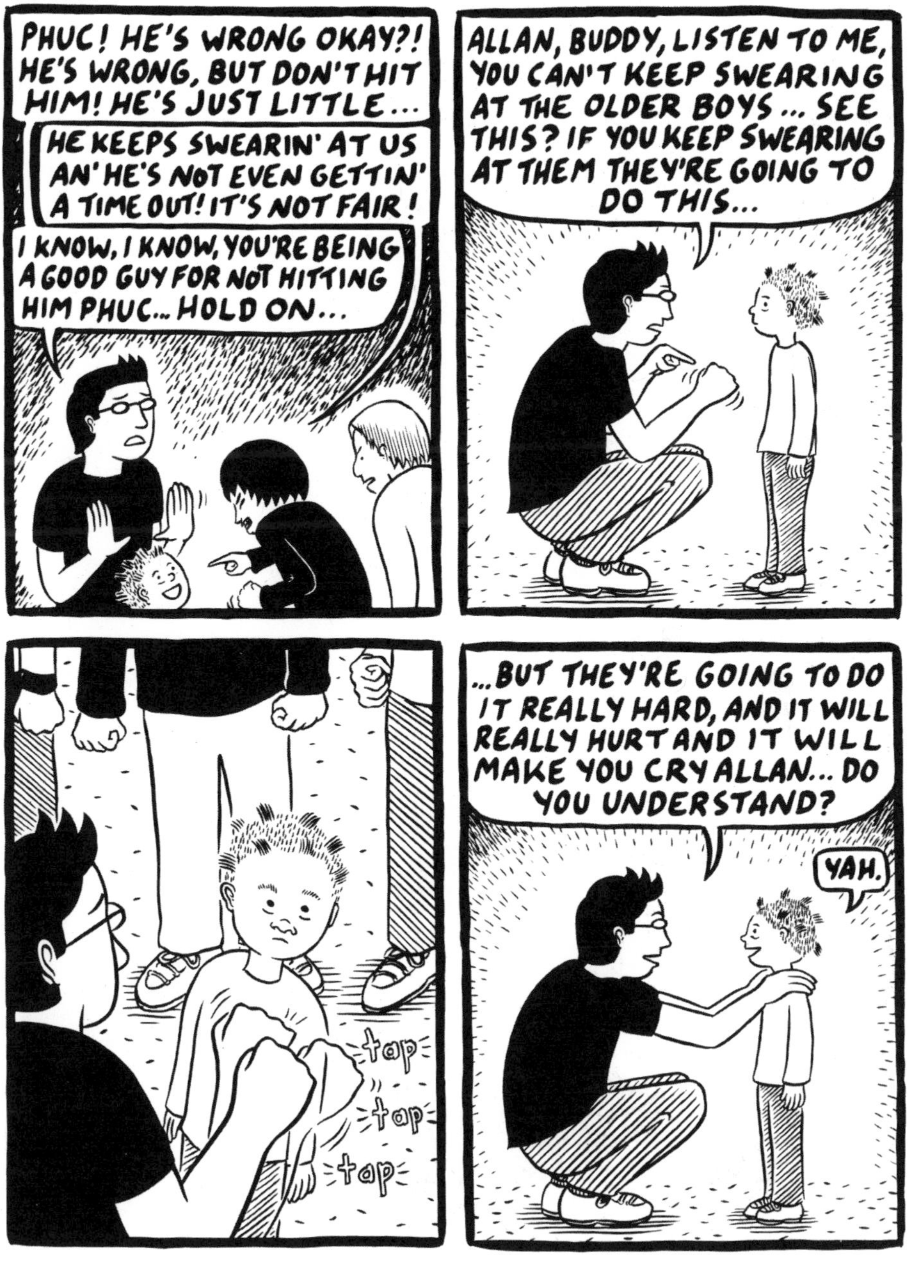

PHUC! HE'S WRONG OKAY?! HE'S WRONG, BUT DON'T HIT HIM! HE'S JUST LITTLE...
HE KEEPS SWEARIN' AT US AN' HE'S NOT EVEN GETTIN' A TIME OUT! IT'S NOT FAIR!
I KNOW, I KNOW, YOU'RE BEING A GOOD GUY FOR NOT HITTING HIM PHUC... HOLD ON...
ALLAN, BUDDY, LISTEN TO ME, YOU CAN'T KEEP SWEARING AT THE OLDER BOYS... SEE THIS? IF YOU KEEP SWEARING AT THEM THEY'RE GOING TO DO THIS...
tap
tap
tap
...BUT THEY'RE GOING TO DO IT REALLY HARD, AND IT WILL REALLY HURT AND IT WILL MAKE YOU CRY ALLAN... DO YOU UNDERSTAND?
YAH.

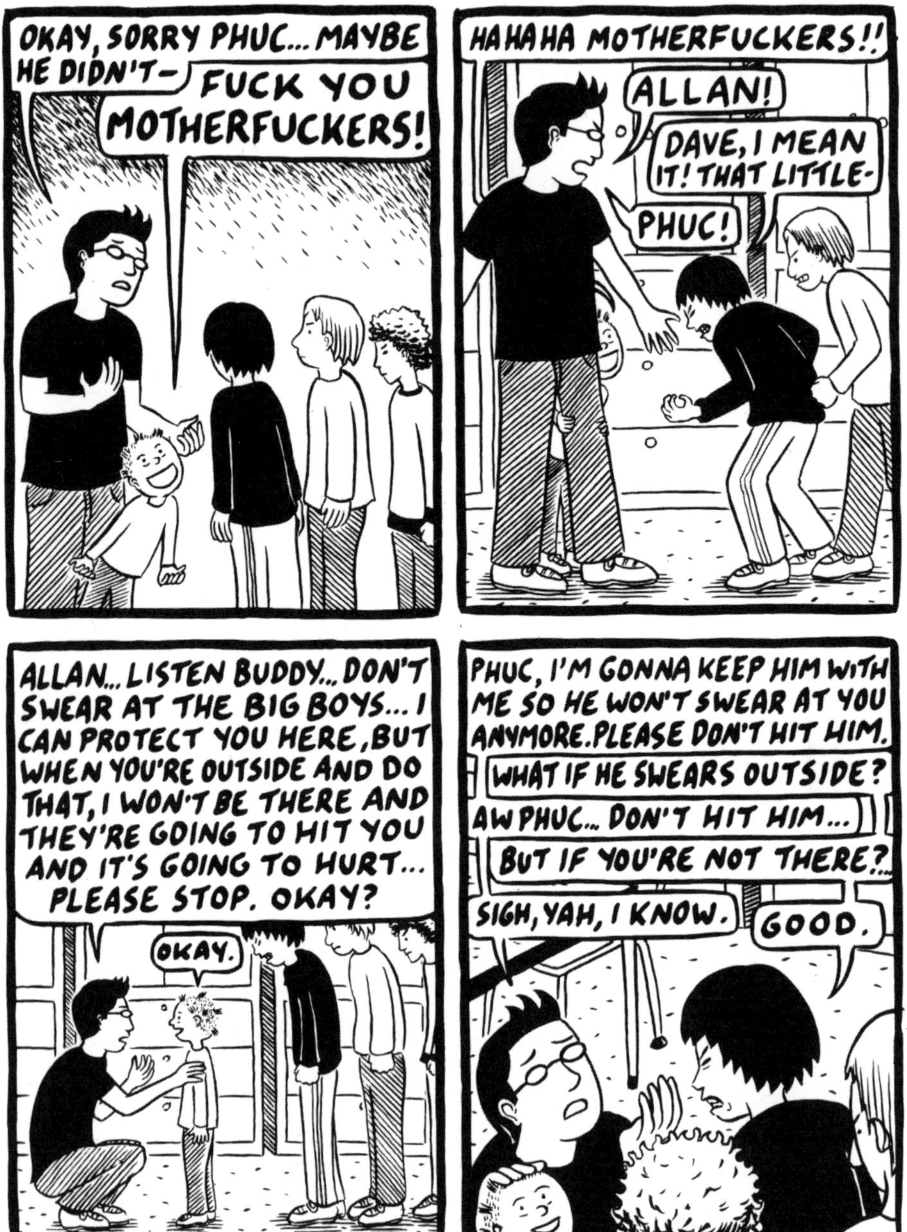

OKAY, SORRY PHUC... MAYBE HE DIDN'T-
FUCK YOU MOTHERFUCKERS!
HAHAHA MOTHERFUCKERS!!
ALLAN!
DAVE, I MEAN IT! THAT LITTLE-
PHUC!
ALLAN... LISTEN BUDDY... DON'T SWEAR AT THE BIG BOYS... I CAN PROTECT YOU HERE, BUT WHEN YOU'RE OUTSIDE AND DO THAT, I WON'T BE THERE AND THEY'RE GOING TO HIT YOU AND IT'S GOING TO HURT... PLEASE STOP. OKAY?
OKAY.
PHUC, I'M GONNA KEEP HIM WITH ME SO HE WON'T SWEAR AT YOU ANYMORE. PLEASE DON'T HIT HIM.
WHAT IF HE SWEARS OUTSIDE?
AW PHUC... DON'T HIT HIM...
BUT IF YOU'RE NOT THERE?...
SIGH, YAH, I KNOW.
GOOD.

maze

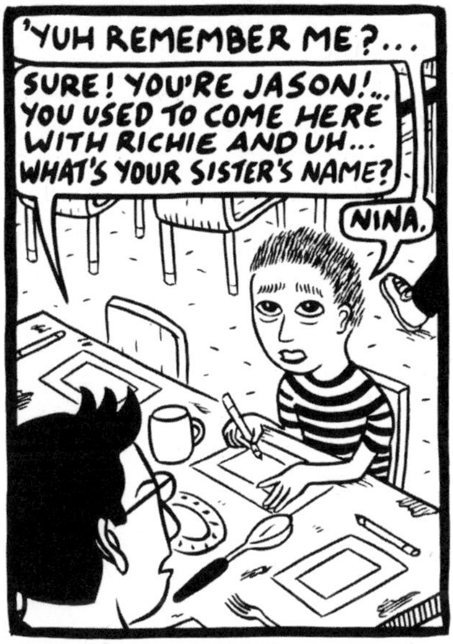
'YUH REMEMBER ME?...
SURE! YOU'RE JASON!... YOU USED TO COME HERE WITH RICHIE AND UH... WHAT'S YOUR SISTER'S NAME?
NINA.

Jason's come into the art centre today... he used to come here with his brother Richie and his sister... he's one of seven kids... haven't seen him here in years...

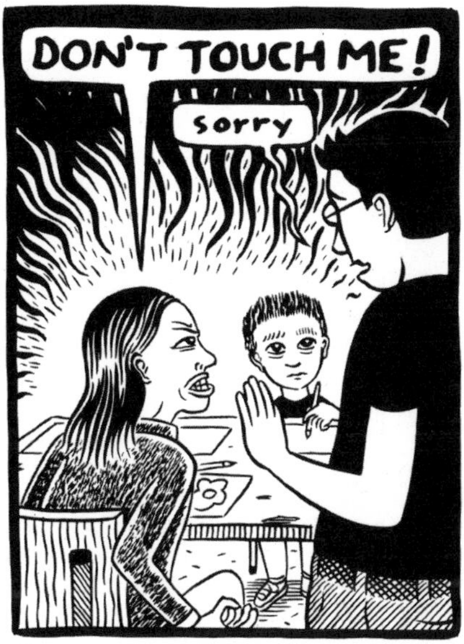
DON'T TOUCH ME!
sorry

I remember first meeting him with Nina... he wouldn't speak, and the way she jolted when I touched her on the shoulder... and her look... sigh... years ago...

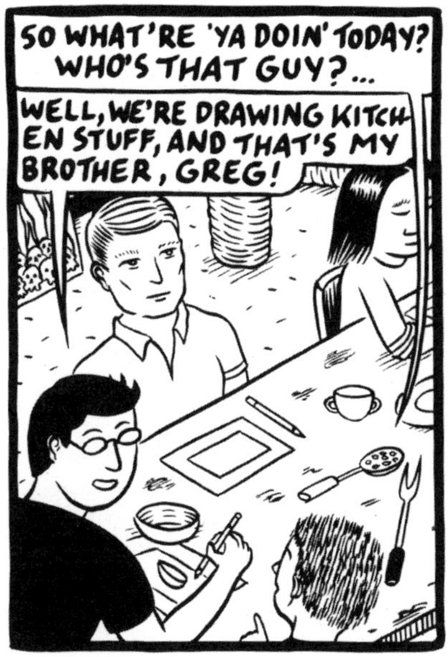
SO WHAT'RE 'YA DOIN' TODAY? WHO'S THAT GUY?...
WELL, WE'RE DRAWING KITCHEN STUFF, AND THAT'S MY BROTHER, GREG!

He doesn't want to draw the kitchen stuff... says 'it's boring'... and I agree... I've got to come up with a better project!

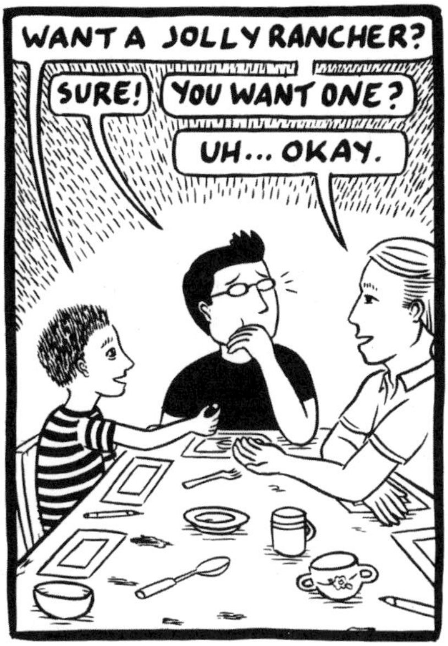
WANT A JOLLY RANCHER?
SURE!
YOU WANT ONE?
UH... OKAY.

Jason offers Greg and I a 'Jolly Rancher' candy and I see my brother is going to decline... I give him a 'look'... that this kid wants to share, it's more than candy...

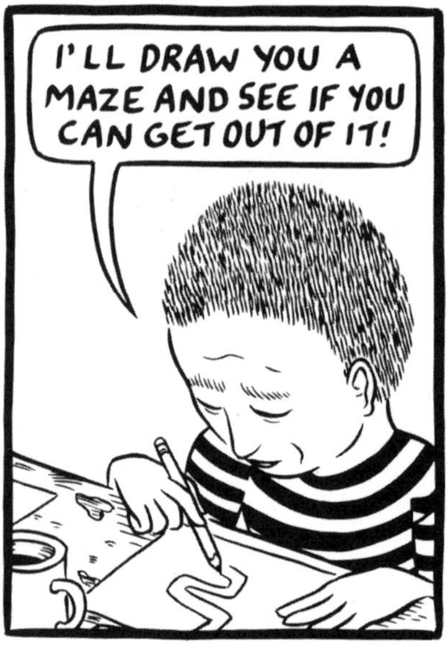
I'LL DRAW YOU A MAZE AND SEE IF YOU CAN GET OUT OF IT!

If something's not working in a project, 'let the students guide you' my sister told me...okay, we're doing mazes...

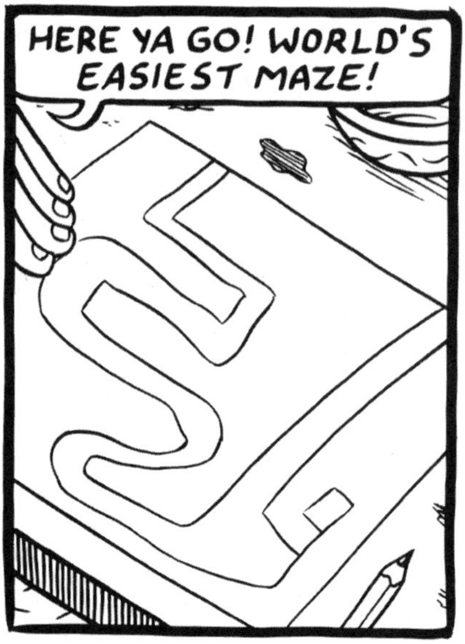
HERE YA GO! WORLD'S EASIEST MAZE!

I ask for the rules... I ask if there's any tricks... I mean it is obviously easy... I don't want to insult him... so I do it, then go and check on some other kids.

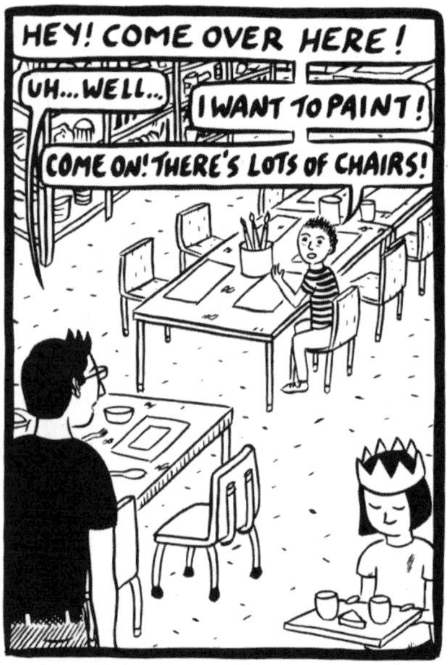
HEY! COME OVER HERE!
UH... WELL...
I WANT TO PAINT!
COME ON! THERE'S LOTS OF CHAIRS!

He's got this insistence... like this is something important... like we must listen to him...what?...

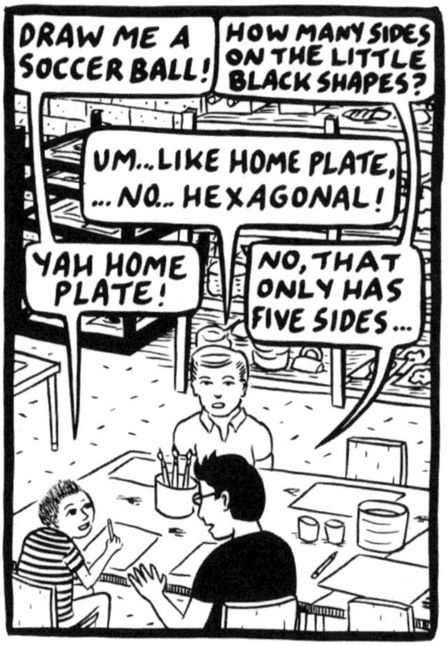
DRAW ME A SOCCER BALL!
HOW MANY SIDES ON THE LITTLE BLACK SHAPES?
UM... LIKE HOME PLATE, ... NO... HEXAGONAL!
YAH HOME PLATE!
NO, THAT ONLY HAS FIVE SIDES...

So we figure out the pattern on a soccer ball...

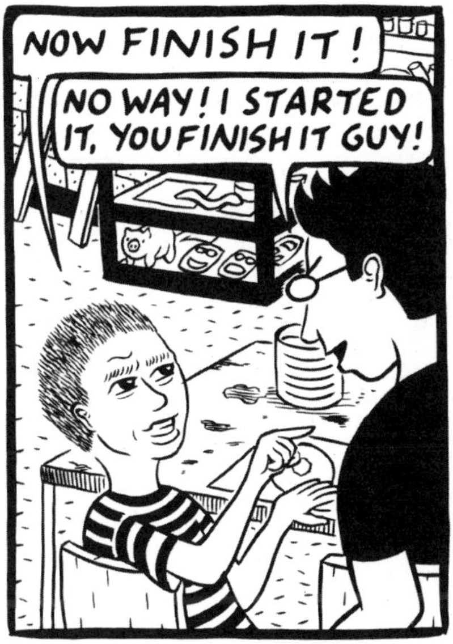
NOW FINISH IT!
NO WAY! I STARTED IT, YOU FINISH IT GUY!

I start the drawing but I want him to finish it... you know, so he learns how to do it himself...

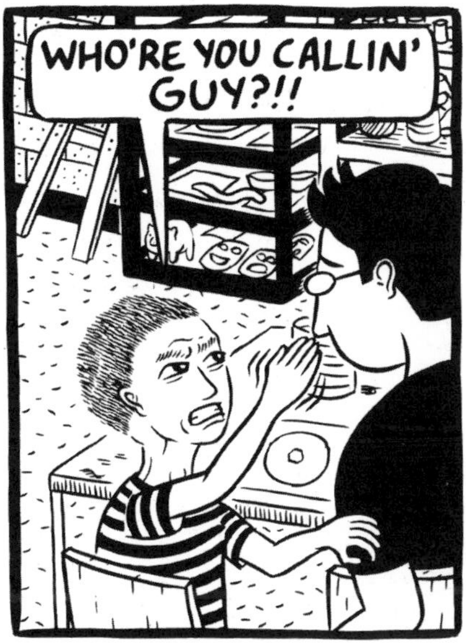
WHO'RE YOU CALLIN' GUY?!!

Suddenly the kid's grabbed my arm staring me angrily in the eye with his back hand ready! Is he really going to smack me?!

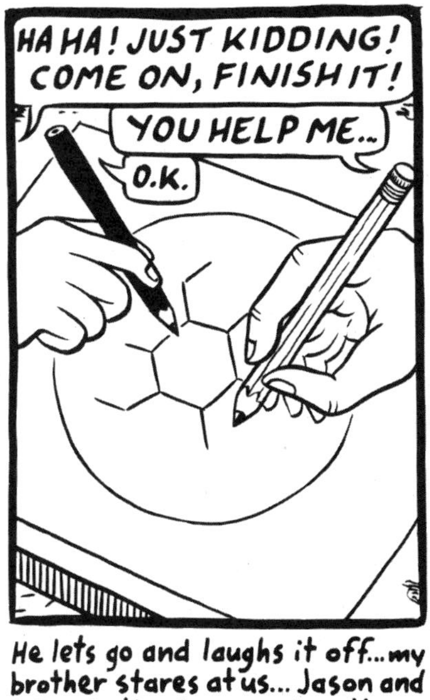
HA HA! JUST KIDDING! COME ON, FINISH IT!
YOU HELP ME...
O.K.

He lets go and laughs it off... my brother stares at us... Jason and I finish the drawing together.

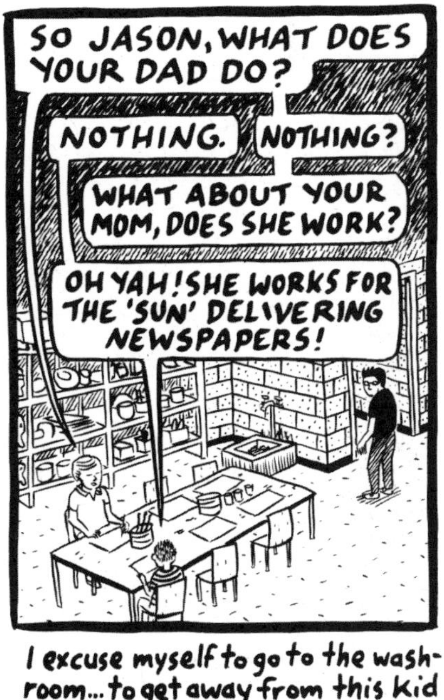
SO JASON, WHAT DOES YOUR DAD DO?
NOTHING.
NOTHING?
WHAT ABOUT YOUR MOM, DOES SHE WORK?
OH YAH! SHE WORKS FOR THE 'SUN' DELIVERING NEWSPAPERS!

I excuse myself to go to the wash-room... to get away from this kid for a minute... I cringe as I hear my brother ask him those questions... how do you get out?...

flytrap

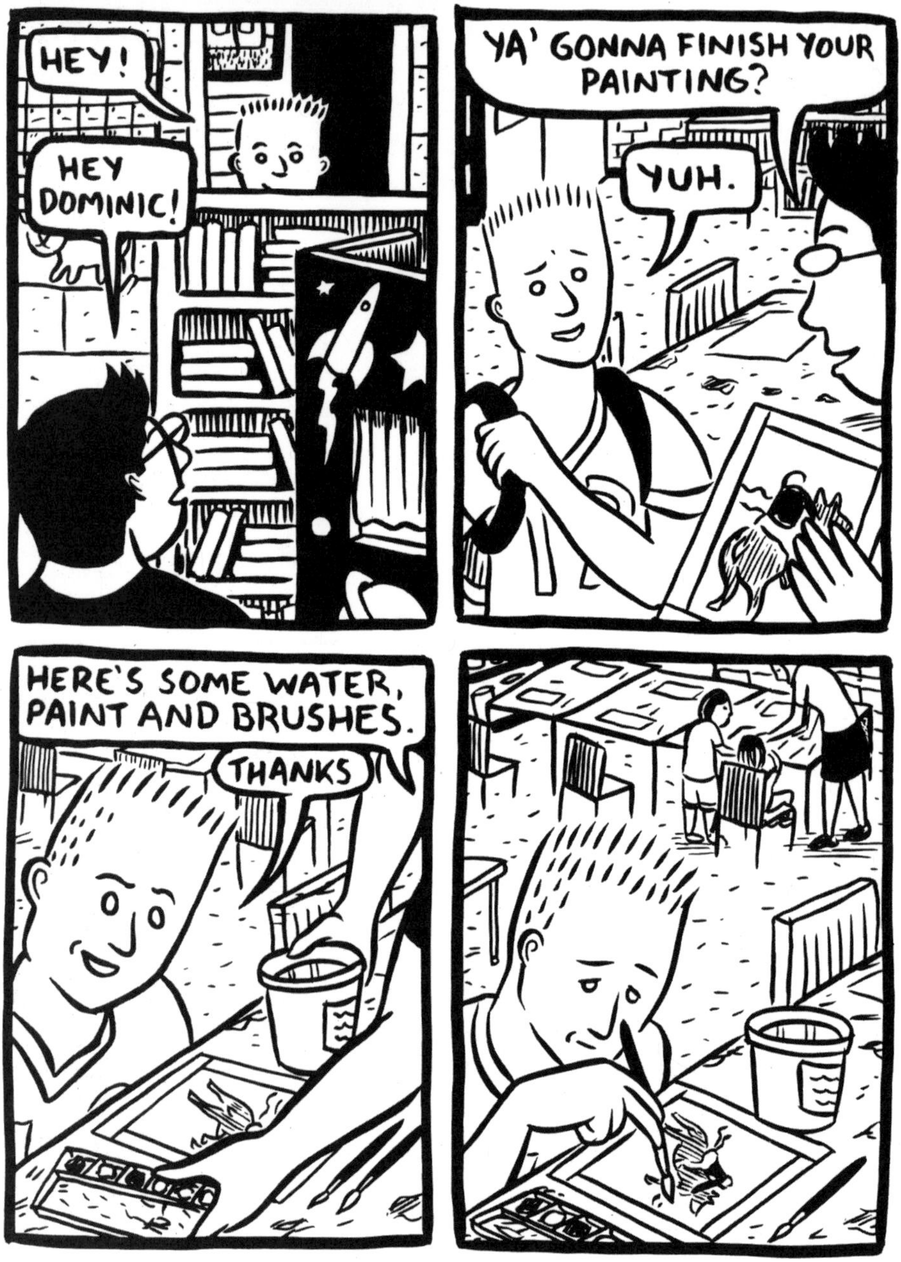
HEY!
HEY DOMINIC!
YA' GONNA FINISH YOUR PAINTING?
YUH.
HERE'S SOME WATER, PAINT AND BRUSHES.
THANKS

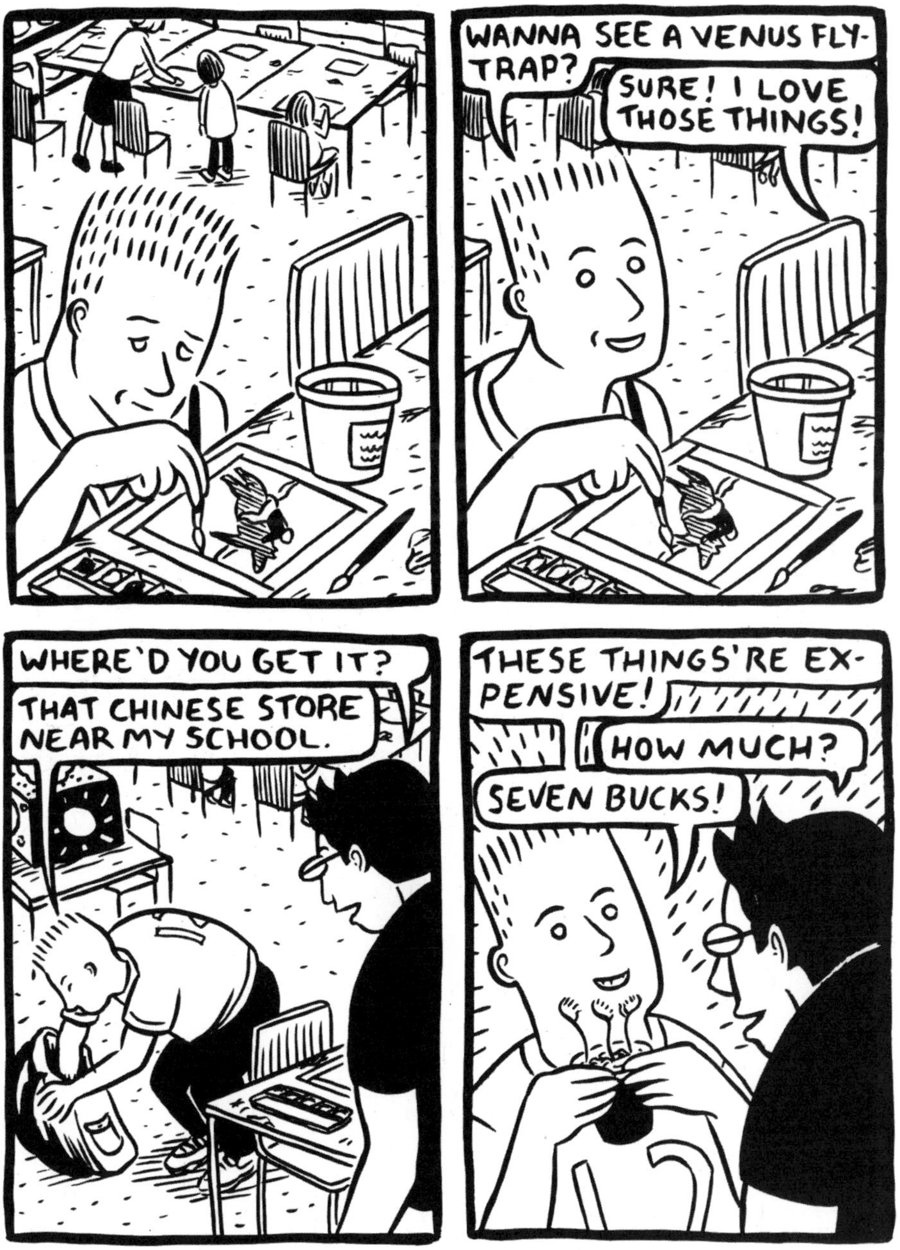
WANNA SEE A VENUS FLY-TRAP?
SURE! I LOVE THOSE THINGS!
WHERE'D YOU GET IT?
THAT CHINESE STORE NEAR MY SCHOOL.
THESE THINGS'RE EX-PENSIVE!
HOW MUCH?
SEVEN BUCKS!

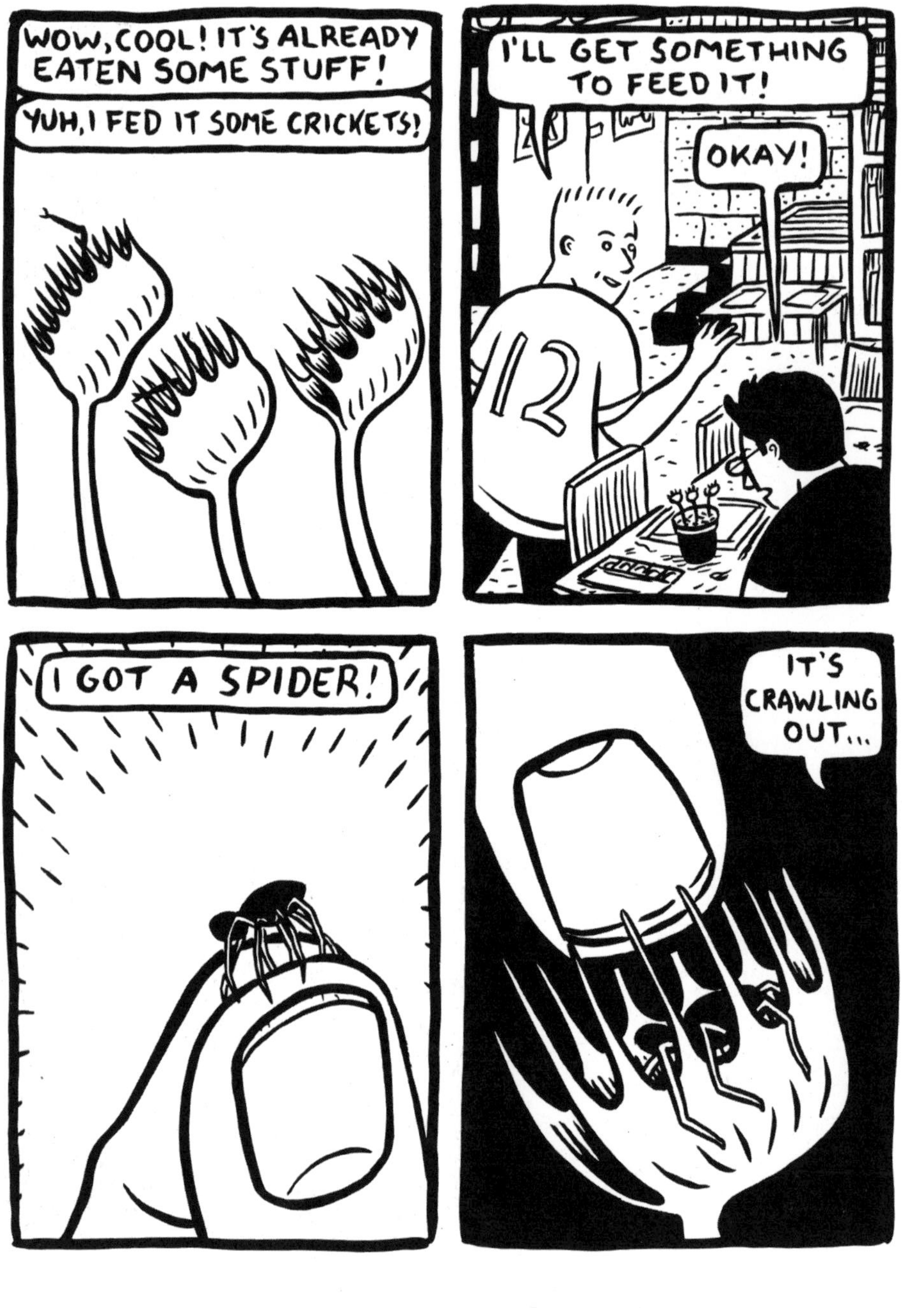
WOW, COOL! IT'S ALREADY EATEN SOME STUFF!
YUH, I FED IT SOME CRICKETS!
I'LL GET SOMETHING TO FEED IT!
OKAY!
I GOT A SPIDER!
IT'S CRAWLING OUT...

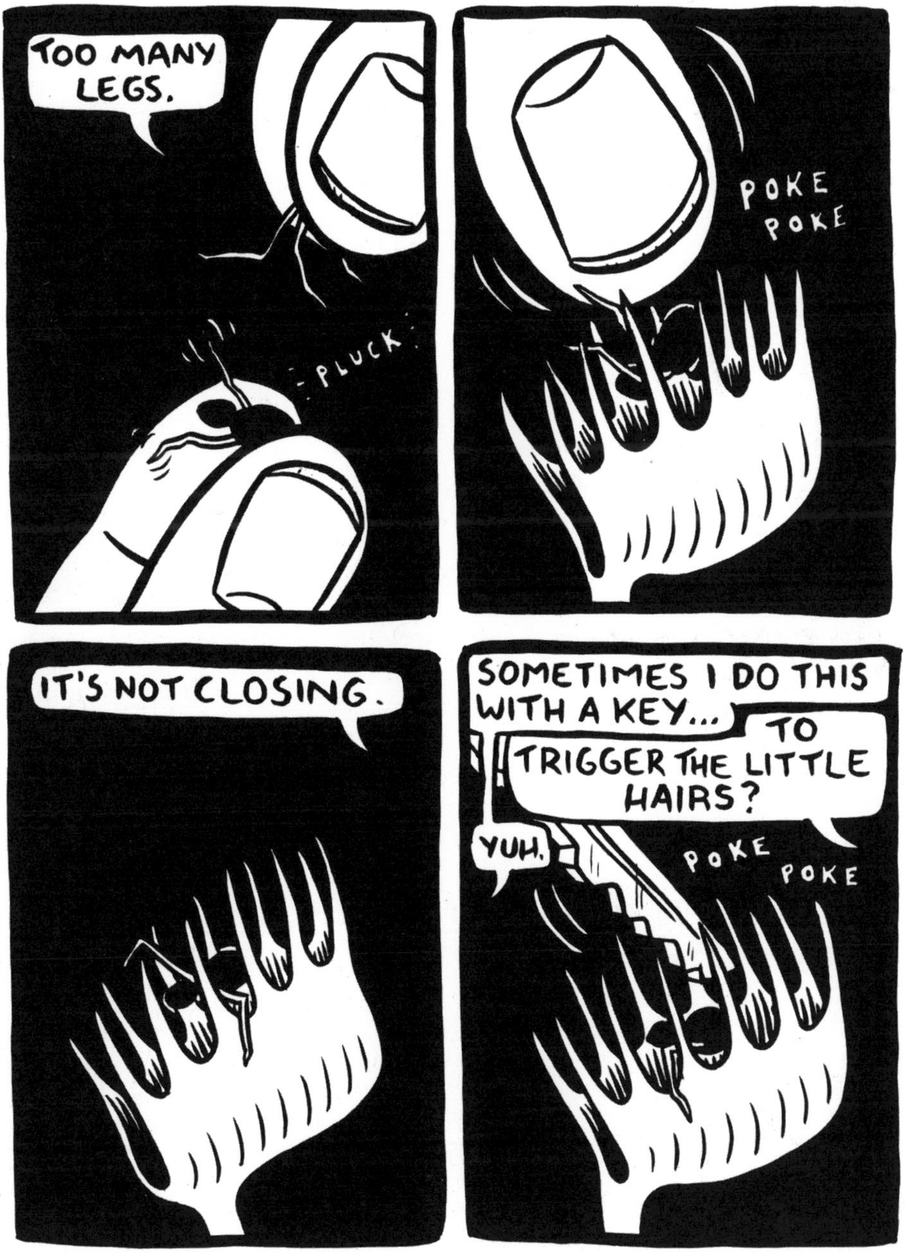

TOO MANY LEGS.
PLUCK
POKE
POKE
IT'S NOT CLOSING.
SOMETIMES I DO THIS WITH A KEY...
TO TRIGGER THE LITTLE HAIRS?
YUH.
POKE
POKE

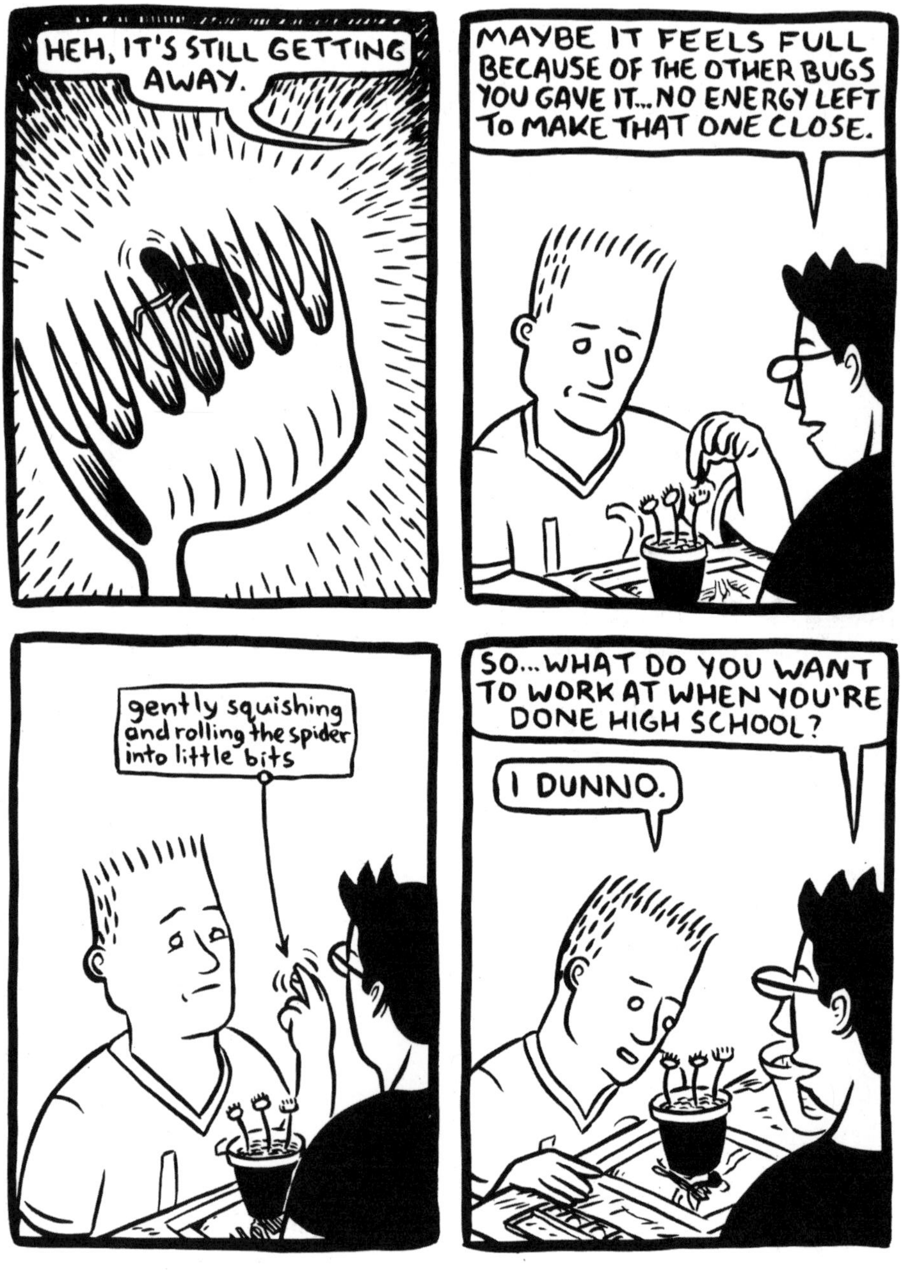
HEH, IT'S STILL GETTING AWAY.
MAYBE IT FEELS FULL BECAUSE OF THE OTHER BUGS YOU GAVE IT... NO ENERGY LEFT TO MAKE THAT ONE CLOSE.
gently squishing and rolling the spider into little bits
SO... WHAT DO YOU WANT TO WORK AT WHEN YOU'RE DONE HIGH SCHOOL?
I DUNNO.

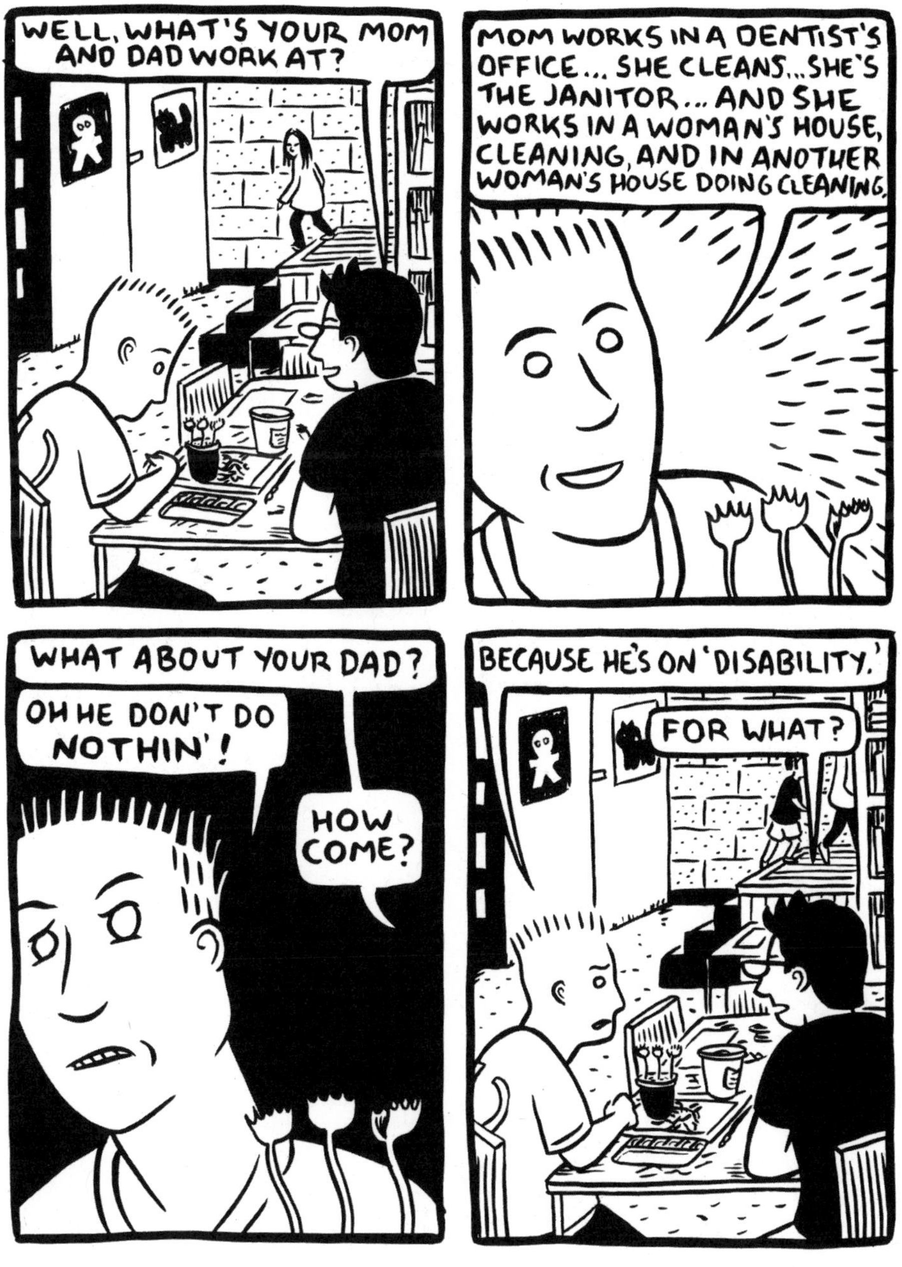
WELL, WHAT'S YOUR MOM AND DAD WORK AT?
MOM WORKS IN A DENTIST'S OFFICE... SHE CLEANS... SHE'S THE JANITOR... AND SHE WORKS IN A WOMAN'S HOUSE, CLEANING, AND IN ANOTHER WOMAN'S HOUSE DOING CLEANING.
WHAT ABOUT YOUR DAD?
OH HE DON'T DO NOTHIN'!
HOW COME?
BECAUSE HE'S ON 'DISABILITY.'
FOR WHAT?

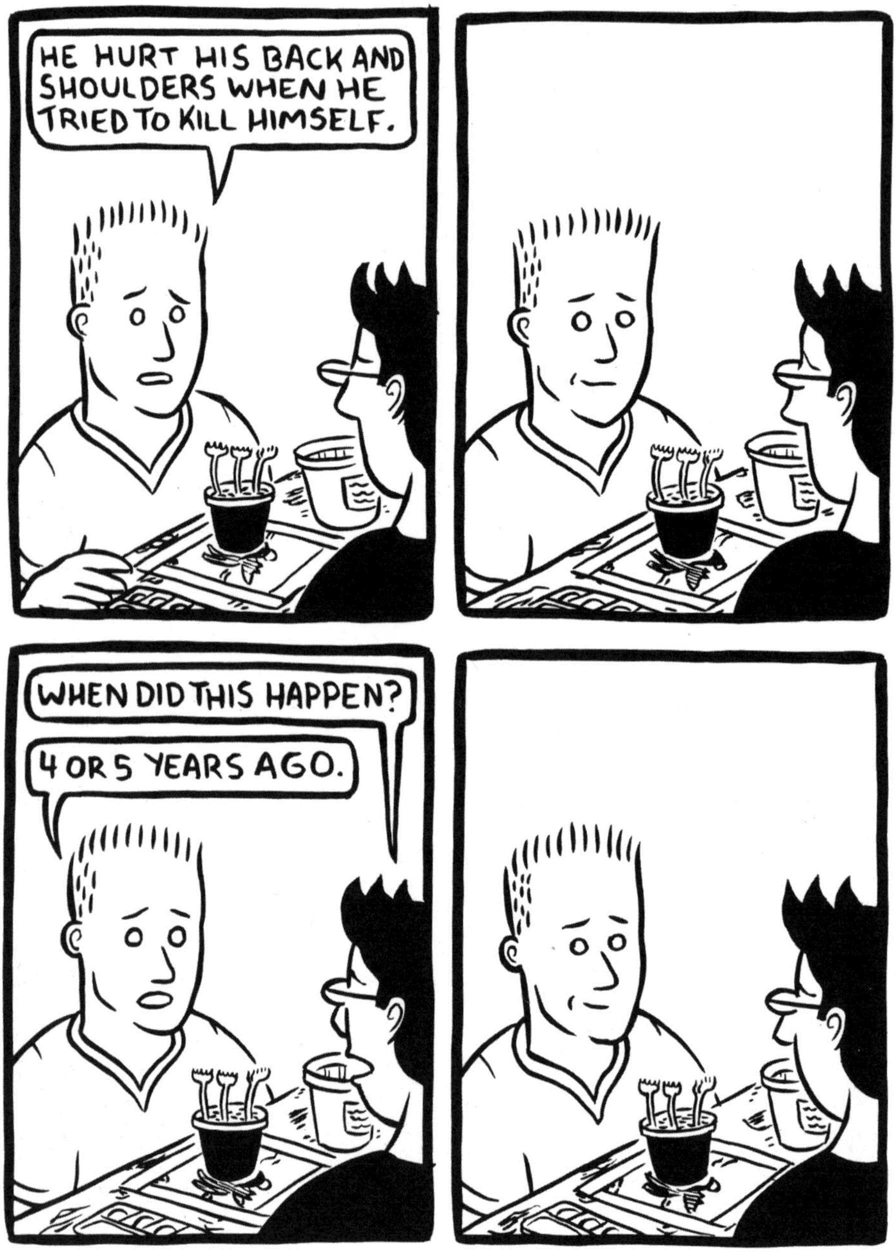
HE HURT HIS BACK AND SHOULDERS WHEN HE TRIED TO KILL HIMSELF.
WHEN DID THIS HAPPEN?
4 OR 5 YEARS AGO.

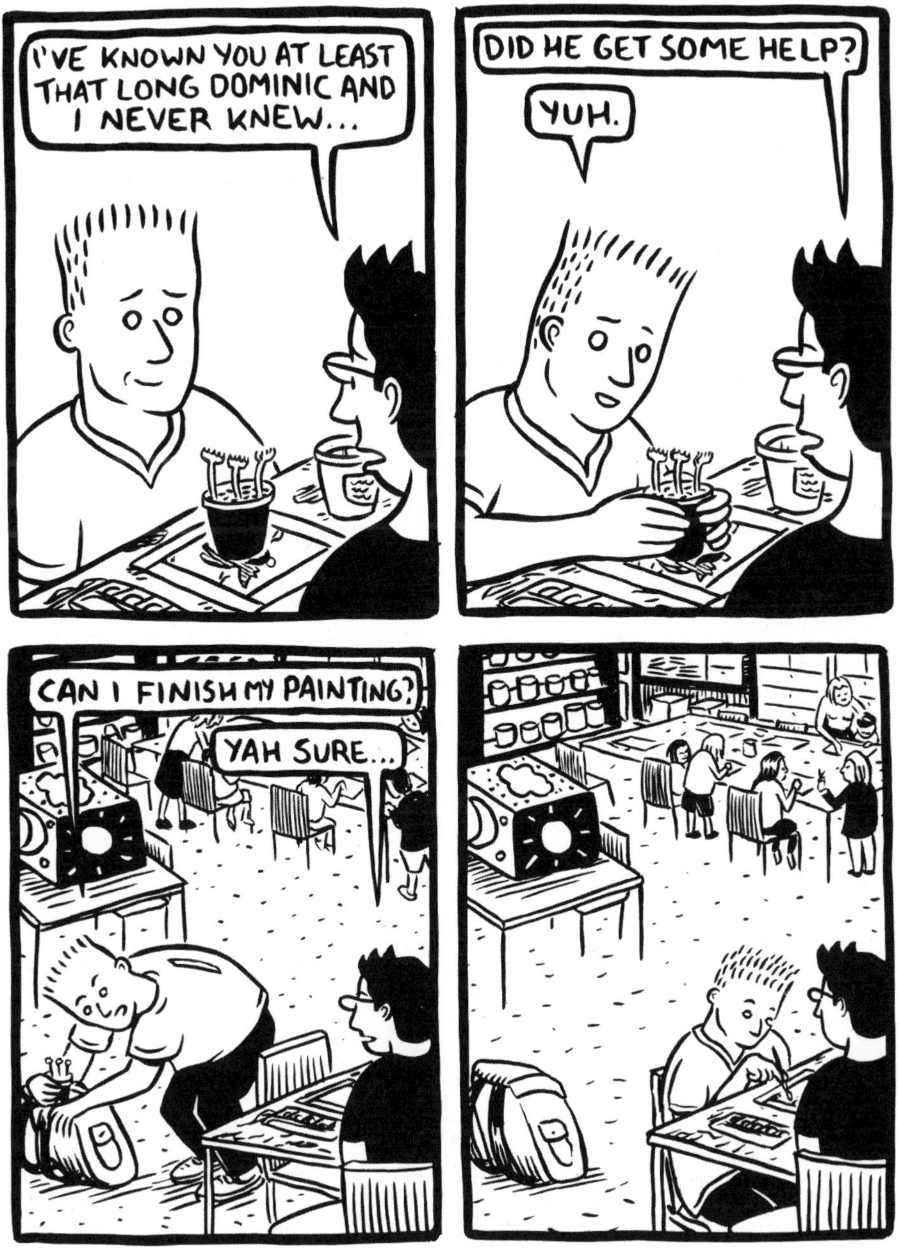
I'VE KNOWN YOU AT LEAST THAT LONG DOMINIC AND I NEVER KNEW...
DID HE GET SOME HELP?
YUH.
CAN I FINISH MY PAINTING?
YAH SURE...

before work

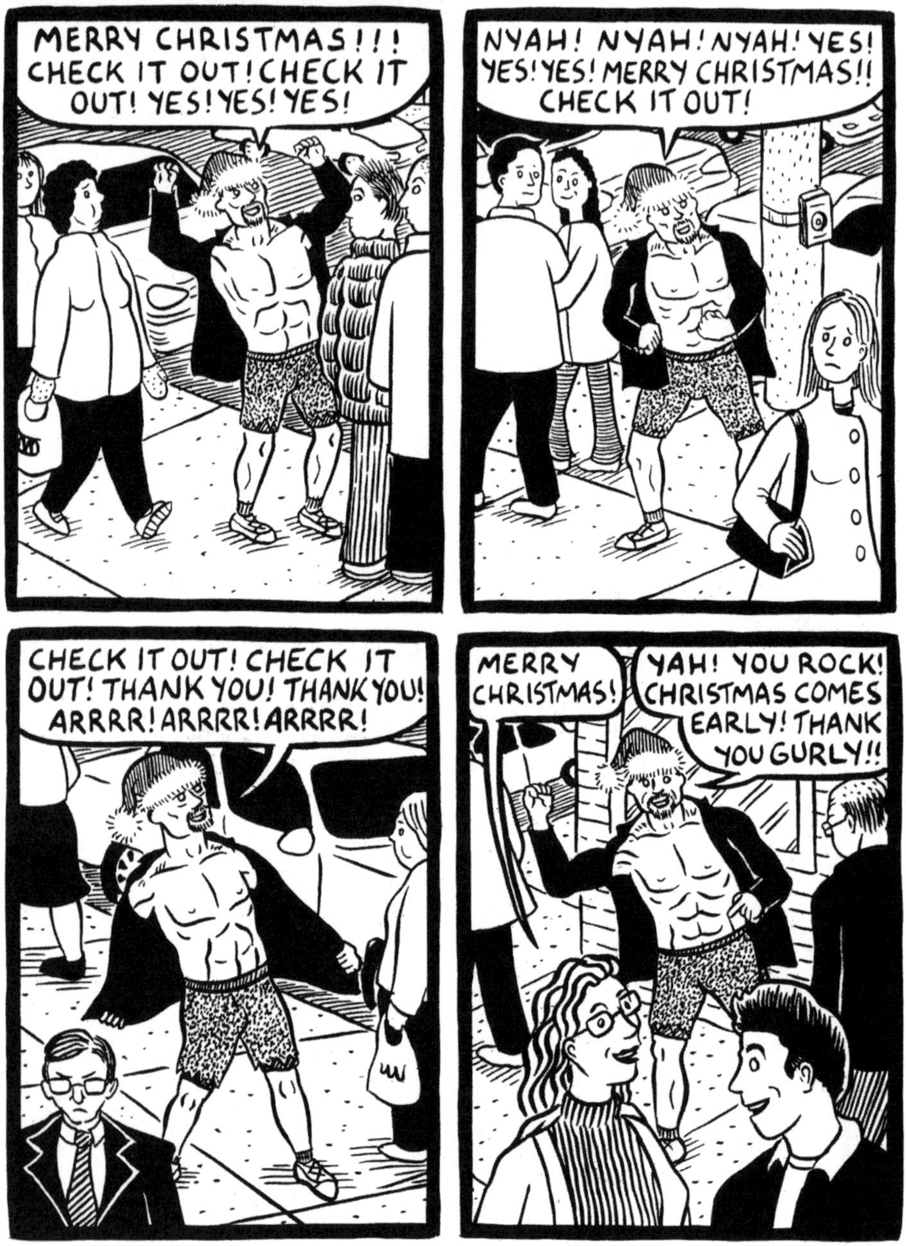

MERRY CHRISTMAS!!! CHECK IT OUT! CHECK IT OUT! YES! YES! YES!
NYAH! NYAH! NYAH! YES! YES! YES! MERRY CHRISTMAS!! CHECK IT OUT!
CHECK IT OUT! CHECK IT OUT! THANK YOU! THANK YOU! ARRRR! ARRRR! ARRRR!
MERRY CHRISTMAS!
YAH! YOU ROCK! CHRISTMAS COMES EARLY! THANK YOU GURLY!!

shoe

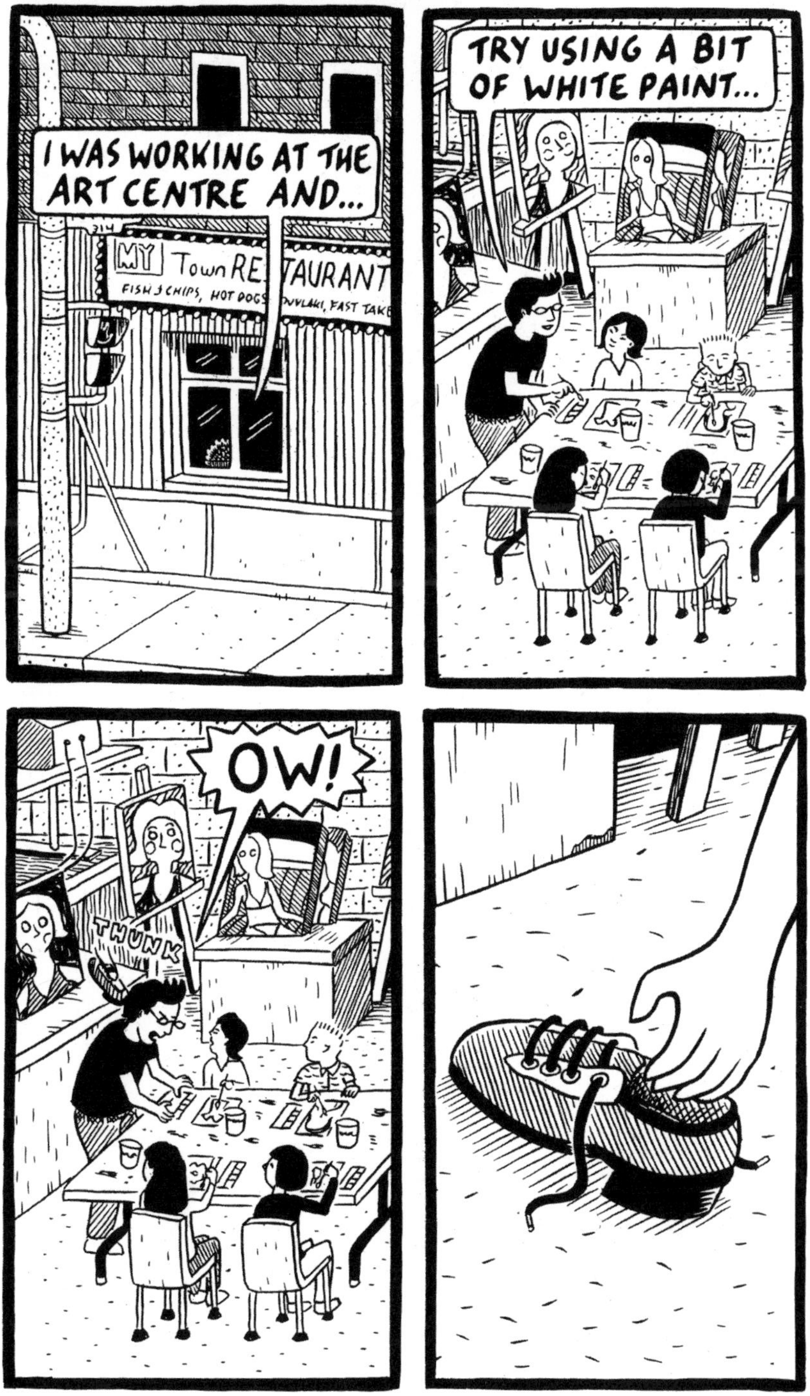
I WAS WORKING AT THE ART CENTRE AND...
MY Town RE TAURANT
FISH & CHIPS, HOT DOGS
TRY USING A BIT OF WHITE PAINT...
OW!
THUNK

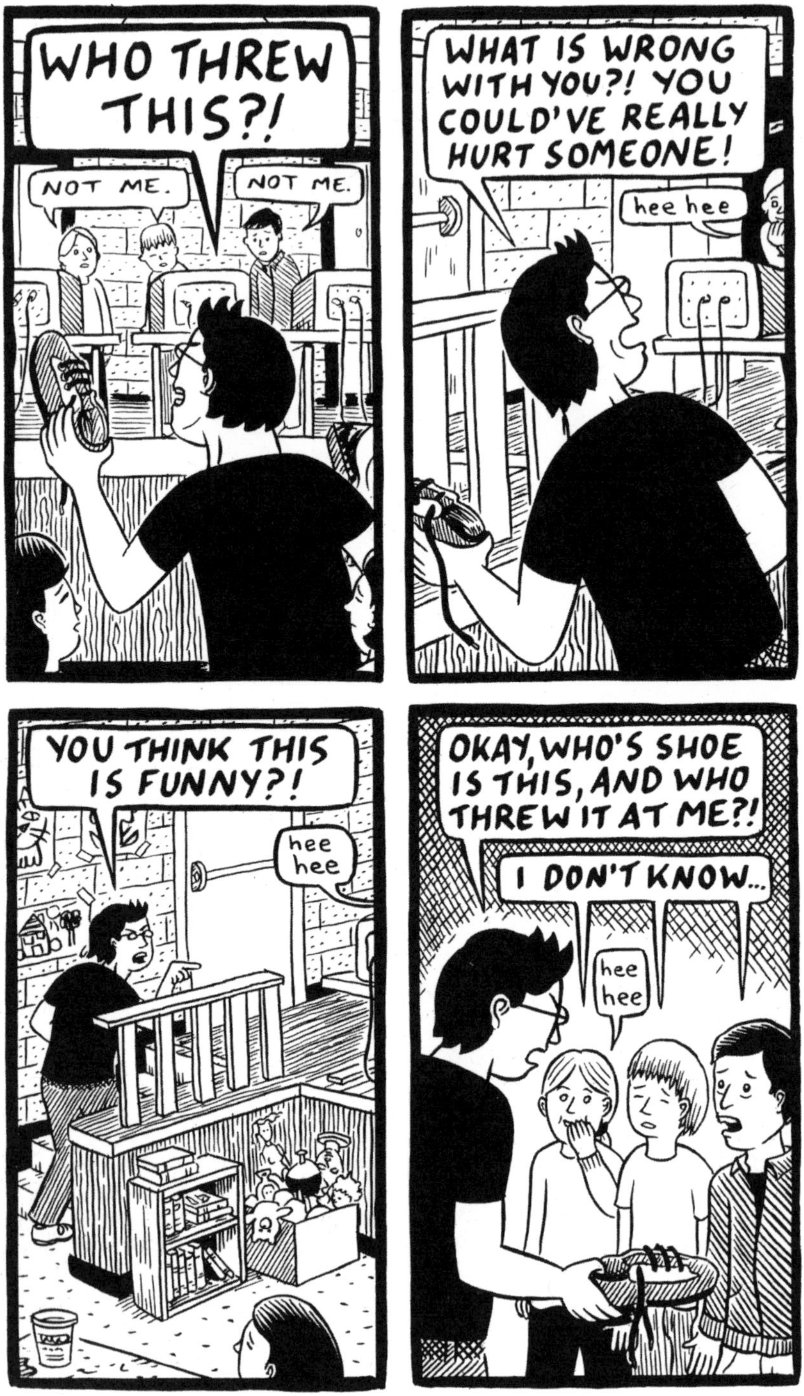
WHO THREW THIS?!
NOT ME.
NOT ME.
WHAT IS WRONG WITH YOU?! YOU COULD'VE REALLY HURT SOMEONE!
hee hee
YOU THINK THIS IS FUNNY?!
hee hee
OKAY, WHO'S SHOE IS THIS, AND WHO THREW IT AT ME?!
I DON'T KNOW...
hee hee

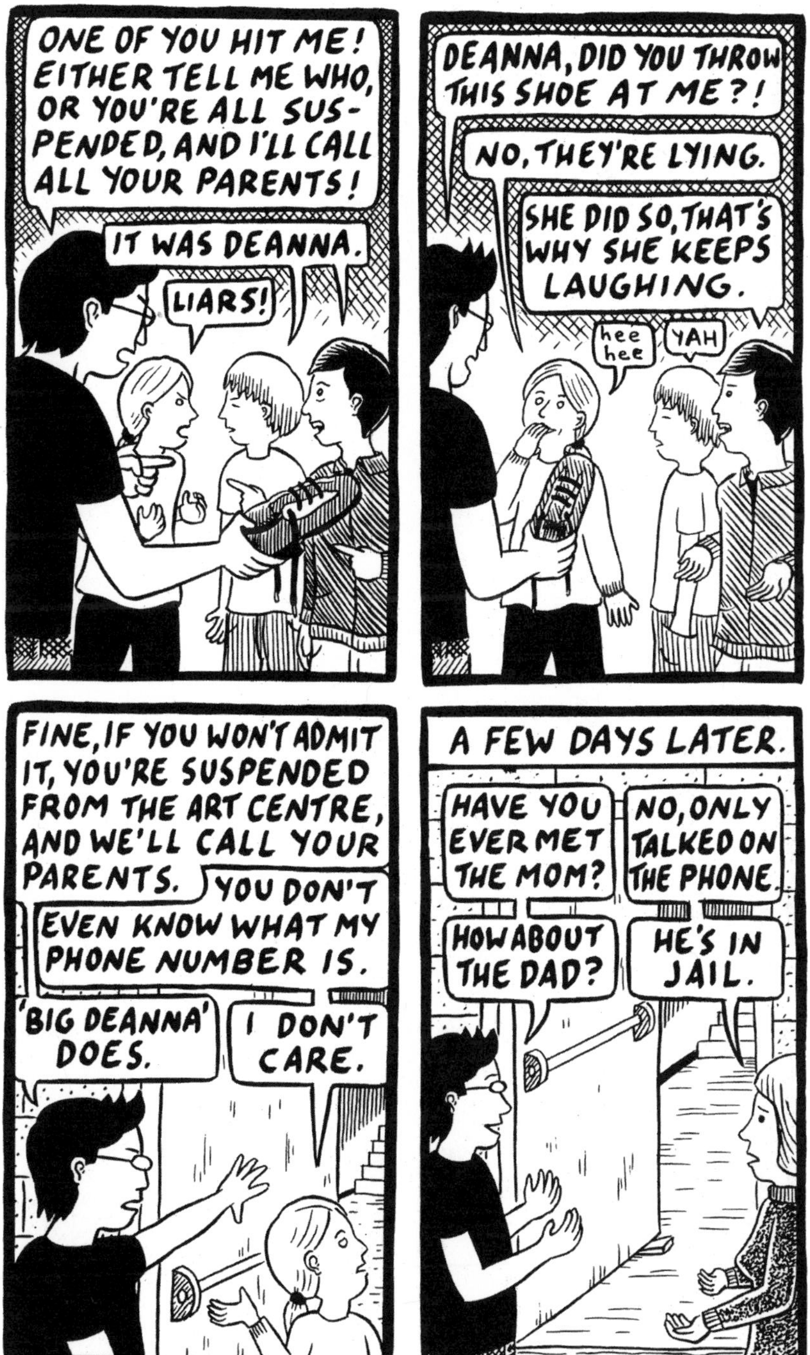
ONE OF YOU HIT ME! EITHER TELL ME WHO, OR YOU'RE ALL SUS-PENDED, AND I'LL CALL ALL YOUR PARENTS!
IT WAS DEANNA.
LIARS!
DEANNA, DID YOU THROW THIS SHOE AT ME?!
NO, THEY'RE LYING.
SHE DID SO, THAT'S WHY SHE KEEPS LAUGHING.
hee hee
YAH
FINE, IF YOU WON'T ADMIT IT, YOU'RE SUSPENDED FROM THE ART CENTRE, AND WE'LL CALL YOUR PARENTS.
YOU DON'T EVEN KNOW WHAT MY PHONE NUMBER IS.
'BIG DEANNA' DOES.
I DON'T CARE.
A FEW DAYS LATER.
HAVE YOU EVER MET THE MOM?
NO, ONLY TALKED ON THE PHONE.
HOW ABOUT THE DAD?
HE'S IN JAIL.

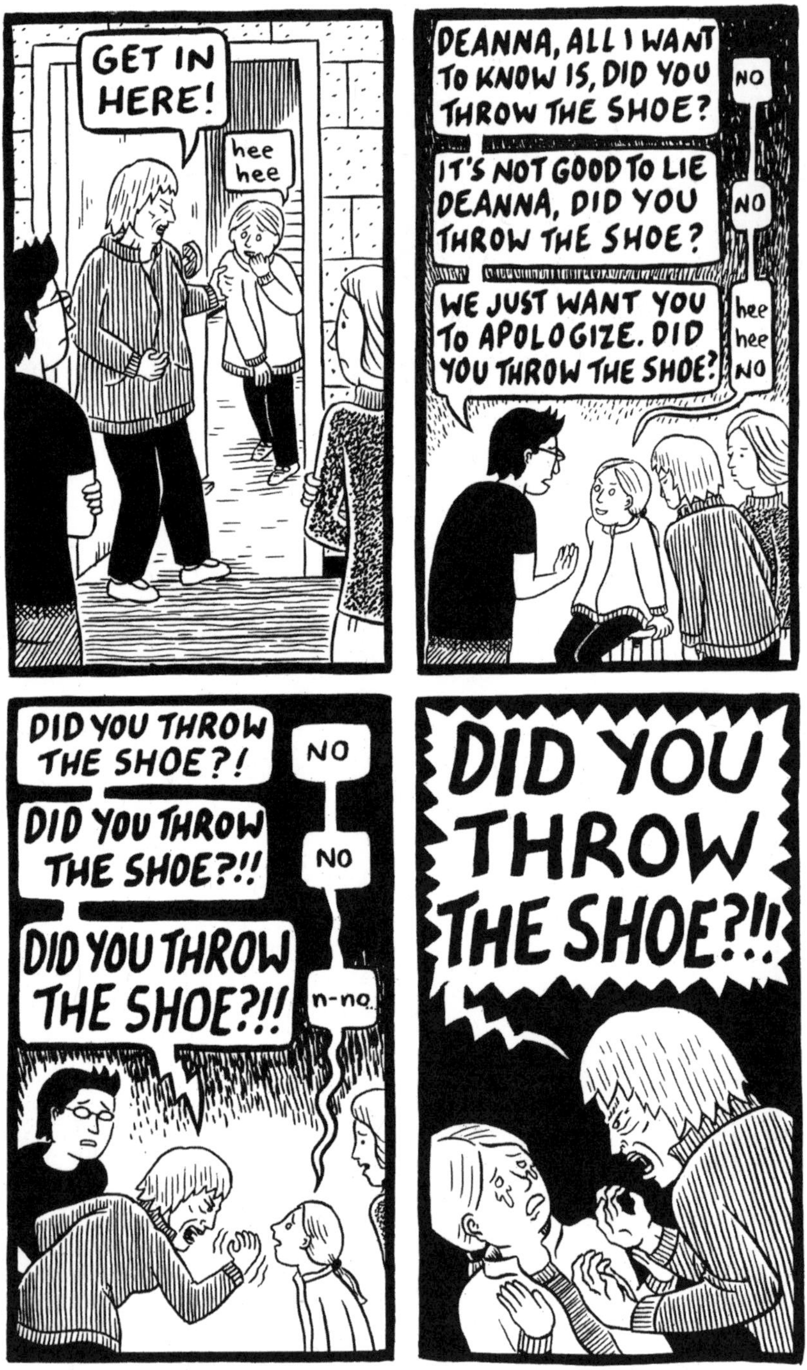
GET IN HERE!
hee hee
DEANNA, ALL I WANT TO KNOW IS, DID YOU THROW THE SHOE?
NO
IT'S NOT GOOD TO LIE DEANNA, DID YOU THROW THE SHOE?
NO
WE JUST WANT YOU TO APOLOGIZE. DID YOU THROW THE SHOE?
hee hee NO
DID YOU THROW THE SHOE?!
NO
DID YOU THROW THE SHOE?!!
NO
DID YOU THROW THE SHOE?!!
n-no..
DID YOU THROW THE SHOE?!!

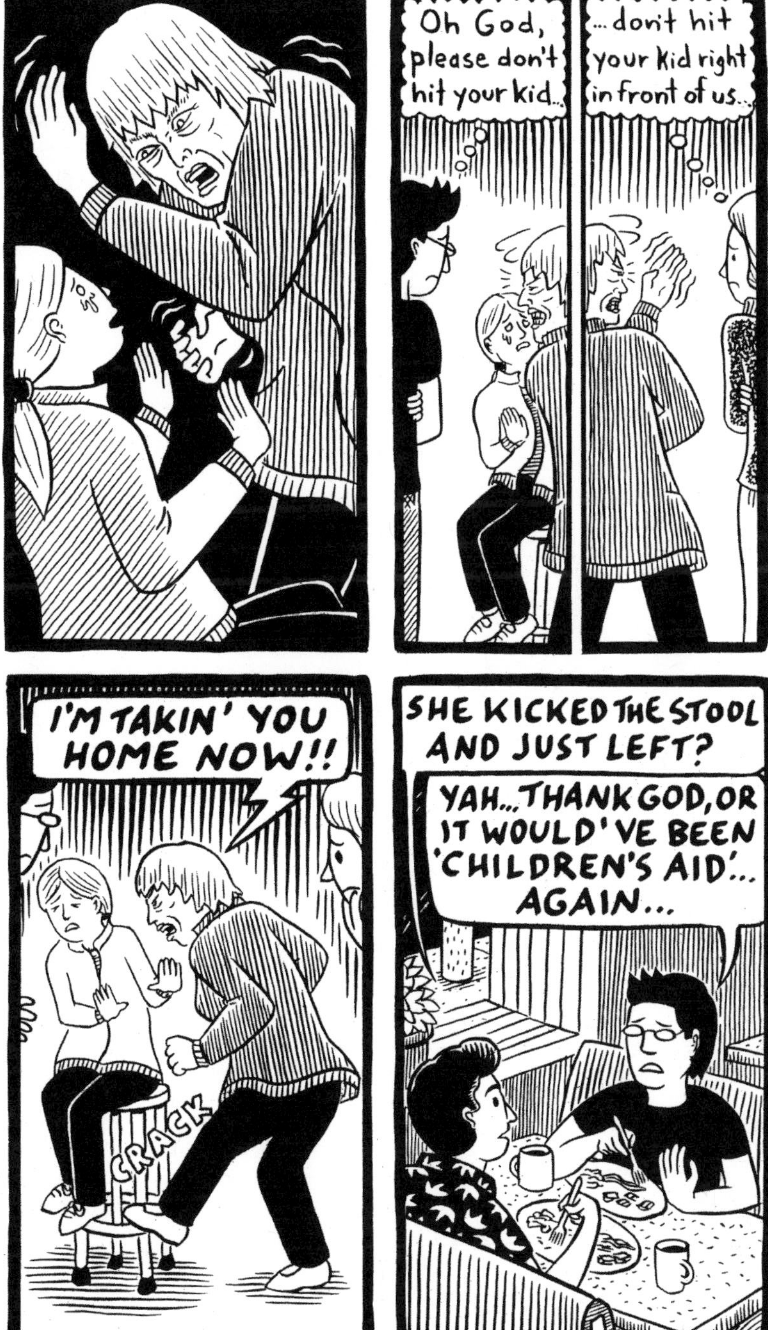

Oh God, please don't hit your kid...
...don't hit your kid right in front of us...
I'M TAKIN' YOU HOME NOW!!
CRACK
SHE KICKED THE STOOL AND JUST LEFT?
YAH... THANK GOD, OR IT WOULD'VE BEEN 'CHILDREN'S AID'... AGAIN...

tamagotchi

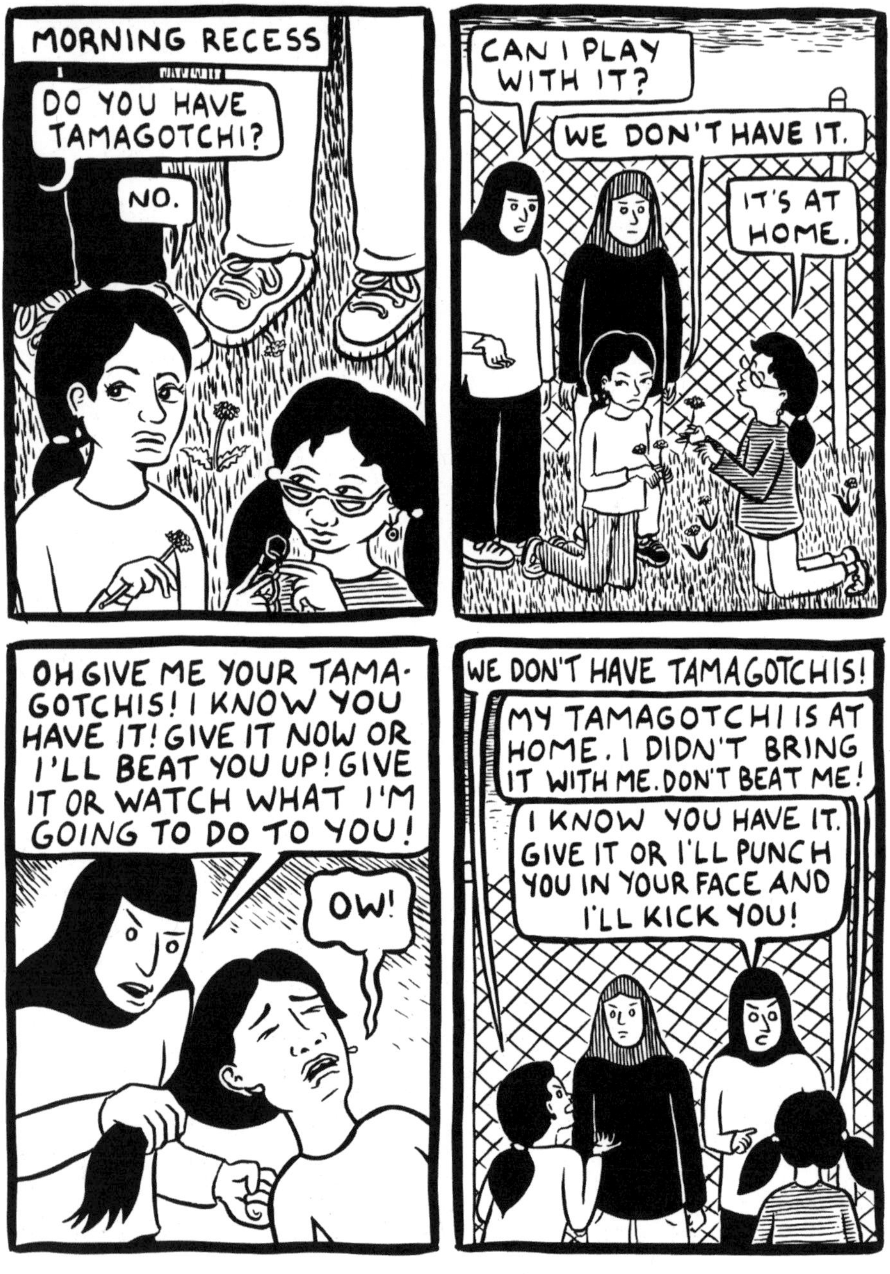
MORNING RECESS
DO YOU HAVE TAMAGOTCHI?
NO.
CAN I PLAY WITH IT?
WE DON'T HAVE IT.
IT'S AT HOME.
OH GIVE ME YOUR TAMA-GOTCHIS! I KNOW YOU HAVE IT! GIVE IT NOW OR I'LL BEAT YOU UP! GIVE IT OR WATCH WHAT I'M GOING TO DO TO YOU!
OW!
WE DON'T HAVE TAMAGOTCHIS!
MY TAMAGOTCHI IS AT HOME. I DIDN'T BRING IT WITH ME. DON'T BEAT ME!
I KNOW YOU HAVE IT. GIVE IT OR I'LL PUNCH YOU IN YOUR FACE AND I'LL KICK YOU!

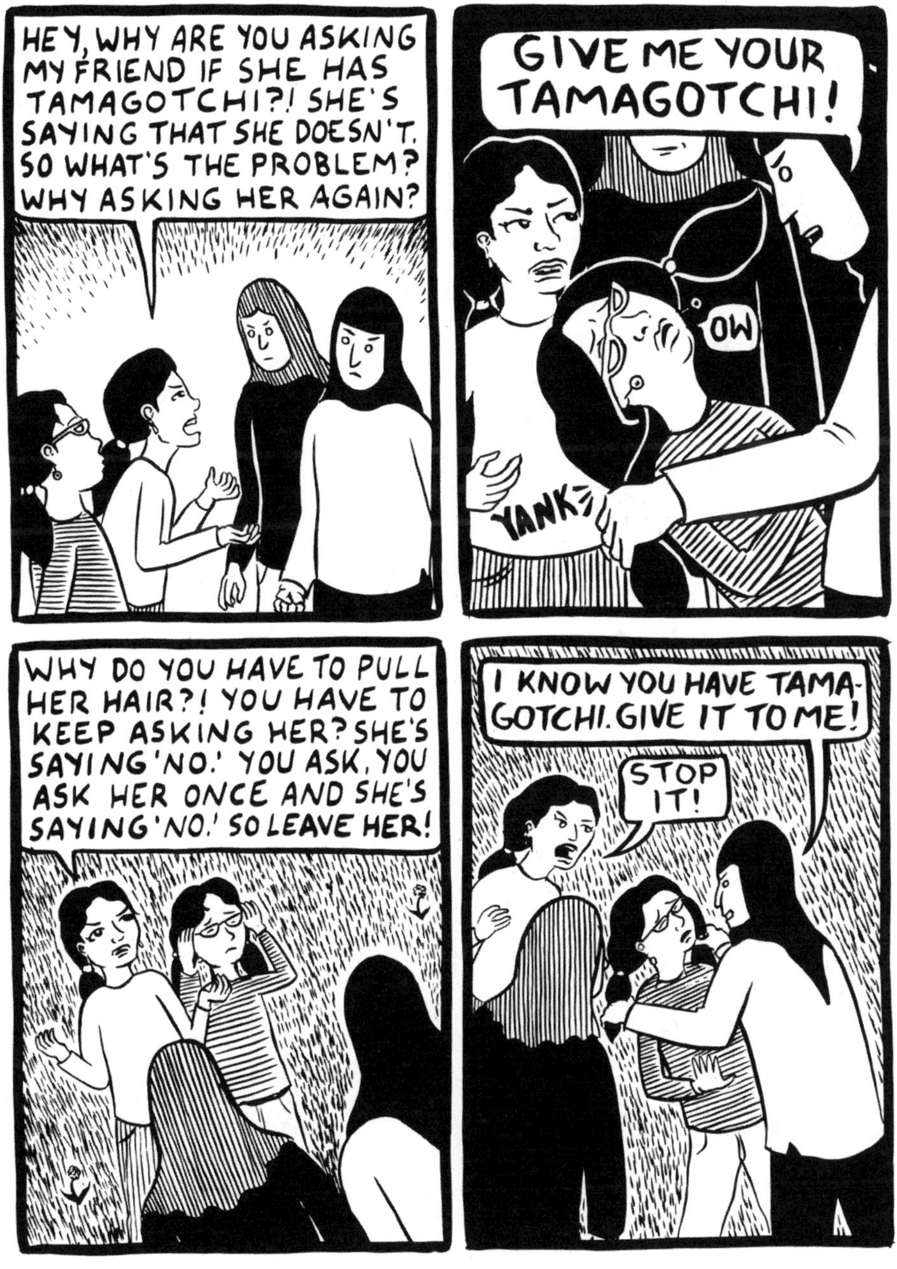
HEY, WHY ARE YOU ASKING MY FRIEND IF SHE HAS TAMAGOTCHI?! SHE'S SAYING THAT SHE DOESN'T. SO WHAT'S THE PROBLEM? WHY ASKING HER AGAIN?
GIVE ME YOUR TAMAGOTCHI!
OW
YANK
WHY DO YOU HAVE TO PULL HER HAIR?! YOU HAVE TO KEEP ASKING HER? SHE'S SAYING 'NO.' YOU ASK, YOU ASK HER ONCE AND SHE'S SAYING 'NO.' SO LEAVE HER!
I KNOW YOU HAVE TAMAGOTCHI. GIVE IT TO ME!
STOP IT!

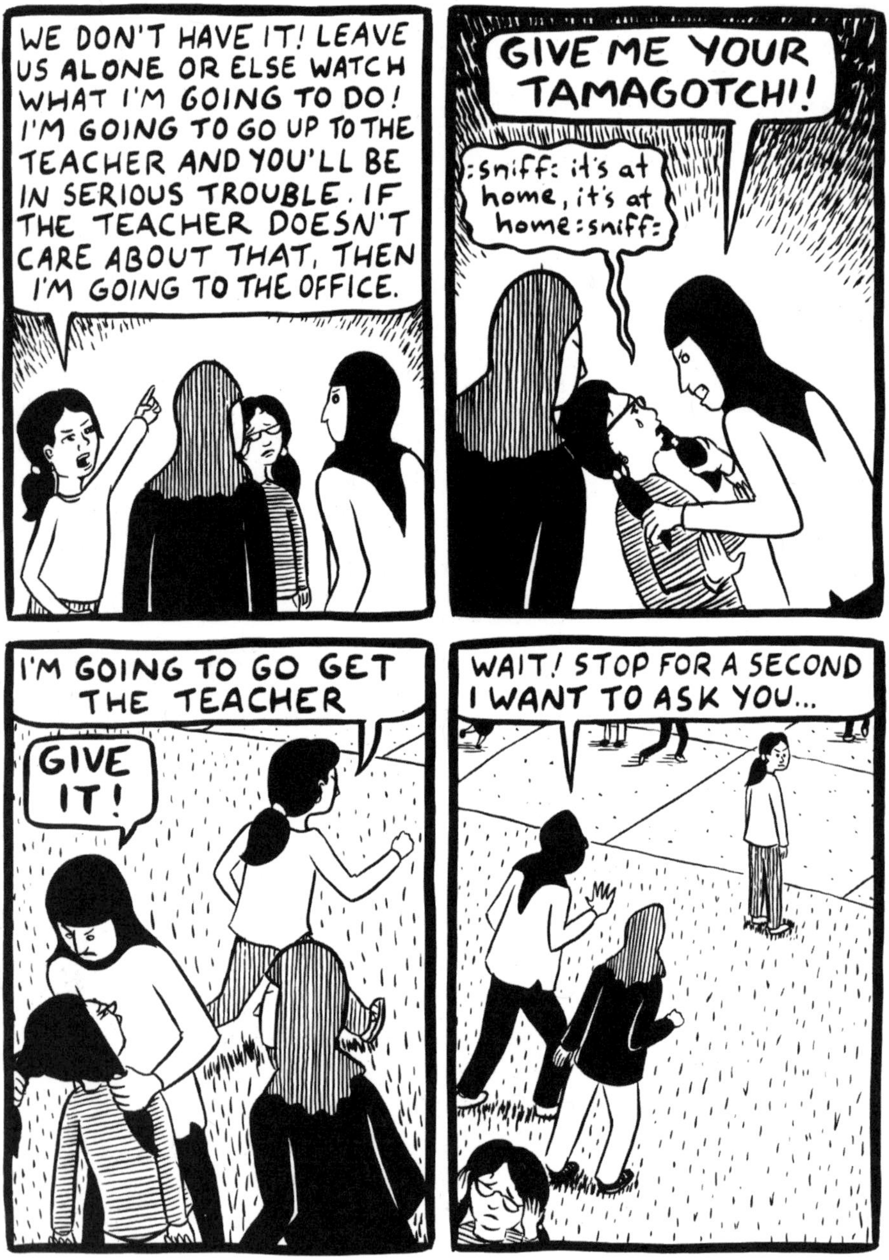
WE DON'T HAVE IT! LEAVE US ALONE OR ELSE WATCH WHAT I'M GOING TO DO! I'M GOING TO GO UP TO THE TEACHER AND YOU'LL BE IN SERIOUS TROUBLE. IF THE TEACHER DOESN'T CARE ABOUT THAT, THEN I'M GOING TO THE OFFICE.
GIVE ME YOUR TAMAGOTCHI!
:sniff: it's at home, it's at home :sniff:
I'M GOING TO GO GET THE TEACHER
GIVE IT!
WAIT! STOP FOR A SECOND I WANT TO ASK YOU...

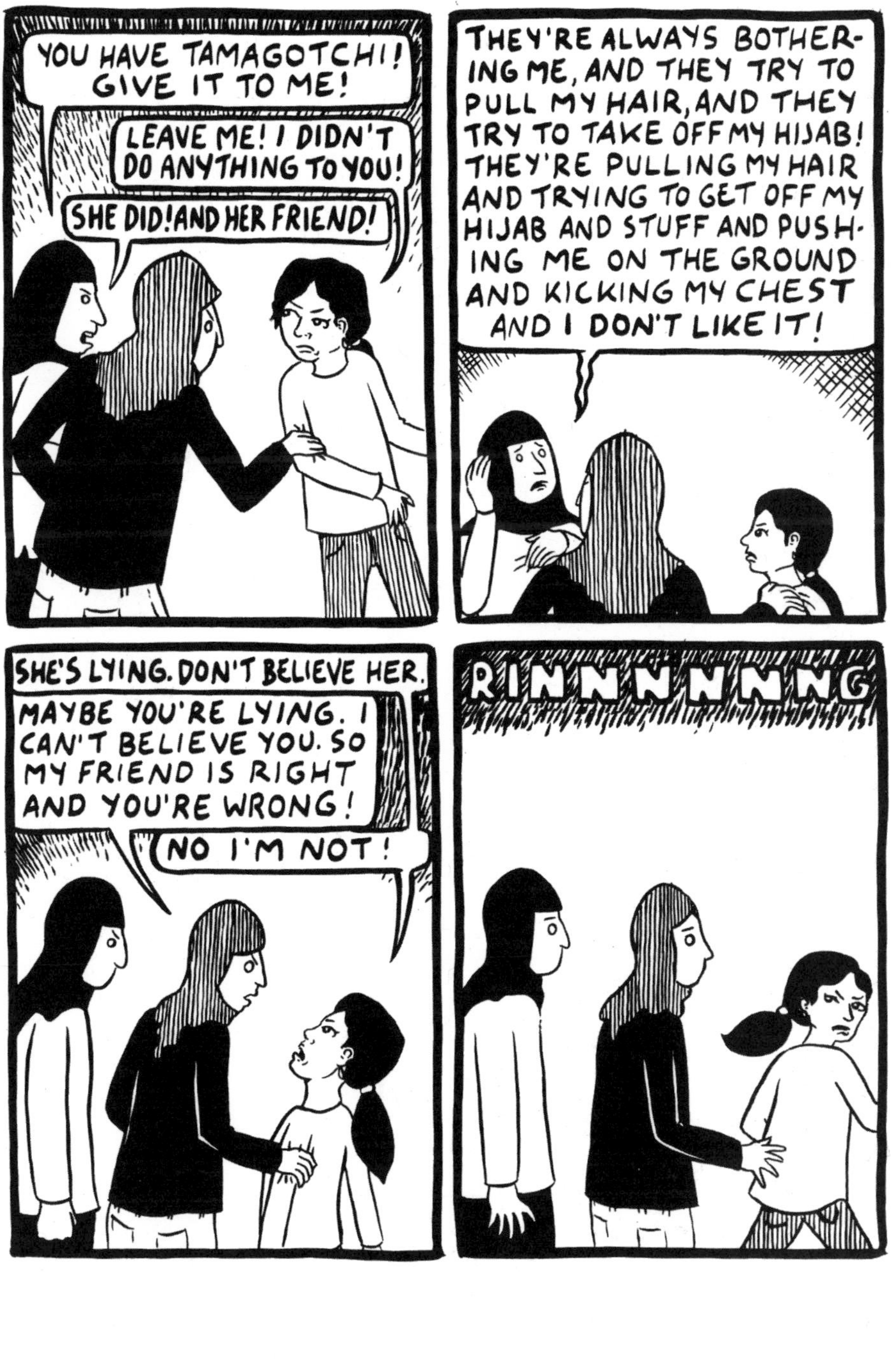
YOU HAVE TAMAGOTCHI! GIVE IT TO ME!
LEAVE ME! I DIDN'T DO ANYTHING TO YOU!
SHE DID! AND HER FRIEND!
THEY'RE ALWAYS BOTHERING ME, AND THEY TRY TO PULL MY HAIR, AND THEY TRY TO TAKE OFF MY HIJAB! THEY'RE PULLING MY HAIR AND TRYING TO GET OFF MY HIJAB AND STUFF AND PUSHING ME ON THE GROUND AND KICKING MY CHEST AND I DON'T LIKE IT!
SHE'S LYING. DON'T BELIEVE HER.
MAYBE YOU'RE LYING. I CAN'T BELIEVE YOU. SO MY FRIEND IS RIGHT AND YOU'RE WRONG!
NO I'M NOT!
RINNNNNNNG

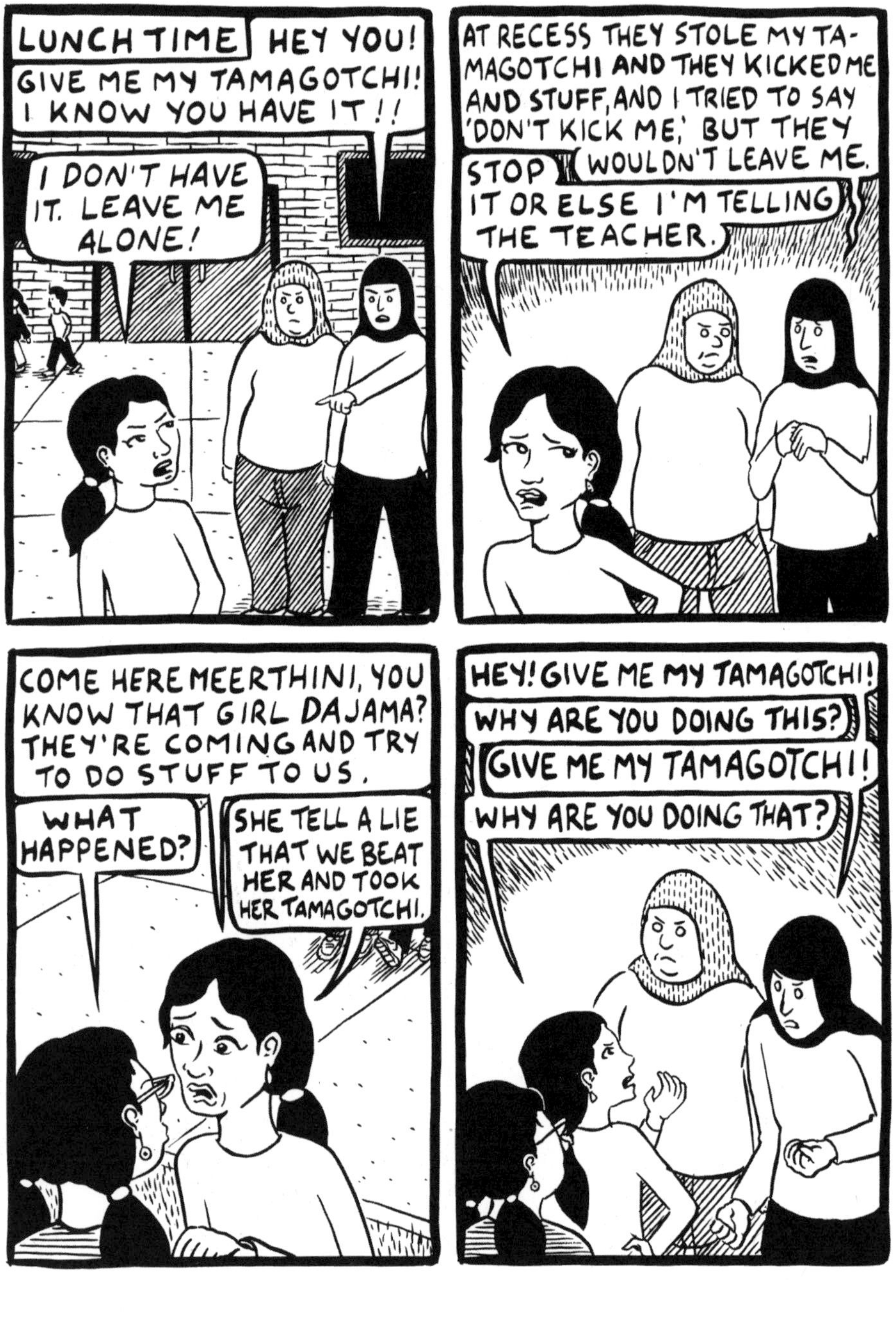
LUNCH TIME
HEY YOU!
GIVE ME MY TAMAGOTCHI! I KNOW YOU HAVE IT!!
I DON'T HAVE IT. LEAVE ME ALONE!
AT RECESS THEY STOLE MY TAMAGOTCHI AND THEY KICKED ME AND STUFF, AND I TRIED TO SAY 'DON'T KICK ME,' BUT THEY WOULDN'T LEAVE ME.
STOP IT OR ELSE I'M TELLING THE TEACHER.
COME HERE MEERTHINI, YOU KNOW THAT GIRL DAJAMA? THEY'RE COMING AND TRY TO DO STUFF TO US.
WHAT HAPPENED?
SHE TELL A LIE THAT WE BEAT HER AND TOOK HER TAMAGOTCHI.
HEY! GIVE ME MY TAMAGOTCHI!
WHY ARE YOU DOING THIS?
GIVE ME MY TAMAGOTCHI!
WHY ARE YOU DOING THAT?

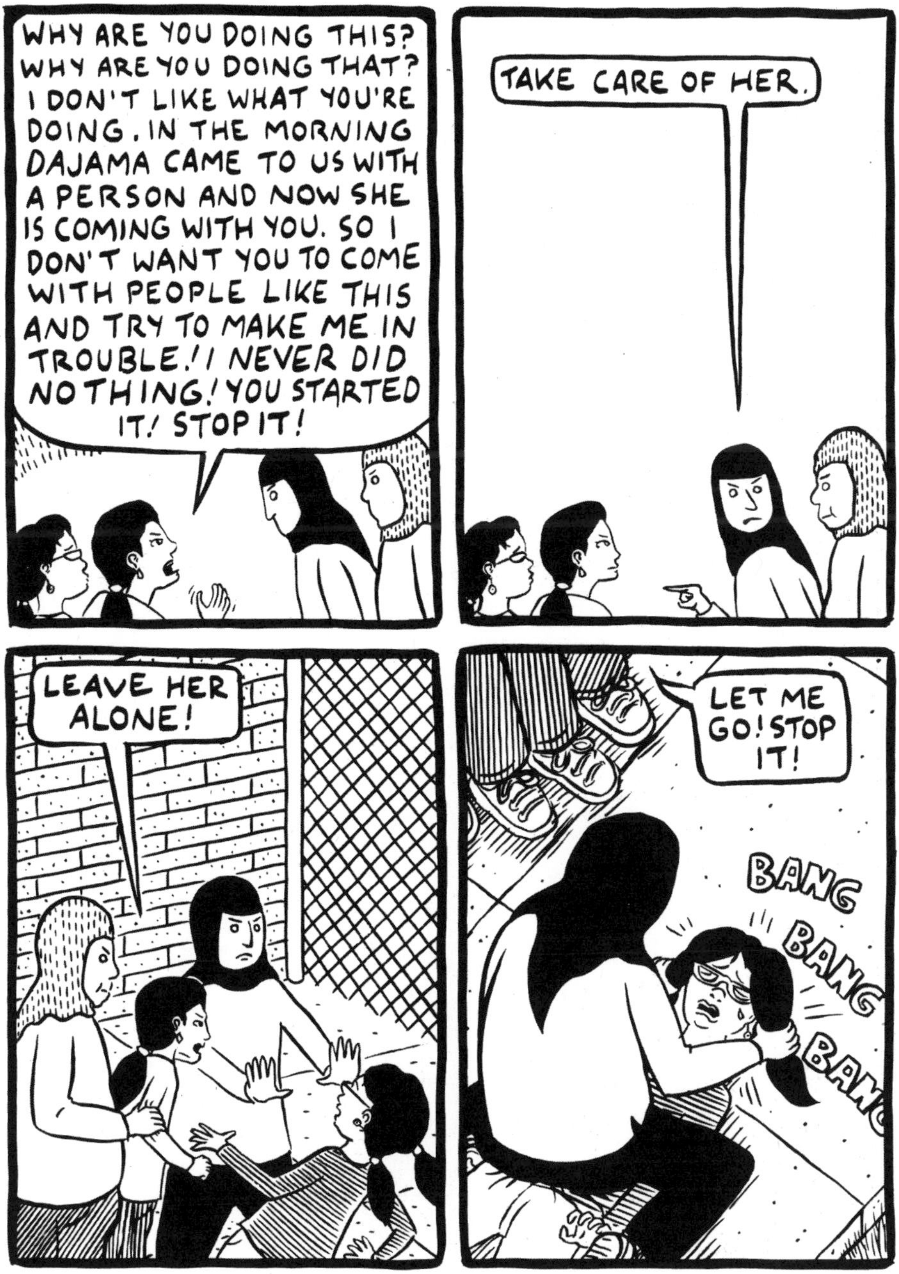
WHY ARE YOU DOING THIS? WHY ARE YOU DOING THAT? I DON'T LIKE WHAT YOU'RE DOING. IN THE MORNING DAJAMA CAME TO US WITH A PERSON AND NOW SHE IS COMING WITH YOU. SO I DON'T WANT YOU TO COME WITH PEOPLE LIKE THIS AND TRY TO MAKE ME IN TROUBLE! I NEVER DID NOTHING! YOU STARTED IT! STOP IT!
TAKE CARE OF HER.
LEAVE HER ALONE!
LET ME GO! STOP IT!
BANG
BANG
BANG
BANG

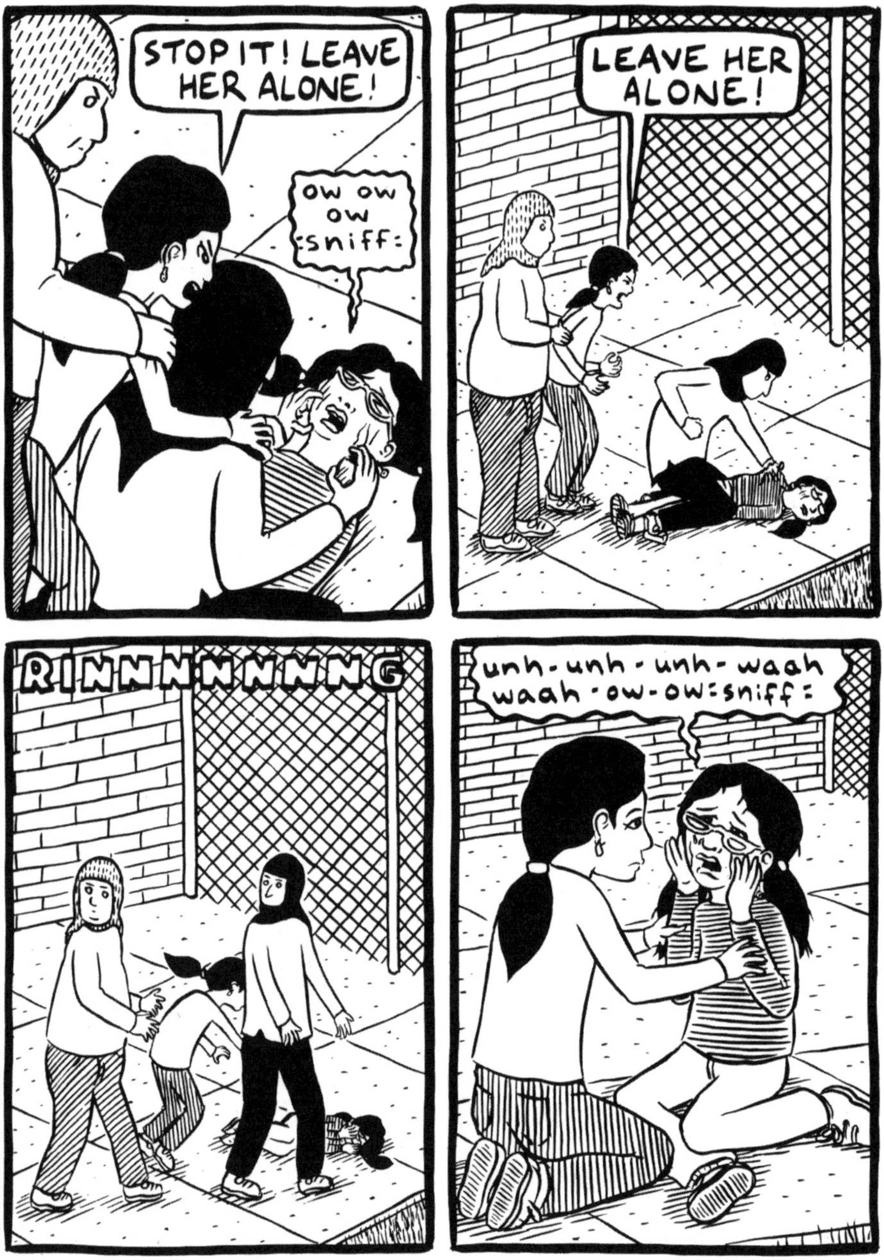
STOP IT! LEAVE HER ALONE!
OW OW OW :SNIFF:
LEAVE HER ALONE!
RINNNNNNNNG
unh-unh-unh-waah waah-ow-ow:sniff:

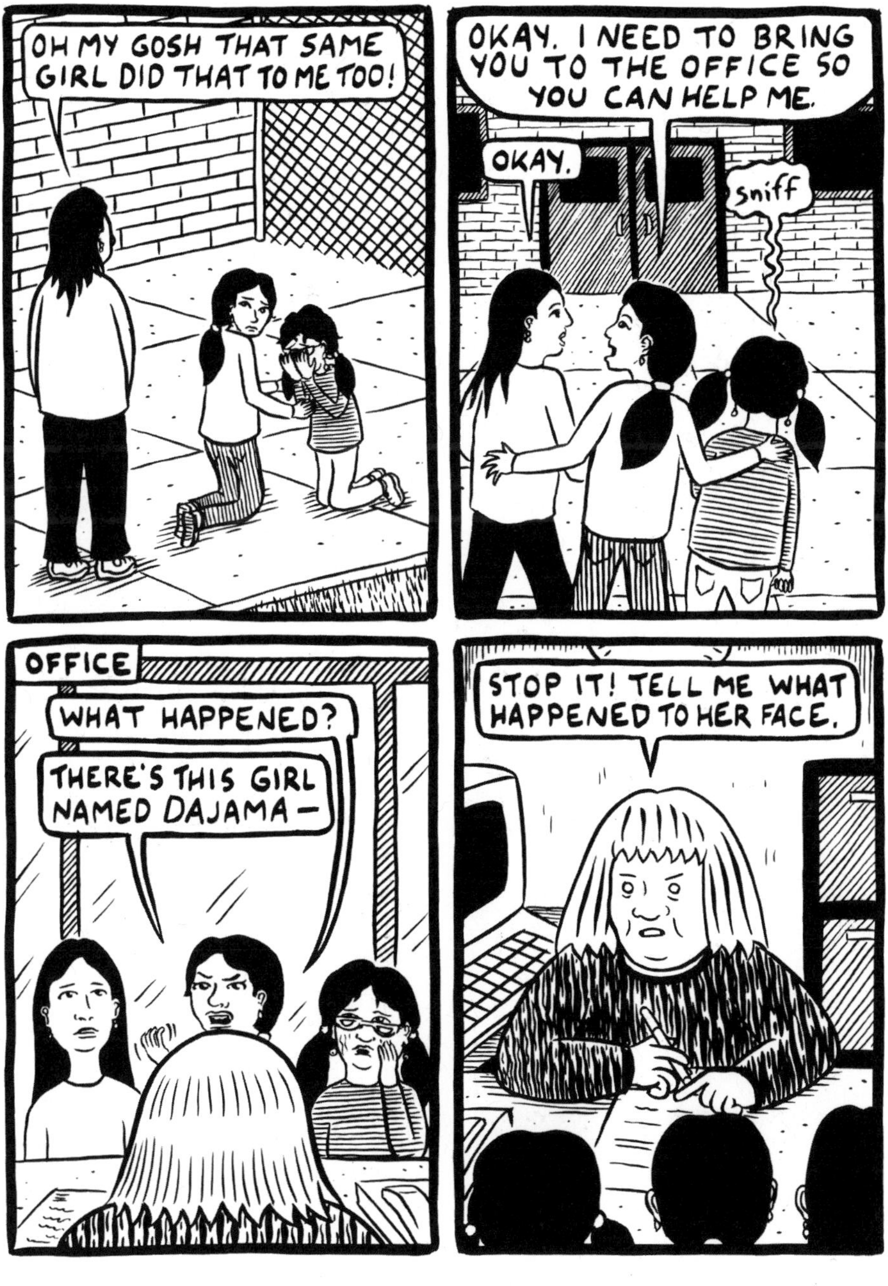
OH MY GOSH THAT SAME GIRL DID THAT TO ME TOO!
OKAY. I NEED TO BRING YOU TO THE OFFICE SO YOU CAN HELP ME.
OKAY.
sniff
OFFICE
WHAT HAPPENED?
THERE'S THIS GIRL NAMED DAJAMA—
STOP IT! TELL ME WHAT HAPPENED TO HER FACE.

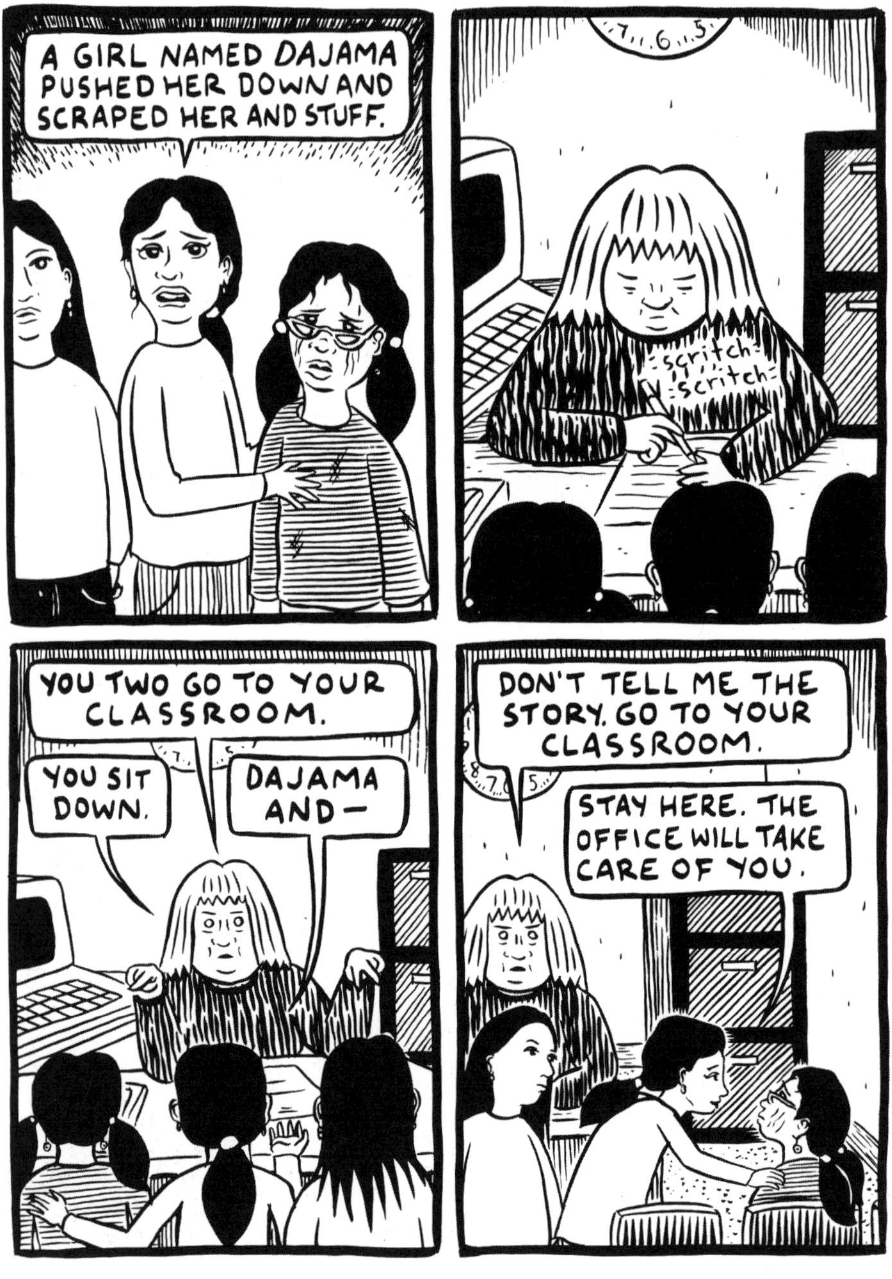
A GIRL NAMED DAJAMA PUSHED HER DOWN AND SCRAPED HER AND STUFF.
-SCRITCH-
-SCRITCH-
YOU TWO GO TO YOUR CLASSROOM.
YOU SIT DOWN.
DAJAMA AND—
DON'T TELL ME THE STORY. GO TO YOUR CLASSROOM.
STAY HERE. THE OFFICE WILL TAKE CARE OF YOU.

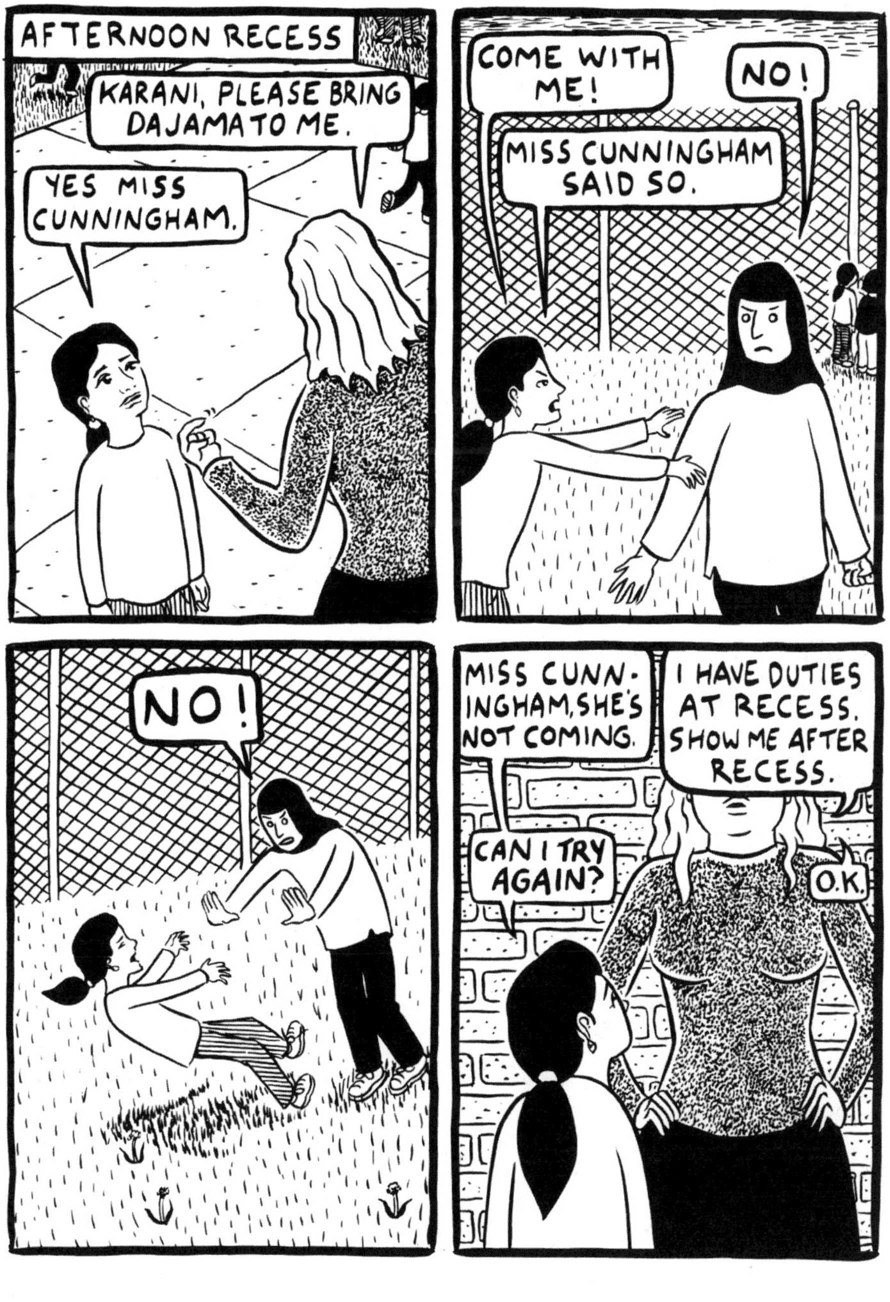
AFTERNOON RECESS
KARANI, PLEASE BRING DAJAMA TO ME.
YES MISS CUNNINGHAM.
COME WITH ME!
MISS CUNNINGHAM SAID SO.
NO!
NO!
MISS CUNN-INGHAM, SHE'S NOT COMING.
I HAVE DUTIES AT RECESS. SHOW ME AFTER RECESS.
CAN I TRY AGAIN?
O.K.

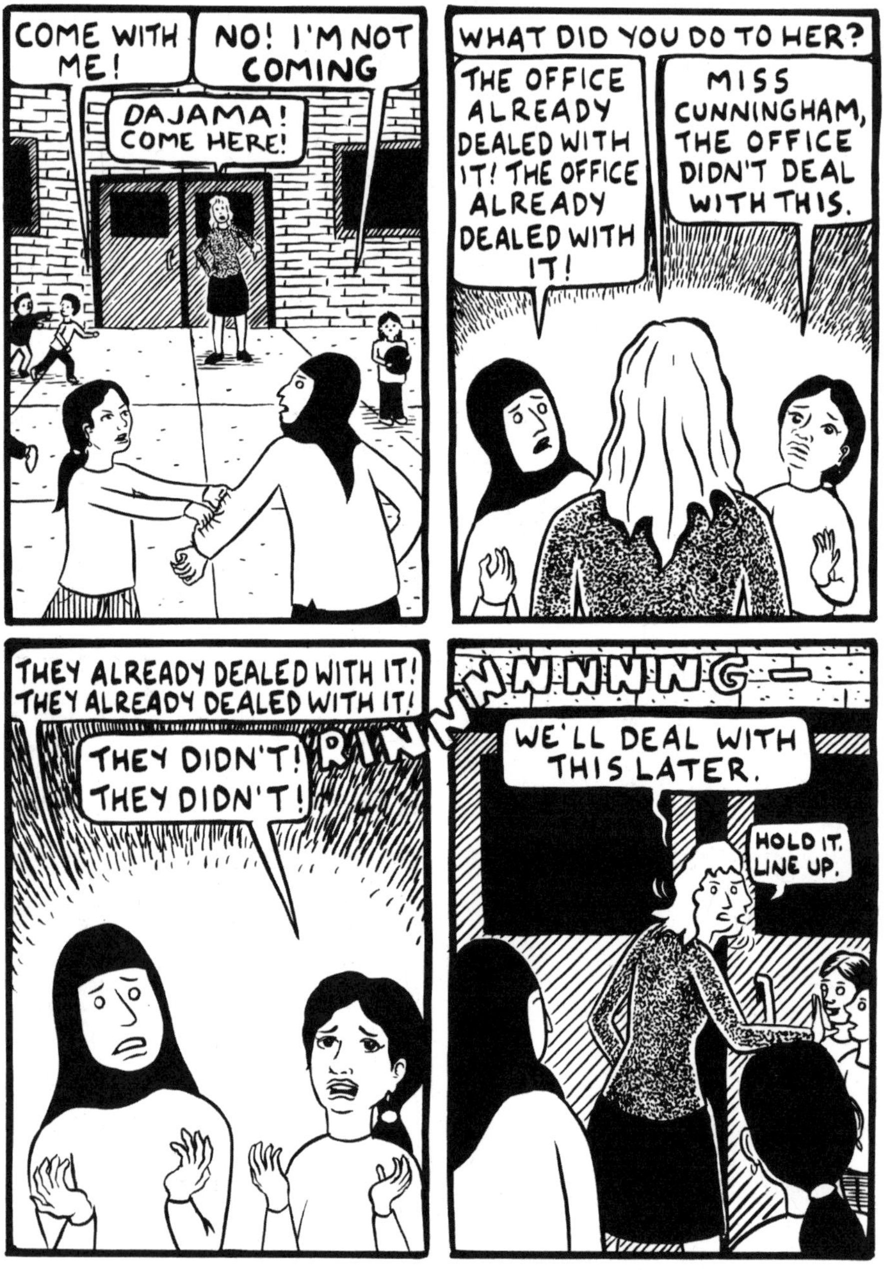
COME WITH ME!
NO! I'M NOT COMING
DAJAMA! COME HERE!
WHAT DID YOU DO TO HER?
THE OFFICE ALREADY DEALED WITH IT! THE OFFICE ALREADY DEALED WITH IT!
MISS CUNNINGHAM, THE OFFICE DIDN'T DEAL WITH THIS.
THEY ALREADY DEALED WITH IT! THEY ALREADY DEALED WITH IT!
THEY DIDN'T! THEY DIDN'T!
RINNNNNNNNG —
WE'LL DEAL WITH THIS LATER.
HOLD IT. LINE UP.

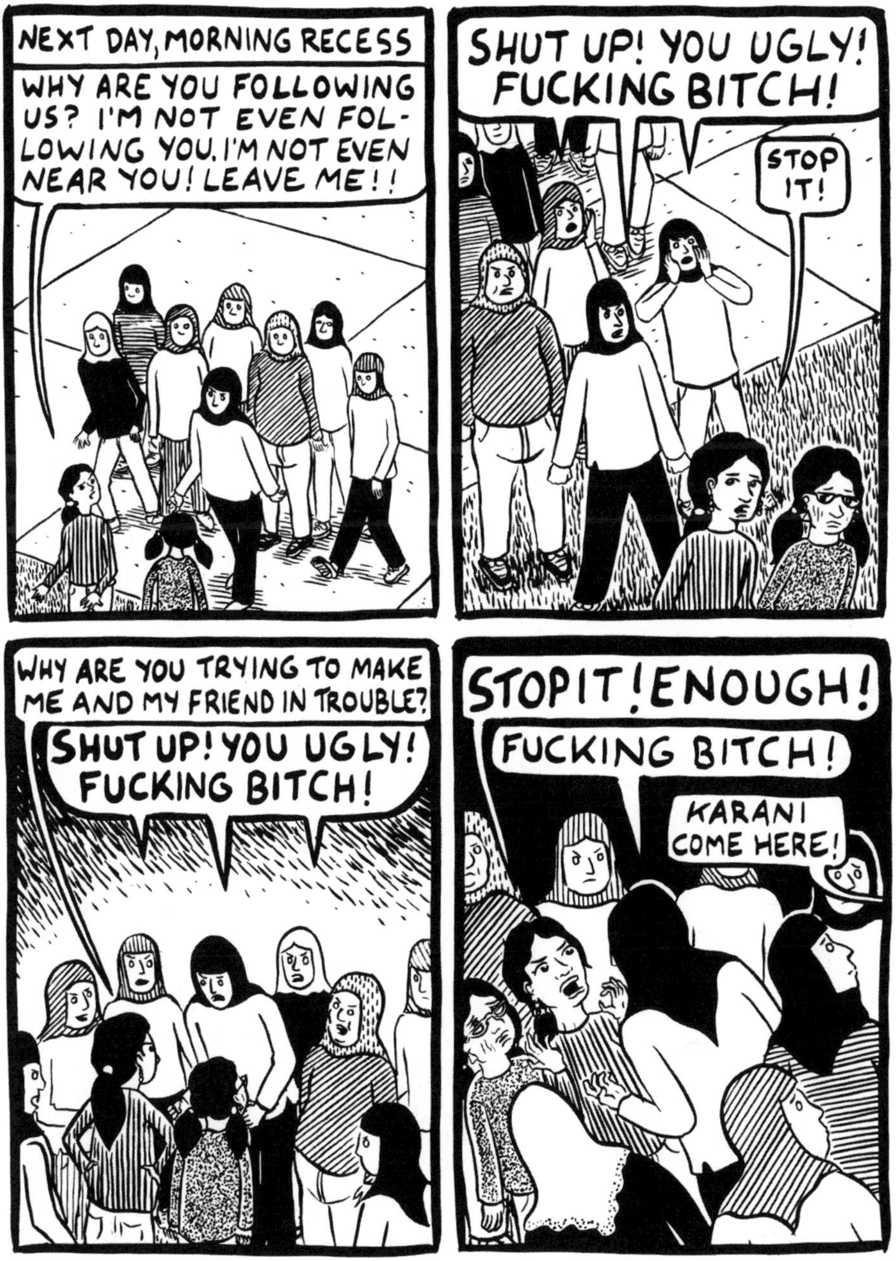
NEXT DAY, MORNING RECESS
WHY ARE YOU FOLLOWING US? I'M NOT EVEN FOL-LOWING YOU. I'M NOT EVEN NEAR YOU! LEAVE ME!!
SHUT UP! YOU UGLY! FUCKING BITCH!
STOP IT!
WHY ARE YOU TRYING TO MAKE ME AND MY FRIEND IN TROUBLE?
SHUT UP! YOU UGLY! FUCKING BITCH!
STOP IT! ENOUGH!
FUCKING BITCH!
KARANI COME HERE!

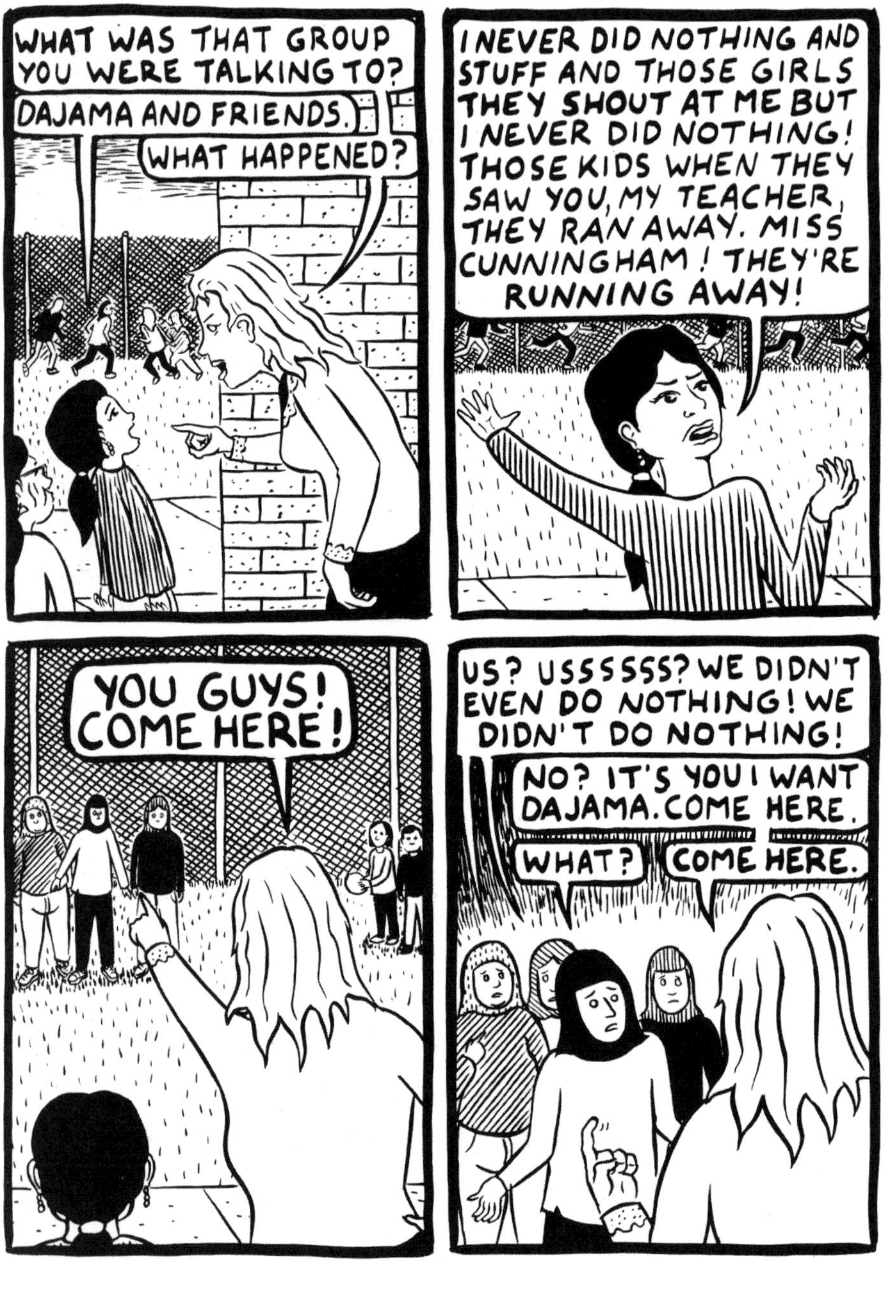
WHAT WAS THAT GROUP YOU WERE TALKING TO?
DAJAMA AND FRIENDS.
WHAT HAPPENED?
I NEVER DID NOTHING AND STUFF AND THOSE GIRLS THEY SHOUT AT ME BUT I NEVER DID NOTHING! THOSE KIDS WHEN THEY SAW YOU, MY TEACHER, THEY RAN AWAY. MISS CUNNINGHAM! THEY'RE RUNNING AWAY!
YOU GUYS! COME HERE!
US? USSSSSS? WE DIDN'T EVEN DO NOTHING! WE DIDN'T DO NOTHING!
NO? IT'S YOU I WANT DAJAMA. COME HERE.
WHAT?
COME HERE.

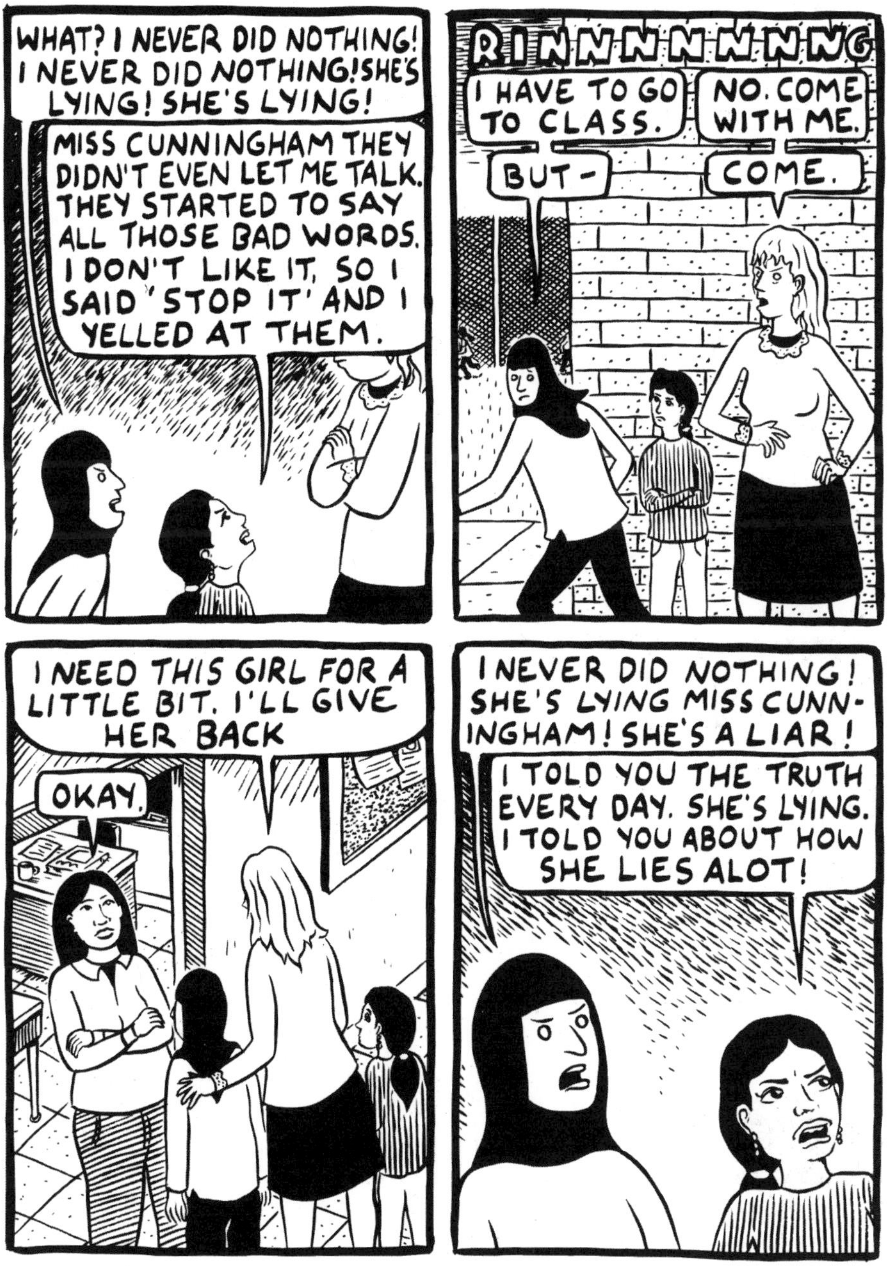

WHAT? I NEVER DID NOTHING! I NEVER DID NOTHING! SHE'S LYING! SHE'S LYING!
MISS CUNNINGHAM THEY DIDN'T EVEN LET ME TALK. THEY STARTED TO SAY ALL THOSE BAD WORDS. I DON'T LIKE IT, SO I SAID 'STOP IT' AND I YELLED AT THEM.
RINNNNNNNNG
I HAVE TO GO TO CLASS.
NO. COME WITH ME.
BUT-
COME.
I NEED THIS GIRL FOR A LITTLE BIT. I'LL GIVE HER BACK
OKAY.
I NEVER DID NOTHING! SHE'S LYING MISS CUNNINGHAM! SHE'S A LIAR!
I TOLD YOU THE TRUTH EVERY DAY. SHE'S LYING. I TOLD YOU ABOUT HOW SHE LIES ALOT!

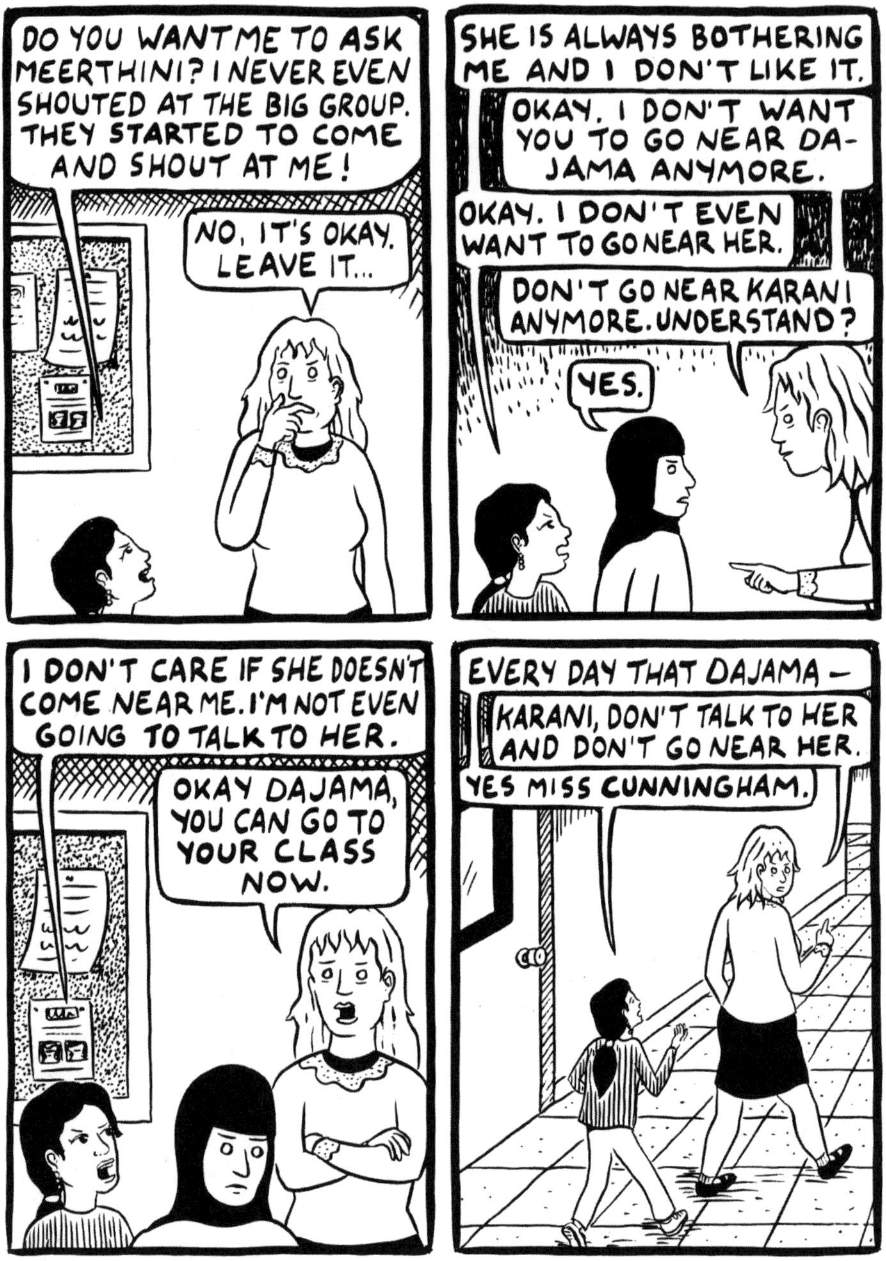
DO YOU WANT ME TO ASK MEERTHINI? I NEVER EVEN SHOUTED AT THE BIG GROUP. THEY STARTED TO COME AND SHOUT AT ME!
NO, IT'S OKAY. LEAVE IT...
SHE IS ALWAYS BOTHERING ME AND I DON'T LIKE IT.
OKAY. I DON'T WANT YOU TO GO NEAR DA-JAMA ANYMORE.
OKAY. I DON'T EVEN WANT TO GO NEAR HER.
DON'T GO NEAR KARANI ANYMORE. UNDERSTAND?
YES.
I DON'T CARE IF SHE DOESN'T COME NEAR ME. I'M NOT EVEN GOING TO TALK TO HER.
OKAY DAJAMA, YOU CAN GO TO YOUR CLASS NOW.
EVERY DAY THAT DAJAMA —
KARANI, DON'T TALK TO HER AND DON'T GO NEAR HER.
YES MISS CUNNINGHAM.

field

The four of us are in a small field and the kids I'm with all fear this long grass... I see a spit bug's nest.

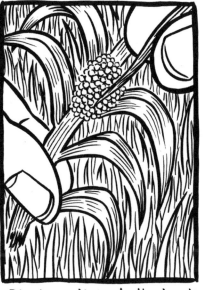

Plucking the stalk, I poke the tiny mass of bubbles with a twig...

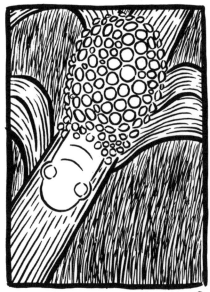

...until a pale yellow leaf hopper larva emerges...

...this little insect home drops away as I spy another.

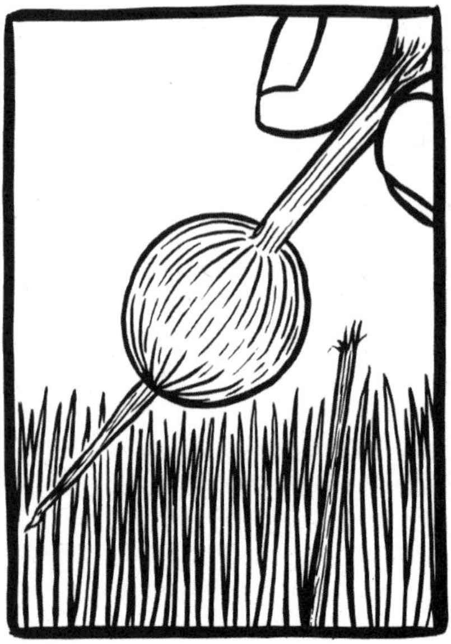

It's a swollen goldenrod stem and there's sure to be something in it!

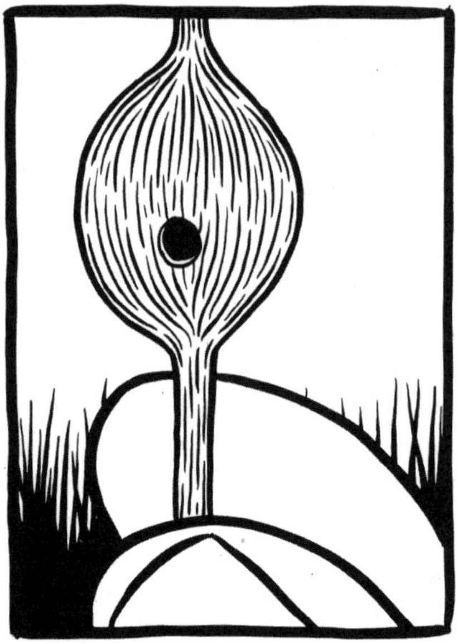

This hole indicates the tenant has left, but we can still examine the premises...

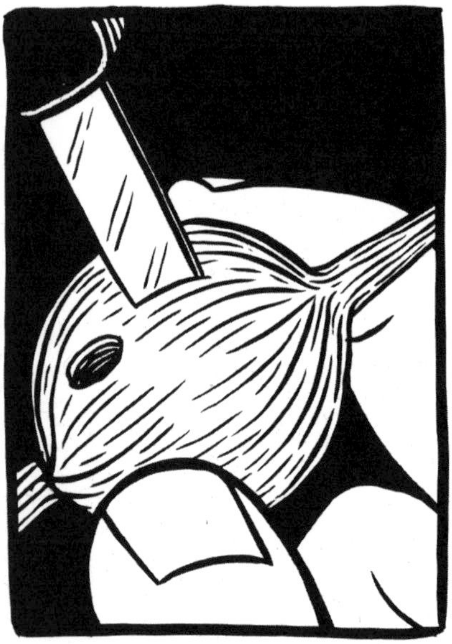

I deftly slice open the vacant home with my jack knife ...

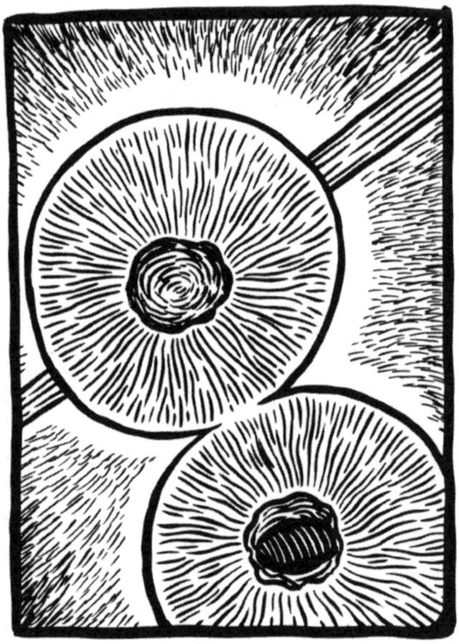

...revealing a small dark cavity with a remnant carapace...

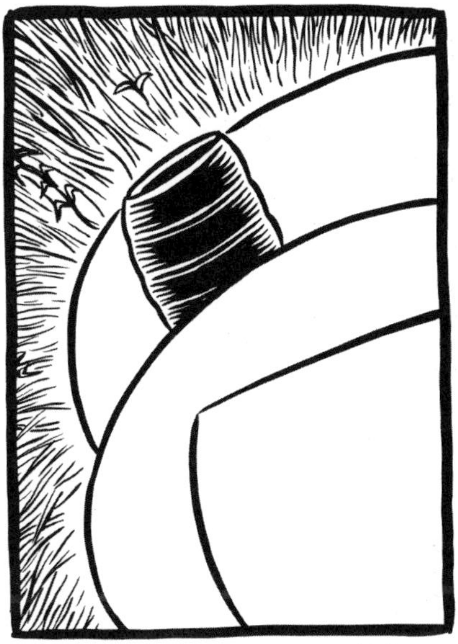

The kids are afraid of this dark empty cocoon. I hold it between my finger tips to show them there's nothing in it ... they're still afraid...!

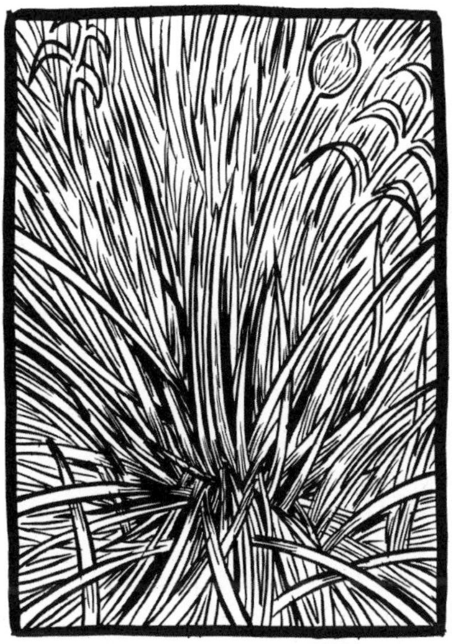

The cocoon slips and dis-appears into the grass ... I feel I've lost something... Do I really need to search for it?

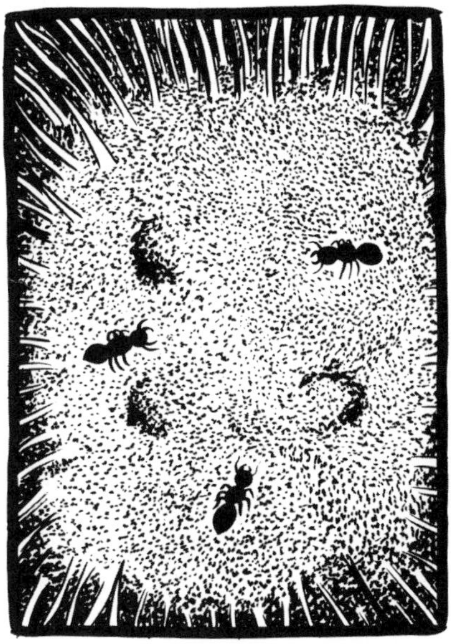

We're on the periphery of the field...a couple of ant mounds are clumped there.

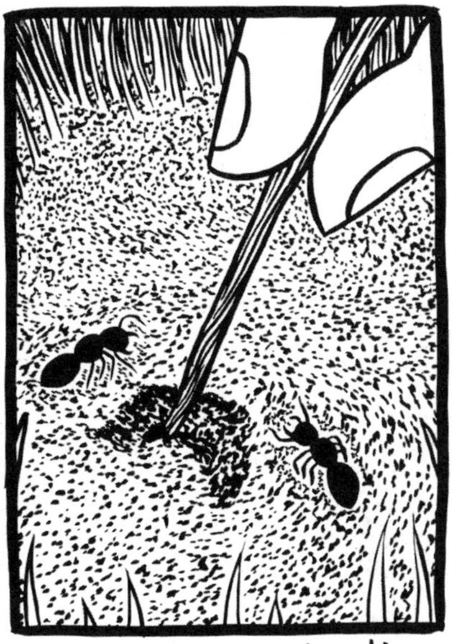

I poke the mound with a stick to show the kids the wrath an intruder will incur!

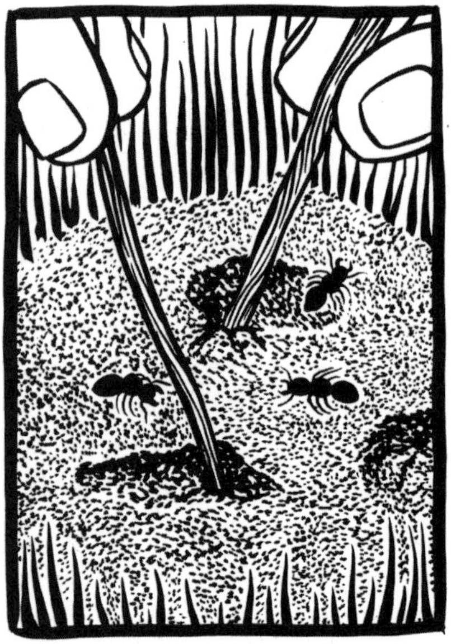

We poke several holes but there's very little wrath... maybe the ants are sleeping.

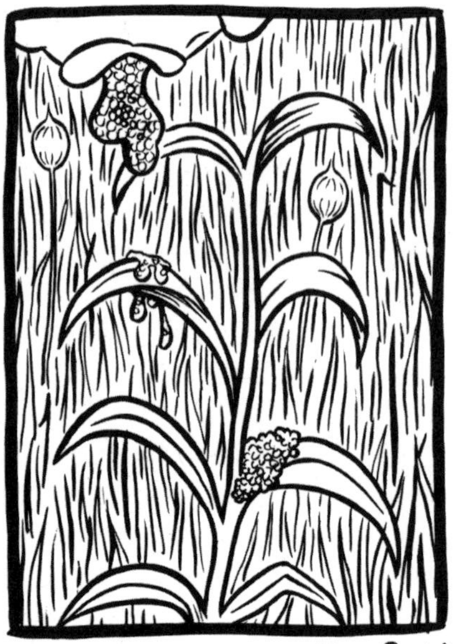

It's time to leave the field... the kids don't fear it so much now and they want to stay. Hien adds spit to a spit bug's nest.

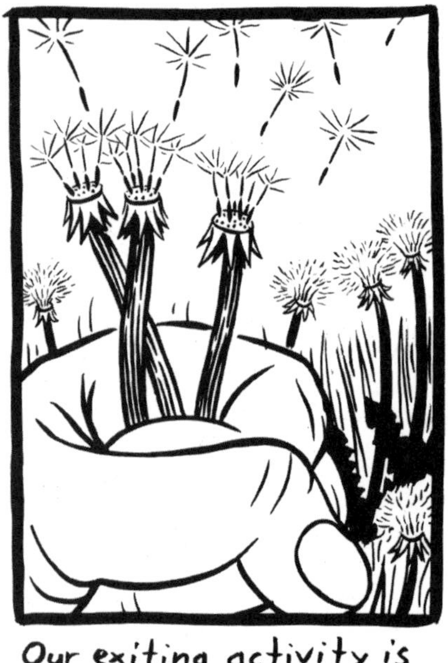

Our exiting activity is picking dandelion stems and blowing them at each other.

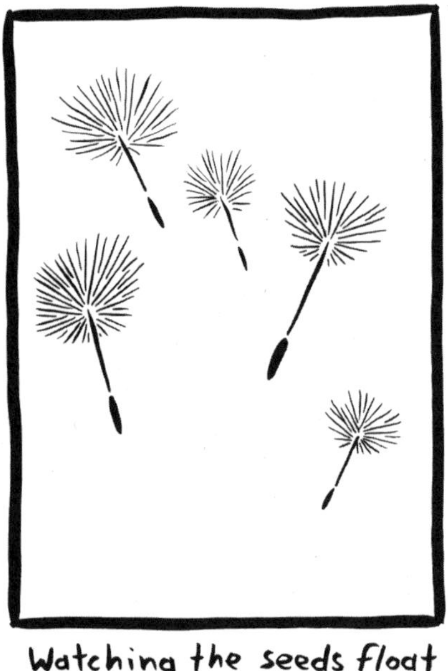

Watching the seeds float in the air, I'm glad we're leaving without destroying any more homes.

pho

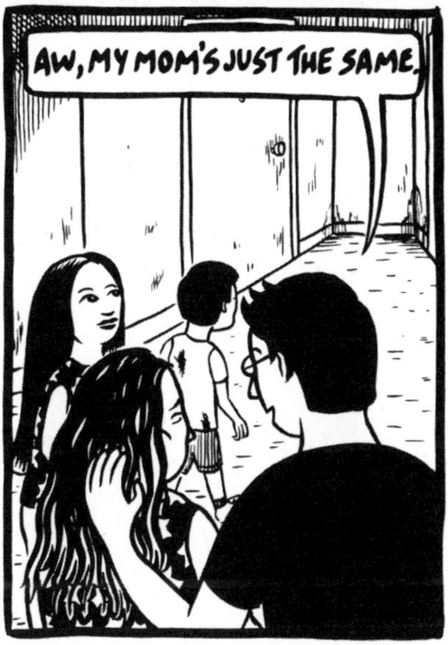
AW, MY MOM'S JUST THE SAME.

In the hallway, they're speaking their language... I pat the mom on the back and try to reassure her... she's worrying about the mess inside.

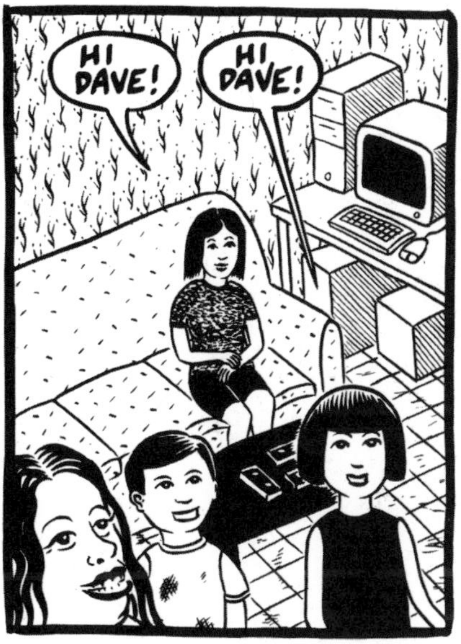
HI DAVE!
HI DAVE!

It's not so bad... someone must have cleaned up... the mom is relieved... big smile!

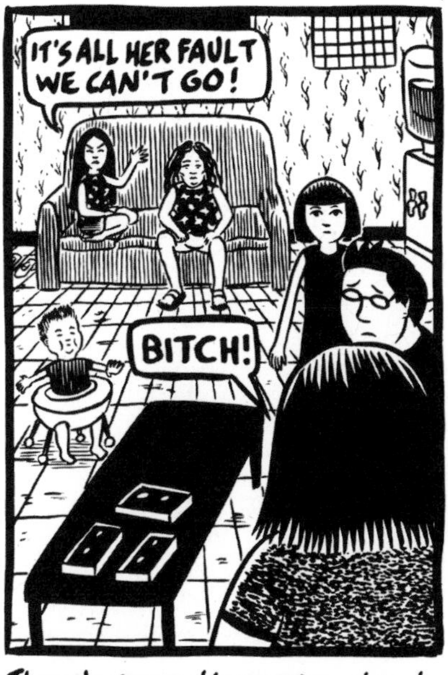
IT'S ALL HER FAULT WE CAN'T GO!
BITCH!

There's some discussion about the oldest girls going away somewhere over night... mom says 'no.' The girls are not happy...

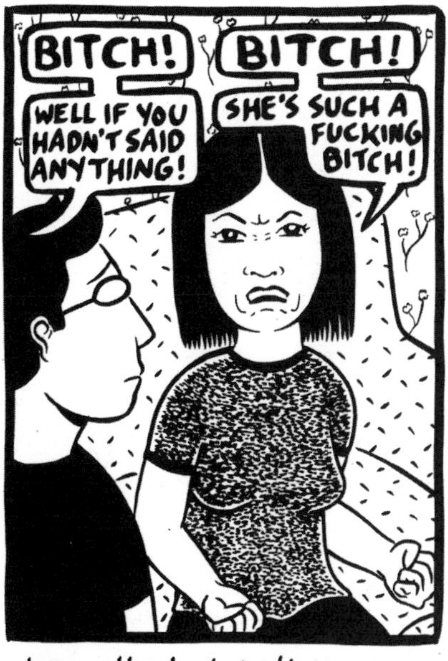
BITCH!
WELL IF YOU HADN'T SAID ANYTHING!
BITCH!
SHE'S SUCH A FUCKING BITCH!

Jeez... the look in their eyes... they're going to fight in a minute... I can't see that happen right in front of me!

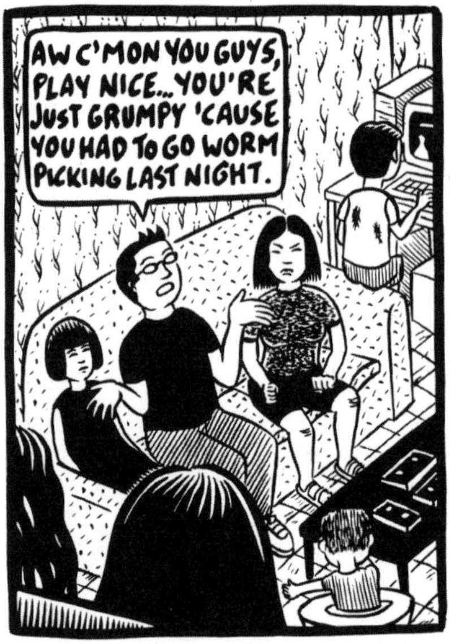
AW C'MON YOU GUYS, PLAY NICE... YOU'RE JUST GRUMPY 'CAUSE YOU HAD TO GO WORM PICKING LAST NIGHT.

The family's tense... the dad's gone off to Denmark for a month's vacation... up and left for a month and he took all the worm money...

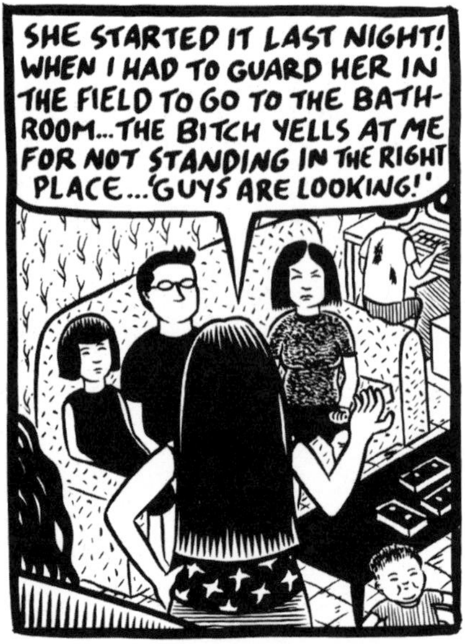
SHE STARTED IT LAST NIGHT! WHEN I HAD TO GUARD HER IN THE FIELD TO GO TO THE BATH-ROOM... THE BITCH YELLS AT ME FOR NOT STANDING IN THE RIGHT PLACE... 'GUYS ARE LOOKING!'

I was later told that the rest of the family didn't go there because the place is too small and you have to wash with a bucket... and it's not safe to leave their home empty for so long.

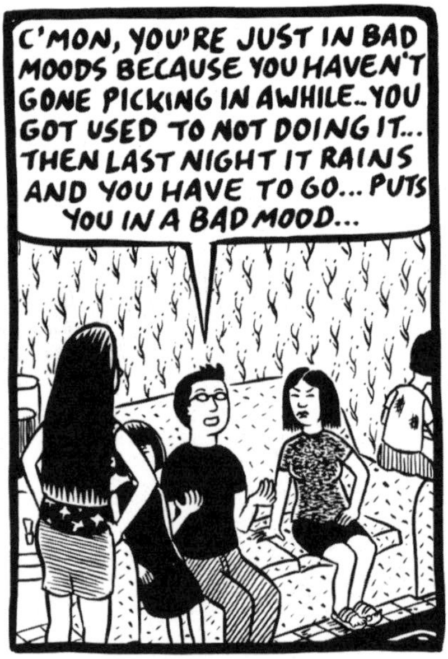
C'MON, YOU'RE JUST IN BAD MOODS BECAUSE YOU HAVEN'T GONE PICKING IN AWHILE.. YOU GOT USED TO NOT DOING IT... THEN LAST NIGHT IT RAINS AND YOU HAVE TO GO... PUTS YOU IN A BAD MOOD...

Their little sister once tied a string from their old dog to the door handle... a drug addict seeing the door ajar wandered in... because there were people inside she left.

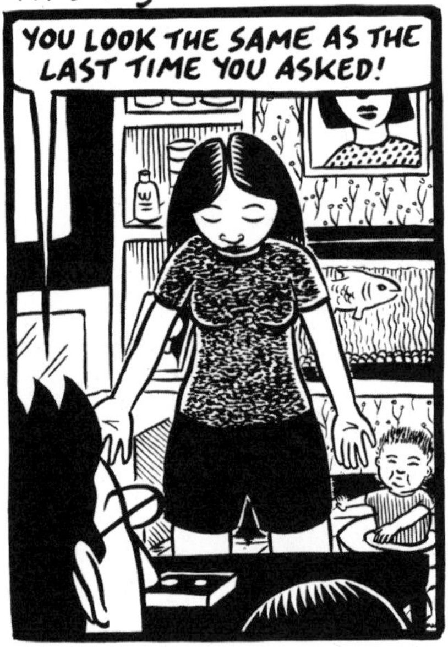
YOU LOOK THE SAME AS THE LAST TIME YOU ASKED!

The storm passes and Hoi asks if she looks fat. Always she asks... and asks, and asks!

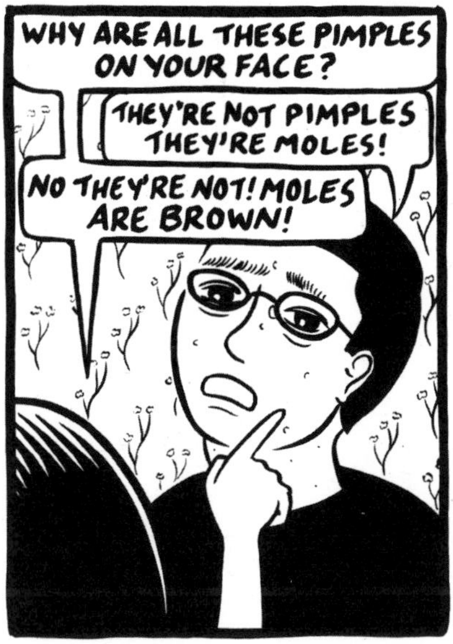
WHY ARE ALL THESE PIMPLES ON YOUR FACE?
THEY'RE NOT PIMPLES THEY'RE MOLES!
NO THEY'RE NOT! MOLES ARE BROWN!

Well, she'd been resting her head on my shoulder and examining my arm hair... she's now kneeling on the couch examining my face... poke, poke, poke...

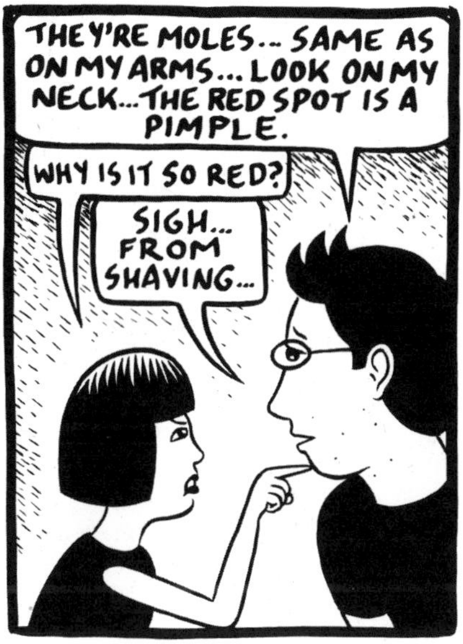
THEY'RE MOLES... SAME AS ON MY ARMS... LOOK ON MY NECK... THE RED SPOT IS A PIMPLE.
WHY IS IT SO RED?
SIGH... FROM SHAVING...

... poke, poke, poke...

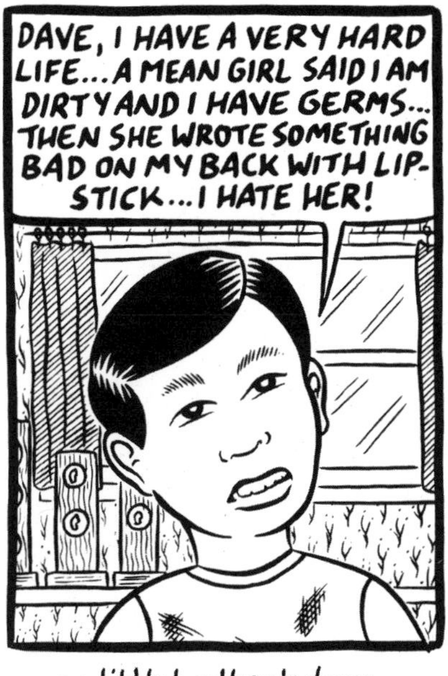
DAVE, I HAVE A VERY HARD LIFE... A MEAN GIRL SAID I AM DIRTY AND I HAVE GERMS... THEN SHE WROTE SOMETHING BAD ON MY BACK WITH LIP-STICK... I HATE HER!

...now little brother's turn...

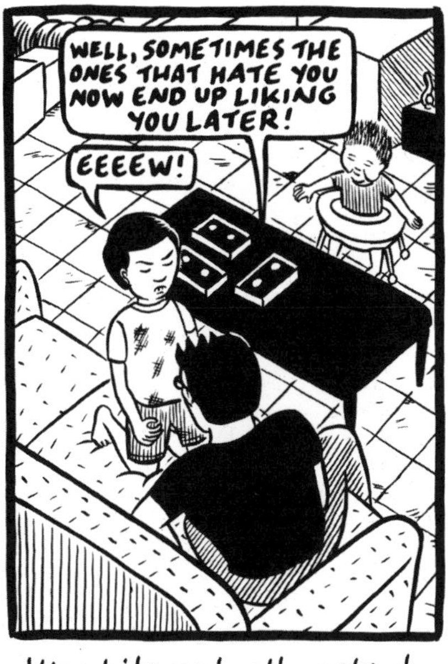
WELL, SOMETIMES THE ONES THAT HATE YOU NOW END UP LIKING YOU LATER!
EEEEW!

His white and yellow shirt really is dirty... but bait and switch y'know...

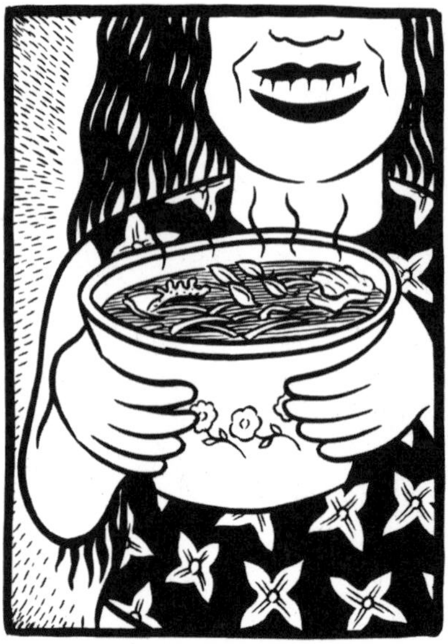

So I visit awhile and the mom makes me some 'Pho'...Vietnamese noodle soup and I apologetically ask for a separate plate so I can pick out all the weird stuff...

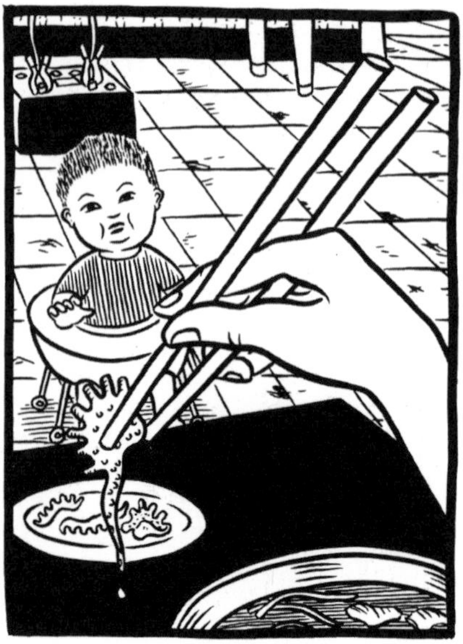

I apologize again and again for being so fussy... I pick out all the tendon and tripe...which the the baby tries to grab at!

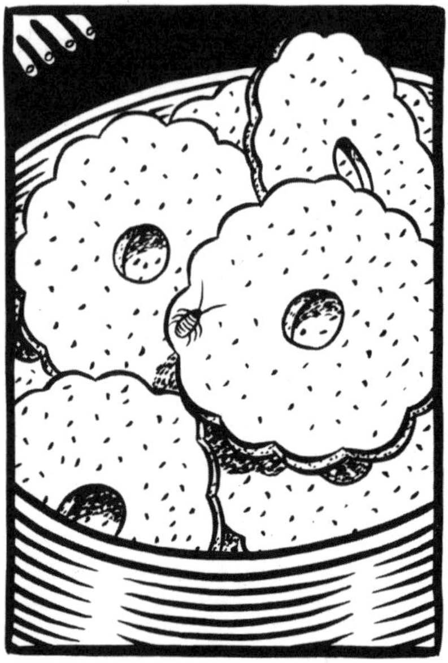

The oldest daughter brings me some 'normal' green sprinkle cookies...after eating three or four, I see a small cockroach crawling on a cookie...

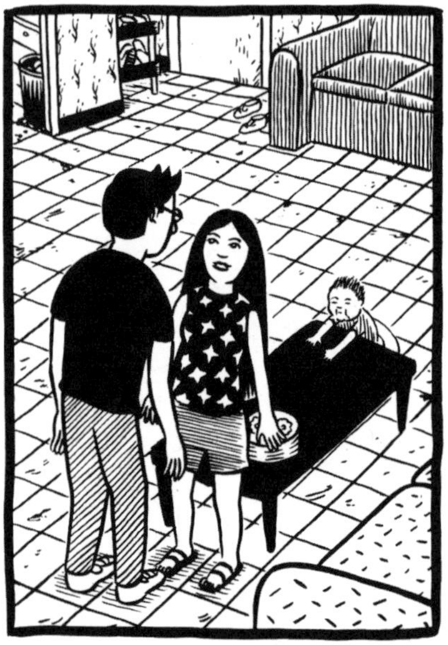

She sees it too... sees me looking and stands in front of the tin... I want to say something protective and funny... just leave it...

thanks

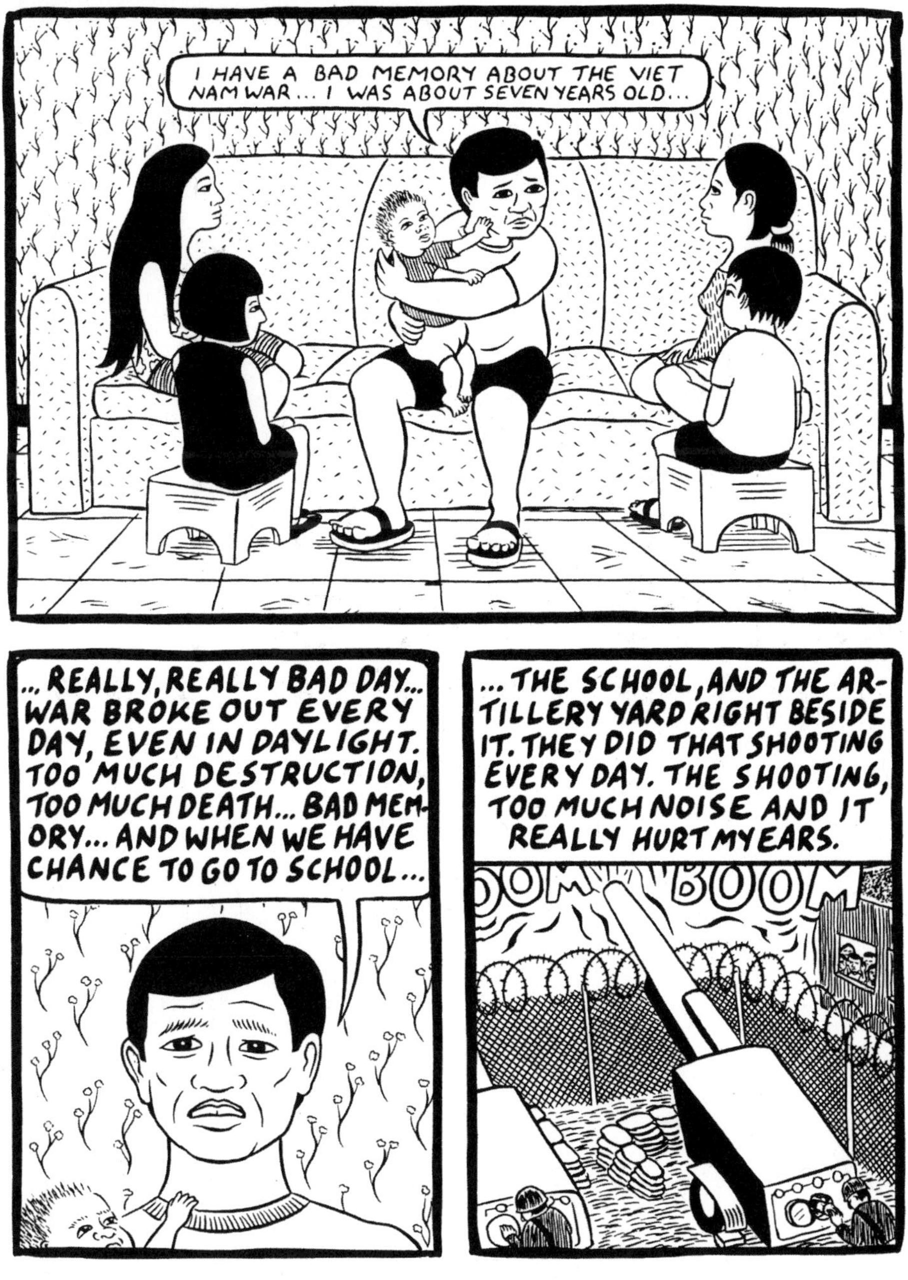

I HAVE A BAD MEMORY ABOUT THE VIET NAM WAR... I WAS ABOUT SEVEN YEARS OLD...
... REALLY, REALLY BAD DAY... WAR BROKE OUT EVERY DAY, EVEN IN DAYLIGHT. TOO MUCH DESTRUCTION, TOO MUCH DEATH... BAD MEMORY... AND WHEN WE HAVE CHANCE TO GO TO SCHOOL...
... THE SCHOOL, AND THE ARTILLERY YARD RIGHT BESIDE IT. THEY DID THAT SHOOTING EVERY DAY. THE SHOOTING, TOO MUCH NOISE AND IT REALLY HURT MY EARS.
BOOM

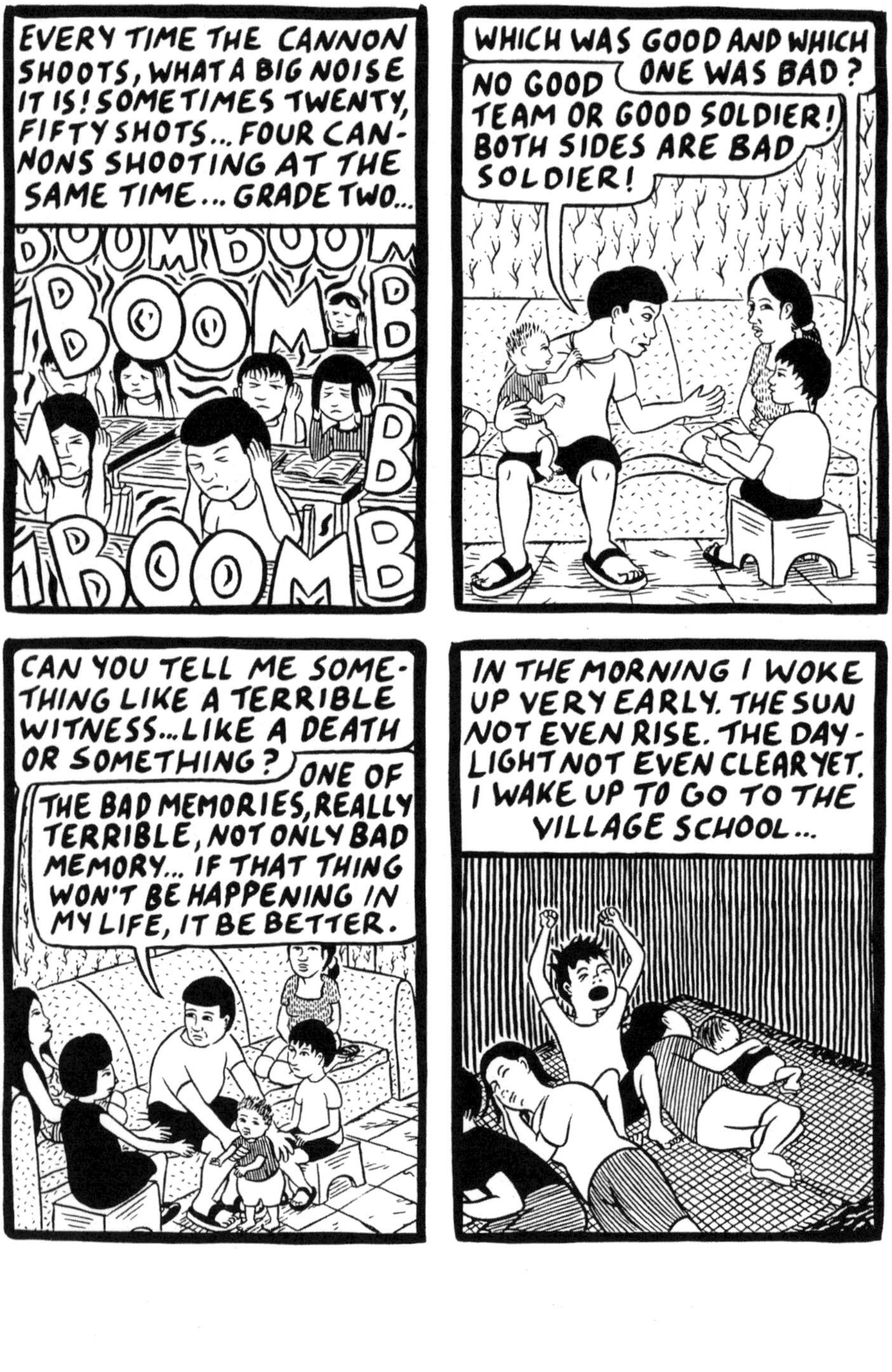
EVERY TIME THE CANNON SHOOTS, WHAT A BIG NOISE IT IS! SOMETIMES TWENTY, FIFTY SHOTS... FOUR CANNONS SHOOTING AT THE SAME TIME... GRADE TWO...
BOOM BOOM
BOOM
BOOM
WHICH WAS GOOD AND WHICH ONE WAS BAD?
NO GOOD TEAM OR GOOD SOLDIER! BOTH SIDES ARE BAD SOLDIER!
CAN YOU TELL ME SOMETHING LIKE A TERRIBLE WITNESS...LIKE A DEATH OR SOMETHING?
ONE OF THE BAD MEMORIES, REALLY TERRIBLE, NOT ONLY BAD MEMORY... IF THAT THING WON'T BE HAPPENING IN MY LIFE, IT BE BETTER.
IN THE MORNING I WOKE UP VERY EARLY. THE SUN NOT EVEN RISE. THE DAYLIGHT NOT EVEN CLEAR YET. I WAKE UP TO GO TO THE VILLAGE SCHOOL...

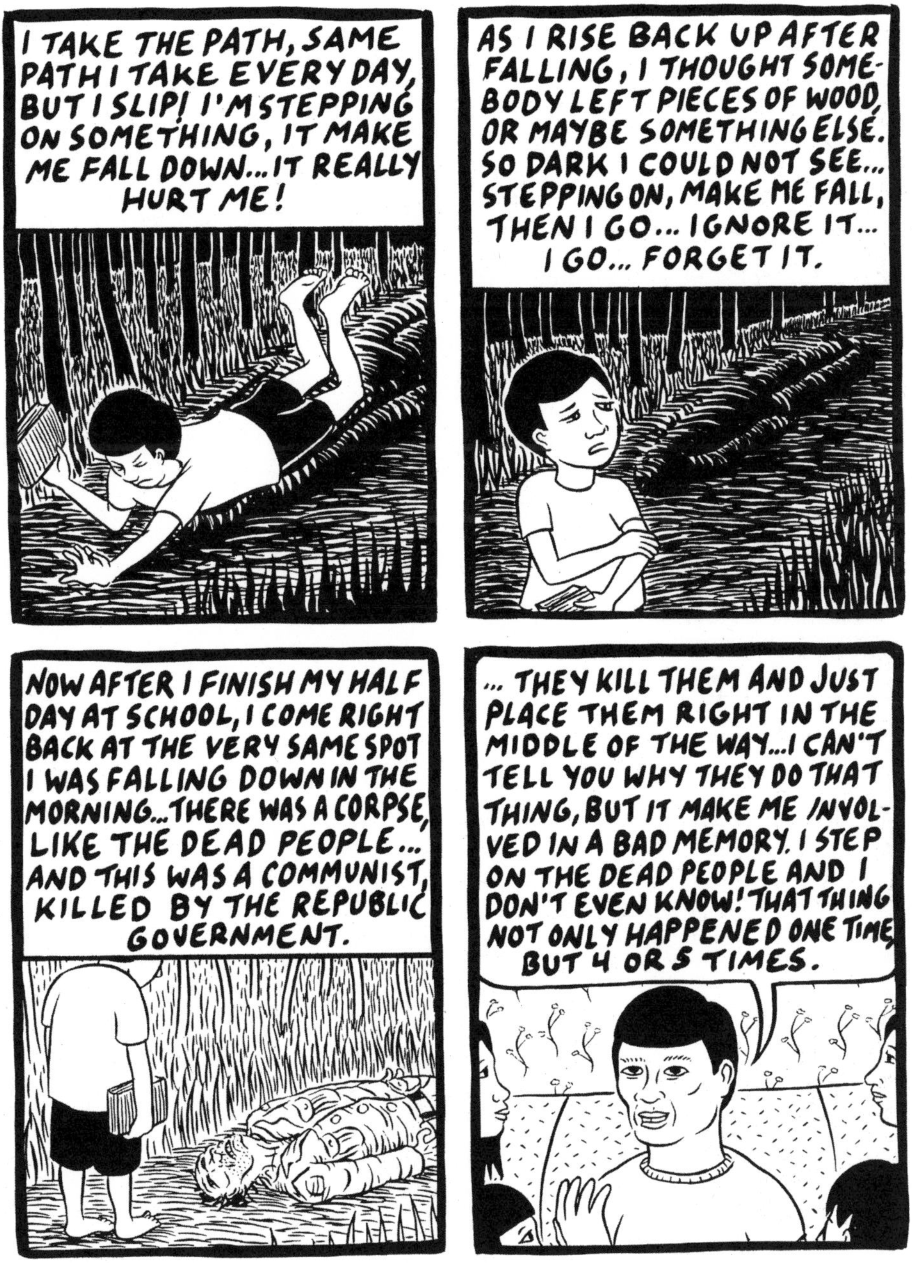
I TAKE THE PATH, SAME PATH I TAKE EVERY DAY, BUT I SLIP! I'M STEPPING ON SOMETHING, IT MAKE ME FALL DOWN... IT REALLY HURT ME!
AS I RISE BACK UP AFTER FALLING, I THOUGHT SOMEBODY LEFT PIECES OF WOOD, OR MAYBE SOMETHING ELSE. SO DARK I COULD NOT SEE... STEPPING ON, MAKE ME FALL, THEN I GO... IGNORE IT... I GO... FORGET IT.
NOW AFTER I FINISH MY HALF DAY AT SCHOOL, I COME RIGHT BACK AT THE VERY SAME SPOT I WAS FALLING DOWN IN THE MORNING... THERE WAS A CORPSE, LIKE THE DEAD PEOPLE... AND THIS WAS A COMMUNIST, KILLED BY THE REPUBLIC GOVERNMENT.
... THEY KILL THEM AND JUST PLACE THEM RIGHT IN THE MIDDLE OF THE WAY... I CAN'T TELL YOU WHY THEY DO THAT THING, BUT IT MAKE ME INVOLVED IN A BAD MEMORY. I STEP ON THE DEAD PEOPLE AND I DON'T EVEN KNOW! THAT THING NOT ONLY HAPPENED ONE TIME, BUT 4 OR 5 TIMES.

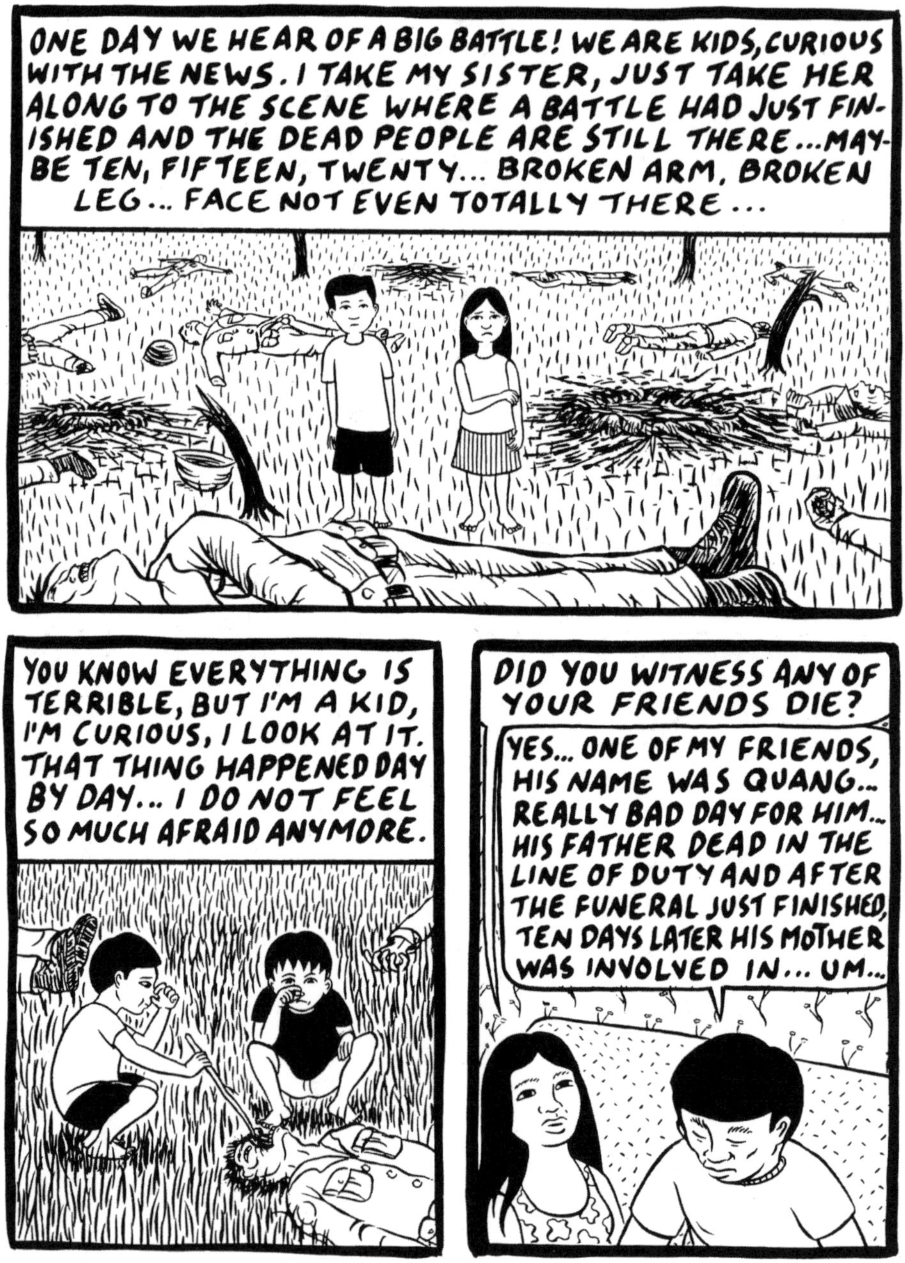

ONE DAY WE HEAR OF A BIG BATTLE! WE ARE KIDS, CURIOUS WITH THE NEWS. I TAKE MY SISTER, JUST TAKE HER ALONG TO THE SCENE WHERE A BATTLE HAD JUST FINISHED AND THE DEAD PEOPLE ARE STILL THERE... MAYBE TEN, FIFTEEN, TWENTY... BROKEN ARM, BROKEN LEG... FACE NOT EVEN TOTALLY THERE...
YOU KNOW EVERYTHING IS TERRIBLE, BUT I'M A KID, I'M CURIOUS, I LOOK AT IT. THAT THING HAPPENED DAY BY DAY... I DO NOT FEEL SO MUCH AFRAID ANYMORE.
DID YOU WITNESS ANY OF YOUR FRIENDS DIE?
YES... ONE OF MY FRIENDS, HIS NAME WAS QUANG... REALLY BAD DAY FOR HIM... HIS FATHER DEAD IN THE LINE OF DUTY AND AFTER THE FUNERAL JUST FINISHED, TEN DAYS LATER HIS MOTHER WAS INVOLVED IN... UM...

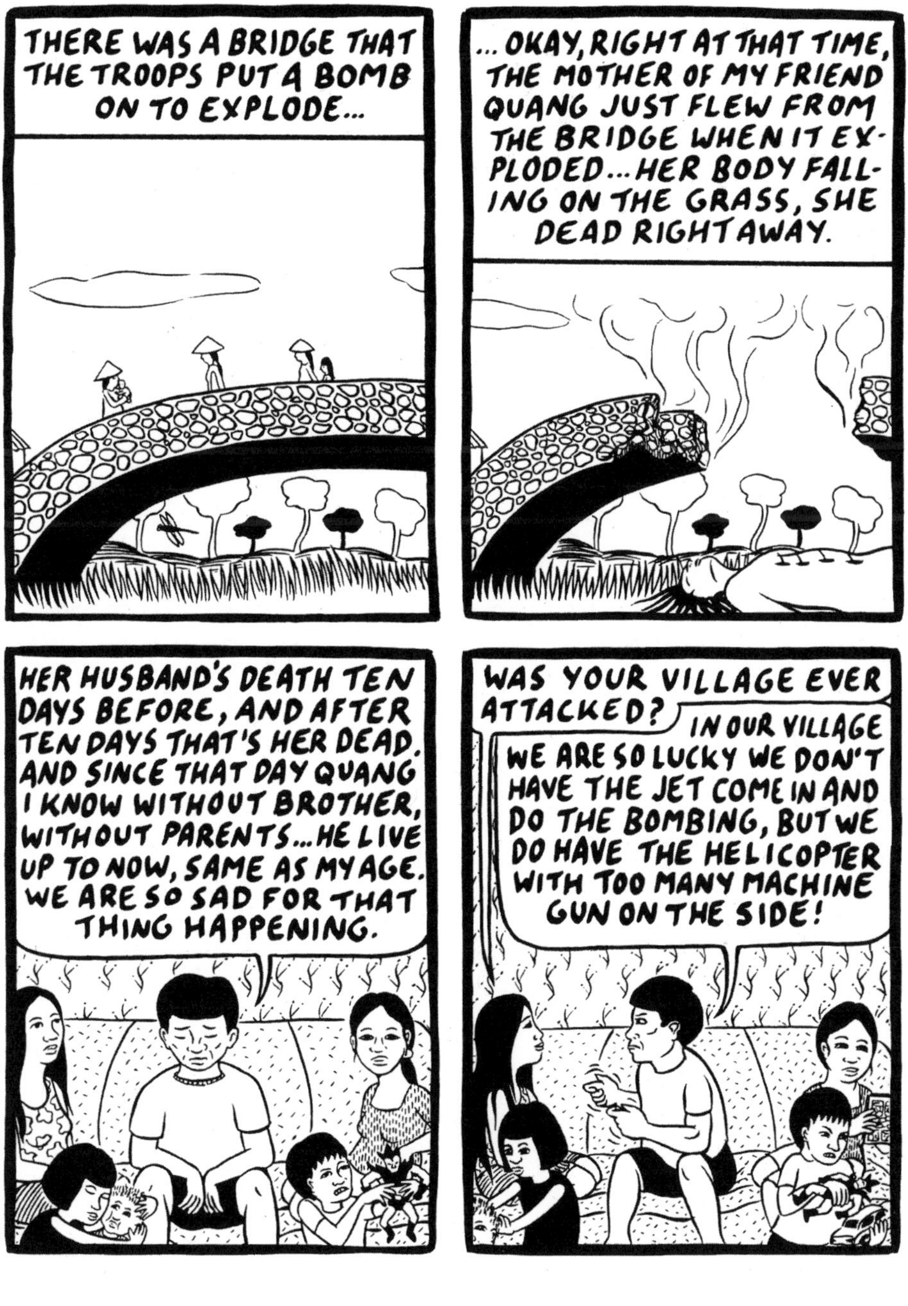
THERE WAS A BRIDGE THAT THE TROOPS PUT A BOMB ON TO EXPLODE...
...OKAY, RIGHT AT THAT TIME, THE MOTHER OF MY FRIEND QUANG JUST FLEW FROM THE BRIDGE WHEN IT EXPLODED... HER BODY FALLING ON THE GRASS, SHE DEAD RIGHTAWAY.
HER HUSBAND'S DEATH TEN DAYS BEFORE, AND AFTER TEN DAYS THAT'S HER DEAD. AND SINCE THAT DAY QUANG I KNOW WITHOUT BROTHER, WITHOUT PARENTS... HE LIVE UP TO NOW, SAME AS MY AGE. WE ARE SO SAD FOR THAT THING HAPPENING.
WAS YOUR VILLAGE EVER ATTACKED?
IN OUR VILLAGE WE ARE SO LUCKY WE DON'T HAVE THE JET COME IN AND DO THE BOMBING, BUT WE DO HAVE THE HELICOPTER WITH TOO MANY MACHINE GUN ON THE SIDE!

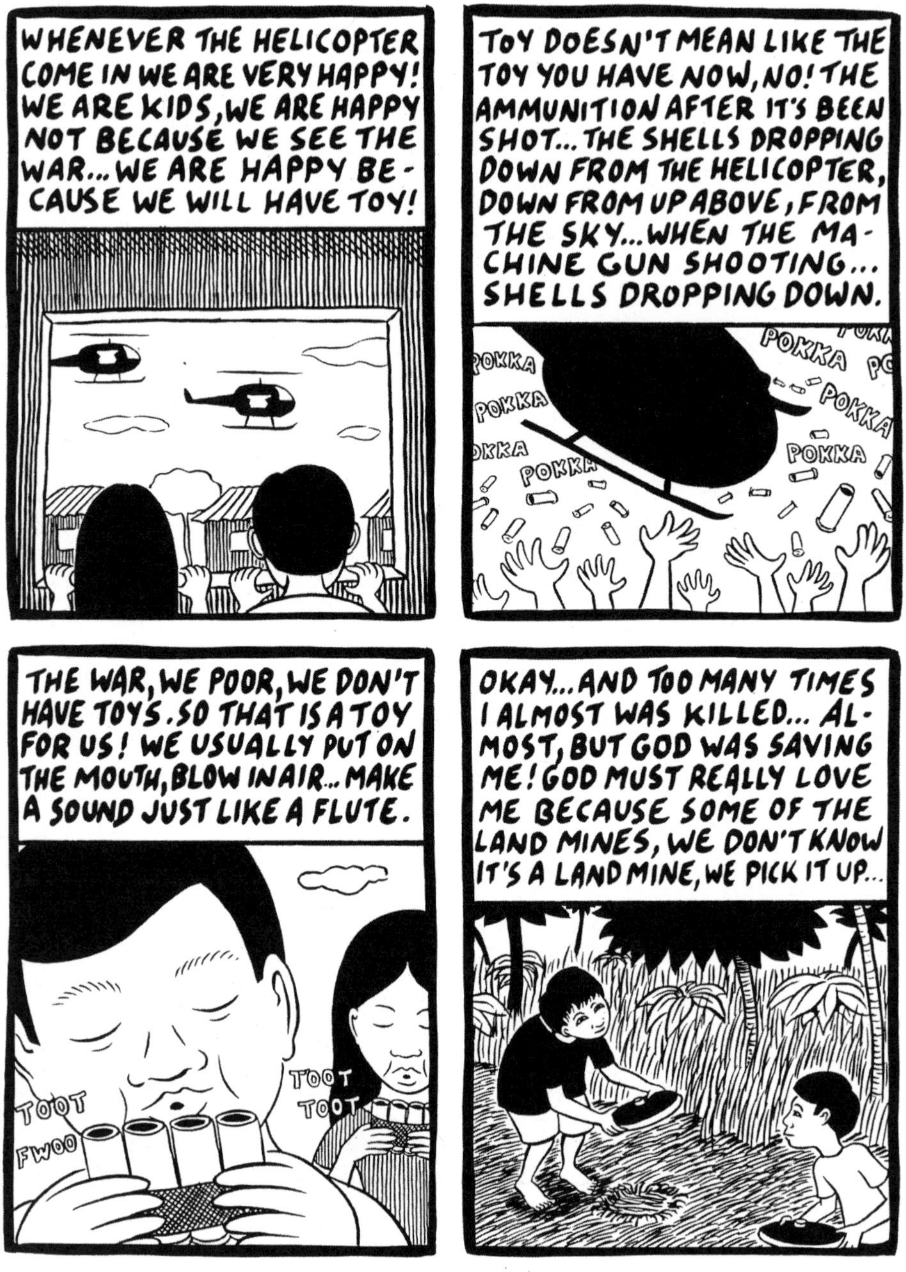
WHENEVER THE HELICOPTER COME IN WE ARE VERY HAPPY! WE ARE KIDS, WE ARE HAPPY NOT BECAUSE WE SEE THE WAR... WE ARE HAPPY BE-CAUSE WE WILL HAVE TOY!
TOY DOESN'T MEAN LIKE THE TOY YOU HAVE NOW, NO! THE AMMUNITION AFTER IT'S BEEN SHOT... THE SHELLS DROPPING DOWN FROM THE HELICOPTER, DOWN FROM UP ABOVE, FROM THE SKY... WHEN THE MA-CHINE GUN SHOOTING... SHELLS DROPPING DOWN.
POKKA
POKKA
POKKA
POKKA
POKKA
POKKA
POKKA
THE WAR, WE POOR, WE DON'T HAVE TOYS. SO THAT IS A TOY FOR US! WE USUALLY PUT ON THE MOUTH, BLOW IN AIR... MAKE A SOUND JUST LIKE A FLUTE.
TOOT
FWOO
TOOT
TOOT
OKAY... AND TOO MANY TIMES I ALMOST WAS KILLED... AL-MOST, BUT GOD WAS SAVING ME! GOD MUST REALLY LOVE ME BECAUSE SOME OF THE LAND MINES, WE DON'T KNOW IT'S A LAND MINE, WE PICK IT UP...

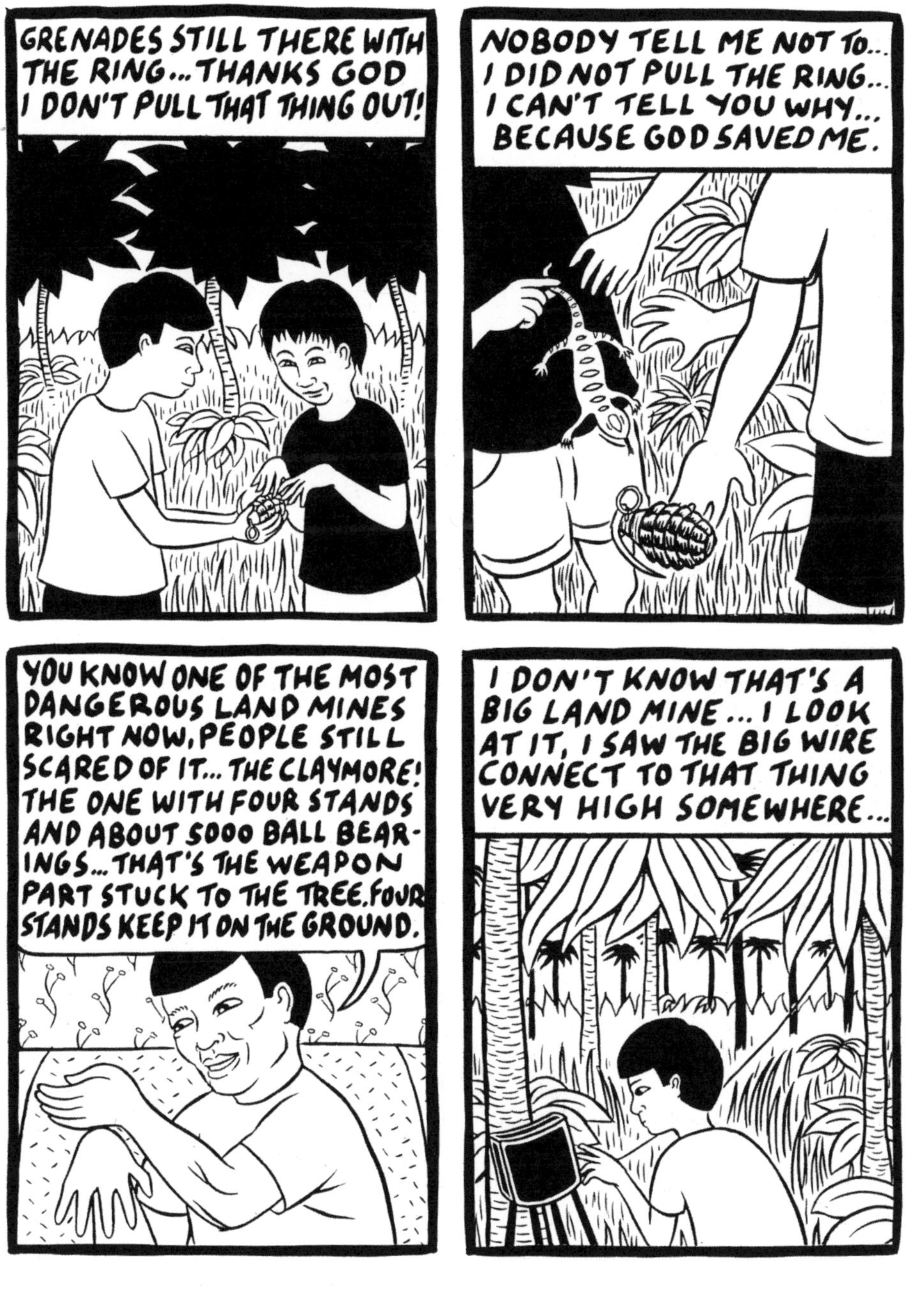
GRENADES STILL THERE WITH THE RING... THANKS GOD I DON'T PULL THAT THING OUT!
NOBODY TELL ME NOT TO... I DID NOT PULL THE RING... I CAN'T TELL YOU WHY... BECAUSE GOD SAVED ME.
YOU KNOW ONE OF THE MOST DANGEROUS LAND MINES RIGHT NOW, PEOPLE STILL SCARED OF IT... THE CLAYMORE! THE ONE WITH FOUR STANDS AND ABOUT 5000 BALL BEARINGS... THAT'S THE WEAPON PART STUCK TO THE TREE. FOUR STANDS KEEP IT ON THE GROUND.
I DON'T KNOW THAT'S A BIG LAND MINE... I LOOK AT IT, I SAW THE BIG WIRE CONNECT TO THAT THING VERY HIGH SOMEWHERE...

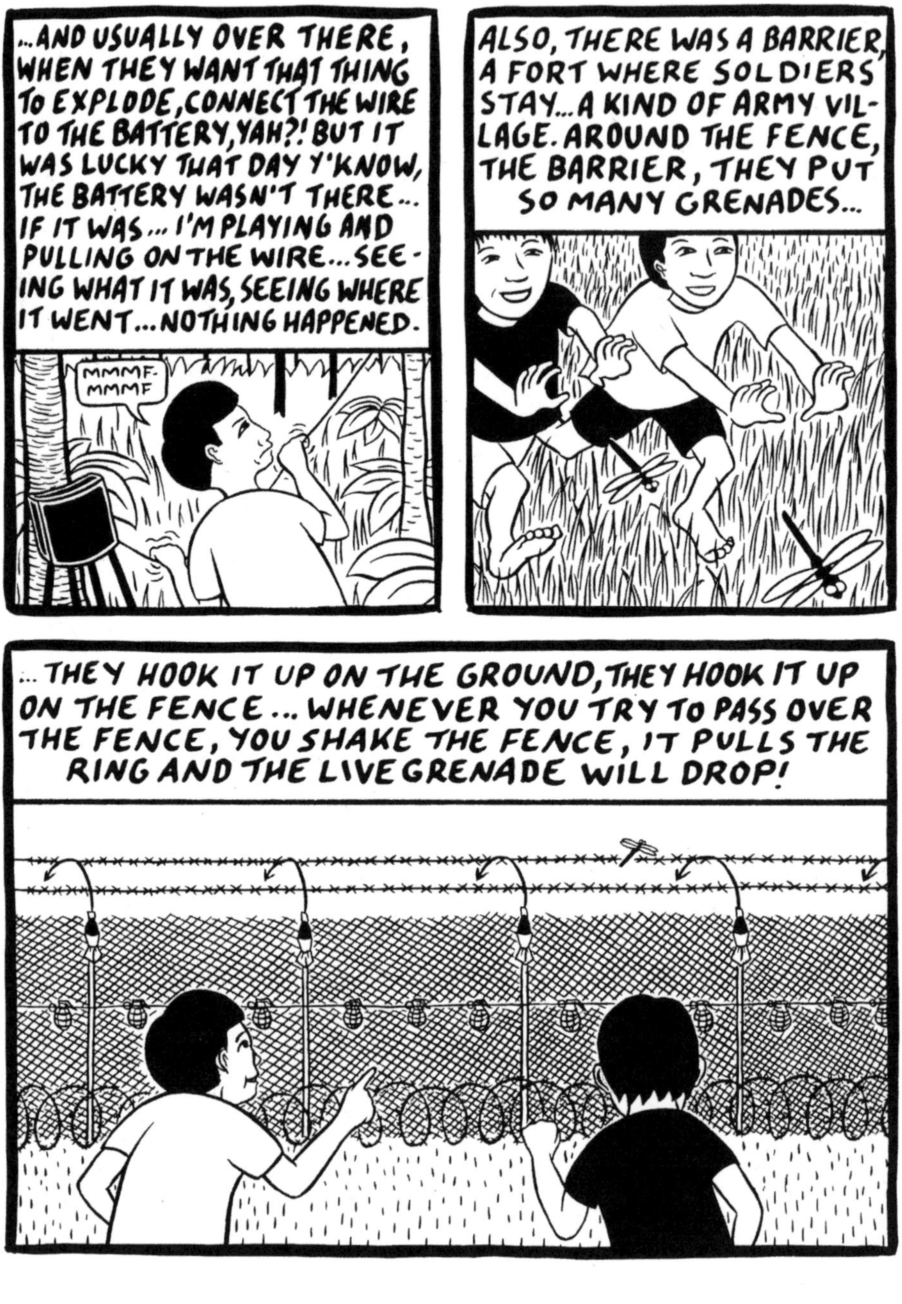
...AND USUALLY OVER THERE, WHEN THEY WANT THAT THING TO EXPLODE, CONNECT THE WIRE TO THE BATTERY, YAH?! BUT IT WAS LUCKY THAT DAY Y'KNOW, THE BATTERY WASN'T THERE... IF IT WAS... I'M PLAYING AND PULLING ON THE WIRE... SEE-ING WHAT IT WAS, SEEING WHERE IT WENT... NOTHING HAPPENED.
MMMF-MMMF
ALSO, THERE WAS A BARRIER, A FORT WHERE SOLDIERS STAY... A KIND OF ARMY VIL-LAGE. AROUND THE FENCE, THE BARRIER, THEY PUT SO MANY GRENADES...
...THEY HOOK IT UP ON THE GROUND, THEY HOOK IT UP ON THE FENCE... WHENEVER YOU TRY TO PASS OVER THE FENCE, YOU SHAKE THE FENCE, IT PULLS THE RING AND THE LIVE GRENADE WILL DROP!

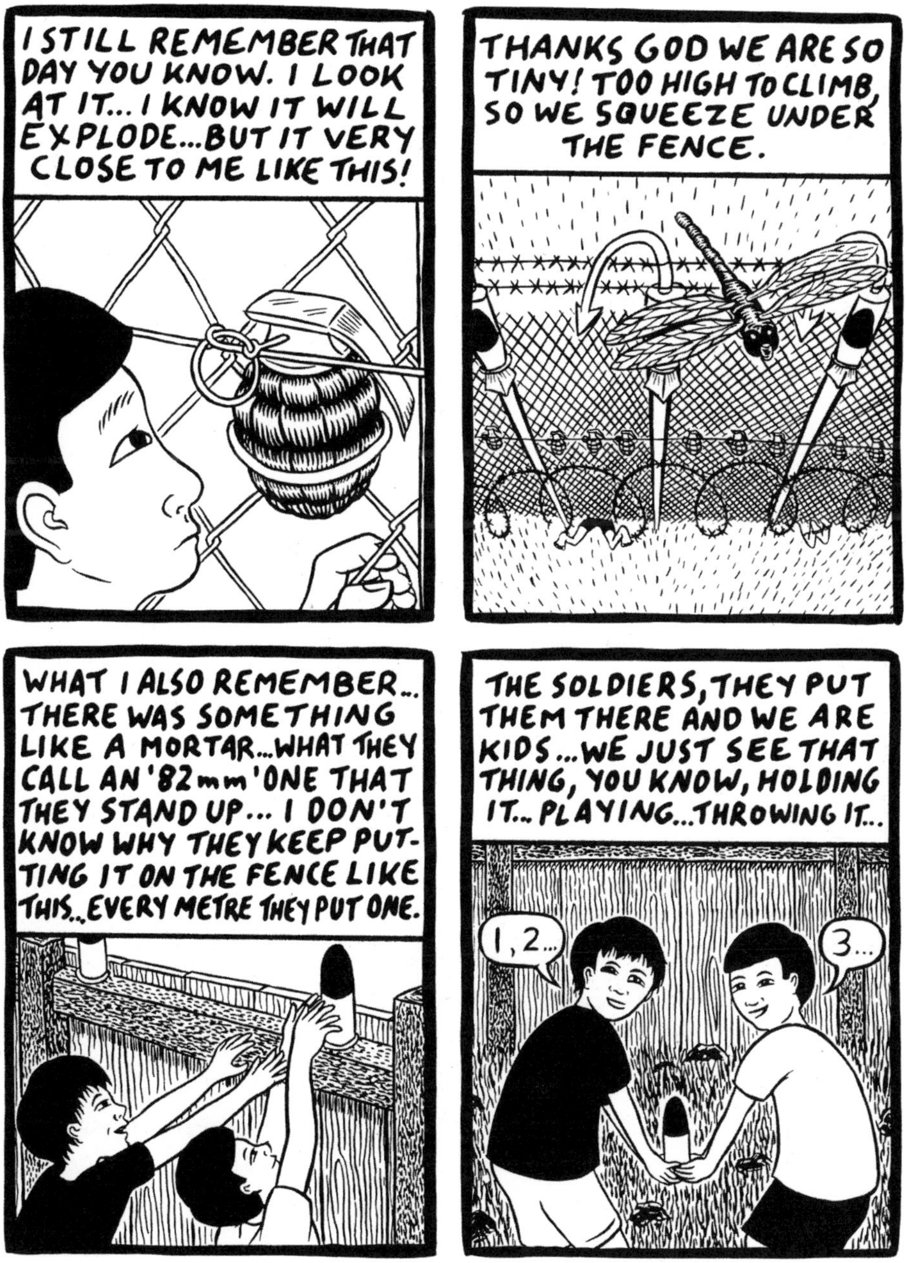
I STILL REMEMBER THAT DAY YOU KNOW. I LOOK AT IT... I KNOW IT WILL EXPLODE...BUT IT VERY CLOSE TO ME LIKE THIS!
THANKS GOD WE ARE SO TINY! TOO HIGH TO CLIMB, SO WE SQUEEZE UNDER THE FENCE.
WHAT I ALSO REMEMBER... THERE WAS SOMETHING LIKE A MORTAR...WHAT THEY CALL AN '82mm' ONE THAT THEY STAND UP... I DON'T KNOW WHY THEY KEEP PUTTING IT ON THE FENCE LIKE THIS...EVERY METRE THEY PUT ONE.
THE SOLDIERS, THEY PUT THEM THERE AND WE ARE KIDS...WE JUST SEE THAT THING, YOU KNOW, HOLDING IT... PLAYING...THROWING IT...
1, 2...
3...

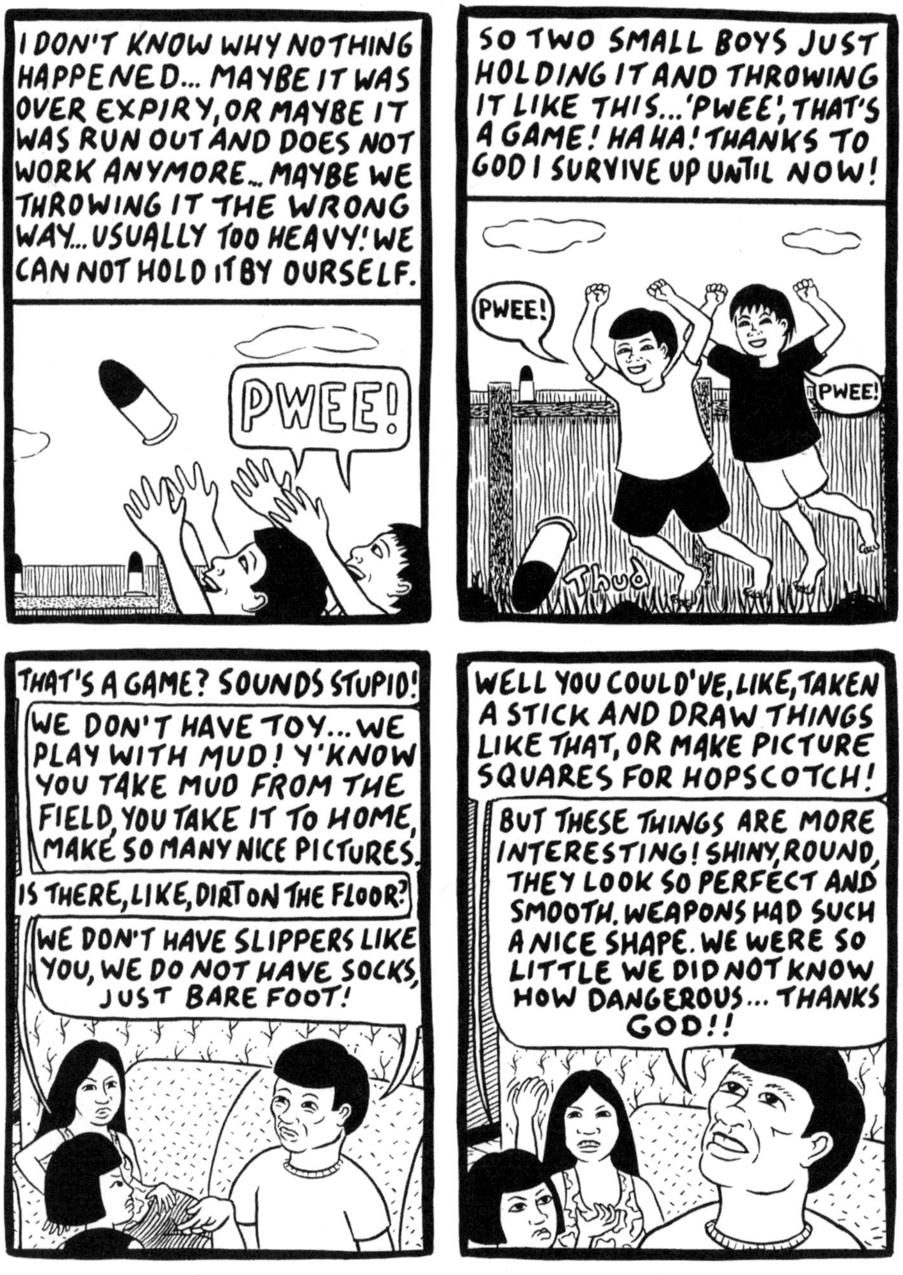
I DON'T KNOW WHY NOTHING HAPPENED... MAYBE IT WAS OVER EXPIRY, OR MAYBE IT WAS RUN OUT AND DOES NOT WORK ANYMORE... MAYBE WE THROWING IT THE WRONG WAY... USUALLY TOO HEAVY! WE CAN NOT HOLD IT BY OURSELF.
PWEE!
SO TWO SMALL BOYS JUST HOLDING IT AND THROWING IT LIKE THIS... 'PWEE', THAT'S A GAME! HA HA! THANKS TO GOD I SURVIVE UP UNTIL NOW!
PWEE!
PWEE!
Thud
THAT'S A GAME? SOUNDS STUPID!
WE DON'T HAVE TOY... WE PLAY WITH MUD! Y'KNOW YOU TAKE MUD FROM THE FIELD, YOU TAKE IT TO HOME, MAKE SO MANY NICE PICTURES.
IS THERE, LIKE, DIRT ON THE FLOOR?
WE DON'T HAVE SLIPPERS LIKE YOU, WE DO NOT HAVE SOCKS, JUST BARE FOOT!
WELL YOU COULD'VE, LIKE, TAKEN A STICK AND DRAW THINGS LIKE THAT, OR MAKE PICTURE SQUARES FOR HOPSCOTCH!
BUT THESE THINGS ARE MORE INTERESTING! SHINY, ROUND, THEY LOOK SO PERFECT AND SMOOTH. WEAPONS HAD SUCH A NICE SHAPE. WE WERE SO LITTLE WE DID NOT KNOW HOW DANGEROUS... THANKS GOD!!

fish

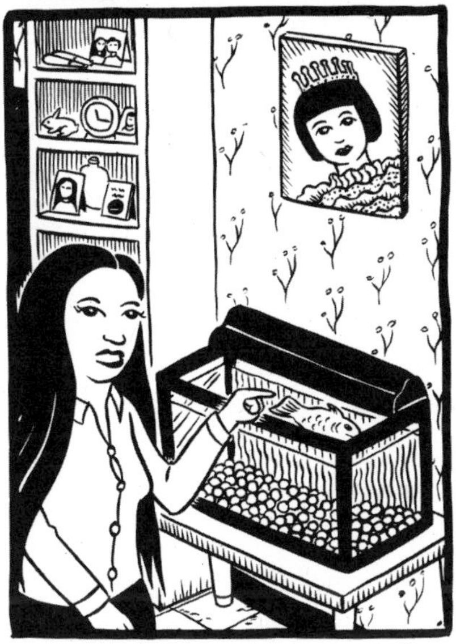

She tells me that the fish is too big for its tank and it hurt itself trying to get out.

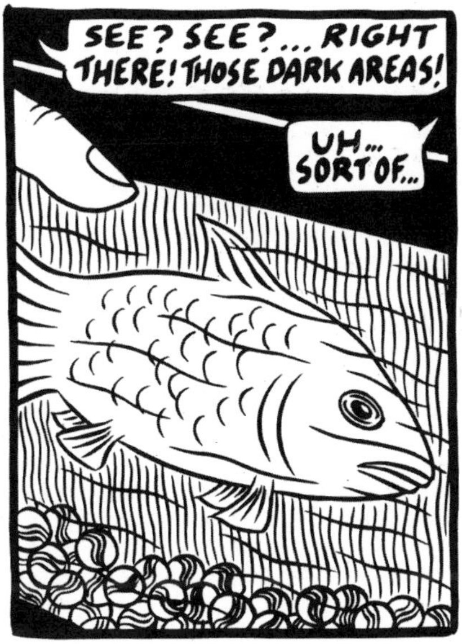
SEE? SEE?... RIGHT THERE! THOSE DARK AREAS!
UH... SORT OF...

The fish just kind of floats there and she is trying to show me the marks of damage from its attempted escape... but I can't see them...

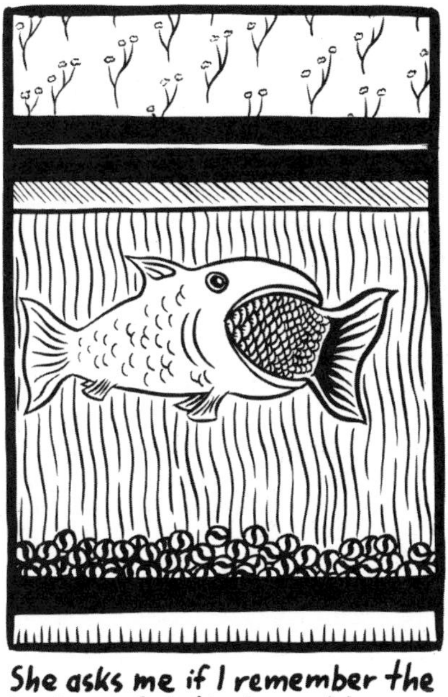

She asks me if I remember the big black fish that used to swim in there... the big white fish ate him!

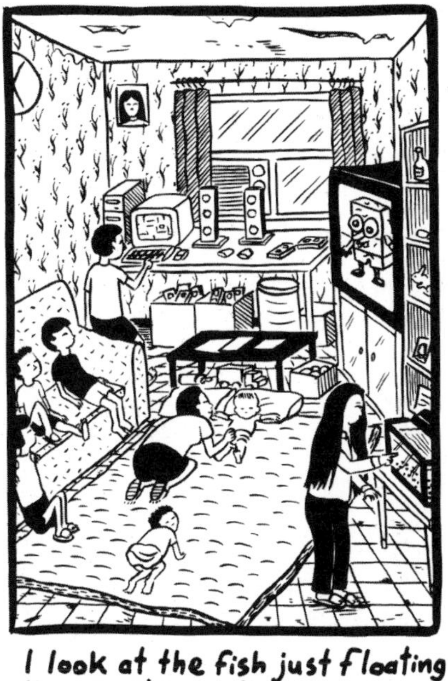

I look at the fish just floating there in its small tank and wonder how it can survive in there at all...

window

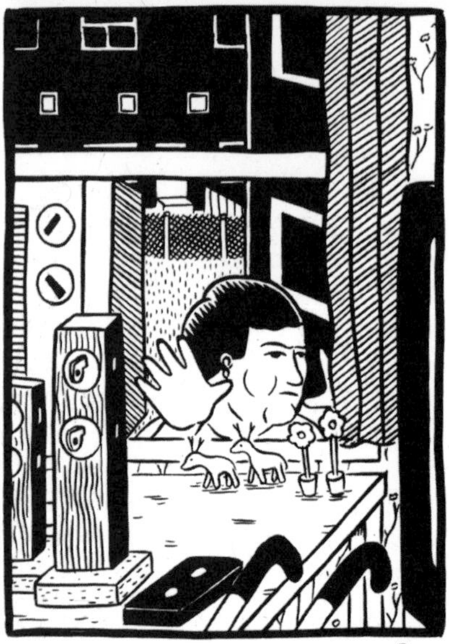

There's someone pushing their face against the window...pushing, peering, looking for someone...something...

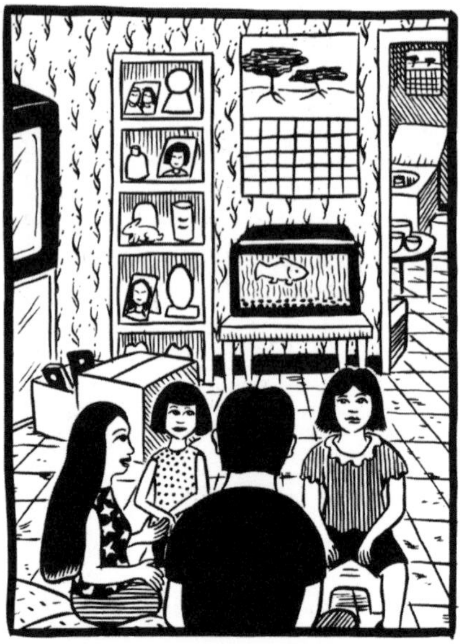

Nobody notices except me, so we just talk on about the 3 sisters' nicknames for each other... 'beef leg', 'pork leg'... and 'chicken leg' who wants to go out and play...

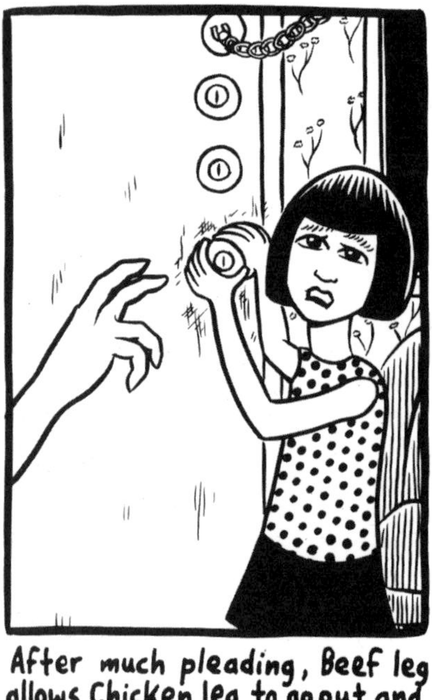

After much pleading, Beef leg allows Chicken leg to go out and play.

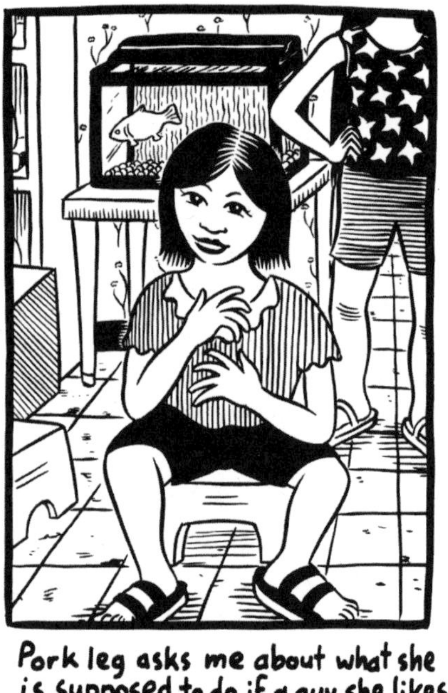

Pork leg asks me about what she is supposed to do if a guy she likes is looking down her top when she is bending over...and 'am I fat?'

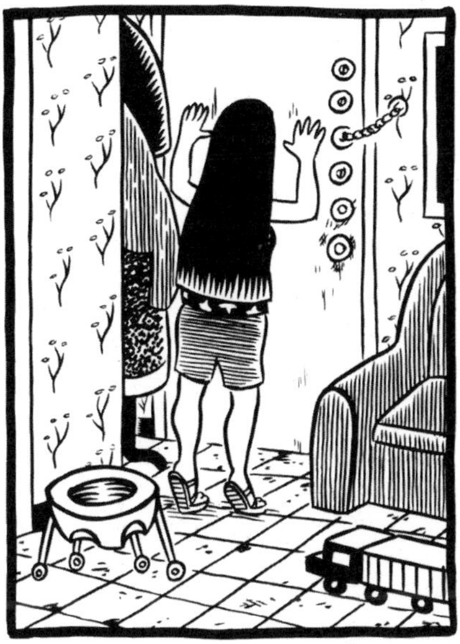

There's a banging at the door and Beef leg checks the eyehole, asks who it is, then unlocks the many locks on the door.

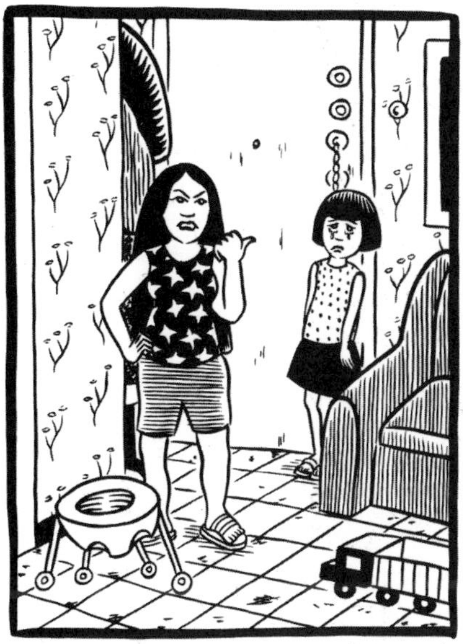

Chicken leg comes in wide eyed and crying... Beef leg yells at her in their language then tells me 'It's her fault! She always does this! This always happens!'

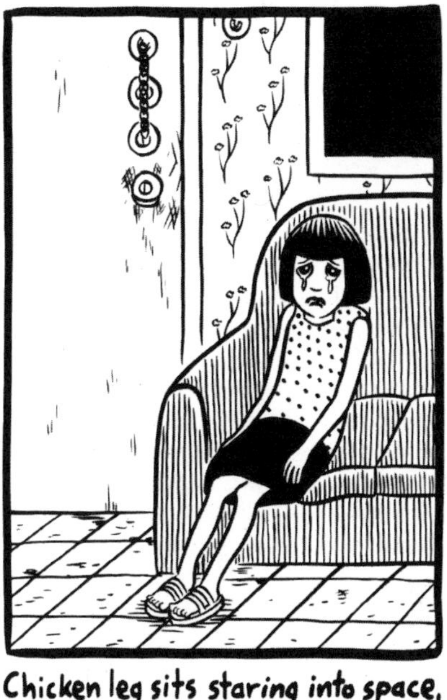

Chicken leg sits staring into space, crying and not moving... Beef leg has stormed out the door...

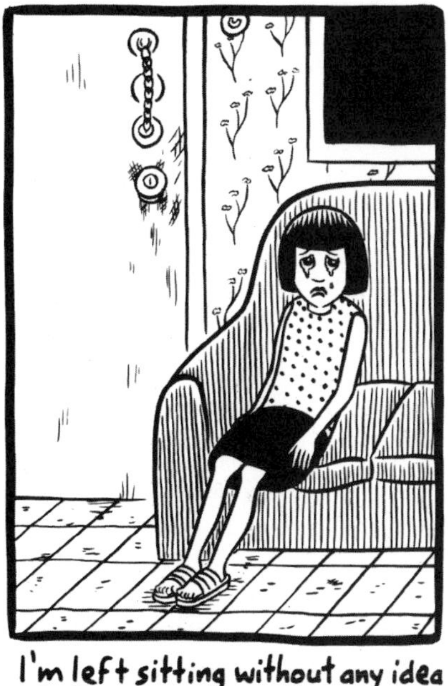

I'm left sitting without any idea what's going on...something happened outside...Chicken leg is sitting there sniffling...what do I do here...?

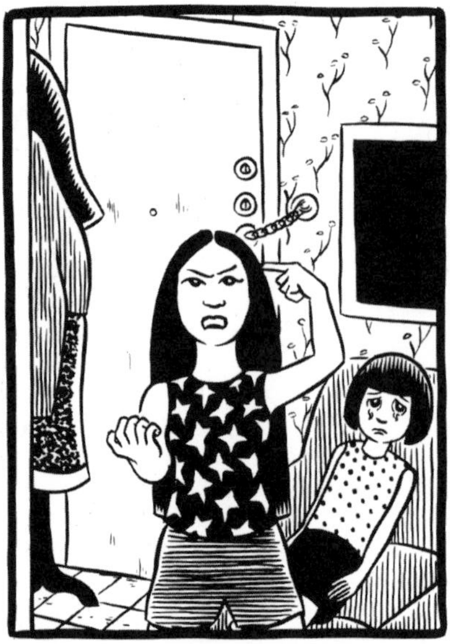

Beef leg has quickly returned...with irritation she informs me that: 'I tried to talk to his mother, but she doesn't speak English and she just kept pointing at her head!'

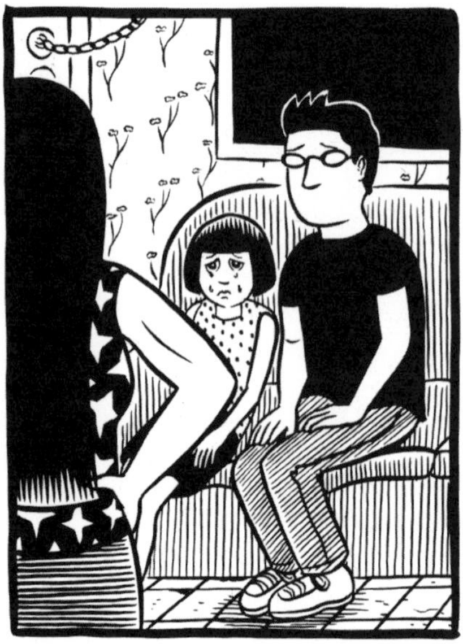

Enough. I go sit beside Chicken leg to ask her what happened...

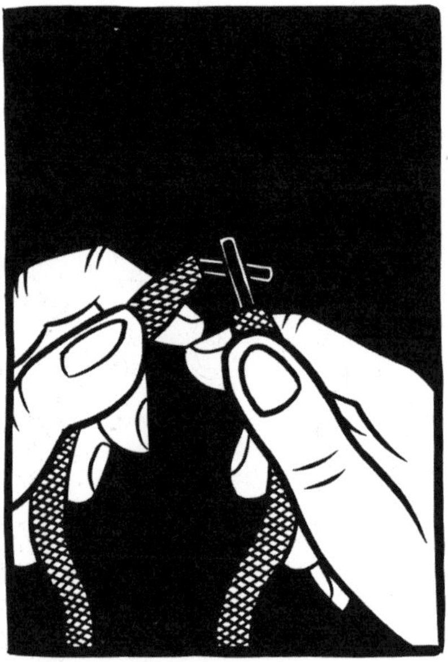

She's unresponsive...absorbing silence... twisting a shoelace between her finger tips. I remember her being like this years ago when she told me 'I have a monster in me' and drawing a picture of it.

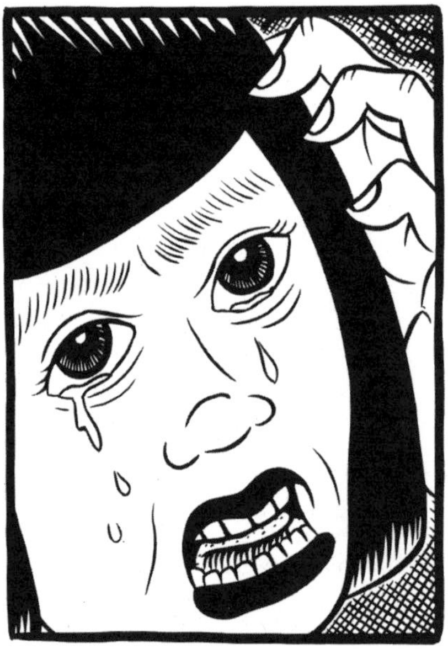

I persist...asking questions until she tells me, 'That boy, you know was banging his bike against mine and wouldn't stop and he liked my hair and grabbed and wouldn't let go and was going to pull it out of my head!'

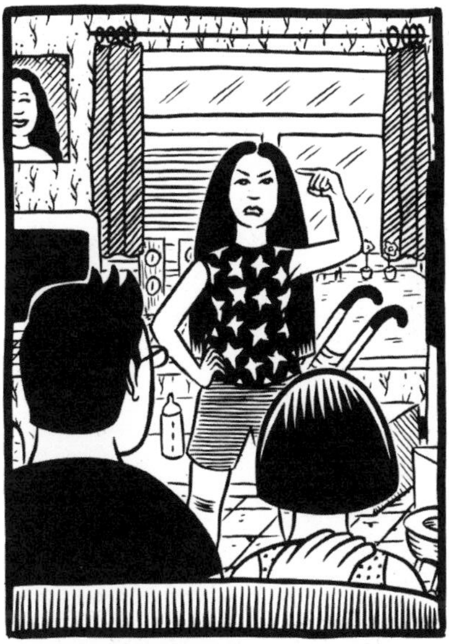

I look to Beef leg for more informa-
tion and I'm told this boy fell down
the stairs when he was two and there's
something wrong with his head.

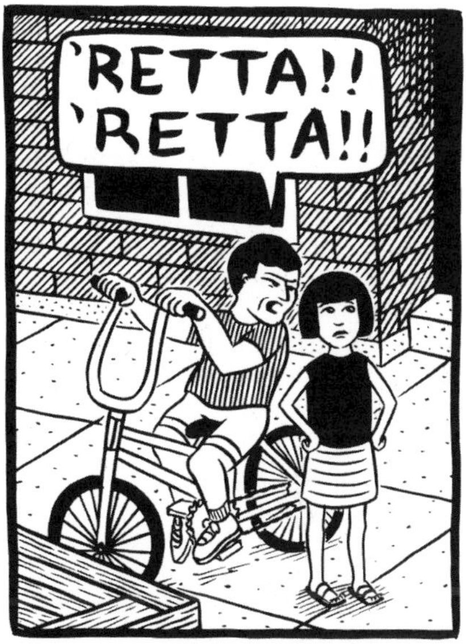
'RETTA!! 'RETTA!!

sigh...the kid's about fourteen now...
must have brain damage...Chicken leg's
afraid to play outside... I remember
a big kid on a bike yelling part of her
name right in her ear and she would
just ignore him...

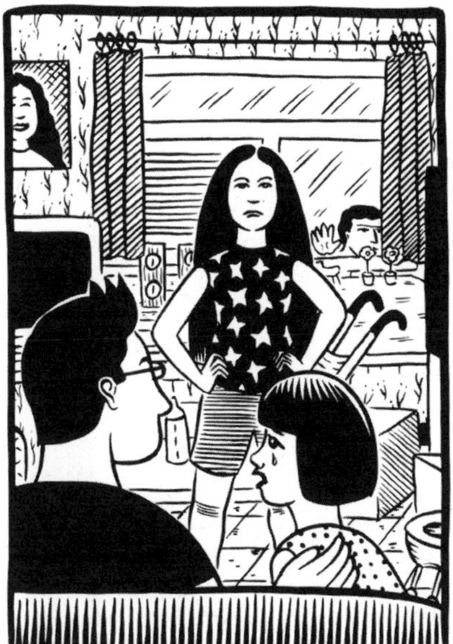

I try to explain to Chicken leg that
he doesn't know what he's doing...he's
not trying to be mean... try not to
play around him... I try to explain
compassion... tolerance...

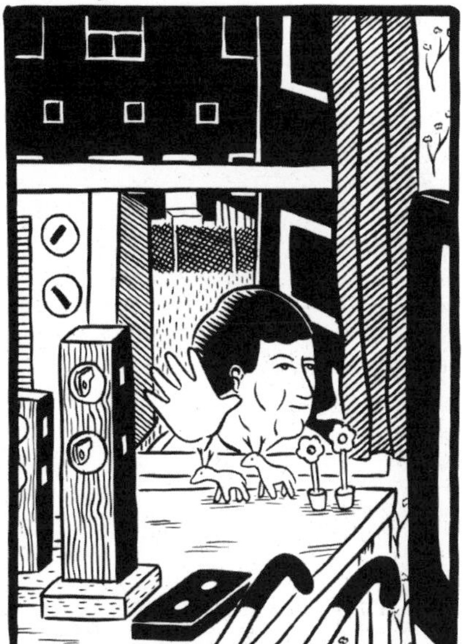

There's someone pushing their face
against the window... again...
pushing, peering, looking for someone... something...

bump

So I visit the girl who's failing summer school math because she picks worms every night until 4 a.m.

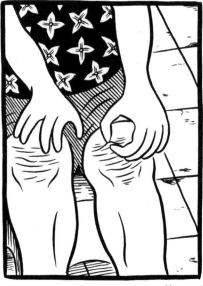

Her knees are dark and calloused from crawling on the ground... she picks at the dry skin.

Her little sister sits on the couch awkwardly because her arm hurts... she wants to say why...'but I can't say why'...her sister gives her a 'look'.

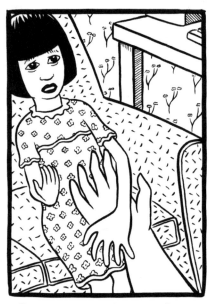

She gives me her arm and asks if I can see a bump.

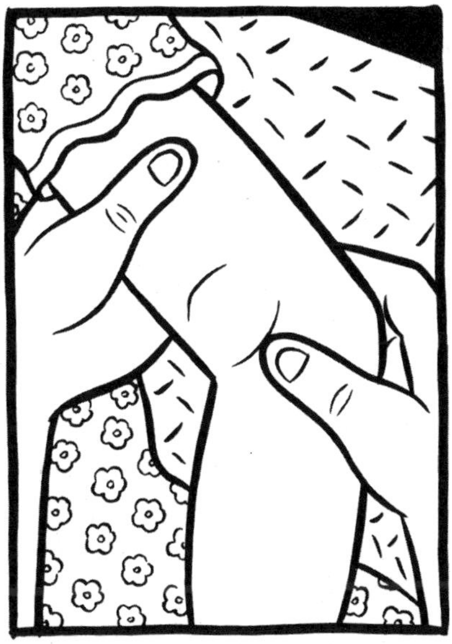

I feel her arm and there's a large, hard, swollen area, but no obvious mark...her sister says 'she deserved it.'

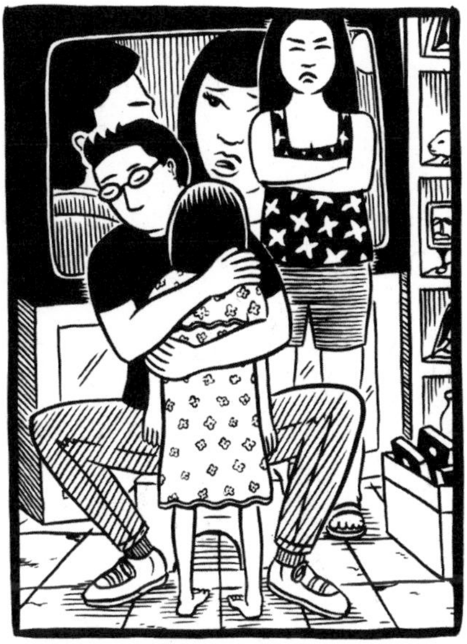

She looks hurt and confused and angry... what can I do?... she leans forward and I give her a hug and a pat on the back.

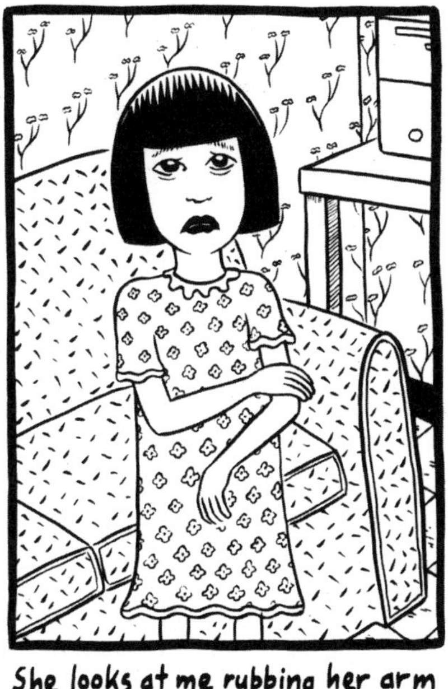

She looks at me rubbing her arm and I wonder how it happened... What she did to deserve it...What can I do? What happens in a family? What can I really do?...

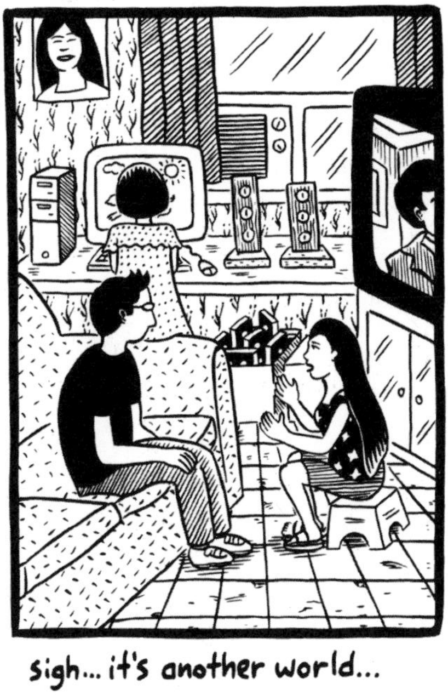

sigh... it's another world...

angels

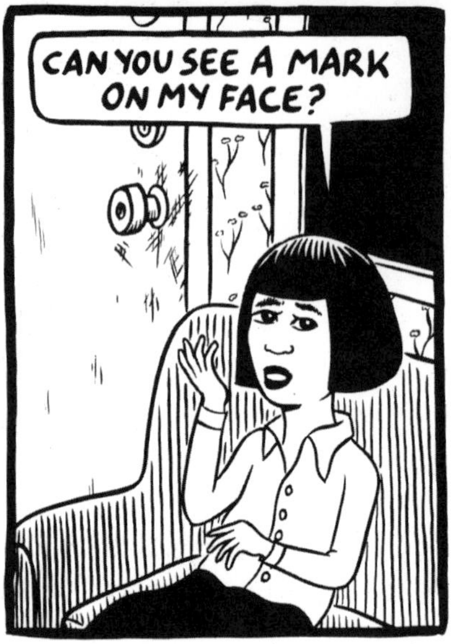
CAN YOU SEE A MARK ON MY FACE?

Aw no... now what's happened to Henrietta...?

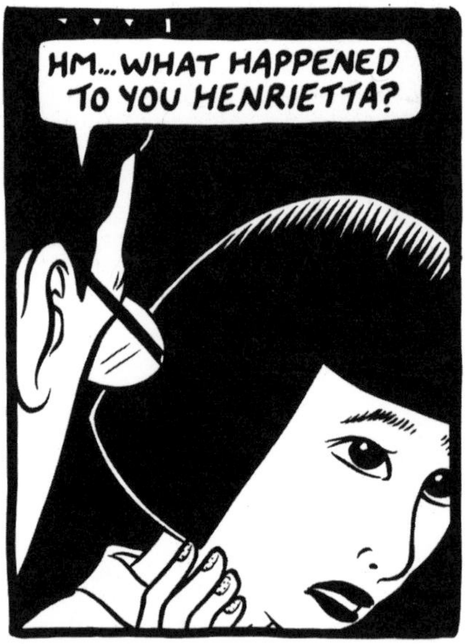
HM...WHAT HAPPENED TO YOU HENRIETTA?

I'm looking... almost not wanting to see anything...

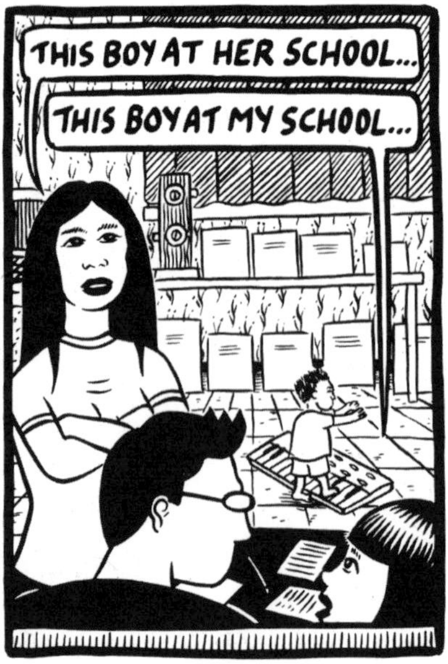
THIS BOY AT HER SCHOOL...
THIS BOY AT MY SCHOOL...

She looks to Hien for approval, then continues...

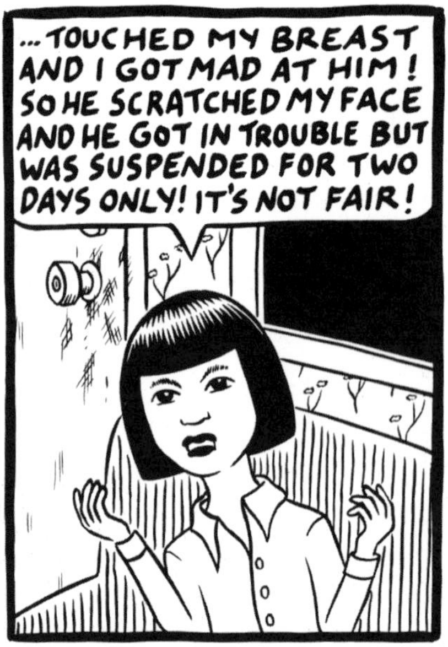
...TOUCHED MY BREAST AND I GOT MAD AT HIM! SO HE SCRATCHED MY FACE AND HE GOT IN TROUBLE BUT WAS SUSPENDED FOR TWO DAYS ONLY! IT'S NOT FAIR!

I wonder what kind of punishment would've satisfied her... I don't want to know... I switch the topic to angels...

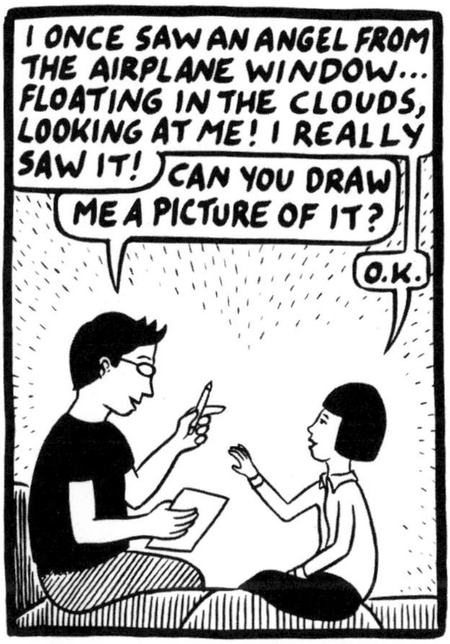
I ONCE SAW AN ANGEL FROM THE AIRPLANE WINDOW... FLOATING IN THE CLOUDS, LOOKING AT ME! I REALLY SAW IT!
CAN YOU DRAW ME A PICTURE OF IT?
O.K.

So I give her a marker and some paper and she starts drawing...

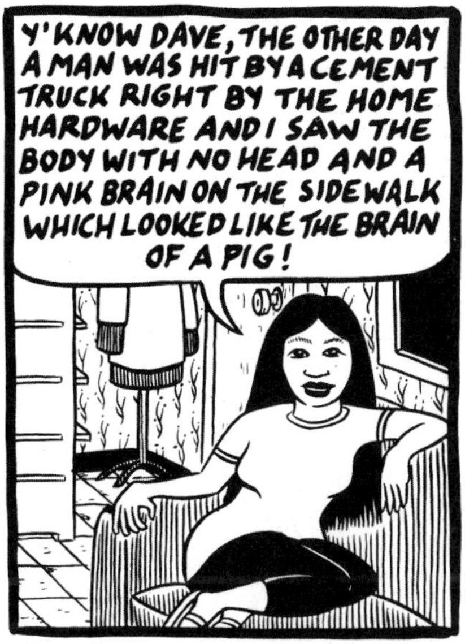
Y'KNOW DAVE, THE OTHER DAY A MAN WAS HIT BY A CEMENT TRUCK RIGHT BY THE HOME HARDWARE AND I SAW THE BODY WITH NO HEAD AND A PINK BRAIN ON THE SIDEWALK WHICH LOOKED LIKE THE BRAIN OF A PIG!

The story is rolled out in one sentence and I'm having trouble understanding... a headless body and a brain on the sidewalk?!

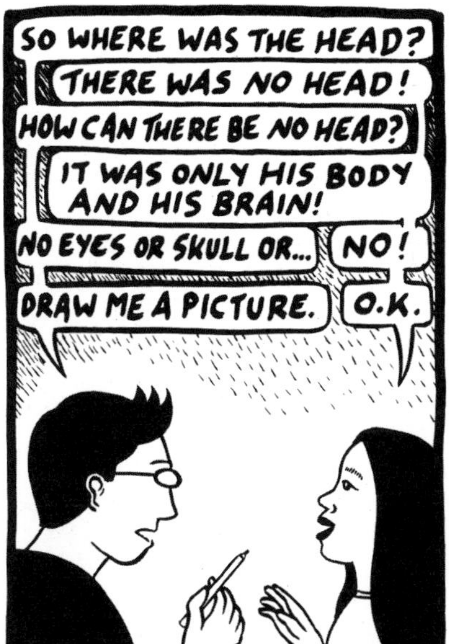
SO WHERE WAS THE HEAD?
THERE WAS NO HEAD!
HOW CAN THERE BE NO HEAD?
IT WAS ONLY HIS BODY AND HIS BRAIN!
NO EYES OR SKULL OR...
NO!
DRAW ME A PICTURE.
O.K.

I really am having trouble with this... so Henrietta's drawing an angel in the clouds and Hien's drawing a brain and a body in front of Home Hardware...

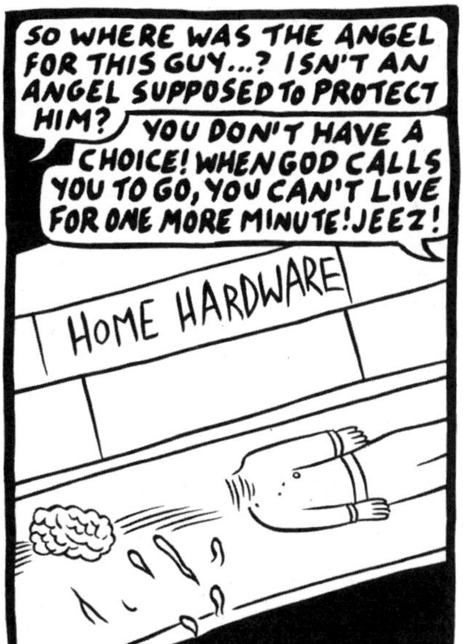
SO WHERE WAS THE ANGEL FOR THIS GUY...? ISN'T AN ANGEL SUPPOSED TO PROTECT HIM?
YOU DON'T HAVE A CHOICE! WHEN GOD CALLS YOU TO GO, YOU CAN'T LIVE FOR ONE MORE MINUTE! JEEZ!
HOME HARDWARE

Okay...like she said... Hien's mom said for her not to walk over that place again because the man's spirit is stuck there and might try to grab her and keep her there! Henrietta's finished her angel drawing.

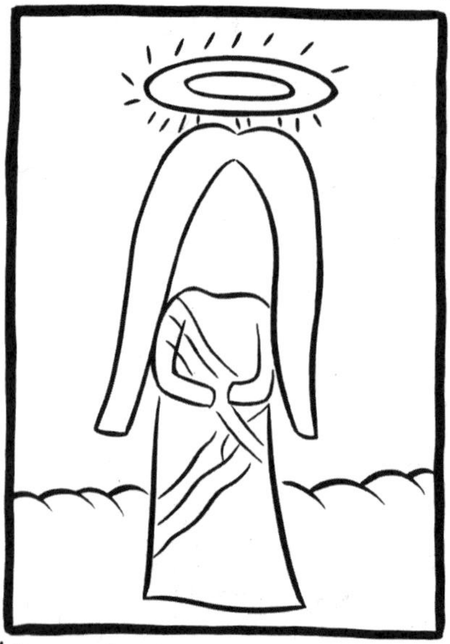

'This angel had only helped me once and it was a miracle and I can never forget about that. And all it did was praying. It was on the clouds and it had no face and no skin, but I can't tell what it did for me.'

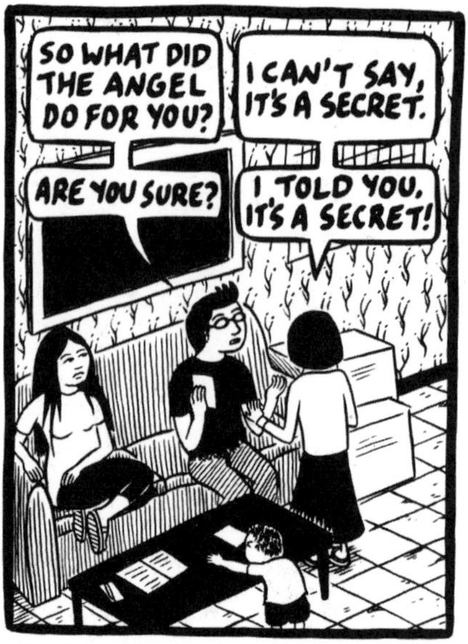
SO WHAT DID THE ANGEL DO FOR YOU?
I CAN'T SAY, IT'S A SECRET.
ARE YOU SURE?
I TOLD YOU, IT'S A SECRET!

Gosh... a secret with an angel... I'm so curious... I really want to know... I ask a couple of times then leave it... maybe angels keep secrets with those they watch over... good secrets...

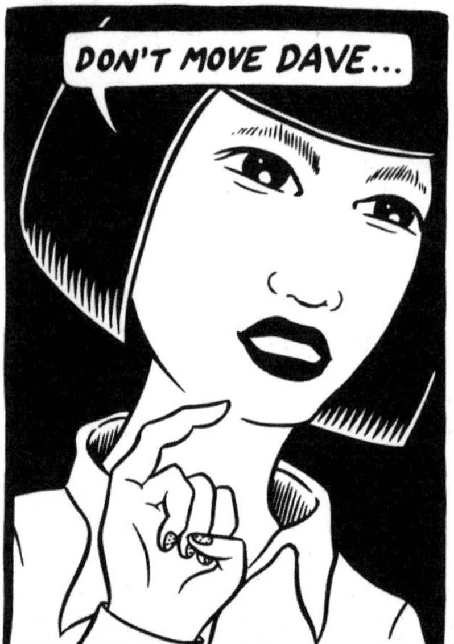
DON'T MOVE DAVE...

Henrietta sees an eyelash on my cheek and removes it with her pinky...

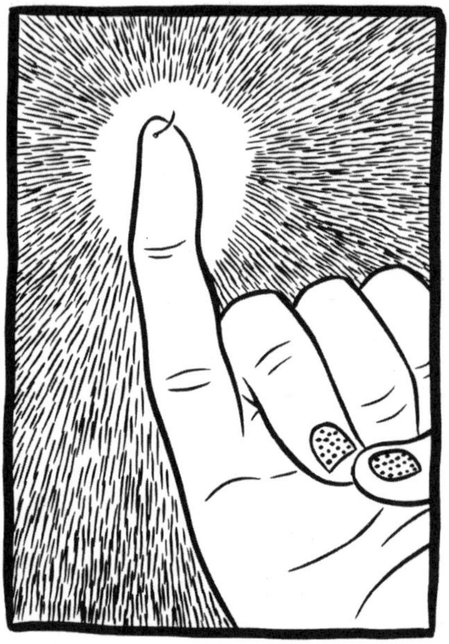

...she presents it to me and tells me to make a wish... then blow it away... I make a secret wish of hope...

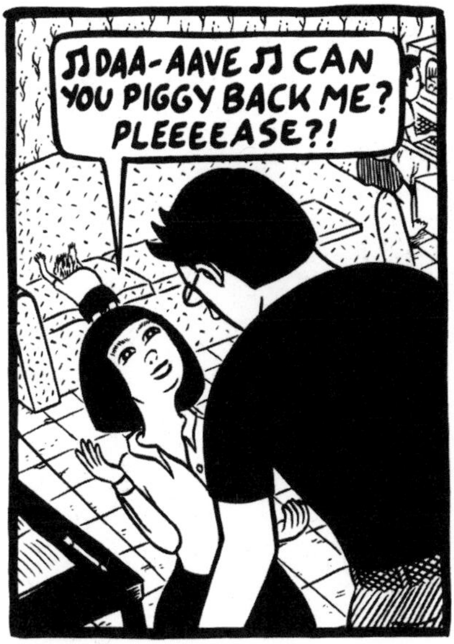
♫DAA-AAVE♫ CAN YOU PIGGY BACK ME? PLEEEEASE?!

Henrietta wants me to piggy back her... God, I hope she's still light enough, it's been a long time...

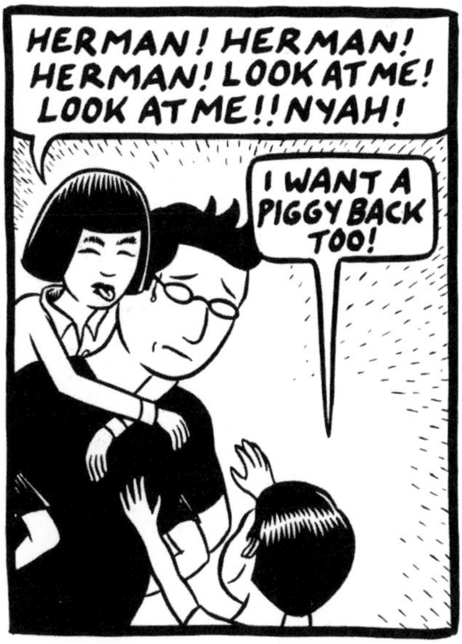
HERMAN! HERMAN! HERMAN! LOOK AT ME! LOOK AT ME!! NYAH!
I WANT A PIGGY BACK TOO!

I should've known... now Herman wants a ride... he also wants to know who's heavier...

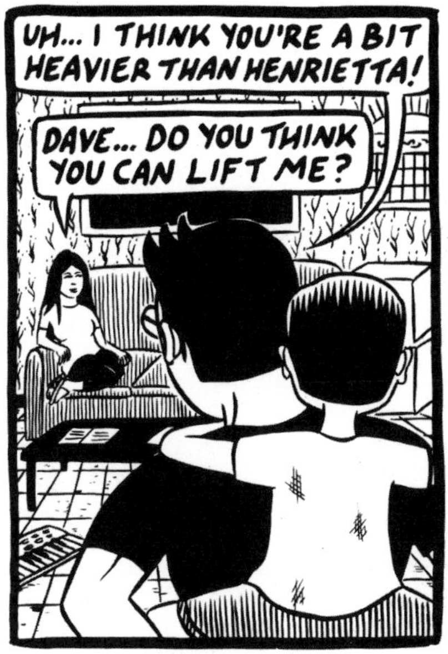
UH... I THINK YOU'RE A BIT HEAVIER THAN HENRIETTA!
DAVE... DO YOU THINK YOU CAN LIFT ME?

I bounce Herman up and down for a bit and Hien mentions how I used to be able to lift her and Hoi at the same time!

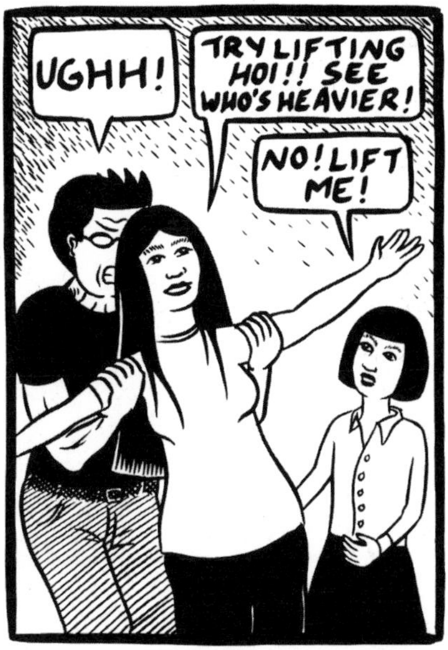
UGHH!
TRY LIFTING HOI!! SEE WHO'S HEAVIER!
NO! LIFT ME!

Standing with her arms outstretched I try, really try to lift her up, but I can just barely get her off the floor!

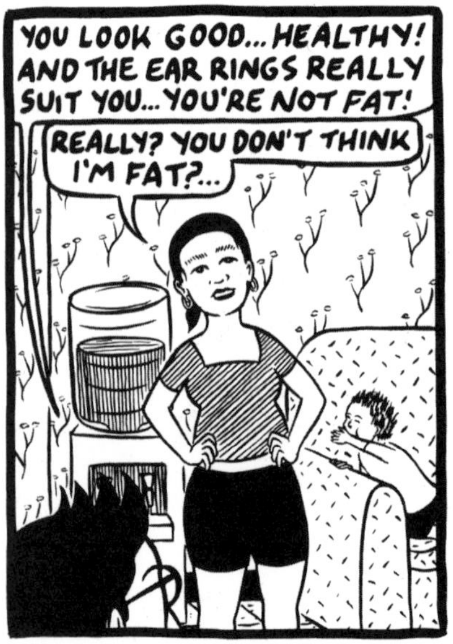
YOU LOOK GOOD... HEALTHY! AND THE EAR RINGS REALLY SUIT YOU... YOU'RE NOT FAT!
REALLY? YOU DON'T THINK I'M FAT?...

Hoi has come into the room and wants to know if she looks fat and if her hoop earrings make her look pretty...

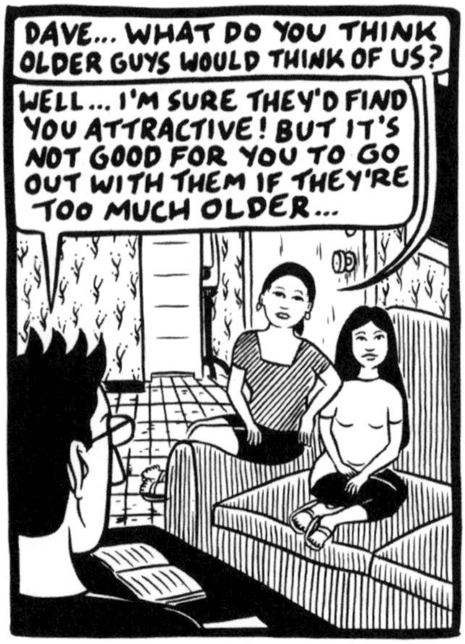
DAVE... WHAT DO YOU THINK OLDER GUYS WOULD THINK OF US?
WELL... I'M SURE THEY'D FIND YOU ATTRACTIVE! BUT IT'S NOT GOOD FOR YOU TO GO OUT WITH THEM IF THEY'RE TOO MUCH OLDER...

Hoi always asks such forthright questions...there's some older guy at her church that she likes...

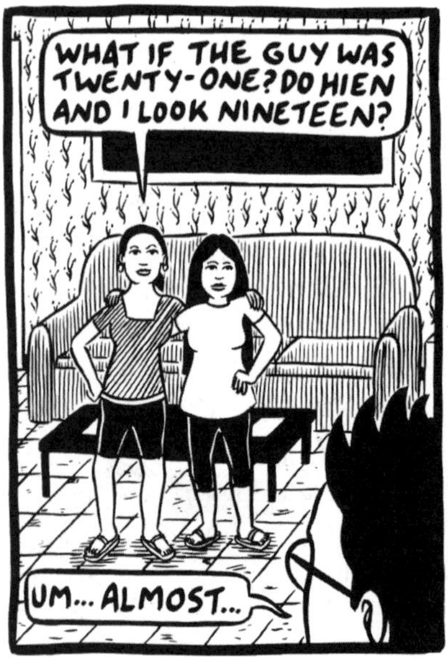
WHAT IF THE GUY WAS TWENTY-ONE? DO HIEN AND I LOOK NINETEEN?
UM... ALMOST...

I tell them that a guy who's twenty-one probably doesn't want to go out with a fifteen year old...and yes, with the right clothes and make-up they might look nineteen...

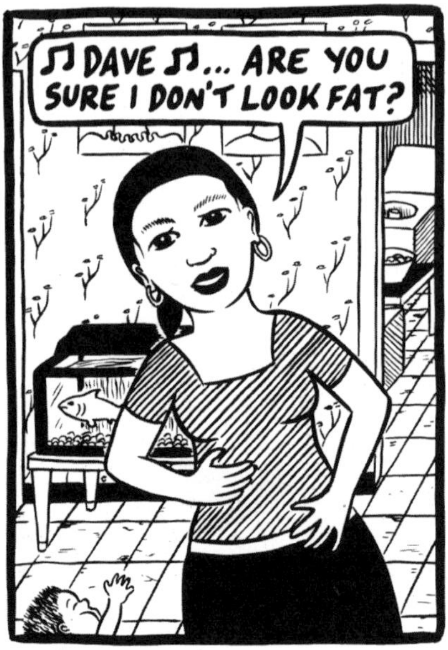
♫ DAVE ♫... ARE YOU SURE I DON'T LOOK FAT?

How many times...?!

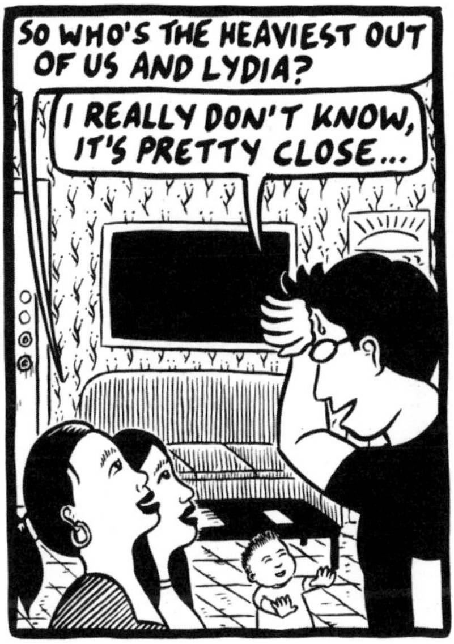
SO WHO'S THE HEAVIEST OUT OF US AND LYDIA?
I REALLY DON'T KNOW, IT'S PRETTY CLOSE...

They want to know who's heavier... my girlfriend or one of them... I try lifting them up again to remember and compare when I get home...

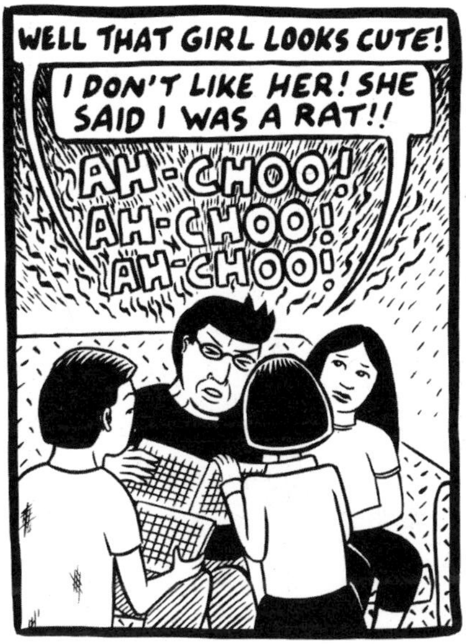
WELL THAT GIRL LOOKS CUTE!
I DON'T LIKE HER! SHE SAID I WAS A RAT!!
AH-CHOO!
AH-CHOO!
AH-CHOO!

Herman and Henrietta want me to see their class pictures...as we discuss who's the best looking classmate, three violent sneezes tear through my body!

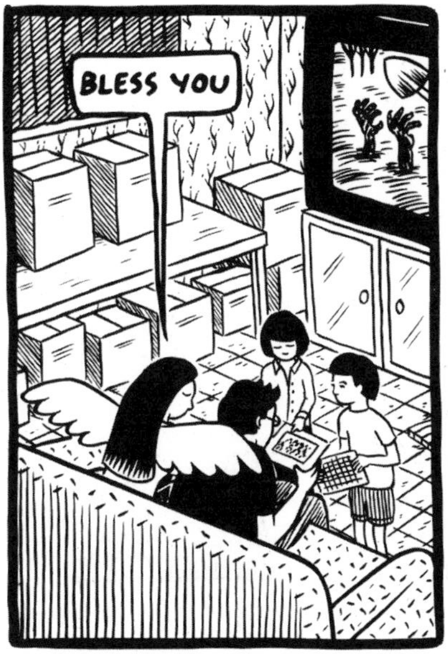
BLESS YOU

Hien puts her arm around me...

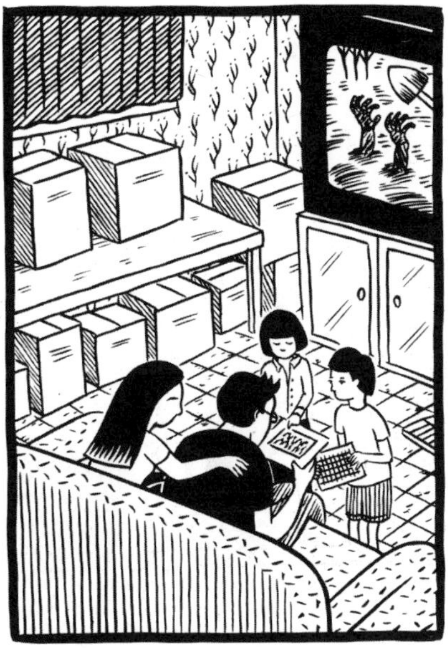

...not a wing.

good ♥

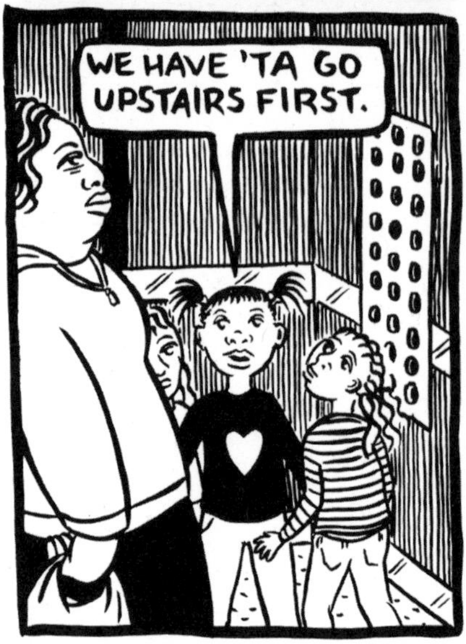
WE HAVE 'TA GO UPSTAIRS FIRST.

I know the one girl, hopefully she'll bring her friends to the art class.

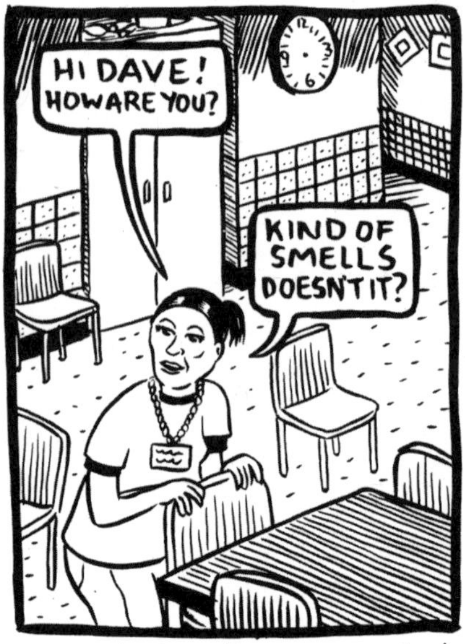
HI DAVE! HOW ARE YOU?
KIND OF SMELLS DOESN'T IT?

Saddest place I've ever worked ... almost barren ... somebody's even taken the hands off the clock...

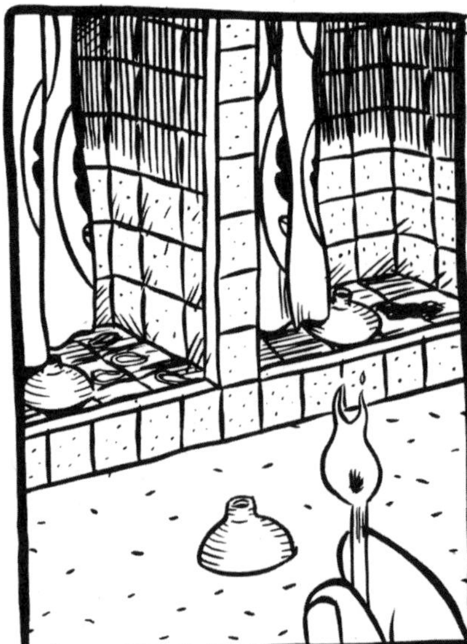

There're two showers in our art room, with three open drains which release warm, moist, foul air ... lighting a match and toilet plunger covers help a bit...

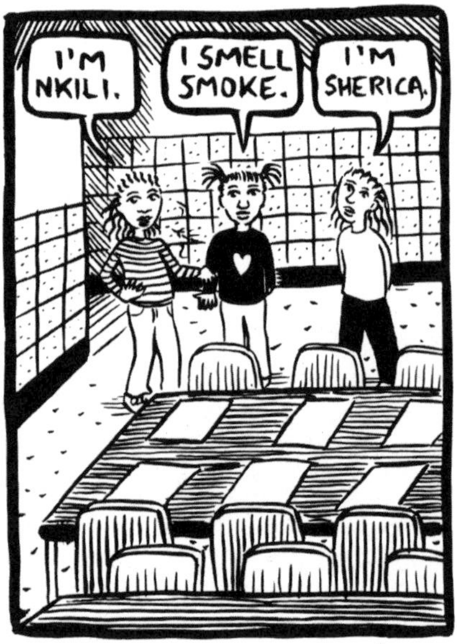
I'M NKILI.
I SMELL SMOKE.
I'M SHERICA.

The girls are back ... Whitney and her two friends.

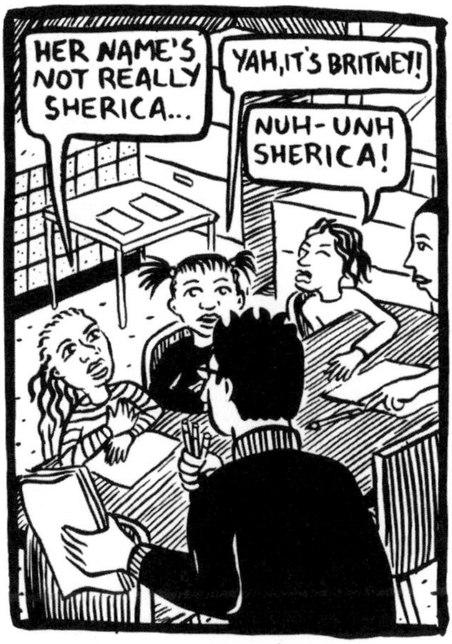
HER NAME'S NOT REALLY SHERICA...
YAH, IT'S BRITNEY!
NUH-UNH SHERICA!

We sit down together and I get some paper and pencils out to start drawing.

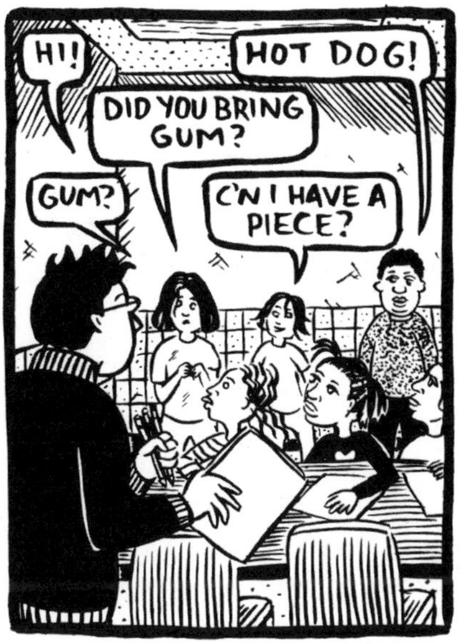
HI!
HOT DOG!
DID YOU BRING GUM?
GUM?
C'N I HAVE A PIECE?

Some more kids from the week before come in and I find them spots around the table.

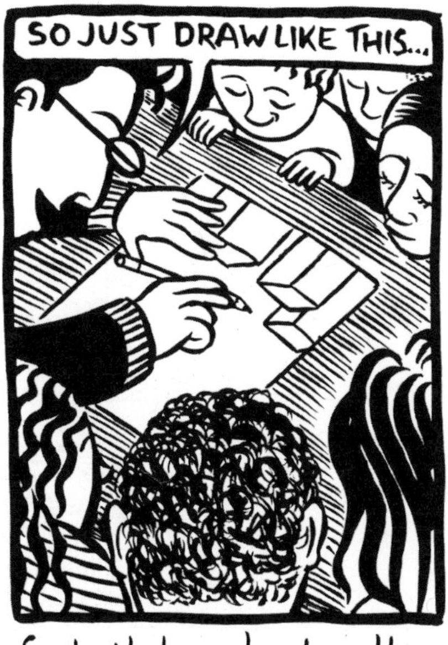
SO JUST DRAW LIKE THIS...

So I sit down to show them a simple drawing trick for drawing a city scene using parallelograms... NKili's right beside me, hands clamped on my thigh... I pull away...

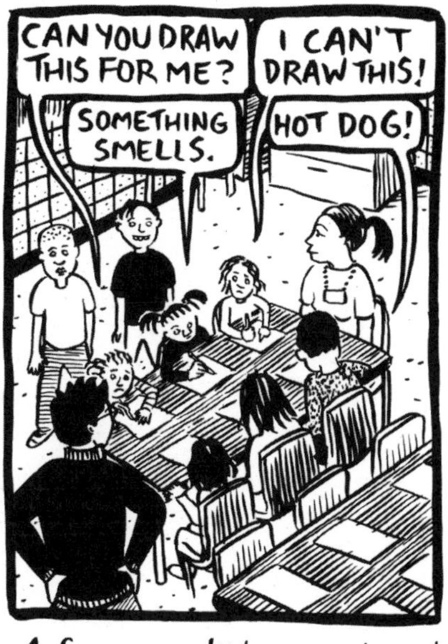
CAN YOU DRAW THIS FOR ME?
I CAN'T DRAW THIS!
SOMETHING SMELLS.
HOT DOG!

A few more kids come in and there's eight now and it's tricky... they all want so much attention...

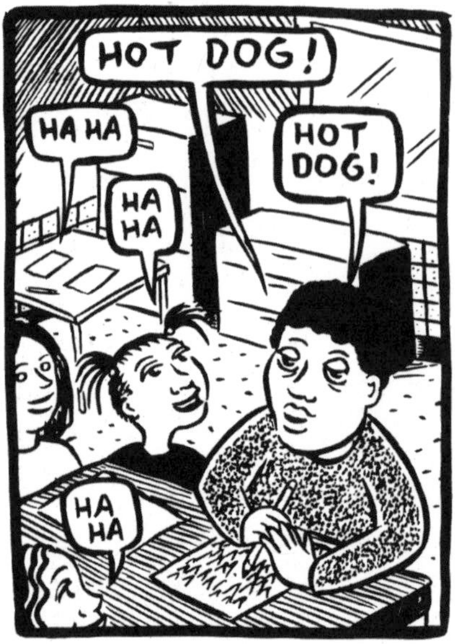
HOT DOG!
HA HA
HA HA
HOT DOG!
HA HA

Poor Kirk... the only thing he draws are these repetitive 'v' shaped scribbles... the only words he says are 'HOT DOG.'

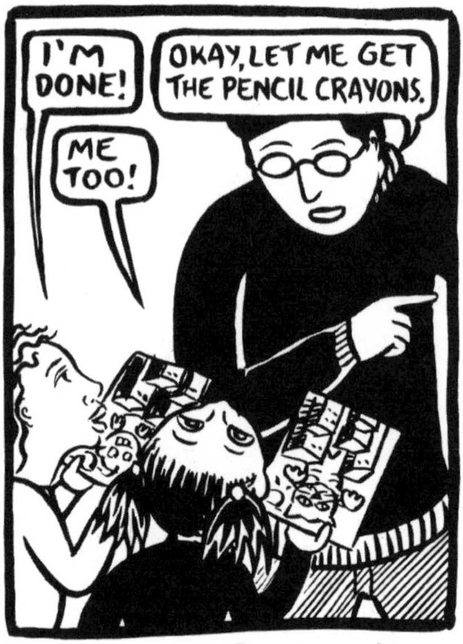
I'M DONE!
OKAY, LET ME GET THE PENCIL CRAYONS.
ME TOO!

The kids are finishing their drawings and they want to colour them. Nkili's drawn a huge heart with arms flying over the city.

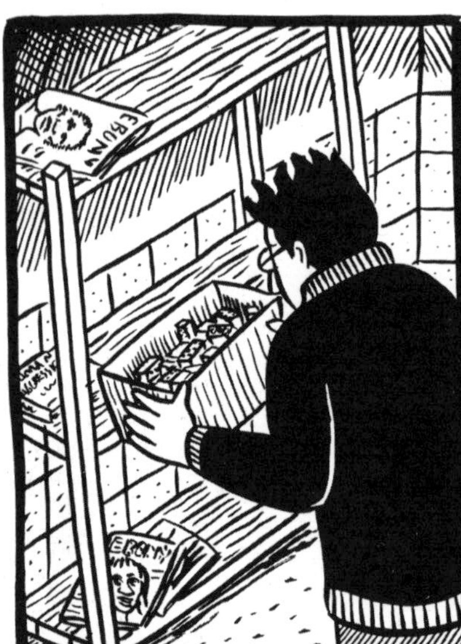

Aw man... this 'art centre' is unbelievable... they had some pencil crayons last week... all gone... empty shelves and a box of Lego.

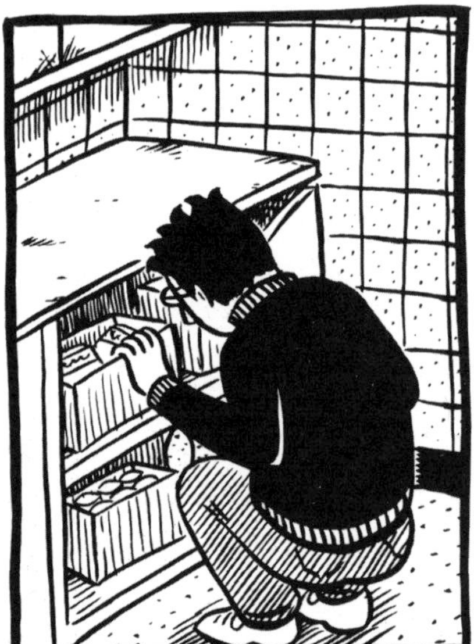

I check the office... cupboard door hanging by a hinge... sigh at least there's some crayons here... gotta fix that door and buy more art supplies!

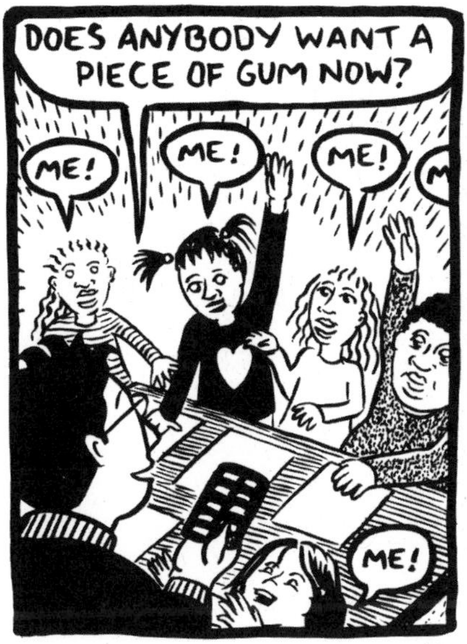
DOES ANYBODY WANT A PIECE OF GUM NOW?
ME!
ME!
ME!
ME!

I've brought some gum... it's amazing how pleased and pacified kids are with a piece of gum!

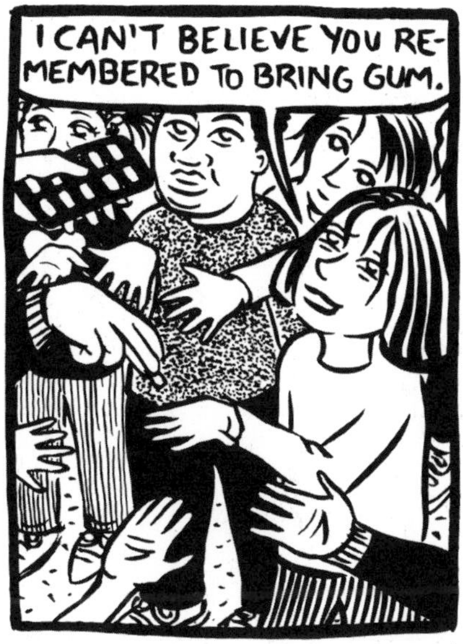
I CAN'T BELIEVE YOU RE-MEMBERED TO BRING GUM.

I explain that I remembered because they were so nice to me last week... helping me clean up and put away stuff.

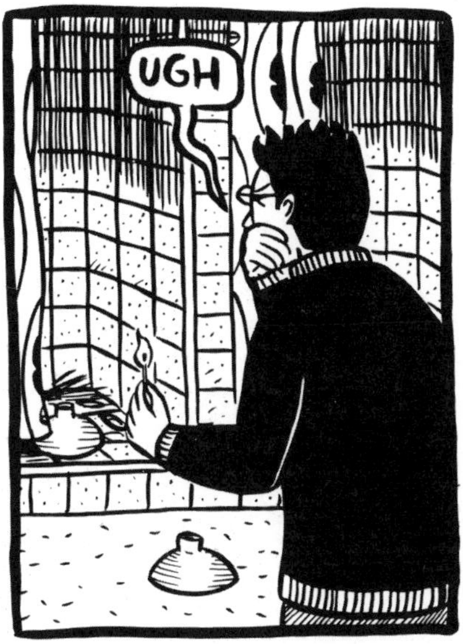
UGH

So they're all pretty happily drawing and chewing... God, that stench... you can't believe it! I hold my breath and light another match.

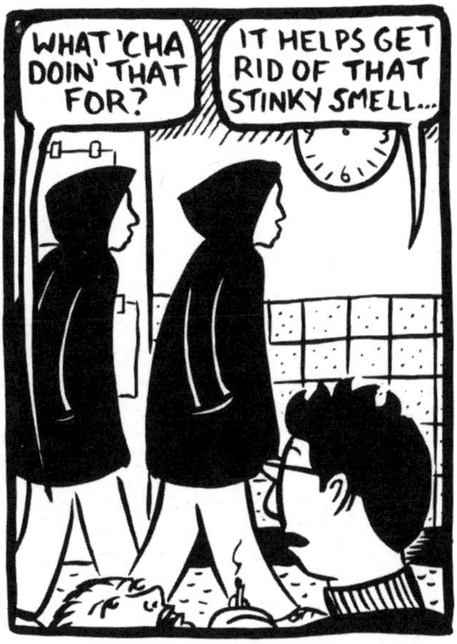
WHAT'CHA DOIN' THAT FOR?
IT HELPS GET RID OF THAT STINKY SMELL...

Huge teens skulk through... they're the 'at risk' group I'm supposed to be working with... honestly, they make me nervous.

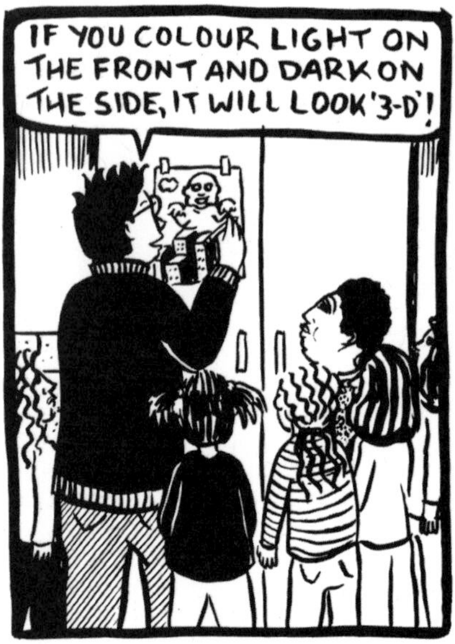
IF YOU COLOUR LIGHT ON THE FRONT AND DARK ON THE SIDE, IT WILL LOOK '3-D'!

I do a little colouring 'demo' with my drawing taped to a storage cabinet...

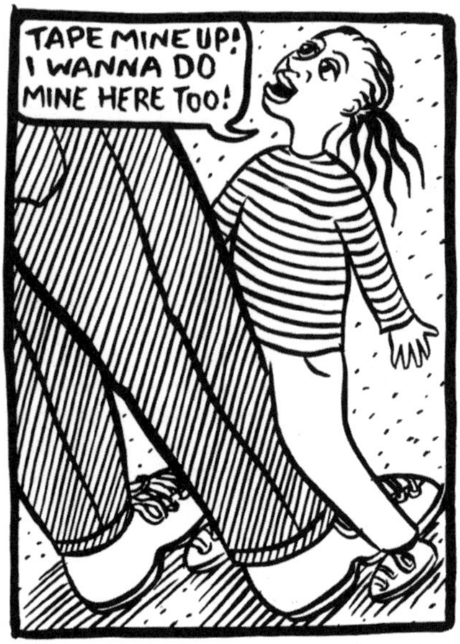
TAPE MINE UP! I WANNA DO MINE HERE TOO!

NKili makes her 'request' wrapped around my leg! She's so clingy!

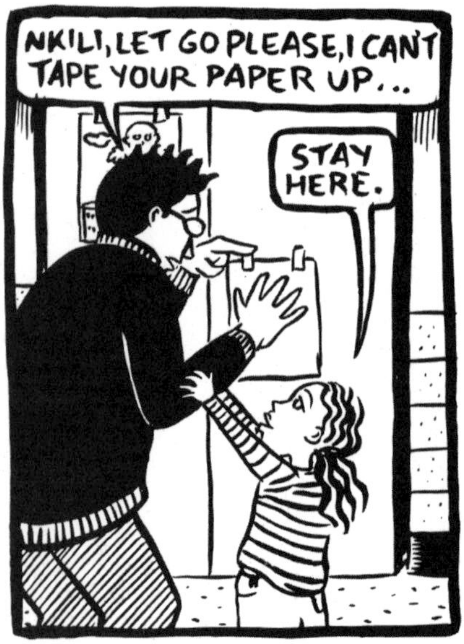
NKILI, LET GO PLEASE, I CAN'T TAPE YOUR PAPER UP...
STAY HERE.

Okay, get her set up and see how the other kids are doing...

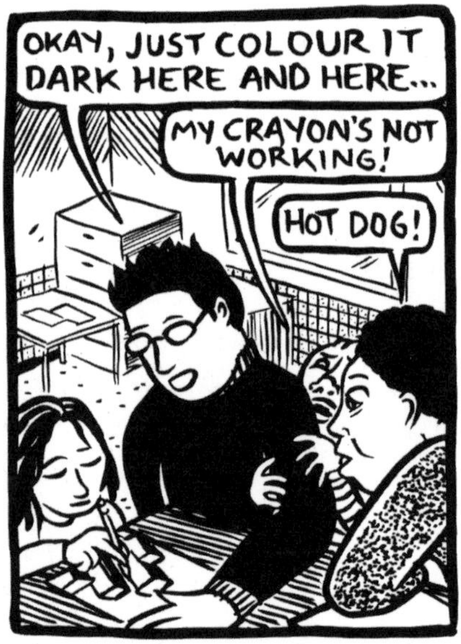
OKAY, JUST COLOUR IT DARK HERE AND HERE...
MY CRAYON'S NOT WORKING!
HOT DOG!

Not five minutes have passed and NKili's clutching at my arm!

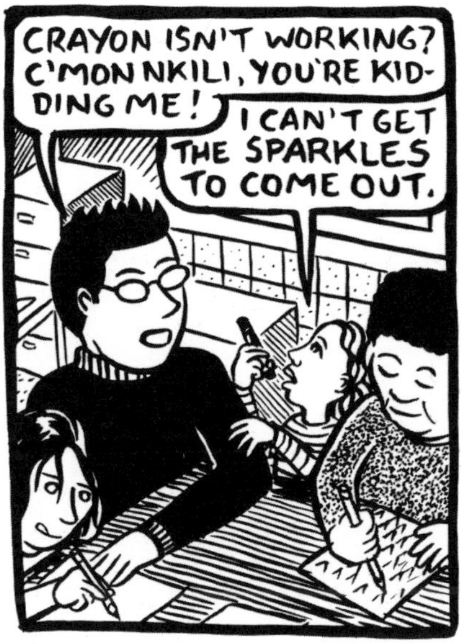
CRAYON ISN'T WORKING? C'MON NKILI, YOU'RE KIDDING ME!
I CAN'T GET THE SPARKLES TO COME OUT.

Sparkles in a crayon?!...Oh all right... she seems to really mean it...

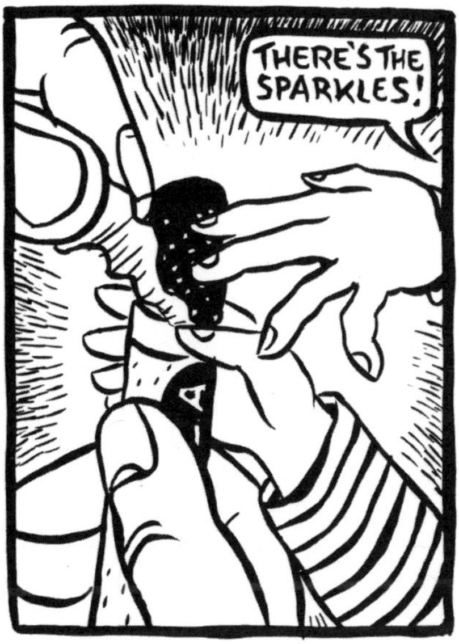
THERE'S THE SPARKLES!

She holds the crayon so gently, so carefully, watching me peel the paper off to reveal... sparkles! ...like magic!

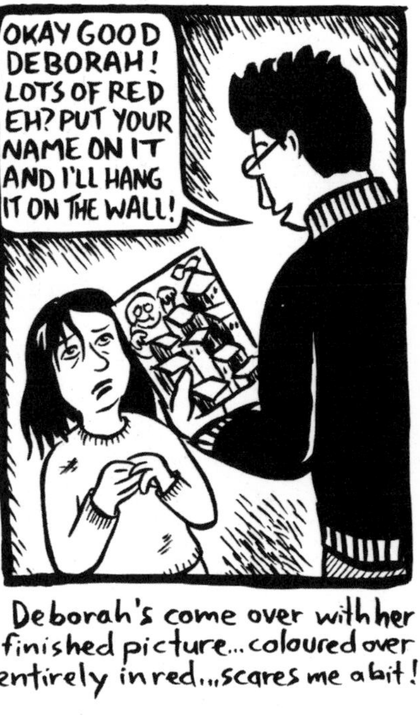
OKAY GOOD DEBORAH! LOTS OF RED EH? PUT YOUR NAME ON IT AND I'LL HANG IT ON THE WALL!

Deborah's come over with her finished picture... coloured over entirely in red... scares me a bit!

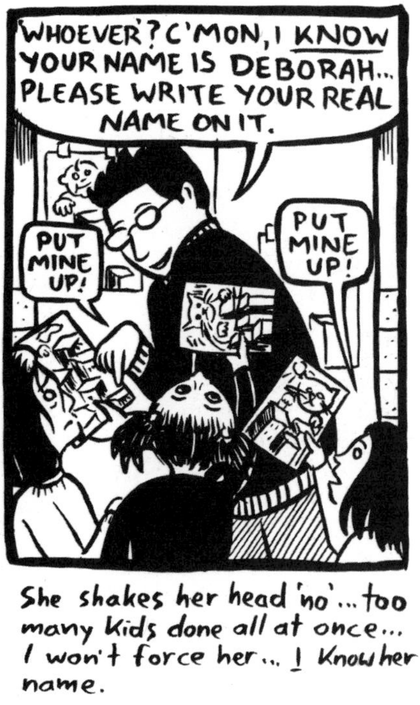
WHOEVER? C'MON, I KNOW YOUR NAME IS DEBORAH... PLEASE WRITE YOUR REAL NAME ON IT.
PUT MINE UP!
PUT MINE UP!

She shakes her head 'no'... too many kids done all at once... I won't force her... I know her name.

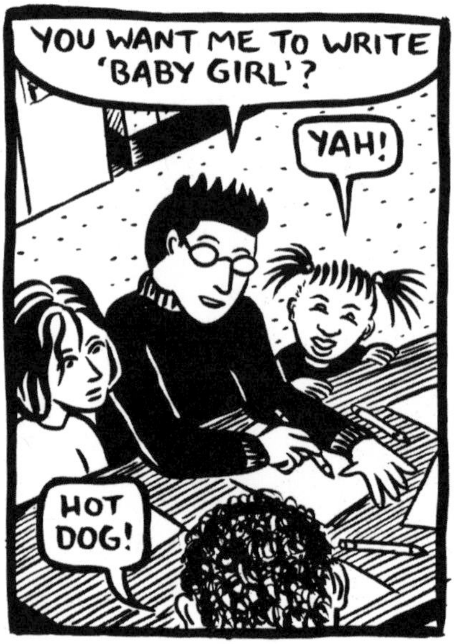
YOU WANT ME TO WRITE 'BABY GIRL'?
YAH!
HOT DOG!

The kids have mostly finished the drawing I asked for, so for 'free time' they want me to help draw 'bubble' letters and hearts.

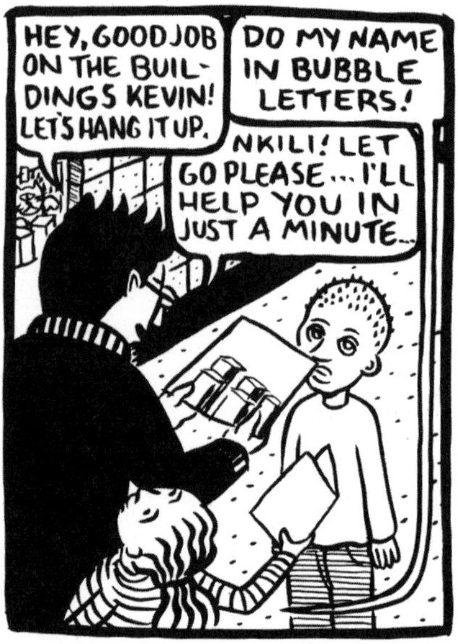
HEY, GOOD JOB ON THE BUILDINGS KEVIN! LET'S HANG IT UP.
DO MY NAME IN BUBBLE LETTERS!
NKILI! LET GO PLEASE... I'LL HELP YOU IN JUST A MINUTE...

NKili's wrapped around my leg again asking for her name in bubble letters on a folded piece of paper... so I sketch it for her... then check more art.

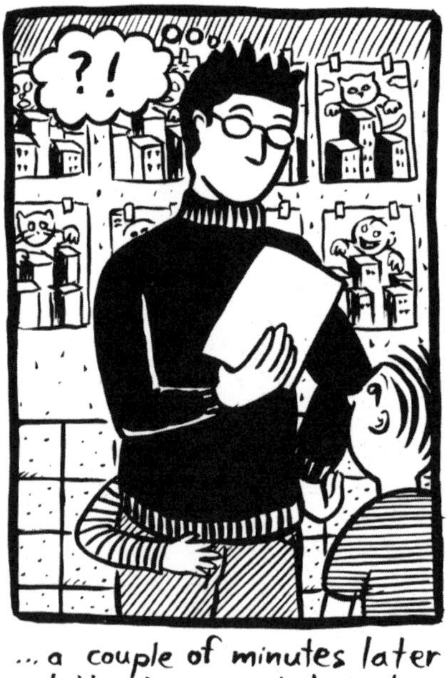
?!

...a couple of minutes later and there's a quick tap at my crotch from behind!...

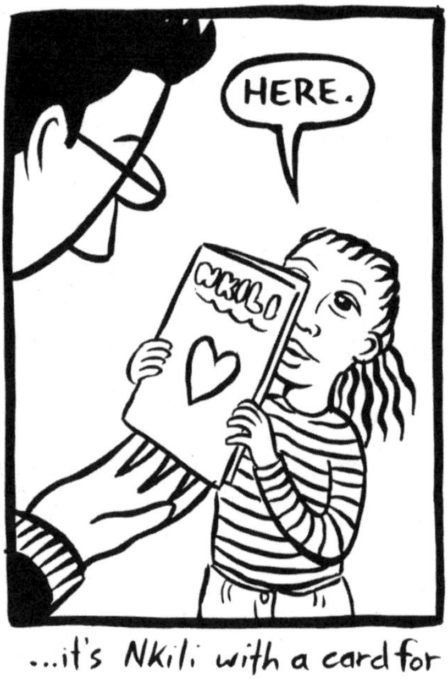
HERE.
NKILI

...it's NKili with a card for me...

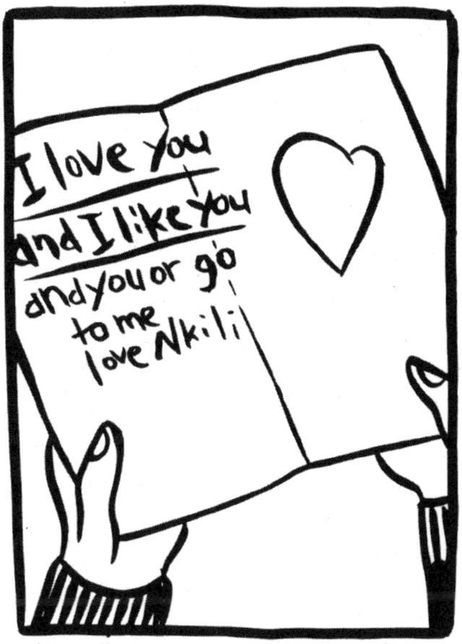
I love you
and I like you
and you or go to me
love Nkili

Jeez! I just met this kid an hour ago... sigh... Wait?! You or go to me??... You are God to me?! Huh?!

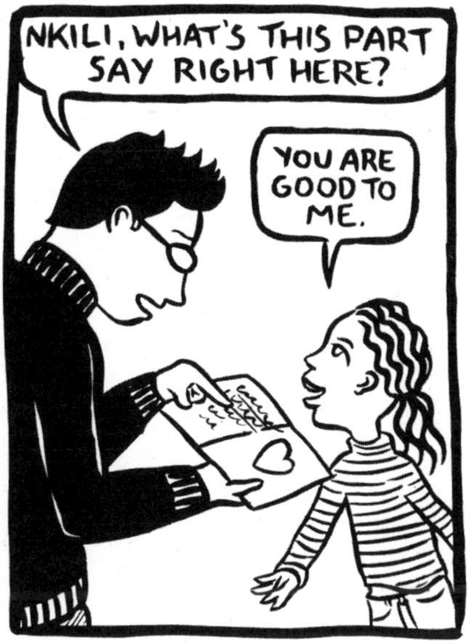
NKILI, WHAT'S THIS PART SAY RIGHT HERE?
YOU ARE GOOD TO ME.

Oh... I'm sorry.

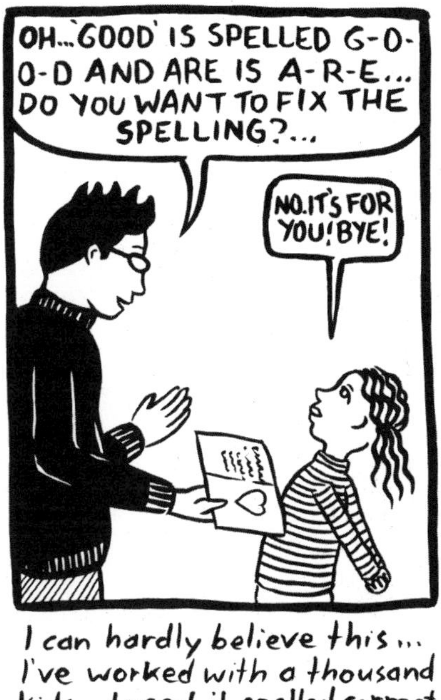
OH... 'GOOD' IS SPELLED G-O-O-D AND ARE IS A-R-E... DO YOU WANT TO FIX THE SPELLING?...
NO. IT'S FOR YOU! BYE!

I can hardly believe this... I've worked with a thousand kids... I need it spelled correctly... because...

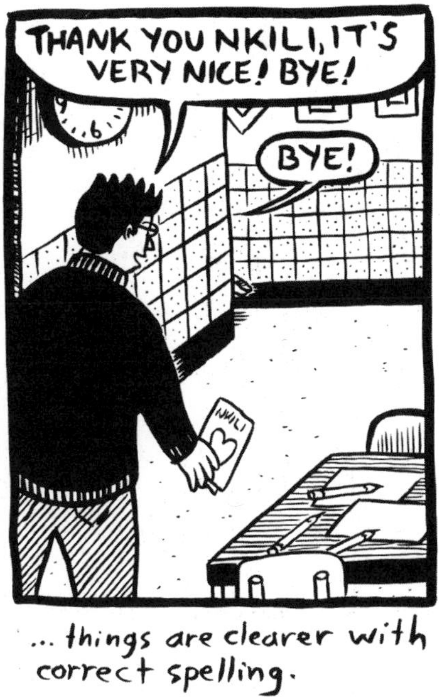
THANK YOU NKILI, IT'S VERY NICE! BYE!
BYE!
NKILI

... things are clearer with correct spelling.

teeth

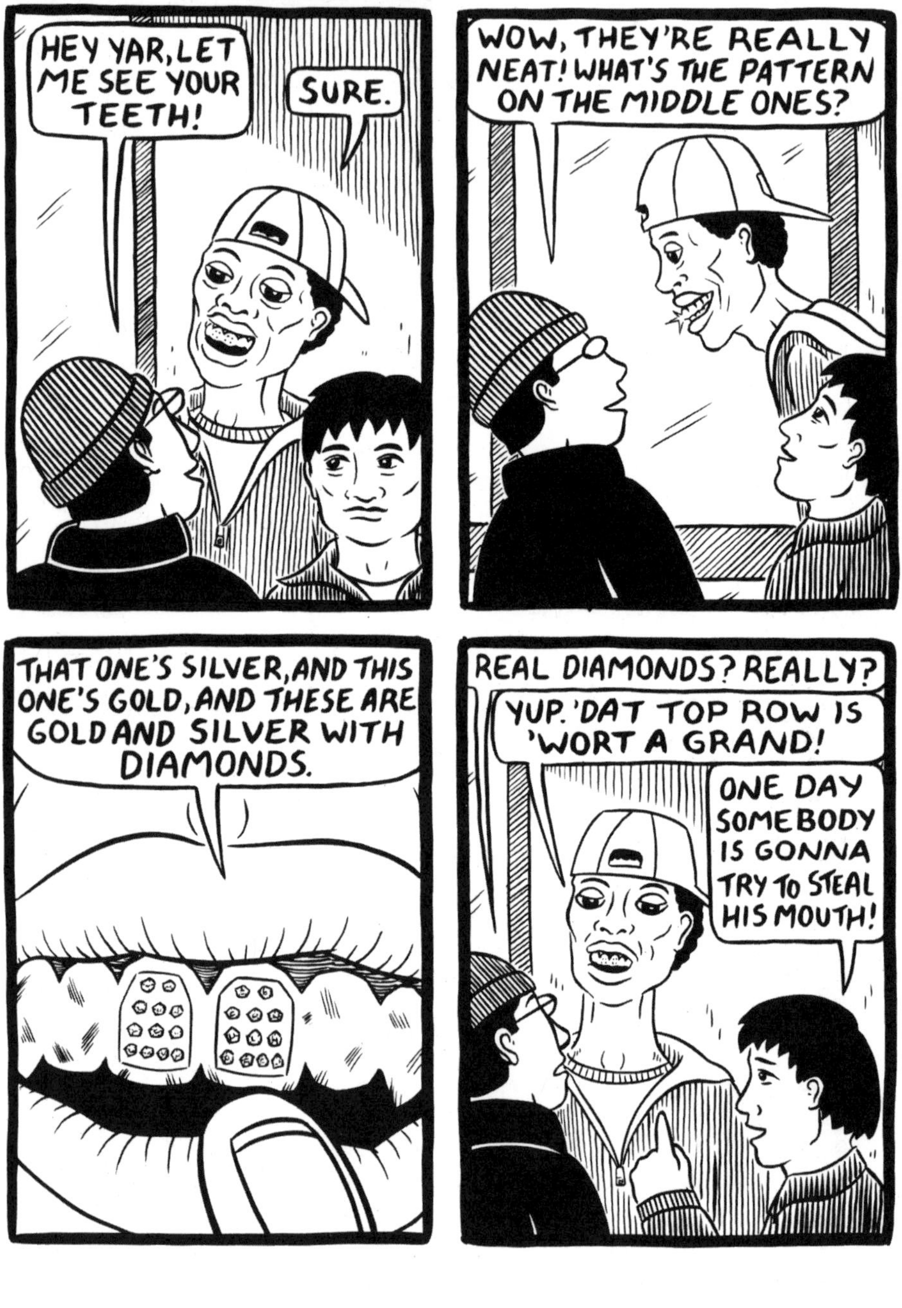
HEY YAR, LET ME SEE YOUR TEETH!
SURE.
WOW, THEY'RE REALLY NEAT! WHAT'S THE PATTERN ON THE MIDDLE ONES?
THAT ONE'S SILVER, AND THIS ONE'S GOLD, AND THESE ARE GOLD AND SILVER WITH DIAMONDS.
REAL DIAMONDS? REALLY?
YUP. 'DAT TOP ROW IS 'WORT A GRAND!
ONE DAY SOMEBODY IS GONNA TRY TO STEAL HIS MOUTH!

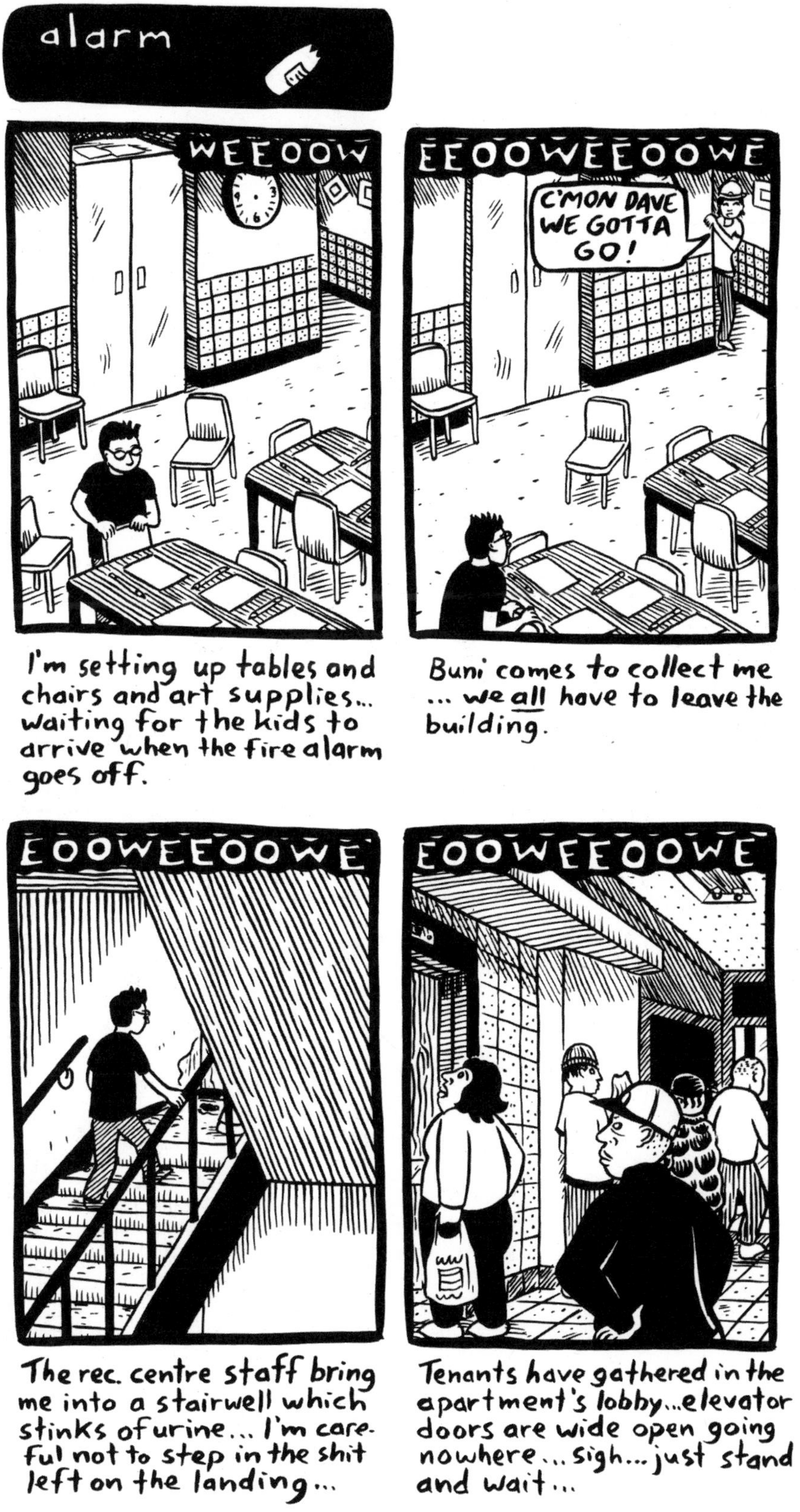
alarm
WEEOOW
I'm setting up tables and chairs and art supplies... waiting for the kids to arrive when the fire alarm goes off.
EEOOWEEOOWE
C'MON DAVE WE GOTTA GO!
Buni comes to collect me ... we all have to leave the building.
EOOWEEOOWE
The rec. centre staff bring me into a stairwell which stinks of urine... I'm careful not to step in the shit left on the landing...
EOOWEEOOWE
Tenants have gathered in the apartment's lobby...elevator doors are wide open going nowhere... sigh... just stand and wait...

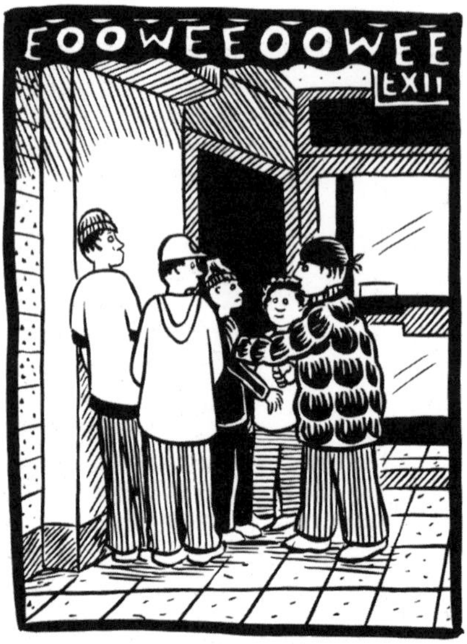
EOOWEEOOWEE
EXIT

Near the front door, three big teens are pushing and shoving two younger boys... play fighting... Yar, a staff member is there...

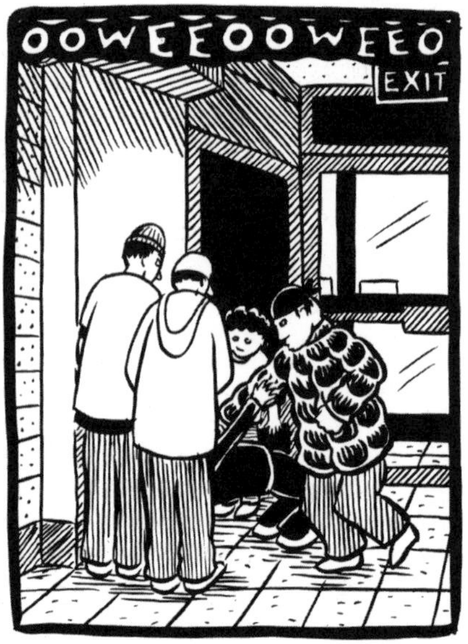
OOWEEOOWEEO
EXIT

The play fighting continues a bit... then the big teen flattens the skinny kid with one really hard punch in the chest! Knocks the kid right to the floor!

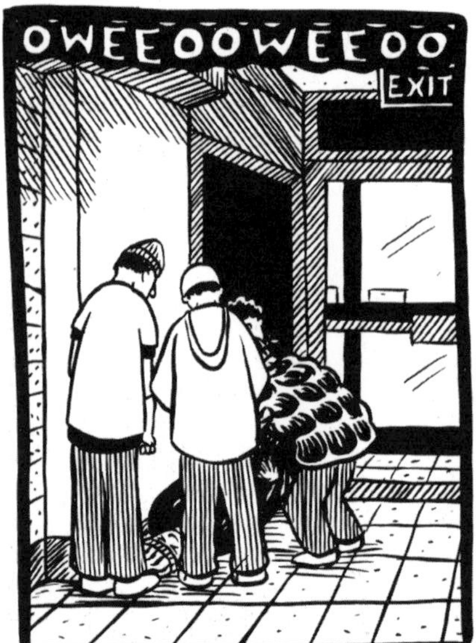
OWEEOOWEEOO
EXIT

Once flattened, the big teen punches the kid in the chest so hard I hear a horrible hollow sound that I've never heard before...

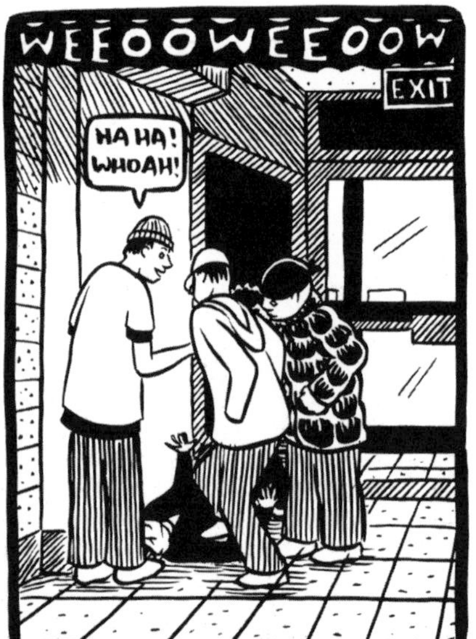
WEEOOWEEOOW
EXIT
HA HA! WHOAH!

The other big teen joins in and kicks the kid in the ribs with the toe of his shoe, there's that sickening hollow sound again...

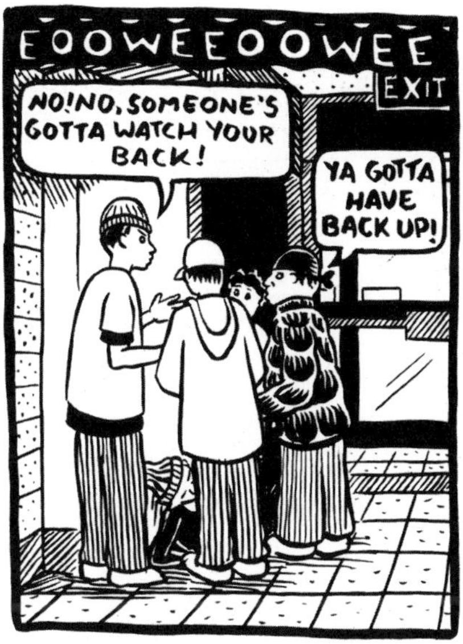
EOOWEEOOWEE
EXIT
NO! NO, SOMEONE'S GOTTA WATCH YOUR BACK!
YA GOTTA HAVE BACK UP!

The kid remains on the floor while the teens stand around giving each other advice.

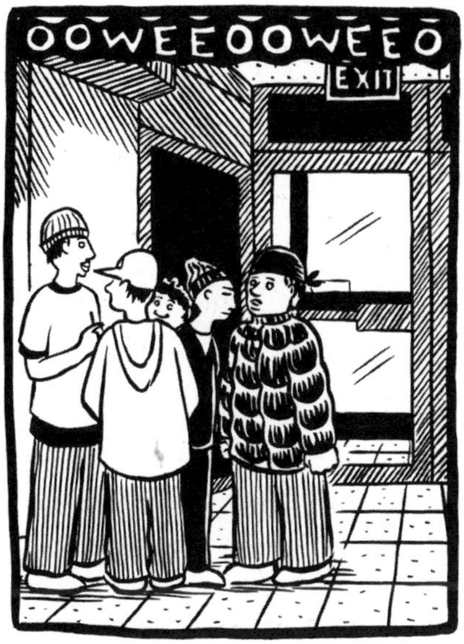
OOWEEOOWEEO
EXIT

Amazingly the skinny kid gets up without crying or showing any signs of pain.

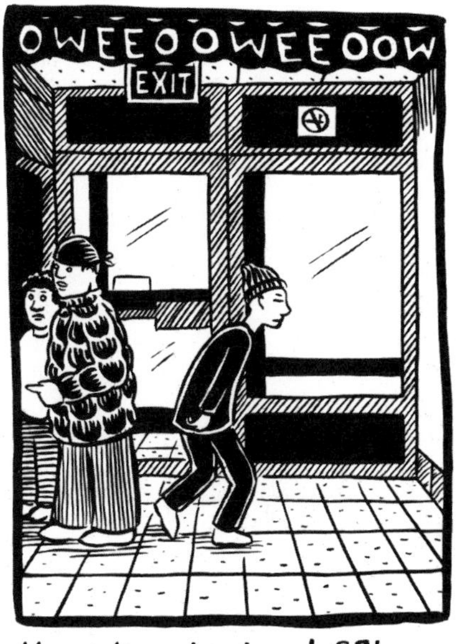
OWEEOOWEEOOW
EXIT

He walks slowly, stiffly... straight to the wall...

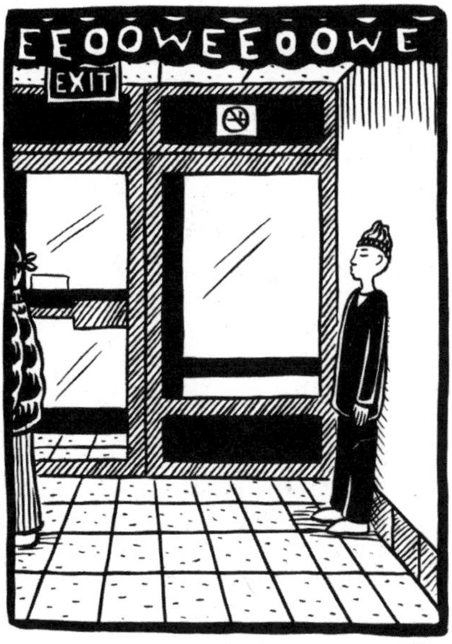
EEOOWEEOOWE
EXIT

...where he stands very still.

EOOWEEOOWEEO
EXIT
OWEEOOWEEOOW
EXIT

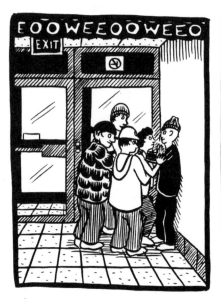

The big teens bring the younger kid over and start shoving him into the skinny kid...

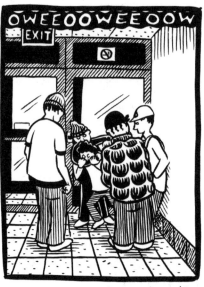

...they push them together until they start to 'play fight.'

EEOOWEEOOWEE
EXIT
BAM BAM
OPEN THE DOOR!!
OPEN THE DOOR!
OOWEEOOWEEOO
EXIT
OPEN THE DOOR!

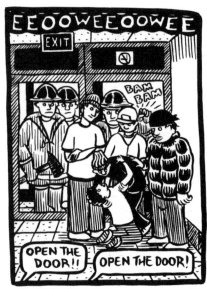

The firemen have arrived. They're waiting to be let in, but the teens won't open the door! People start yelling at them...

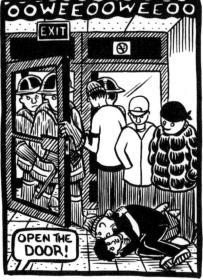

... finally one of the other staff gets Yar's attention, and he casually 'buzzes' them in.

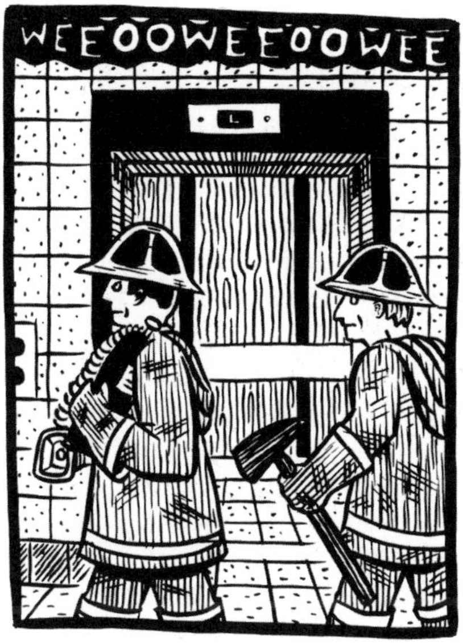
WEEOOWEEOOWEE

The firemen come tromping in and I feel relieved by their authoratative presence.

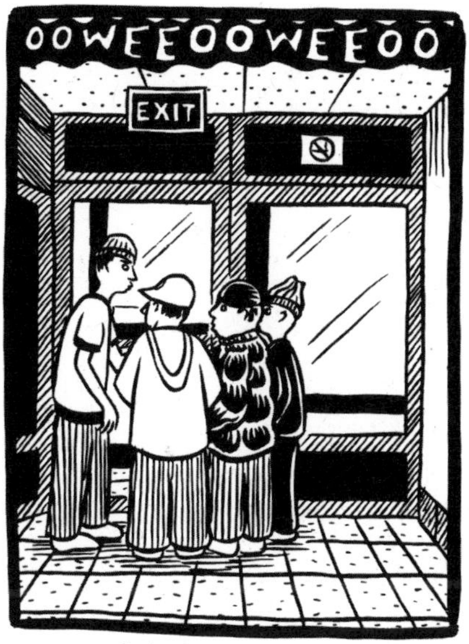
OOWEEOOWEEOO
EXIT

When I look back, the fighting's stopped and the youngest boy is gone...

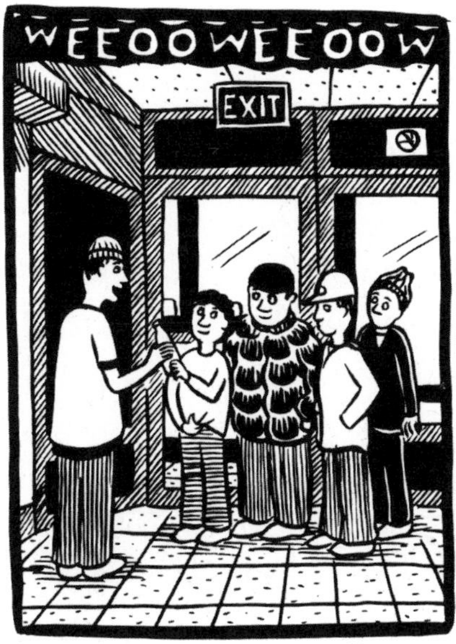
WEEOOWEEOOW
EXIT

... he comes back from the variety store and pulls a bottle of pop from beneath his shirt and presents it to Yar...

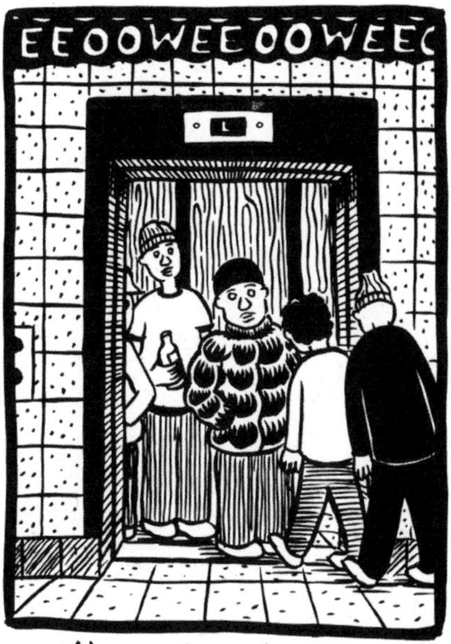
EEOOWEEOOWEE

... it's a glass bottle and they can't open it, so they all come over to the elevator ... to go up and get a bottle opener?...

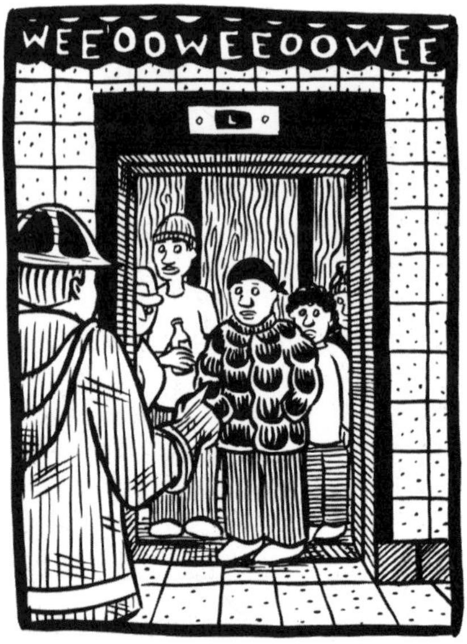
WEEOOWEEOOWEE

A fireman comes by and tells the guys that the elevator won't be going anywhere for quite awhile...

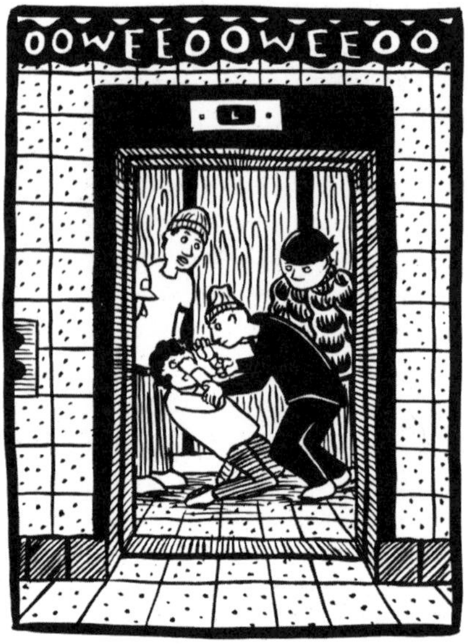
OOWEEOOWEEOO

...so the two younger guys start play fighting again.

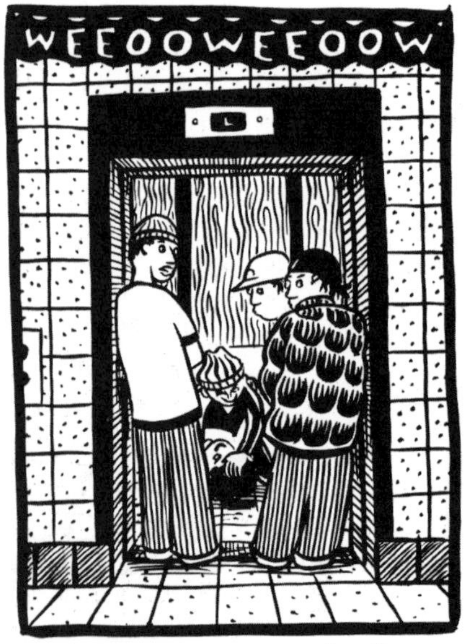
WEEOOWEEOOW

The older guys keep looking over their shoulders and eventually form a wall across the mouth of the elevator.

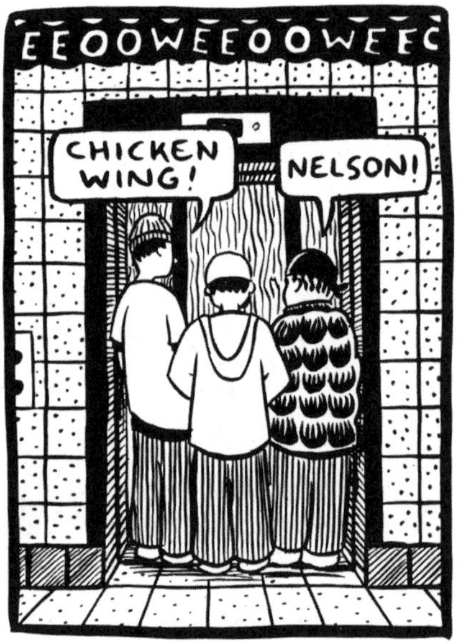
EEOOWEEOOWEEC
CHICKEN WING!
NELSON!

I can't see the fighting now, but I can hear loud thumps and thuds as the boys bang hard against the walls...

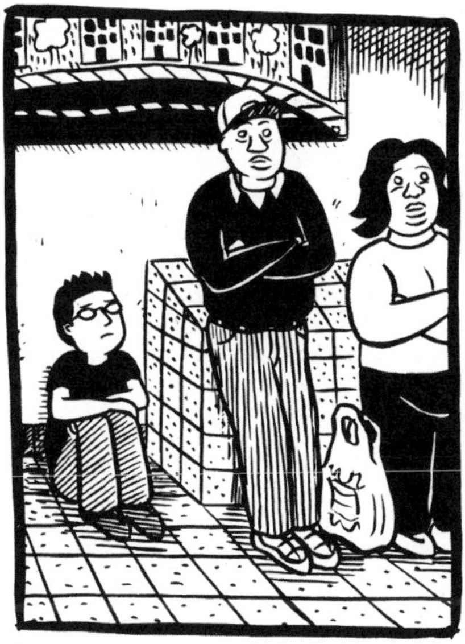

Finally the fire alarm stops... I want to get away from this miserable scene.

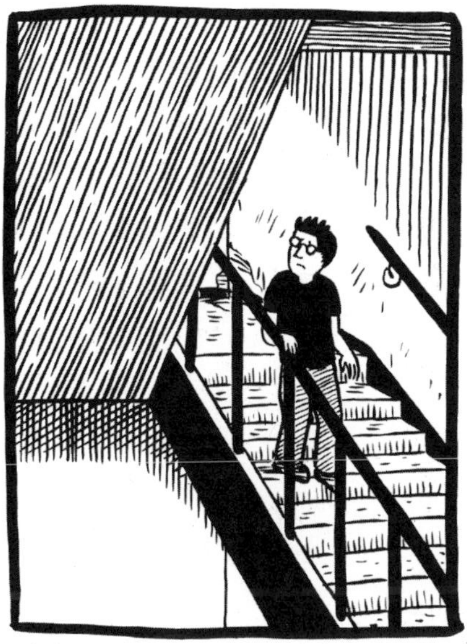

I take the 'piss' stairs back down... I keep checking over my shoulder... I feel like those thugs are right behind me...

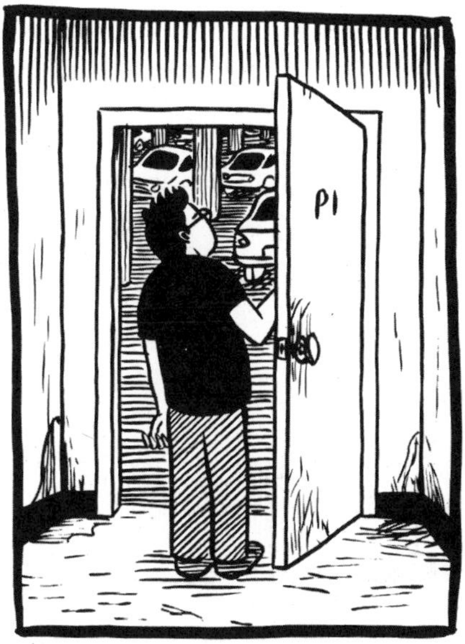
P1

I take a wrong turn and end up at the gloomy parking garage... if I'm gonna get jumped, this is the place...

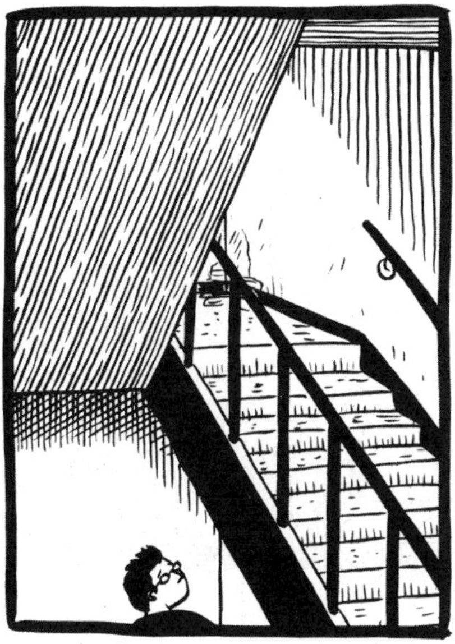

... I step back into the stair-well... no one's there, no one's following me...

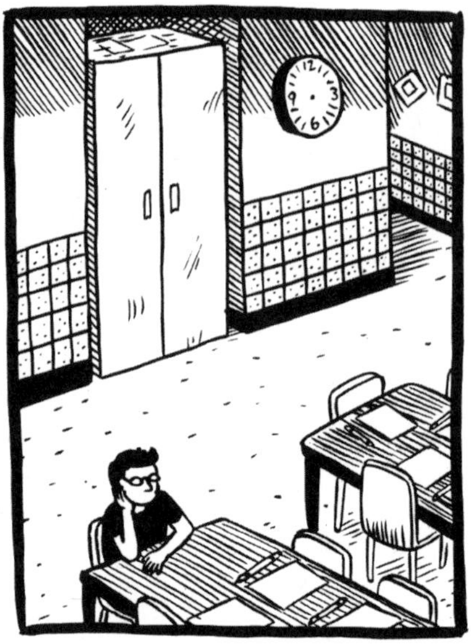

I get back to the art room and sit down... it reeks of pot smoke... I'm supposed to teach little kids in here.

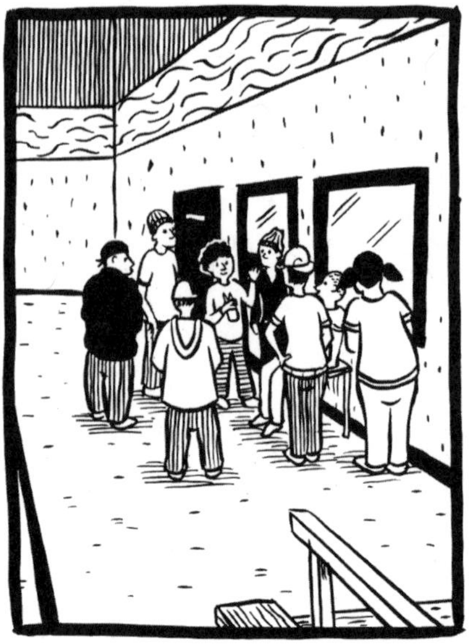

No kids show up so I go to the gym and the guys from the lobby are there... the one kid's got the pop bottle... the top's been smashed off...

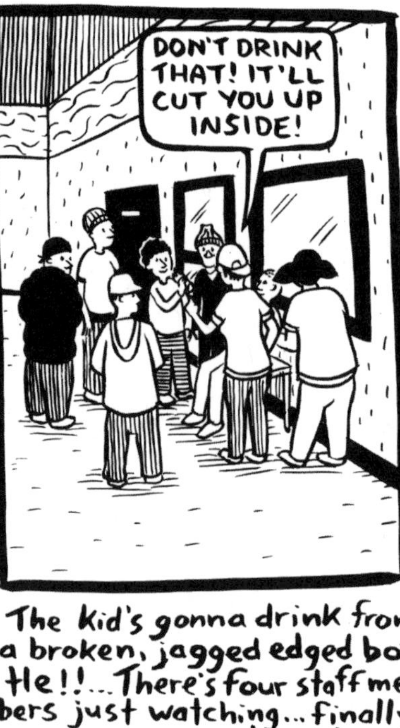
DON'T DRINK THAT! IT'LL CUT YOU UP INSIDE!

The kid's gonna drink from a broken, jagged edged bottle!!... There's four staff members just watching... finally Buni says something!...

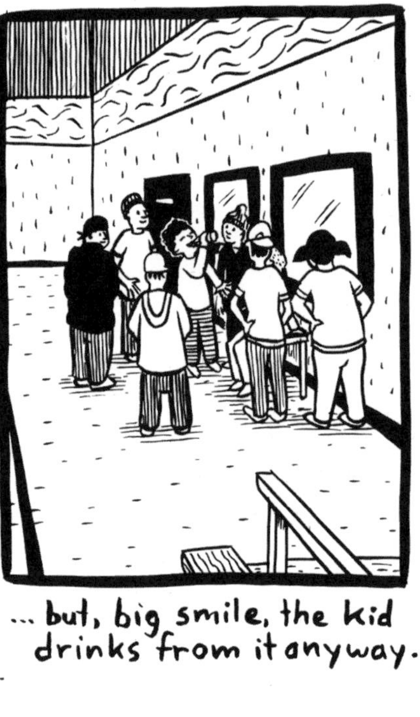

... but, big smile, the kid drinks from it anyway.

ghosts

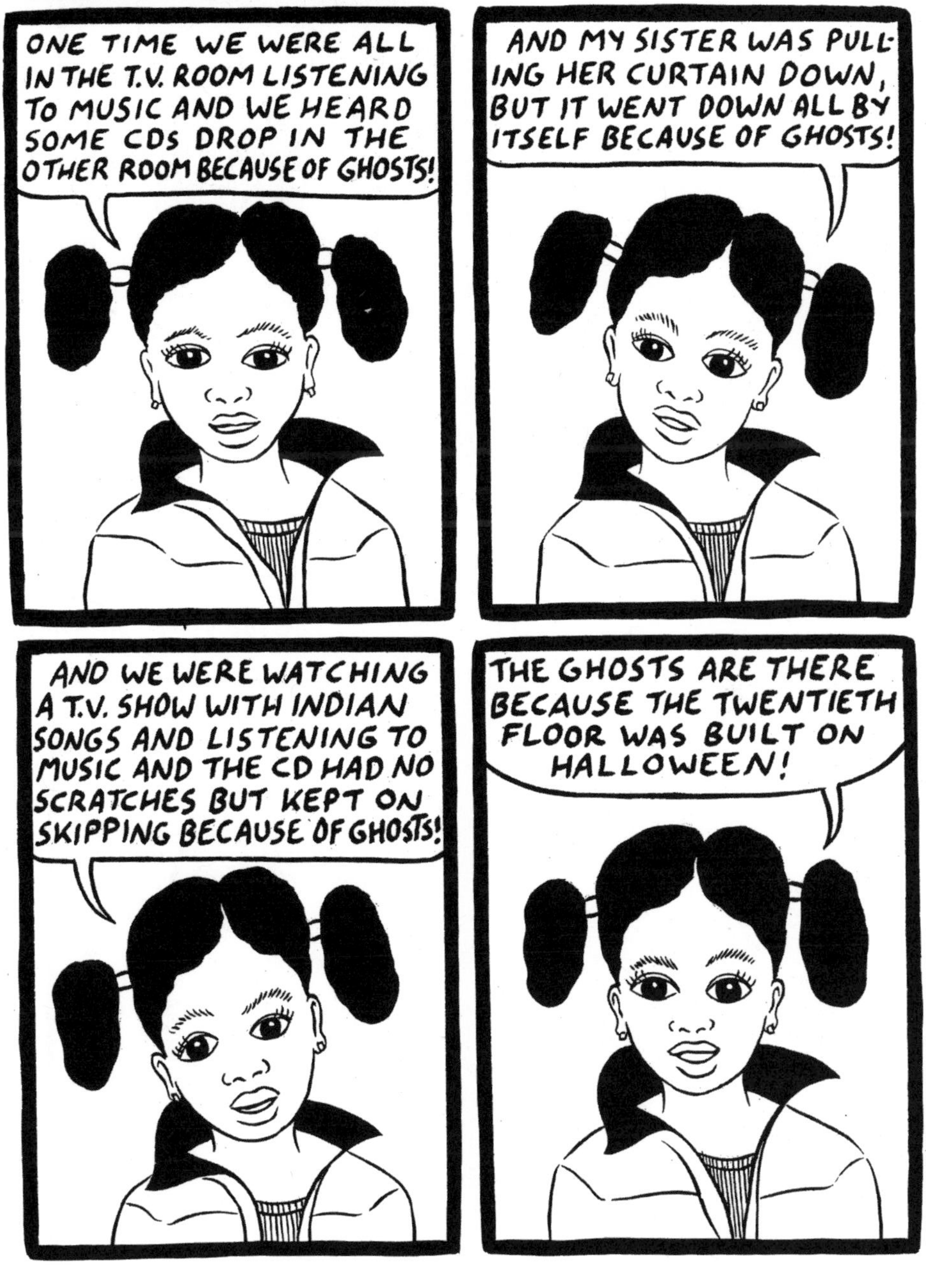
ONE TIME WE WERE ALL IN THE T.V. ROOM LISTENING TO MUSIC AND WE HEARD SOME CDs DROP IN THE OTHER ROOM BECAUSE OF GHOSTS!
AND MY SISTER WAS PULL-ING HER CURTAIN DOWN, BUT IT WENT DOWN ALL BY ITSELF BECAUSE OF GHOSTS!
AND WE WERE WATCHING A T.V. SHOW WITH INDIAN SONGS AND LISTENING TO MUSIC AND THE CD HAD NO SCRATCHES BUT KEPT ON SKIPPING BECAUSE OF GHOSTS!
THE GHOSTS ARE THERE BECAUSE THE TWENTIETH FLOOR WAS BUILT ON HALLOWEEN!

after work

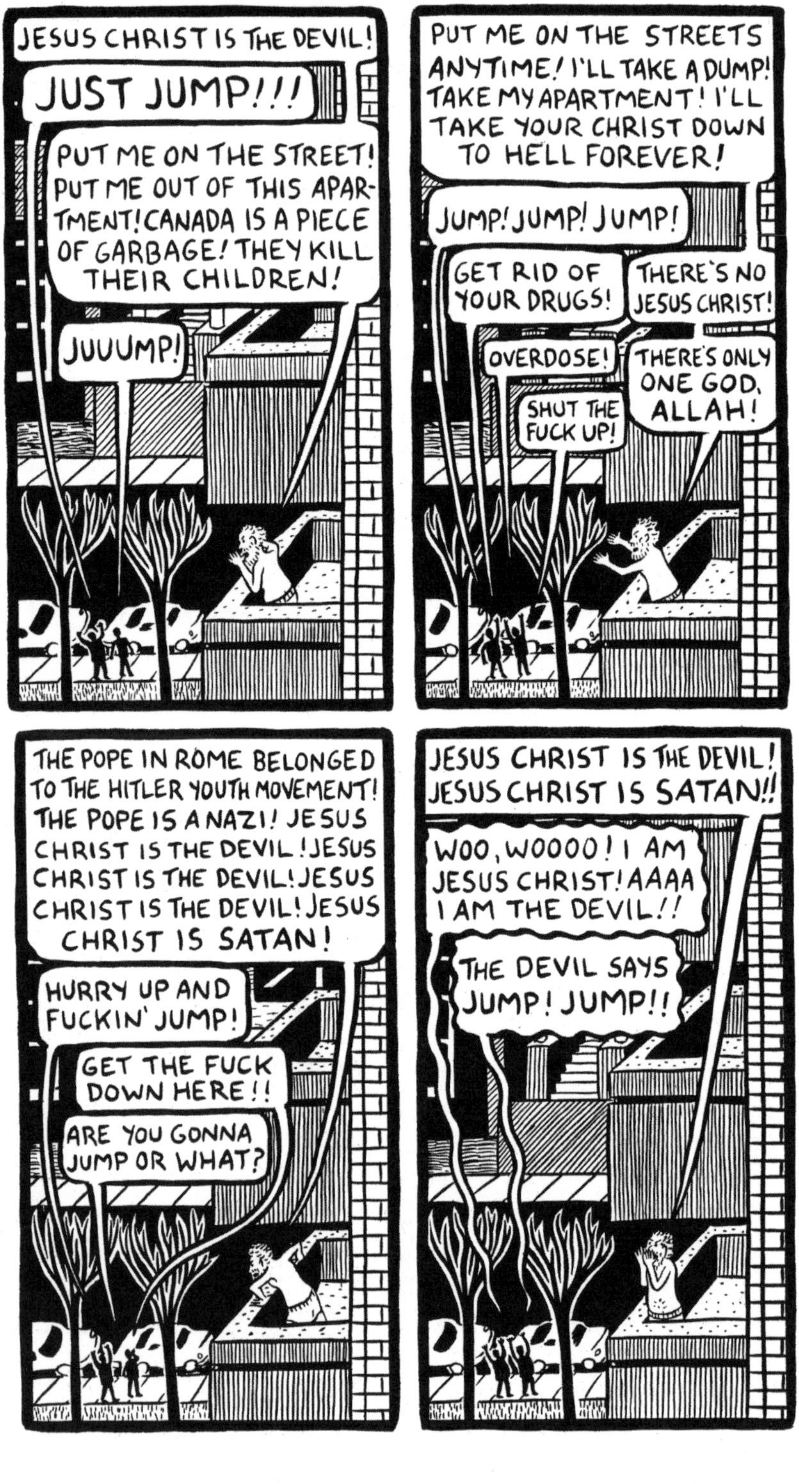

JESUS CHRIST IS THE DEVIL!
JUST JUMP!!!
PUT ME ON THE STREET! PUT ME OUT OF THIS APARTMENT! CANADA IS A PIECE OF GARBAGE! THEY KILL THEIR CHILDREN!
JUUUMP!
PUT ME ON THE STREETS ANYTIME! I'LL TAKE A DUMP! TAKE MY APARTMENT! I'LL TAKE YOUR CHRIST DOWN TO HELL FOREVER!
JUMP! JUMP! JUMP!
GET RID OF YOUR DRUGS!
THERE'S NO JESUS CHRIST!
OVERDOSE!
THERE'S ONLY ONE GOD, ALLAH!
SHUT THE FUCK UP!
THE POPE IN ROME BELONGED TO THE HITLER YOUTH MOVEMENT! THE POPE IS A NAZI! JESUS CHRIST IS THE DEVIL! JESUS CHRIST IS THE DEVIL! JESUS CHRIST IS THE DEVIL! JESUS CHRIST IS SATAN!
HURRY UP AND FUCKIN' JUMP!
GET THE FUCK DOWN HERE!!
ARE YOU GONNA JUMP OR WHAT?
JESUS CHRIST IS THE DEVIL! JESUS CHRIST IS SATAN!!
WOO, WOOOO! I AM JESUS CHRIST! AAAA I AM THE DEVIL!!
THE DEVIL SAYS JUMP! JUMP!!

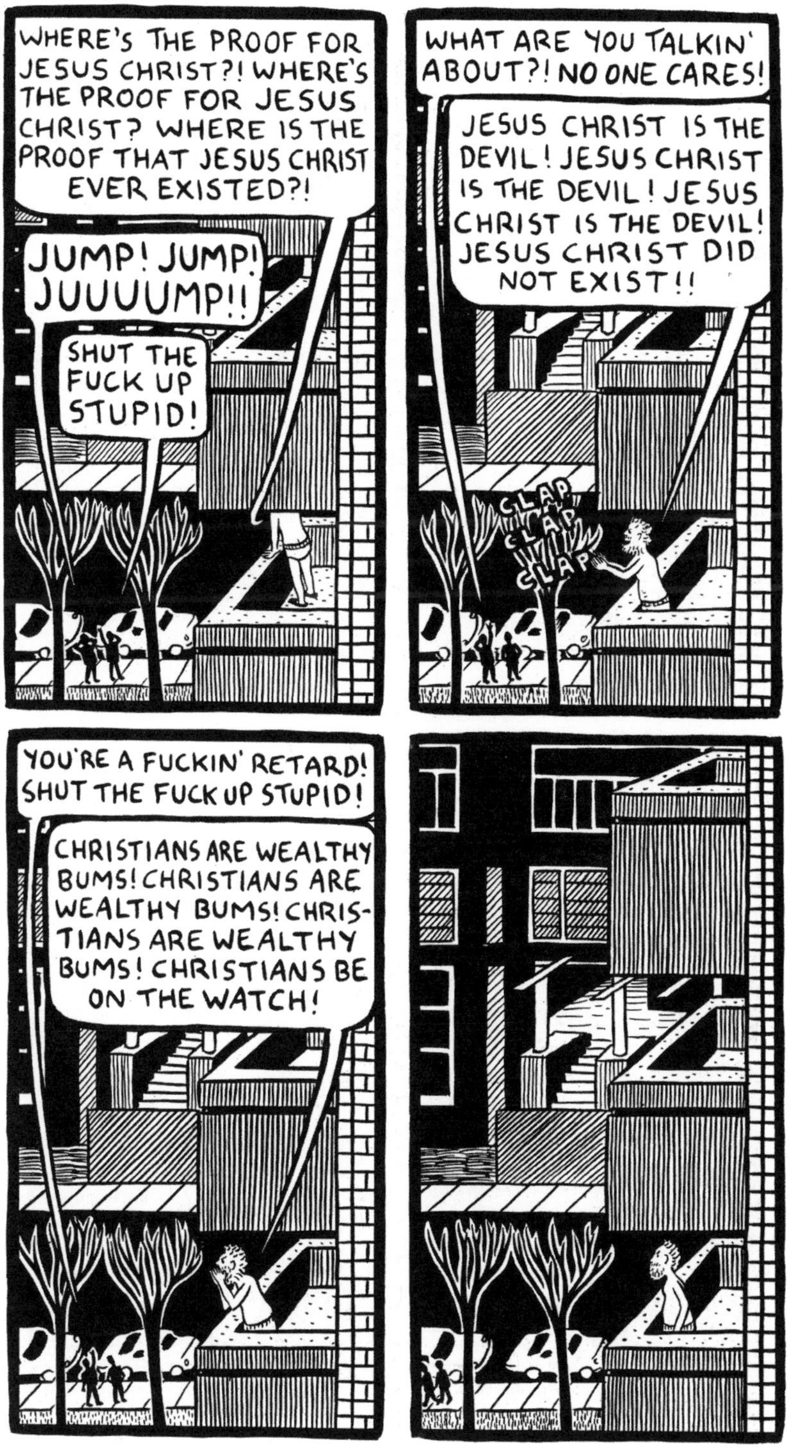
WHERE'S THE PROOF FOR JESUS CHRIST?! WHERE'S THE PROOF FOR JESUS CHRIST? WHERE IS THE PROOF THAT JESUS CHRIST EVER EXISTED?!
JUMP! JUMP! JUUUUMP!!
SHUT THE FUCK UP STUPID!
WHAT ARE YOU TALKIN' ABOUT?! NO ONE CARES!
JESUS CHRIST IS THE DEVIL! JESUS CHRIST IS THE DEVIL! JESUS CHRIST IS THE DEVIL! JESUS CHRIST DID NOT EXIST!!
CLAP CLAP CLAP
YOU'RE A FUCKIN' RETARD! SHUT THE FUCK UP STUPID!
CHRISTIANS ARE WEALTHY BUMS! CHRISTIANS ARE WEALTHY BUMS! CHRISTIANS ARE WEALTHY BUMS! CHRISTIANS BE ON THE WATCH!

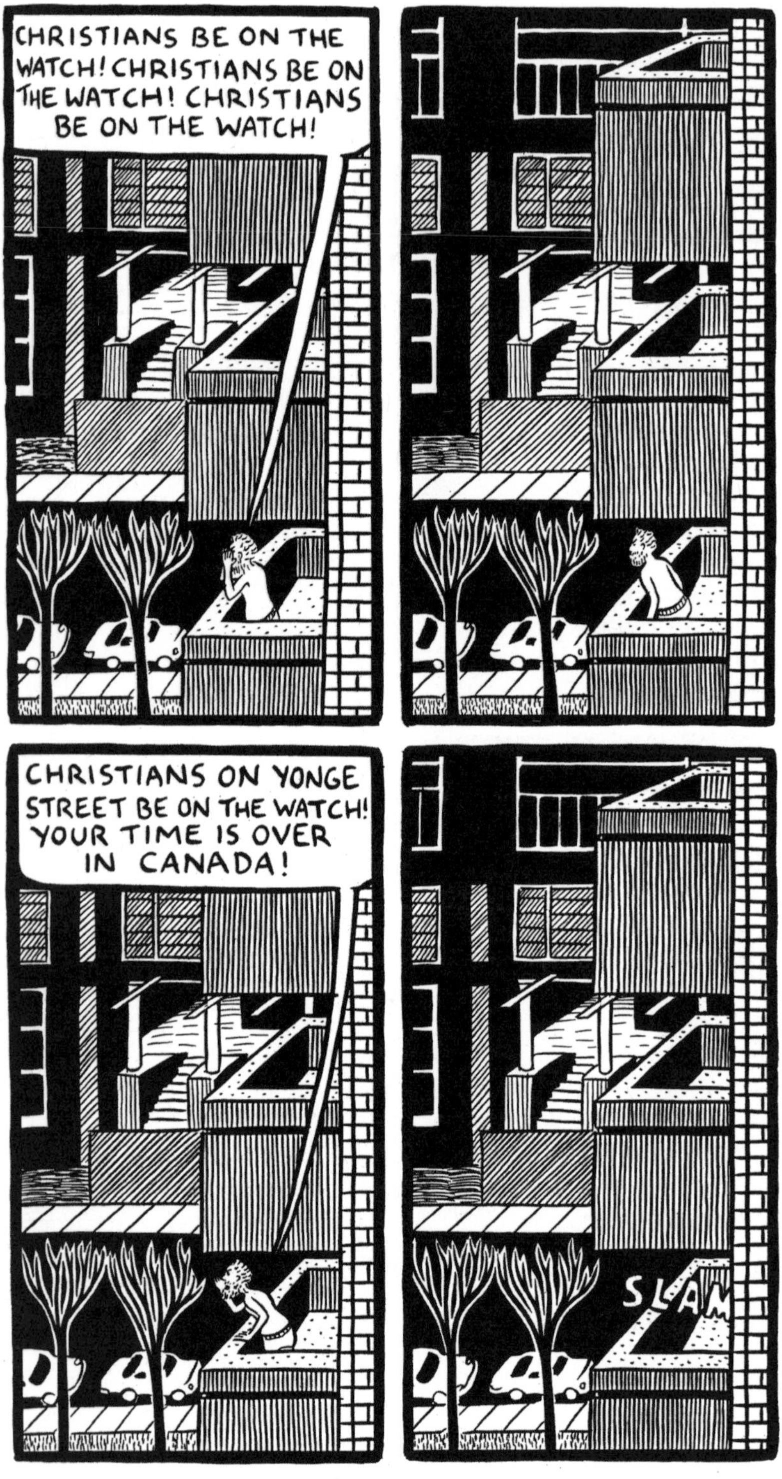
CHRISTIANS BE ON THE WATCH! CHRISTIANS BE ON THE WATCH! CHRISTIANS BE ON THE WATCH!
CHRISTIANS ON YONGE STREET BE ON THE WATCH! YOUR TIME IS OVER IN CANADA!
SLAM

door

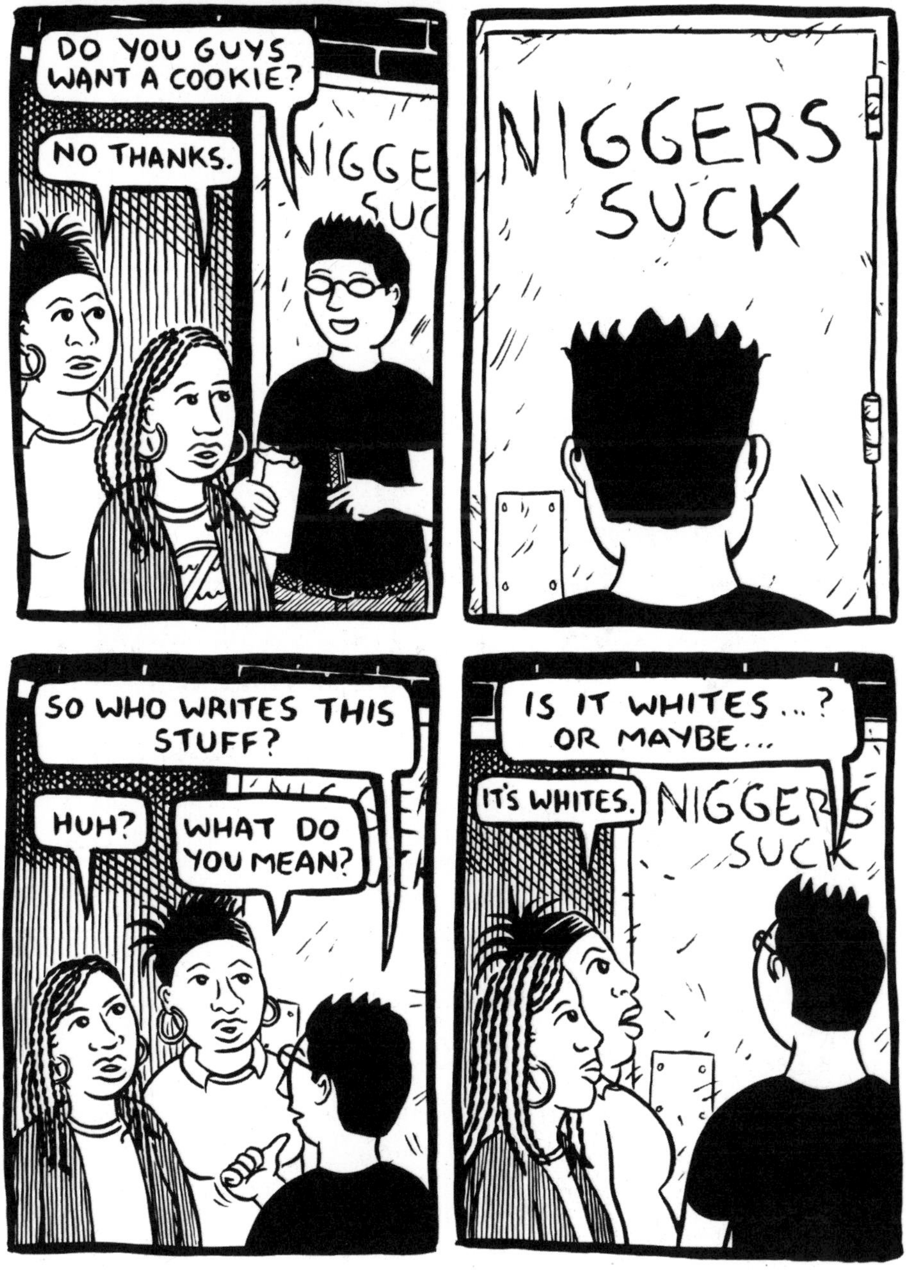
DO YOU GUYS WANT A COOKIE?
NO THANKS.
NIGGERS SUCK
SO WHO WRITES THIS STUFF?
HUH?
WHAT DO YOU MEAN?
IS IT WHITES...? OR MAYBE...
IT'S WHITES.
NIGGERS SUCK

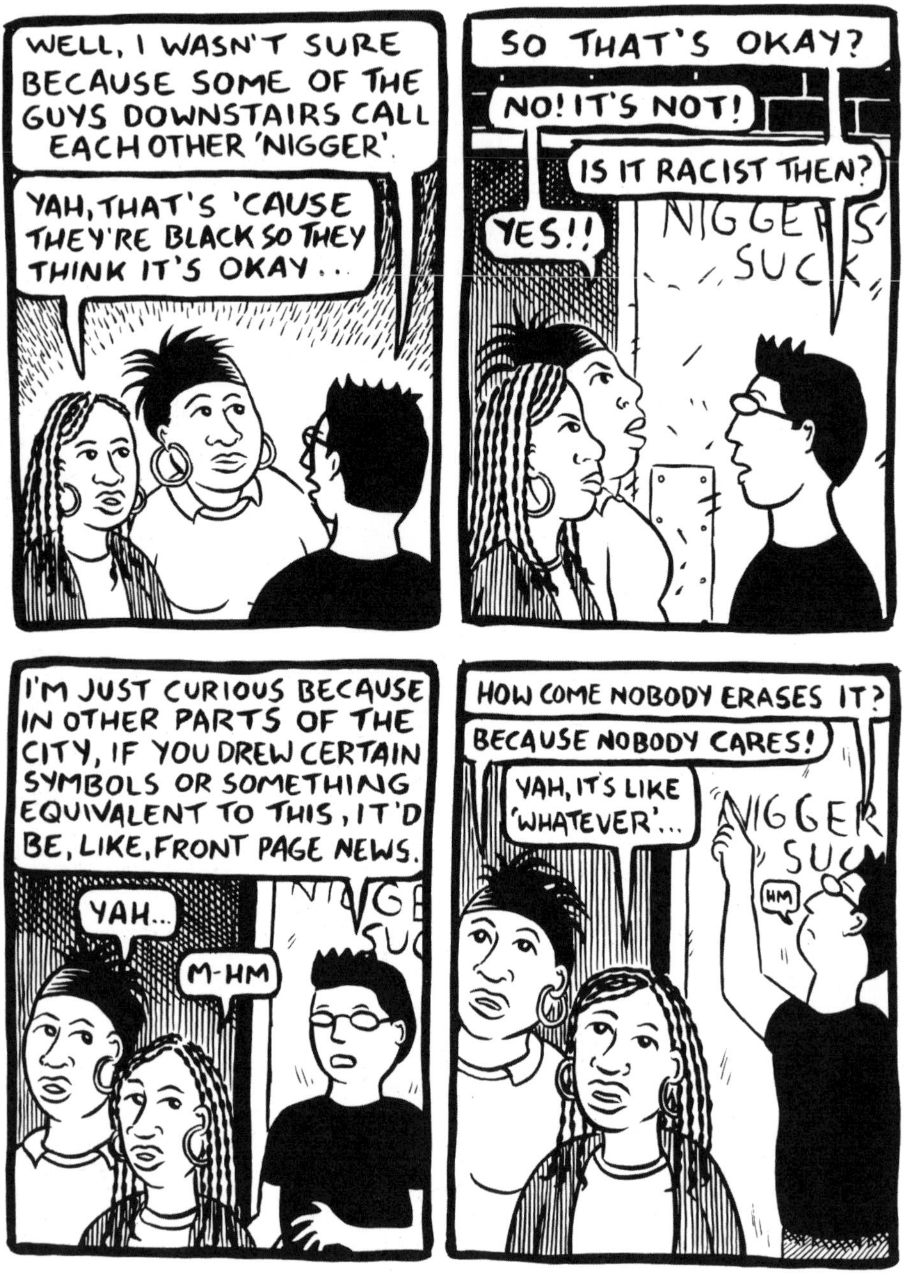
WELL, I WASN'T SURE BECAUSE SOME OF THE GUYS DOWNSTAIRS CALL EACH OTHER 'NIGGER'.
YAH, THAT'S 'CAUSE THEY'RE BLACK SO THEY THINK IT'S OKAY...
SO THAT'S OKAY?
NO! IT'S NOT!
IS IT RACIST THEN?
YES!!
NIGGERS SUCK
I'M JUST CURIOUS BECAUSE IN OTHER PARTS OF THE CITY, IF YOU DREW CERTAIN SYMBOLS OR SOMETHING EQUIVALENT TO THIS, IT'D BE, LIKE, FRONT PAGE NEWS.
YAH...
M-HM
HOW COME NOBODY ERASES IT?
BECAUSE NOBODY CARES!
YAH, IT'S LIKE 'WHATEVER'...
HM

hoar

Hoar

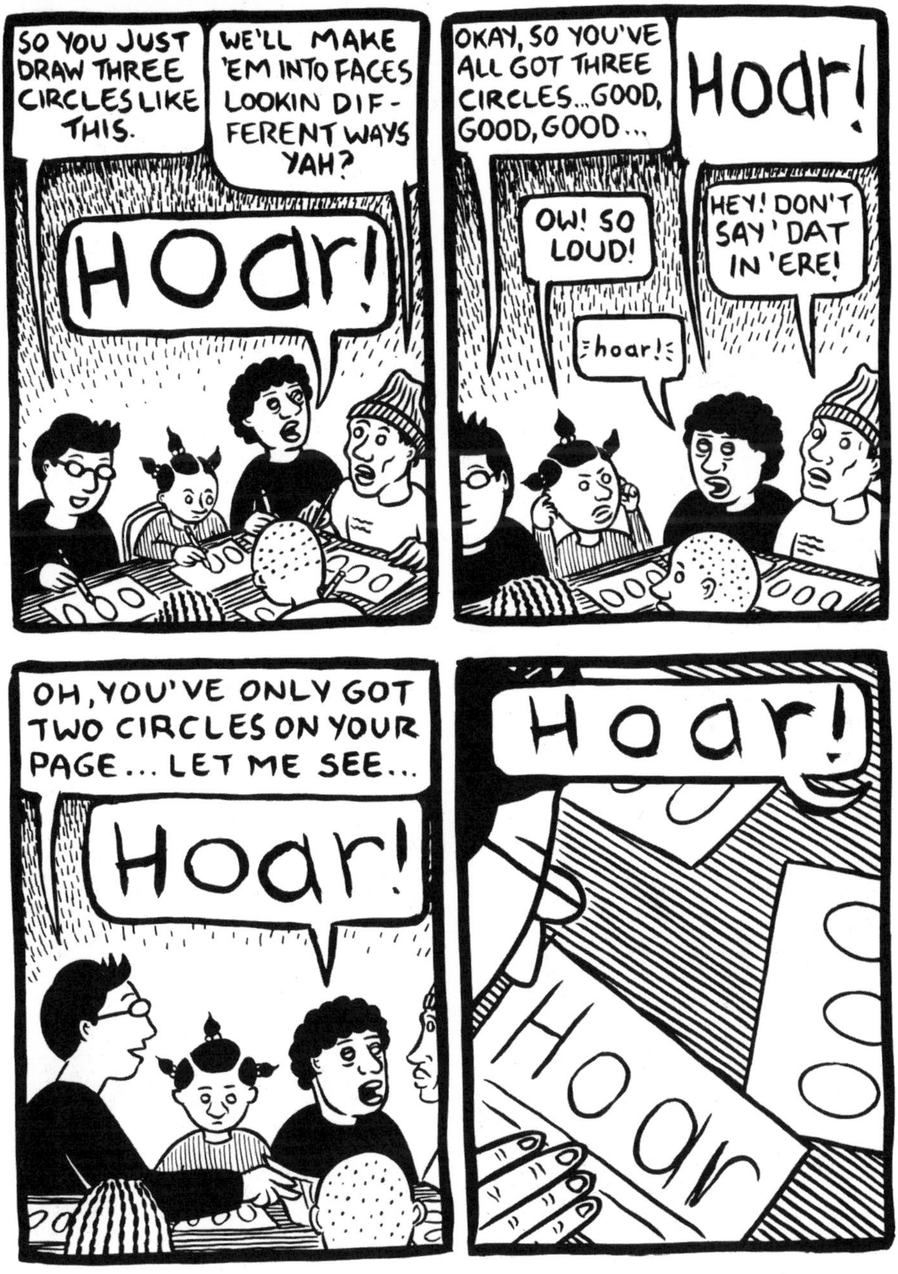

SO YOU JUST DRAW THREE CIRCLES LIKE THIS.
WE'LL MAKE 'EM INTO FACES LOOKIN DIF-FERENT WAYS YAH?
HOAR!
OKAY, SO YOU'VE ALL GOT THREE CIRCLES...GOOD, GOOD, GOOD...
Hoar!
OW! SO LOUD!
hoar!
HEY! DON'T SAY 'DAT IN 'ERE!
OH, YOU'VE ONLY GOT TWO CIRCLES ON YOUR PAGE... LET ME SEE...
Hoar!
Hoar!
Hoar

jump rope

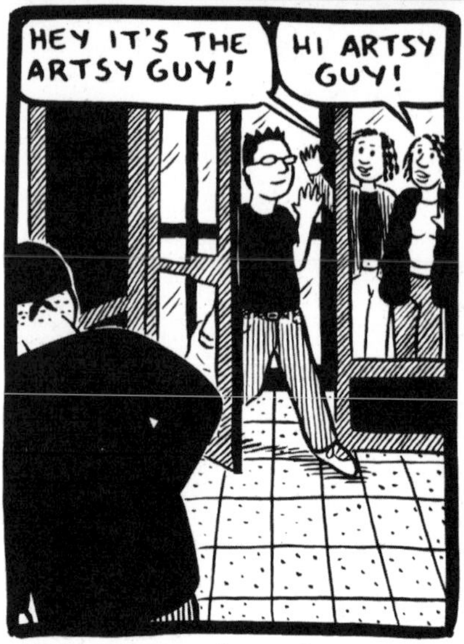
HEY IT'S THE ARTSY GUY!
HI ARTSY GUY!

Nice spring day... teen girls greet me at the front door, I walk in to catch the elevator down to the community centre.

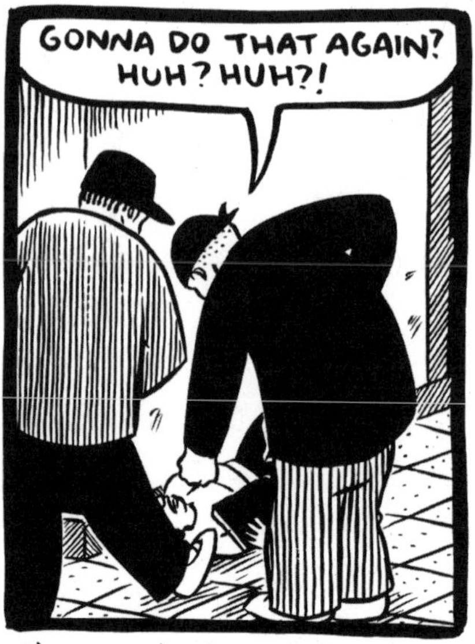
GONNA DO THAT AGAIN? HUH? HUH?!

I've just stepped into the lobby and there's a small boy on the ground being beaten by two huge teens!

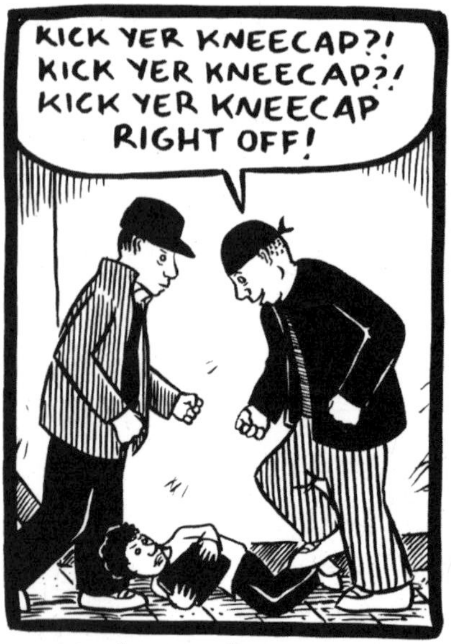
KICK YER KNEECAP?! KICK YER KNEECAP?! KICK YER KNEECAP RIGHT OFF!

...what can I say... I detach... things slow down... Do I recognize the teens? What's going on? ... Are they really hurting him?

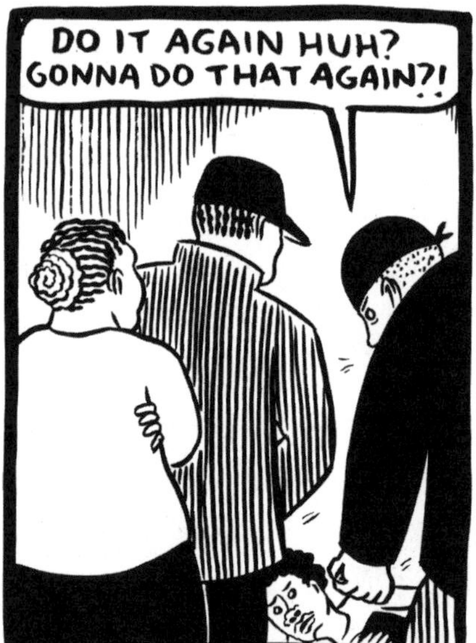
DO IT AGAIN HUH? GONNA DO THAT AGAIN?!

A woman stands beside them watching... waiting for the elevator... she's giving a dirty look while the boy writhes on the floor from random punches and kicks.

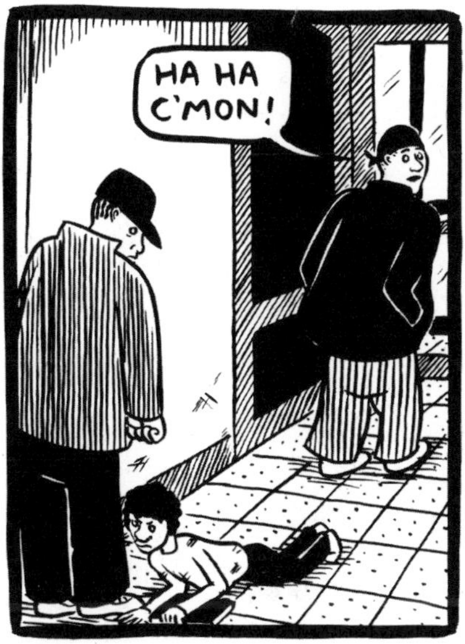
HA HA
C'MON!

The girls at the front door are beckoning the big guys, and one of them leaves laughing... is this a game? a little brother? What's going on?!

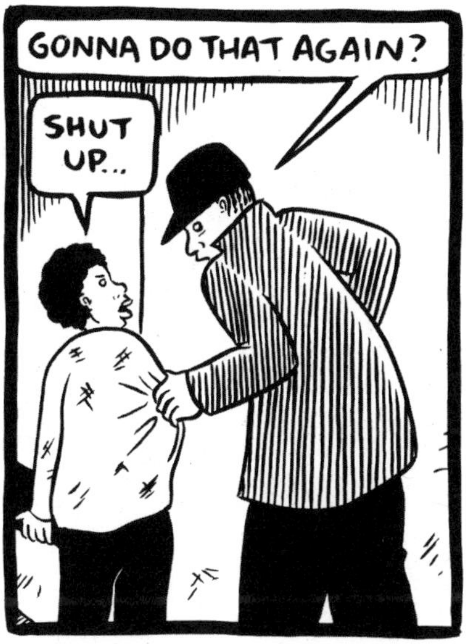
GONNA DO THAT AGAIN?
SHUT UP...

The kid gets up and the teen hovers over him with his fist 'cocked' threatening to punch him...

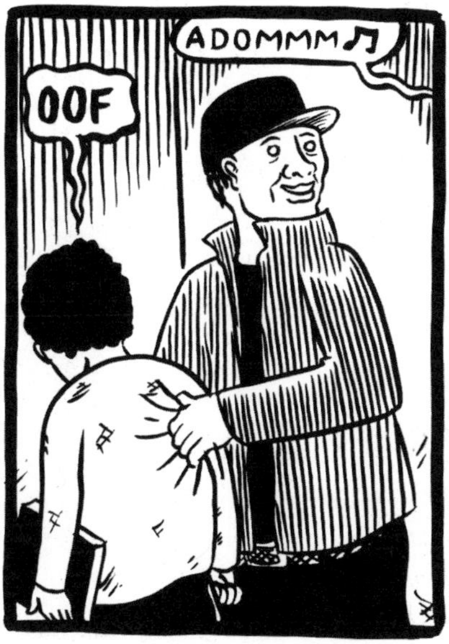
OOF
ADOMMM ♫

The big teen looks genuinely surprised that the kid would still talk back... so he punches him hard.

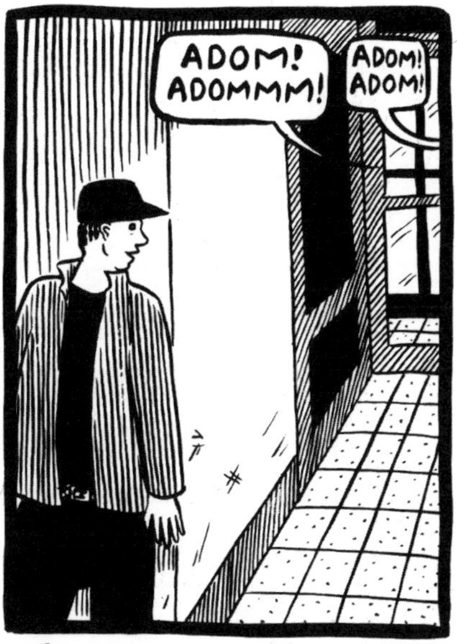
ADOM! ADOMMM!
ADOM! ADOM!

The guy is grinning as he leaves the kid and hides behind the wall... the girls at the front door are screaming his name... elevator's here.

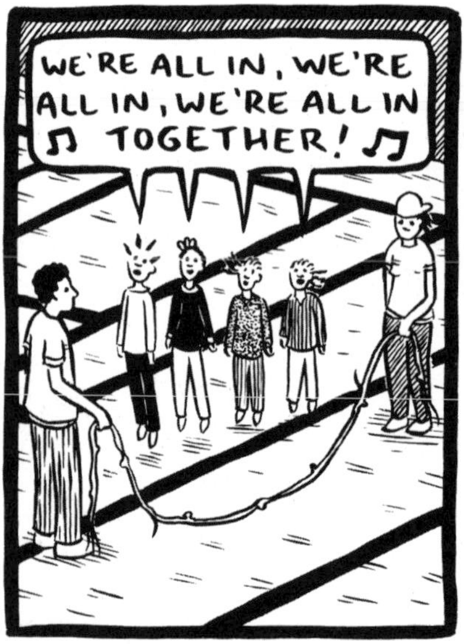
WE'RE ALL IN, WE'RE ALL IN, WE'RE ALL IN ♫ TOGETHER! ♫

I go down to the gym where I do my art classes... staff members Buni and Nebil are playing jump rope with four little girls.

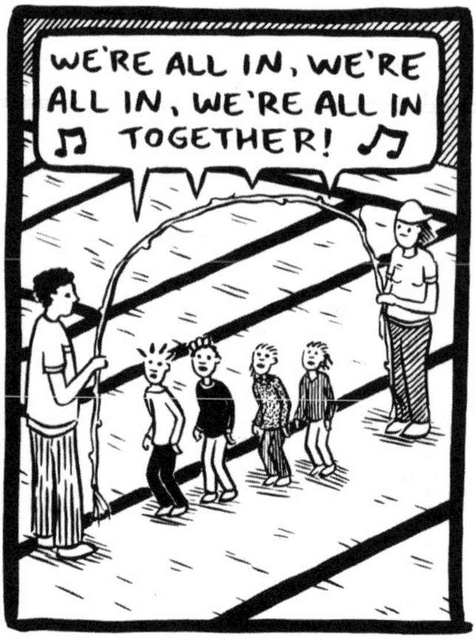
WE'RE ALL IN, WE'RE ALL IN, WE'RE ALL IN ♫ TOGETHER! ♫

I sit and watch the potential process of elimination... if the rope hits you, you're out!

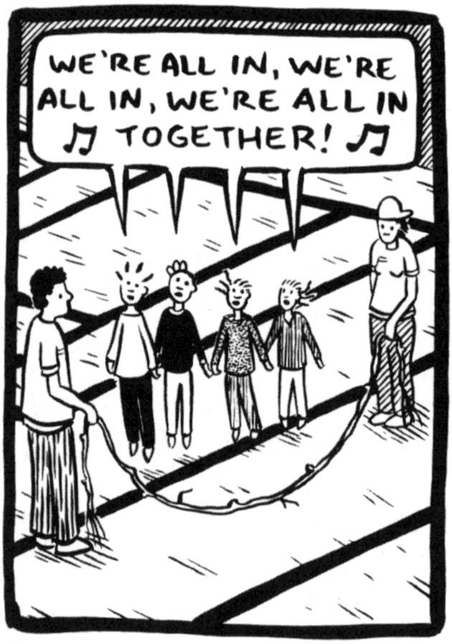
WE'RE ALL IN, WE'RE ALL IN, WE'RE ALL IN ♫ TOGETHER! ♫

It's a nice scene watching all the girls jump in unison... nobody is getting 'out'!

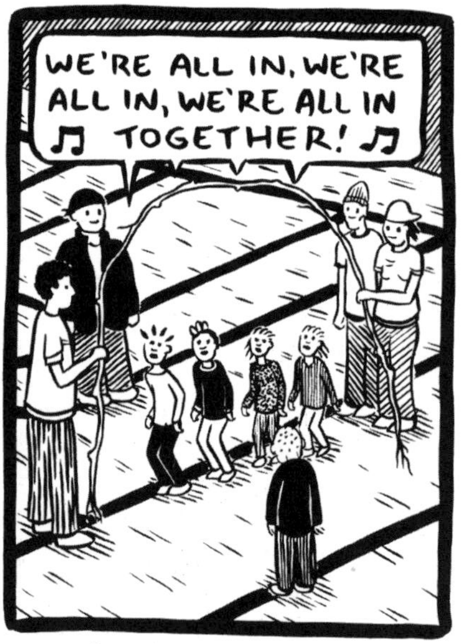
WE'RE ALL IN, WE'RE ALL IN, WE'RE ALL IN ♫ TOGETHER! ♫

Two big teens, Yar a staff member, and Clarance want to join in... so does Kirk... a 'special needs' kid...

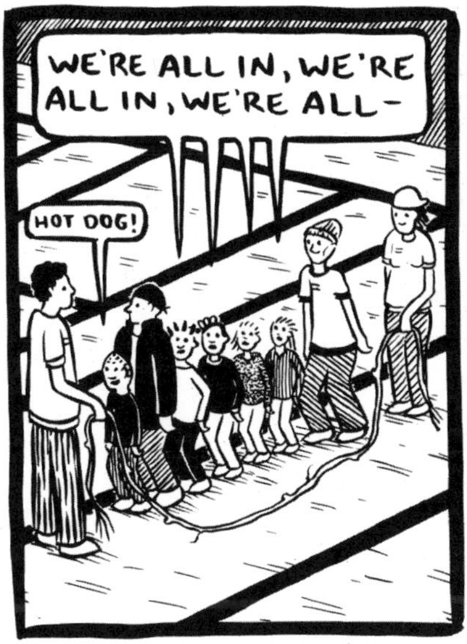
WE'RE ALL IN, WE'RE ALL IN, WE'RE ALL–
HOT DOG!

So funny to watch this strangely sized group trying to jump over the knotted frayed, yellow utility rope...

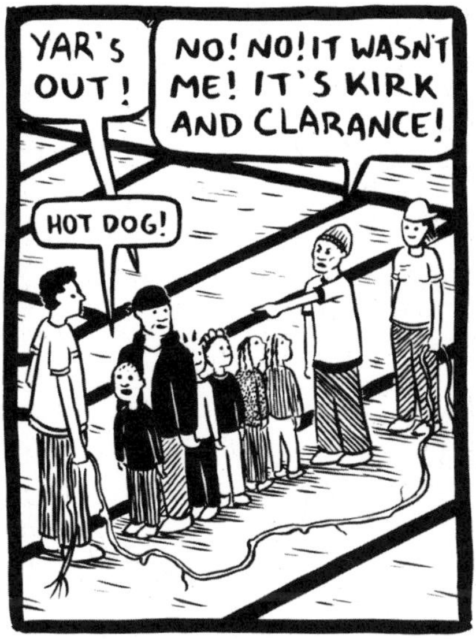
YAR'S OUT!
NO! NO! IT WASN'T ME! IT'S KIRK AND CLARANCE!
HOT DOG!

Yar's getting pretty serious about the 'out' thing... whose feet did the rope hit?

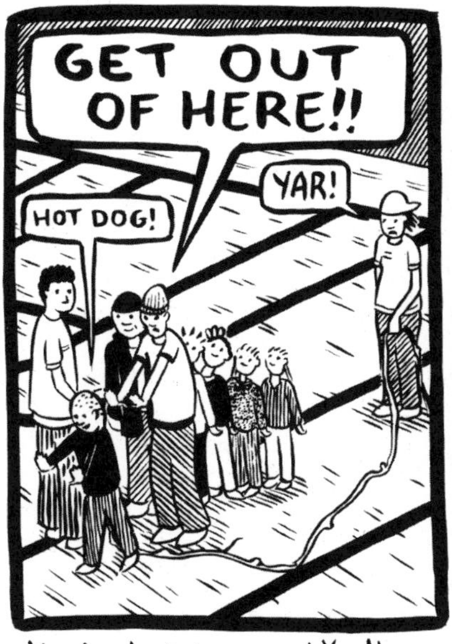
GET OUT OF HERE!!
YAR!
HOT DOG!

Kirk trips up and Yar throws him out forcefully.

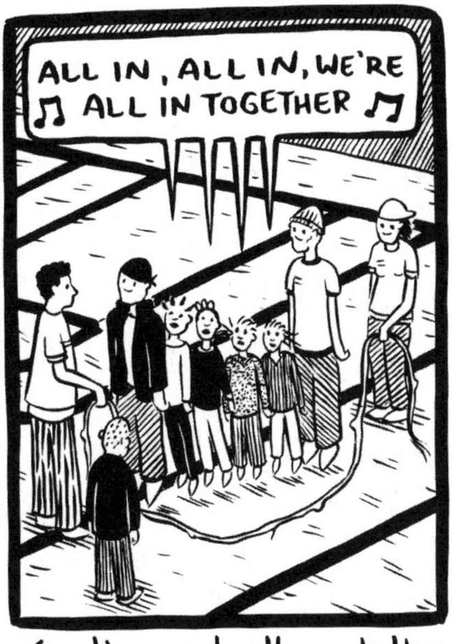
ALL IN, ALL IN, WE'RE ♫ ALL IN TOGETHER ♫

So they actually get the rope around a couple of times! It really is a sweet scene...

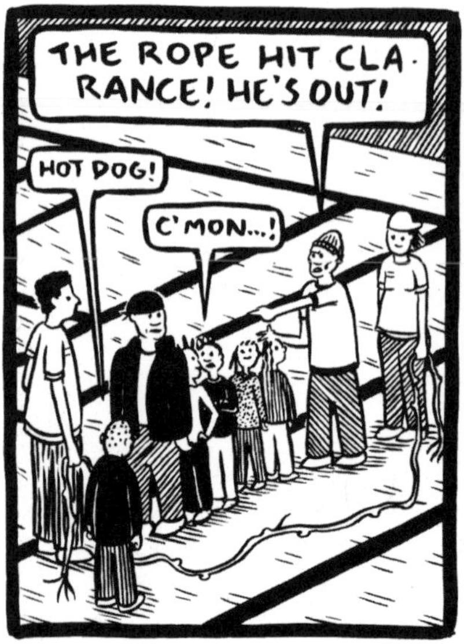
THE ROPE HIT CLA-RANCE! HE'S OUT!
HOT DOG!
C'MON...!

Well... then the rope hits Clarance and Yar demands him out!

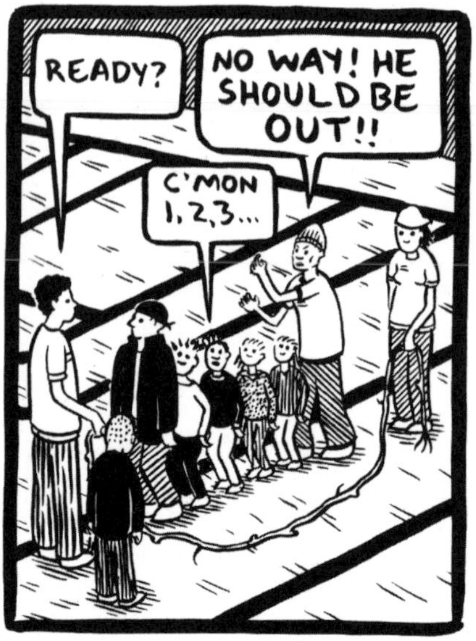
READY?
NO WAY! HE SHOULD BE OUT!!
C'MON 1,2,3...

Clarance won't leave so they turn the rope around and it hits Yar who says it hit Clarance and <u>he</u> should be out!

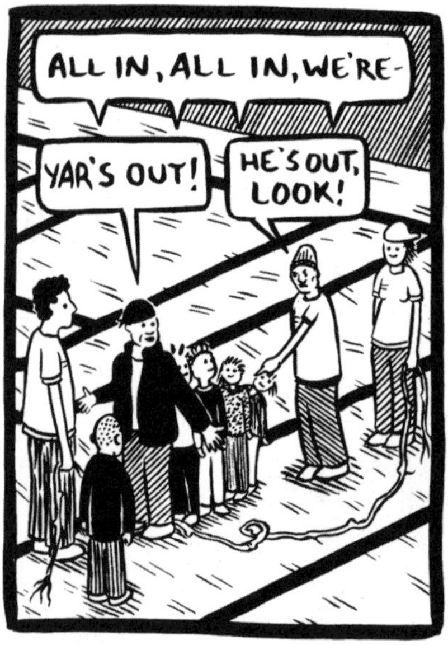
ALL IN, ALL IN, WE'RE-
YAR'S OUT!
HE'S OUT, LOOK!

The rope turns again and hits Clarance and Yar wants him out, but he still won't go.

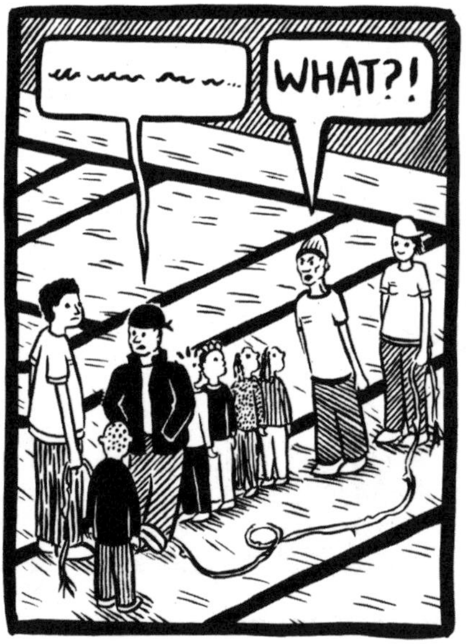
WHAT?!

This time Clarance kind of smiles... the rope <u>is</u> between his feet... he starts to leave... muttering something to Yar...

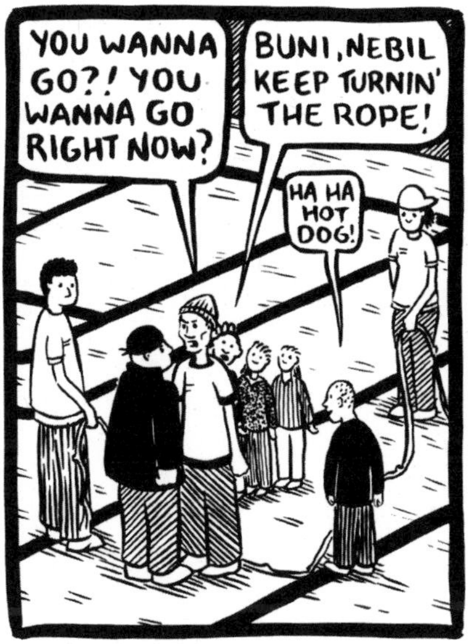
YOU WANNA GO?! YOU WANNA GO RIGHT NOW?
BUNI, NEBIL KEEP TURNIN' THE ROPE!
HA HA HOT DOG!

Suddenly they're face to face... the girls want Buni and Nebil to keep turning the rope.

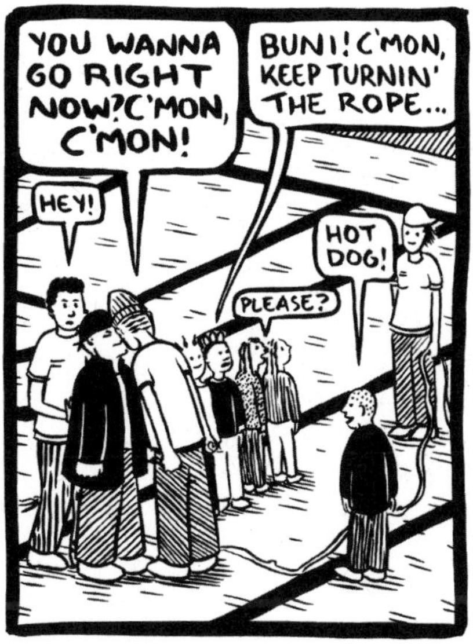
YOU WANNA GO RIGHT NOW? C'MON, C'MON!
BUNI! C'MON, KEEP TURNIN' THE ROPE...
HEY!
HOT DOG!
PLEASE?

Yar snaps his head at Clarance, quick, hard, sharp... just grazing him... not really trying to connect, just goading him.

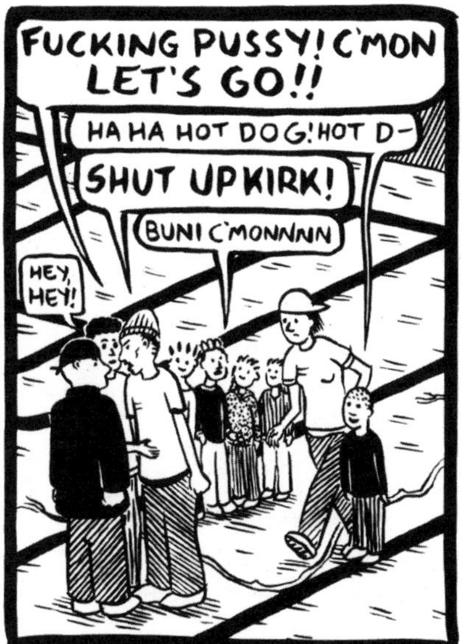
FUCKING PUSSY! C'MON LET'S GO!!
HA HA HOT DOG! HOT D-
SHUT UP KIRK!
BUNI C'MONNNNN
HEY, HEY!

Yar is doing all the talking. Nebil is trying to get between them.

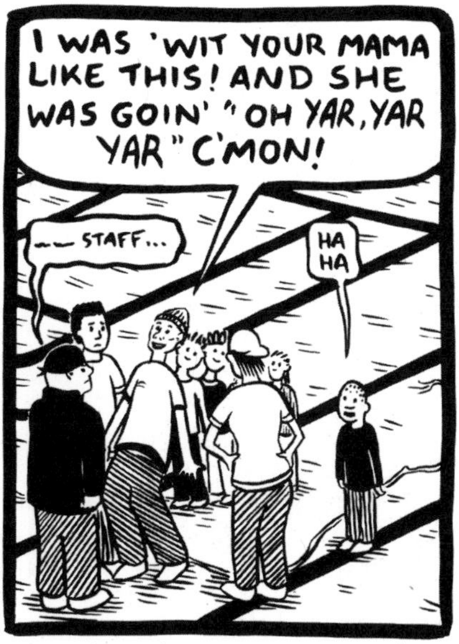
I WAS 'WIT YOUR MAMA LIKE THIS! AND SHE WAS GOIN' "OH YAR, YAR YAR" C'MON!
—— STAFF...
HA HA

Yar is thrusting his pelvis in the air... Clarance seems like he might just walk away... but again he mutters something...

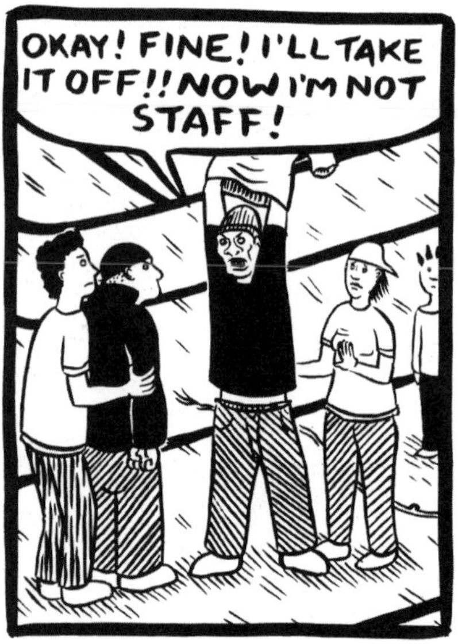
OKAY! FINE! I'LL TAKE IT OFF!! NOW I'M NOT STAFF!

Yar whips off his staff shirt, Nebil is really holding Clarance and Buni is coming in for Yar!

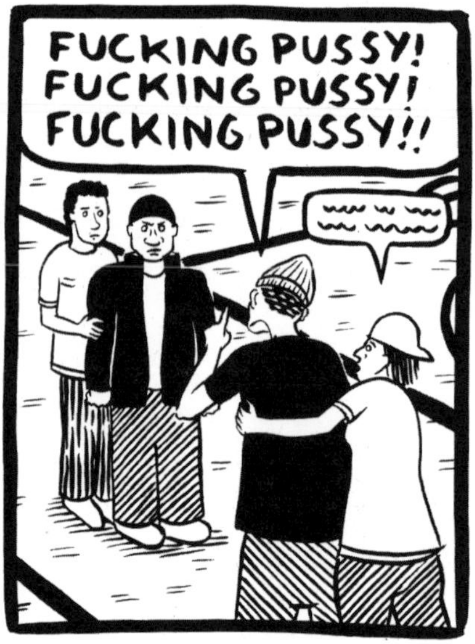
FUCKING PUSSY! FUCKING PUSSY! FUCKING PUSSY!!

Buni is trying to lead Yar to the office... she tries to calm him by saying something in Somalian, but he won't listen and pulls away.

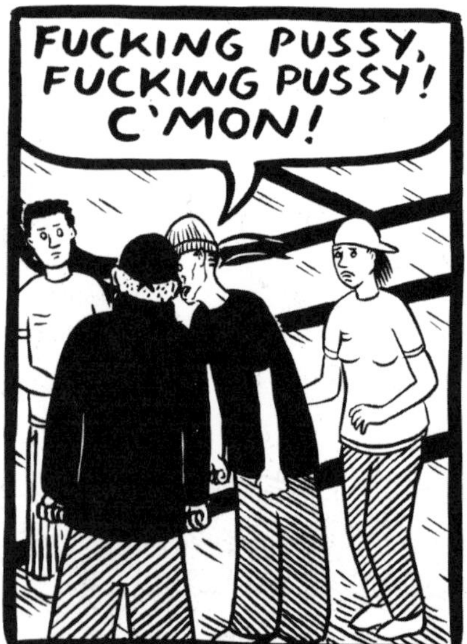
FUCKING PUSSY, FUCKING PUSSY! C'MON!

Yar keeps snapping his head at Clarance... both of them keep their fists clenched at their sides... but Yar, that long neck, and his head... snap, snap, snap!

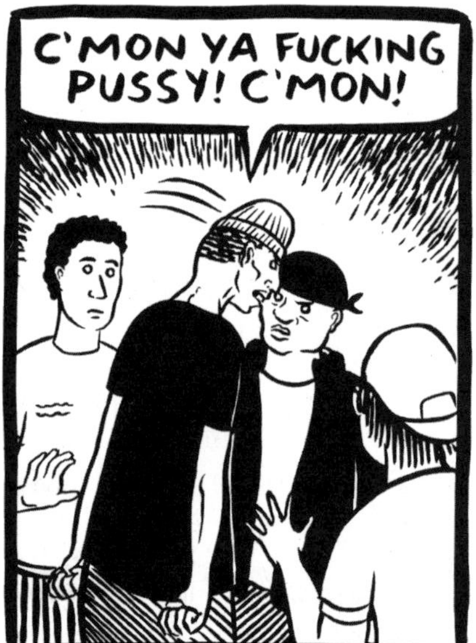
C'MON YA FUCKING PUSSY! C'MON!

The guys keep circling, taunting, looking mean, but neither of them is willing to throw a punch.

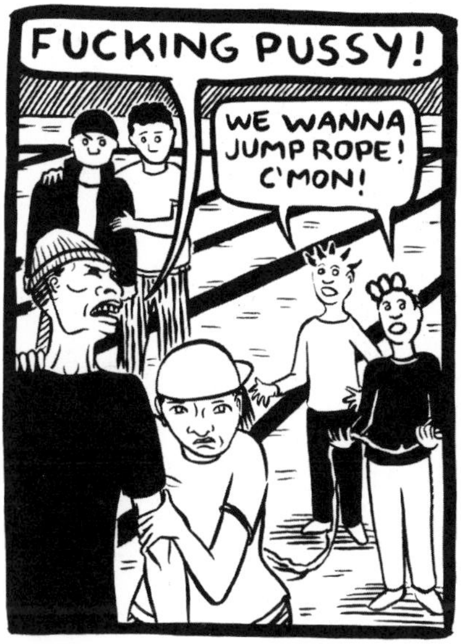
FUCKING PUSSY!
WE WANNA JUMP ROPE! C'MON!

Both teens are really angry, but unwilling to fight... they allow themselves to be led to the office... the girls have been waiting patiently...

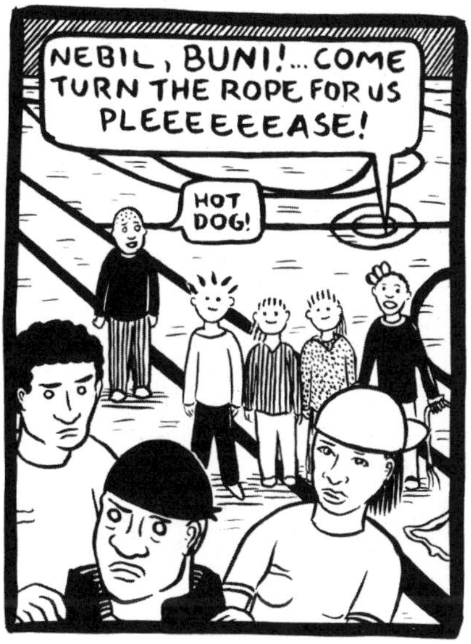
NEBIL, BUNI!...COME TURN THE ROPE FOR US PLEEEEEEEASE!
HOT DOG!

Buni and Nebil get Yar into the office and wait outside to keep an eye on Clarance. The girls want to play.

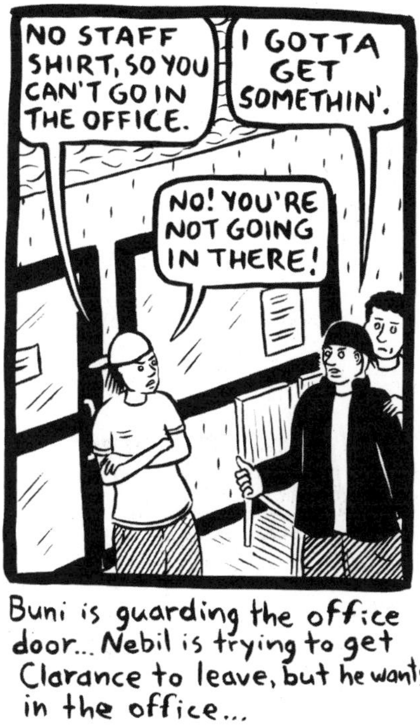
NO STAFF SHIRT, SO YOU CAN'T GO IN THE OFFICE.
I GOTTA GET SOMETHIN'.
NO! YOU'RE NOT GOING IN THERE!

Buni is guarding the office door... Nebil is trying to get Clarance to leave, but he wants in the office...

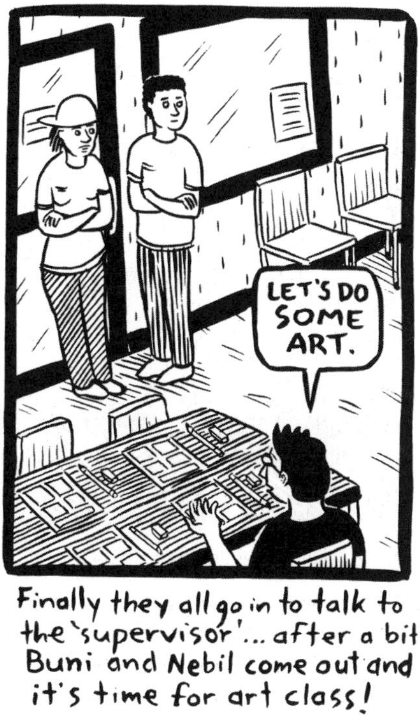
LET'S DO SOME ART.

Finally they all go in to talk to the 'supervisor'... after a bit Buni and Nebil come out and it's time for art class!

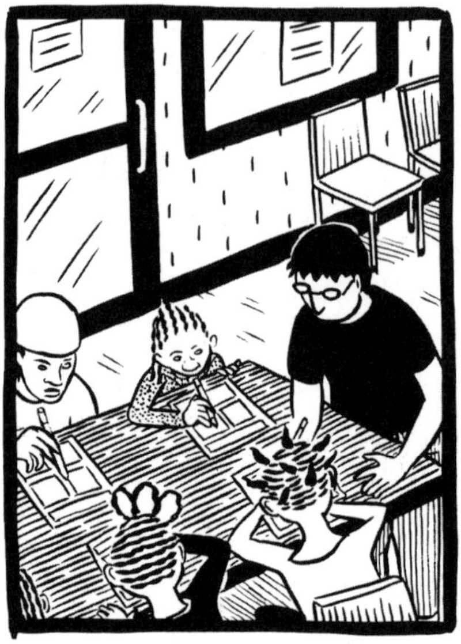

So we actually get to work on some drawing while things go on in the office...

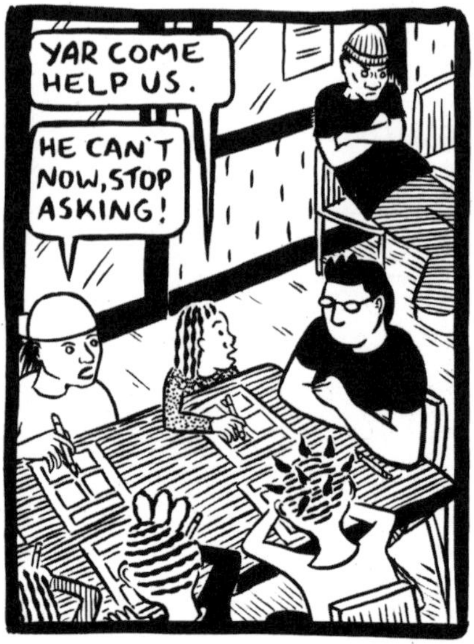
YAR COME HELP US.
HE CAN'T NOW, STOP ASKING!

Yar eventually comes out and parks himself sullenly in a chair... the girls want him to help with their pictures, but he's not allowed to.

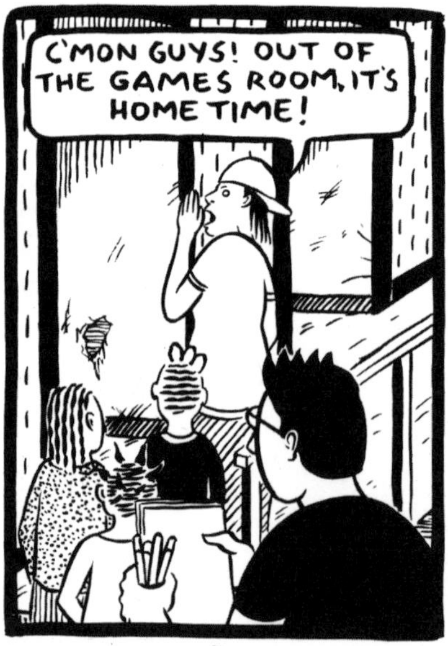
C'MON GUYS! OUT OF THE GAMES ROOM, IT'S HOME TIME!

We've drawn for awhile... Yar and Clarance were sent home... now it's time to go. Buni's been great and I'd like to help her get a good summer job.

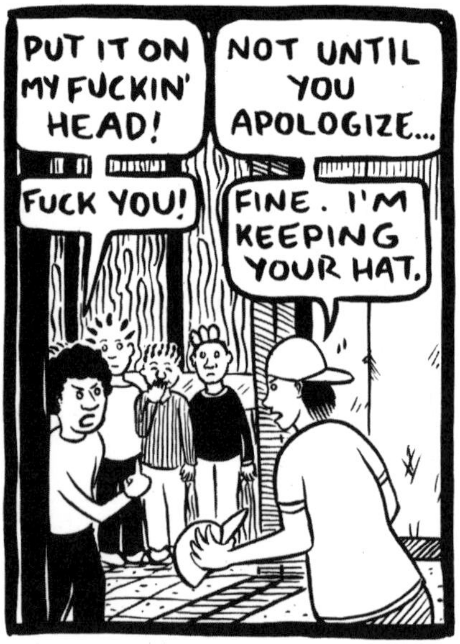
PUT IT ON MY FUCKIN' HEAD!
NOT UNTIL YOU APOLOGIZE...
FUCK YOU!
FINE. I'M KEEPING YOUR HAT.

She's gathered all the kids from the centre and piled them into the elevator for 'home time'.

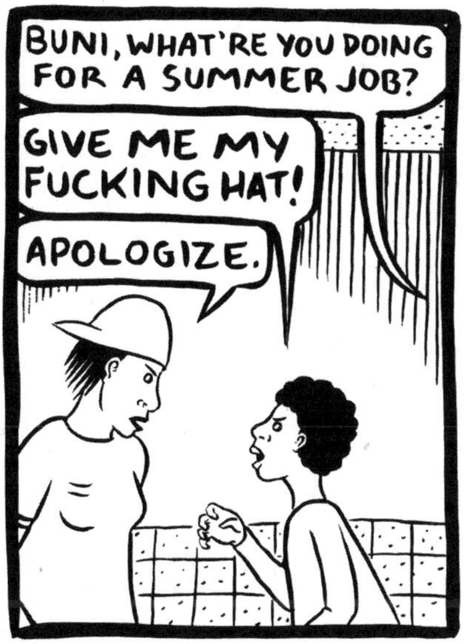
BUNI, WHAT'RE YOU DOING FOR A SUMMER JOB?
GIVE ME MY FUCKING HAT!
APOLOGIZE.

Buni walks away with the kid's hat and I ask her about summer work...

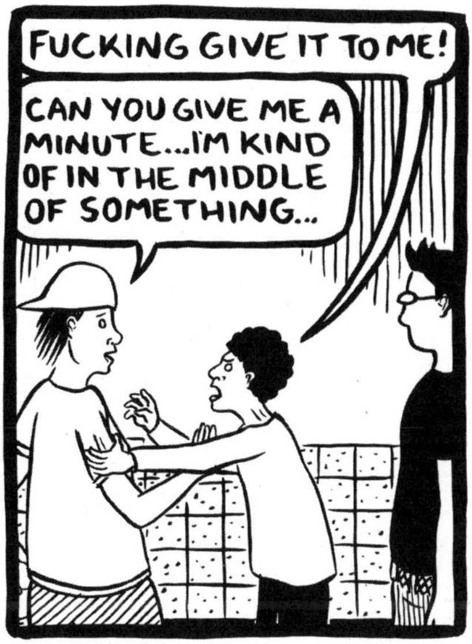
FUCKING GIVE IT TO ME!
CAN YOU GIVE ME A MINUTE...I'M KIND OF IN THE MIDDLE OF SOMETHING...

The kid's grabbing her arm and she's holding him off... I'd like to offer her a job away from this place.

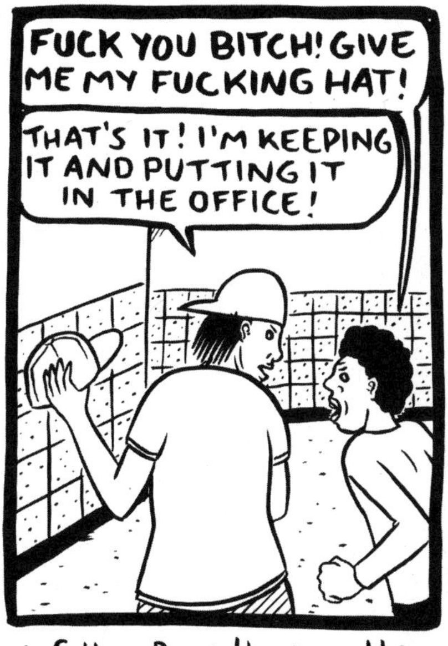
FUCK YOU BITCH! GIVE ME MY FUCKING HAT!
THAT'S IT! I'M KEEPING IT AND PUTTING IT IN THE OFFICE!

I follow Buni thinking this will just take a minute...maybe I can give her the chance to make a little more money... a nicer place...

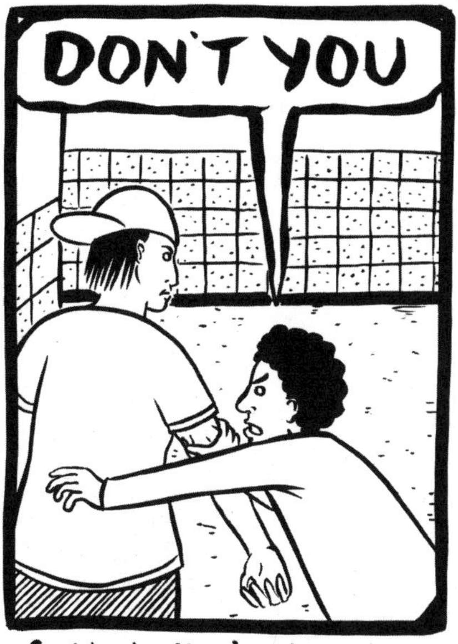
DON'T YOU

Suddenly the kid lunges! Shoving her he grabs for his hat!

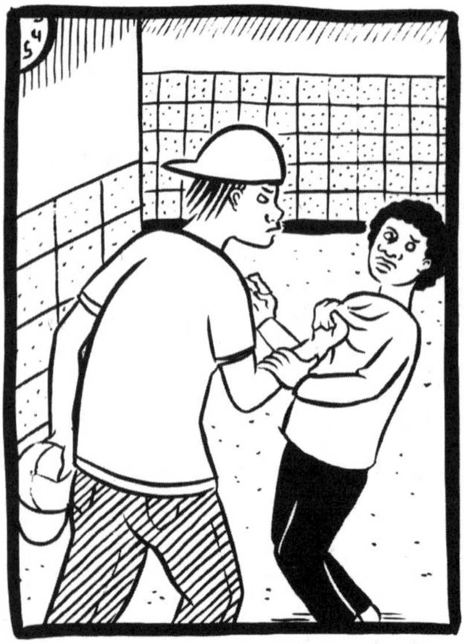

With a quick move she grabs the kid by the front of his shirt...

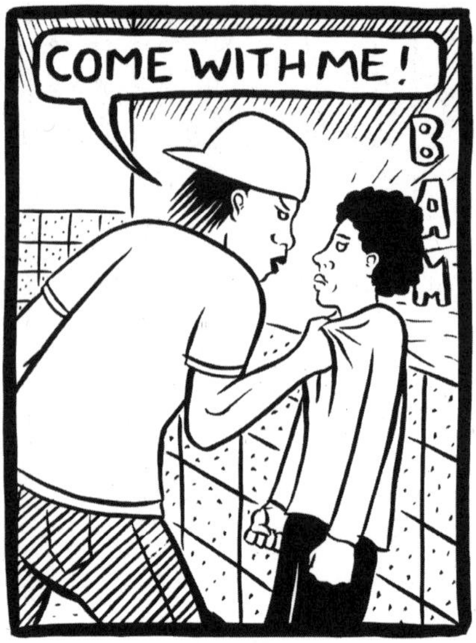
COME WITH ME!
BAM

...and pins him against the wall where she glares at him with a look of such ferocity that the kid's frozen in anger.

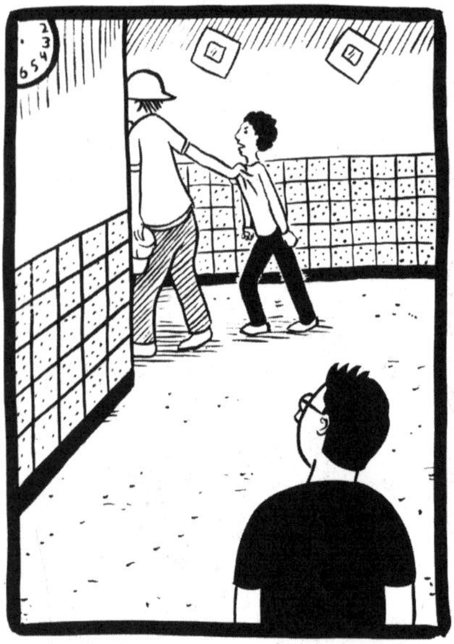

I want to follow her... I want to talk to her... I want to help her... should I follow her...?

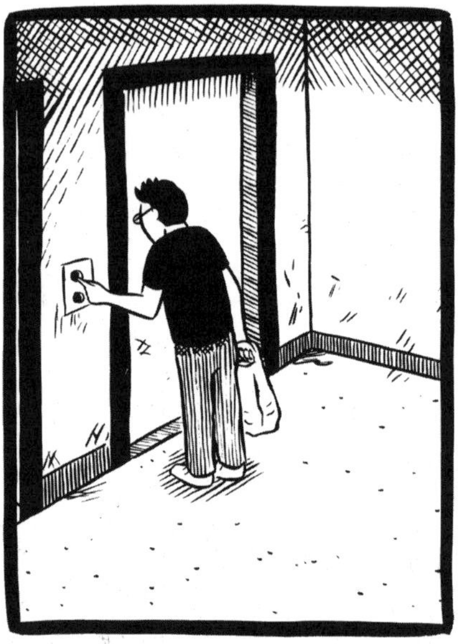

Enough for one day, I'm going home.

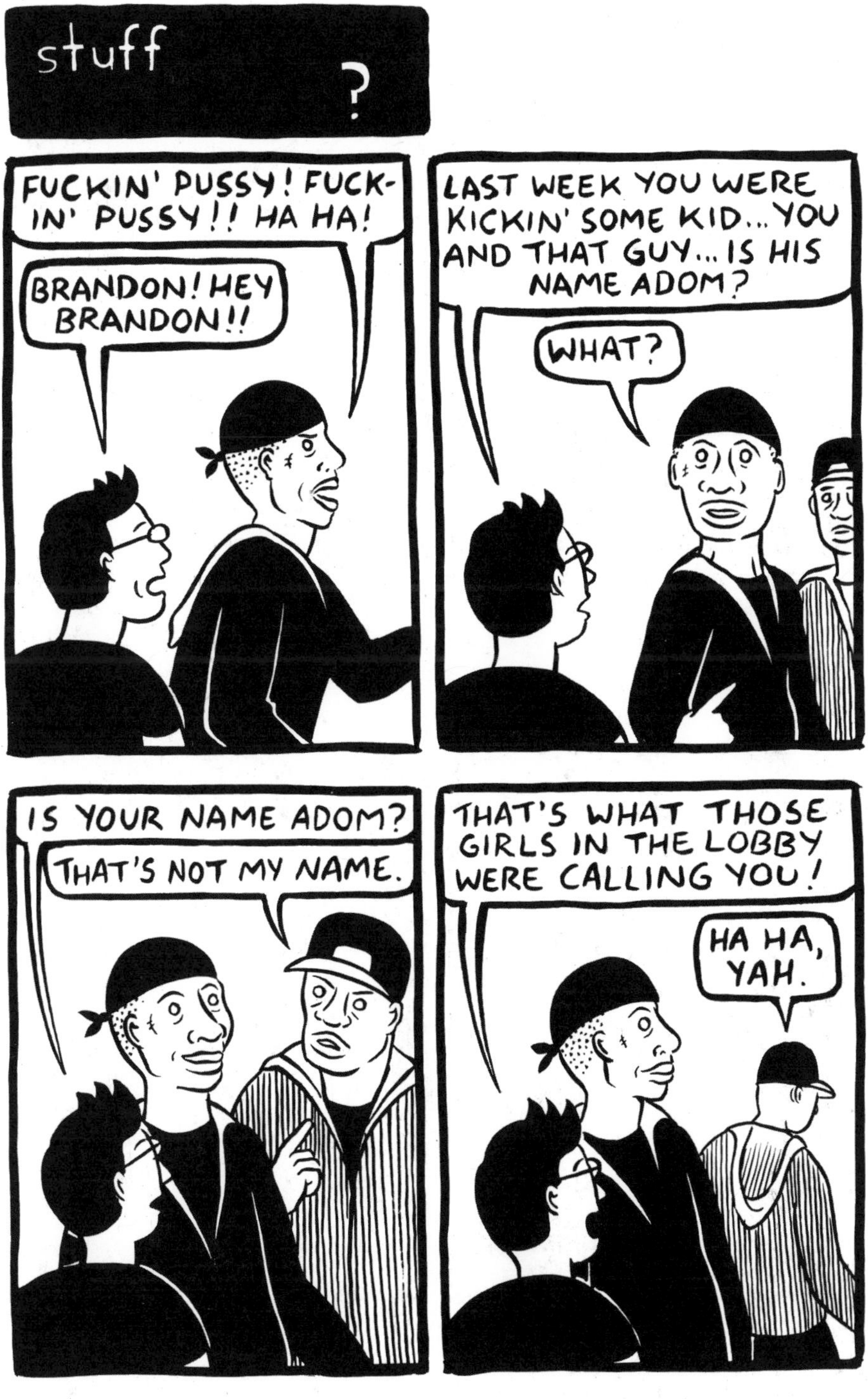
stuff ?
FUCKIN' PUSSY! FUCKIN' PUSSY!! HA HA!
BRANDON! HEY BRANDON!!
LAST WEEK YOU WERE KICKIN' SOME KID... YOU AND THAT GUY... IS HIS NAME ADOM?
WHAT?
IS YOUR NAME ADOM?
THAT'S NOT MY NAME.
THAT'S WHAT THOSE GIRLS IN THE LOBBY WERE CALLING YOU!
HA HA, YAH.

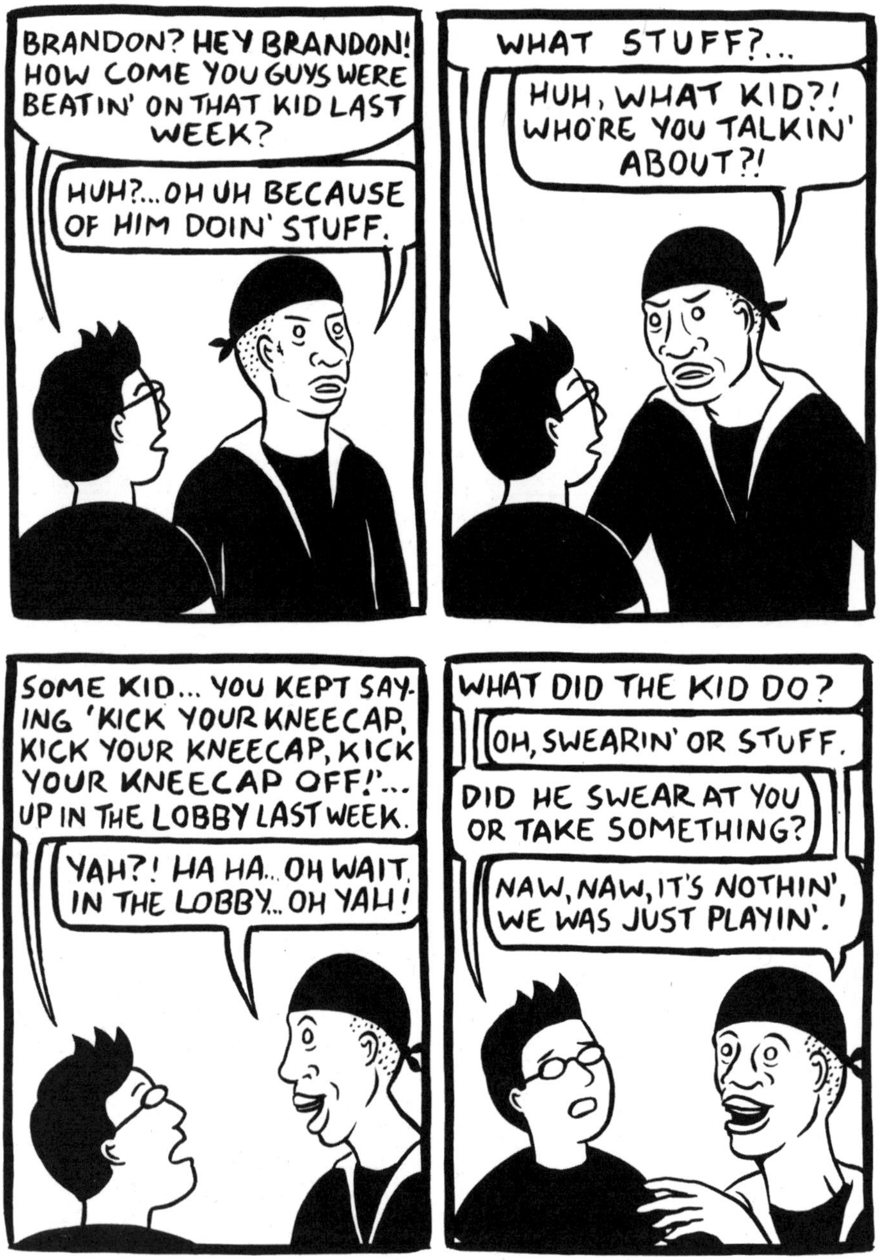
BRANDON? HEY BRANDON! HOW COME YOU GUYS WERE BEATIN' ON THAT KID LAST WEEK?
HUH?...OH UH BECAUSE OF HIM DOIN' STUFF.
WHAT STUFF?...
HUH, WHAT KID?! WHO'RE YOU TALKIN' ABOUT?!
SOME KID... YOU KEPT SAYING 'KICK YOUR KNEECAP, KICK YOUR KNEECAP, KICK YOUR KNEECAP OFF!'... UP IN THE LOBBY LAST WEEK.
YAH?! HA HA... OH WAIT, IN THE LOBBY... OH YAH!
WHAT DID THE KID DO?
OH, SWEARIN' OR STUFF.
DID HE SWEAR AT YOU OR TAKE SOMETHING?
NAW, NAW, IT'S NOTHIN', WE WAS JUST PLAYIN'.

pears

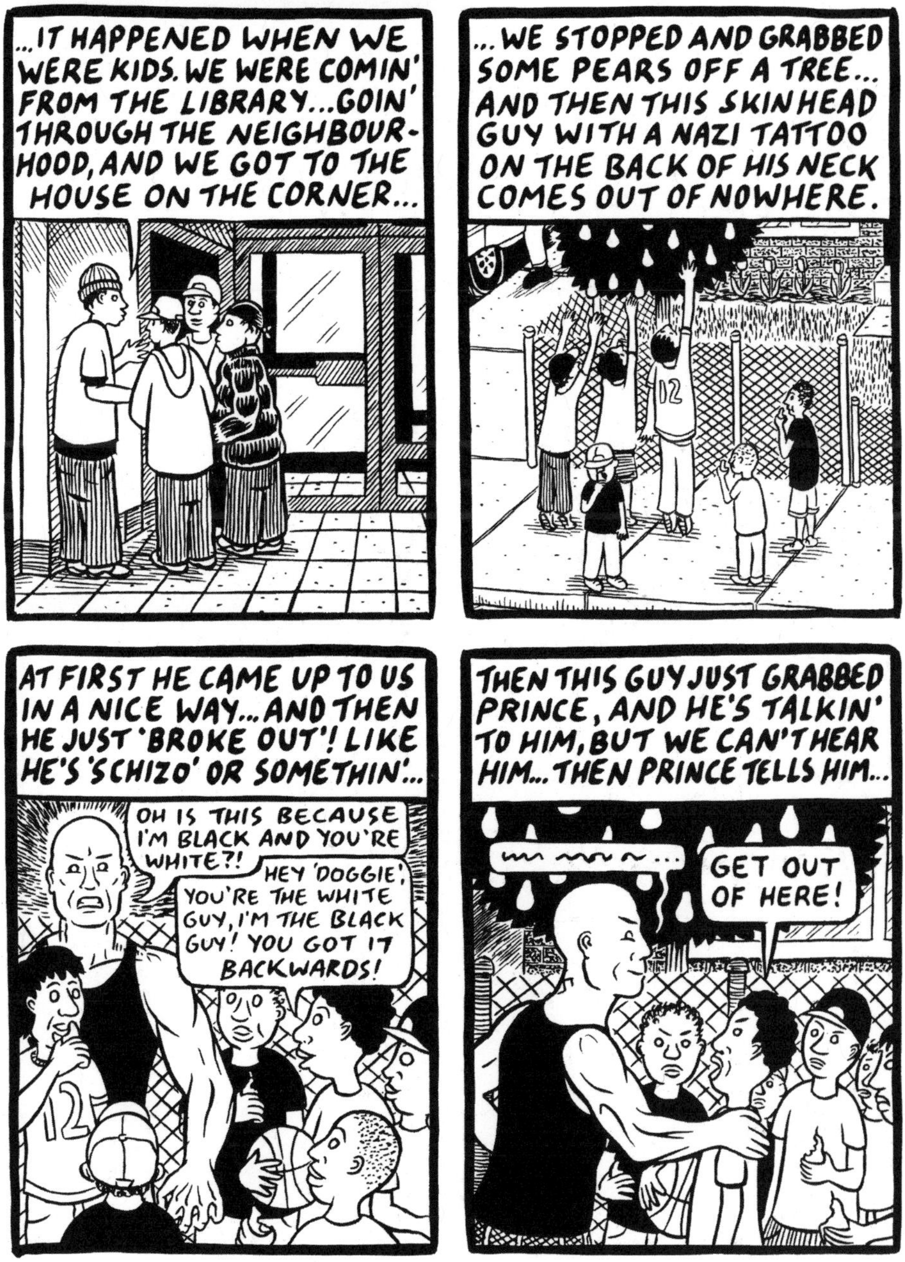
...IT HAPPENED WHEN WE WERE KIDS. WE WERE COMIN' FROM THE LIBRARY...GOIN' THROUGH THE NEIGHBOUR-HOOD, AND WE GOT TO THE HOUSE ON THE CORNER...
...WE STOPPED AND GRABBED SOME PEARS OFF A TREE... AND THEN THIS SKINHEAD GUY WITH A NAZI TATTOO ON THE BACK OF HIS NECK COMES OUT OF NOWHERE.
12
AT FIRST HE CAME UP TO US IN A NICE WAY... AND THEN HE JUST 'BROKE OUT'! LIKE HE'S 'SCHIZO' OR SOMETHIN'...
OH IS THIS BECAUSE I'M BLACK AND YOU'RE WHITE?!
HEY 'DOGGIE', YOU'RE THE WHITE GUY, I'M THE BLACK GUY! YOU GOT IT BACKWARDS!
12
THEN THIS GUY JUST GRABBED PRINCE, AND HE'S TALKIN' TO HIM, BUT WE CAN'T HEAR HIM... THEN PRINCE TELLS HIM...
GET OUT OF HERE!

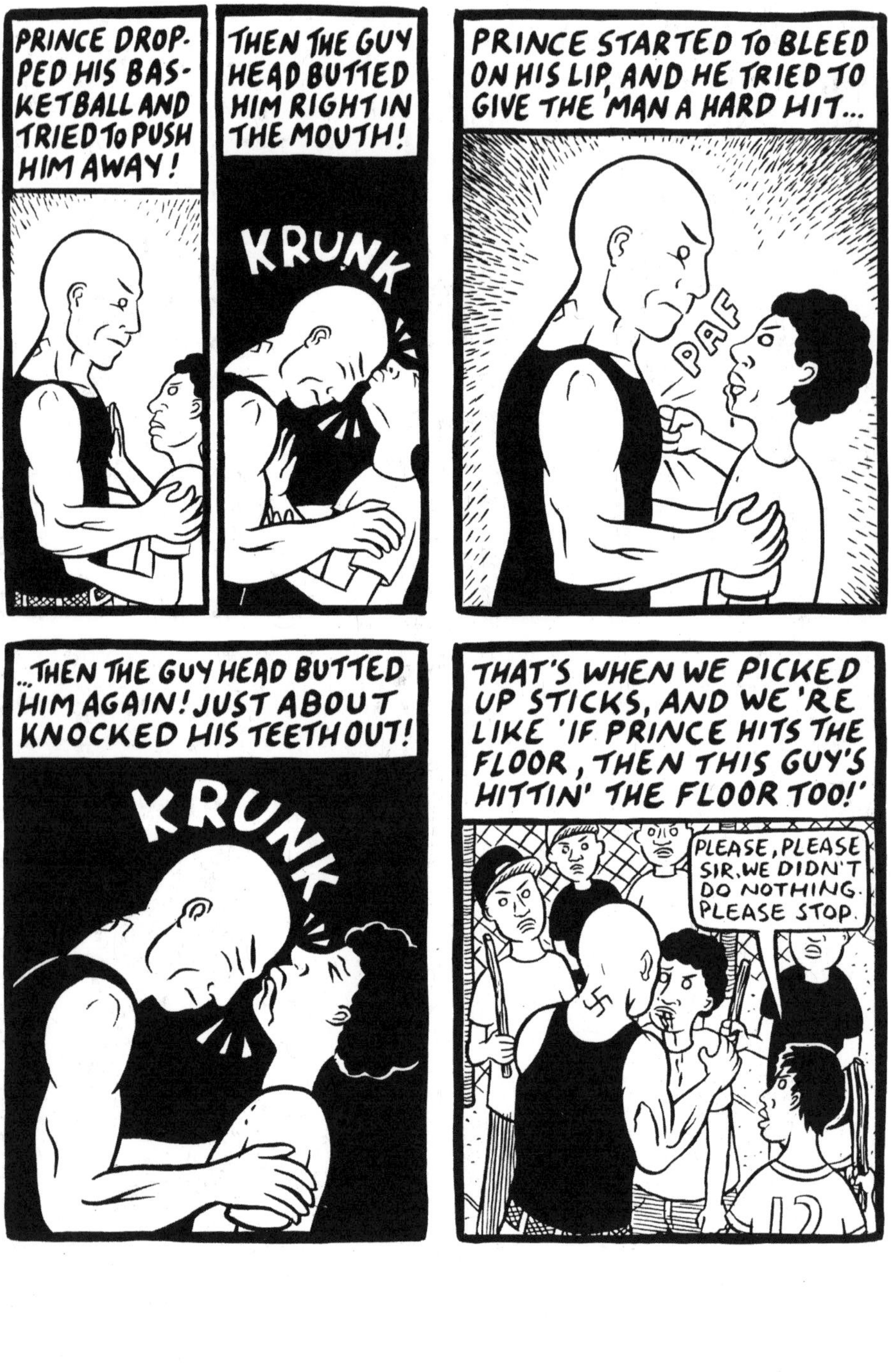
PRINCE DROPPED HIS BASKETBALL AND TRIED TO PUSH HIM AWAY!
THEN THE GUY HEAD BUTTED HIM RIGHT IN THE MOUTH!
KRUNK
PRINCE STARTED TO BLEED ON HIS LIP, AND HE TRIED TO GIVE THE MAN A HARD HIT...
PAF
...THEN THE GUY HEAD BUTTED HIM AGAIN! JUST ABOUT KNOCKED HIS TEETH OUT!
KRUNK
THAT'S WHEN WE PICKED UP STICKS, AND WE'RE LIKE 'IF PRINCE HITS THE FLOOR, THEN THIS GUY'S HITTIN' THE FLOOR TOO!'
PLEASE, PLEASE SIR. WE DIDN'T DO NOTHING. PLEASE STOP.
12

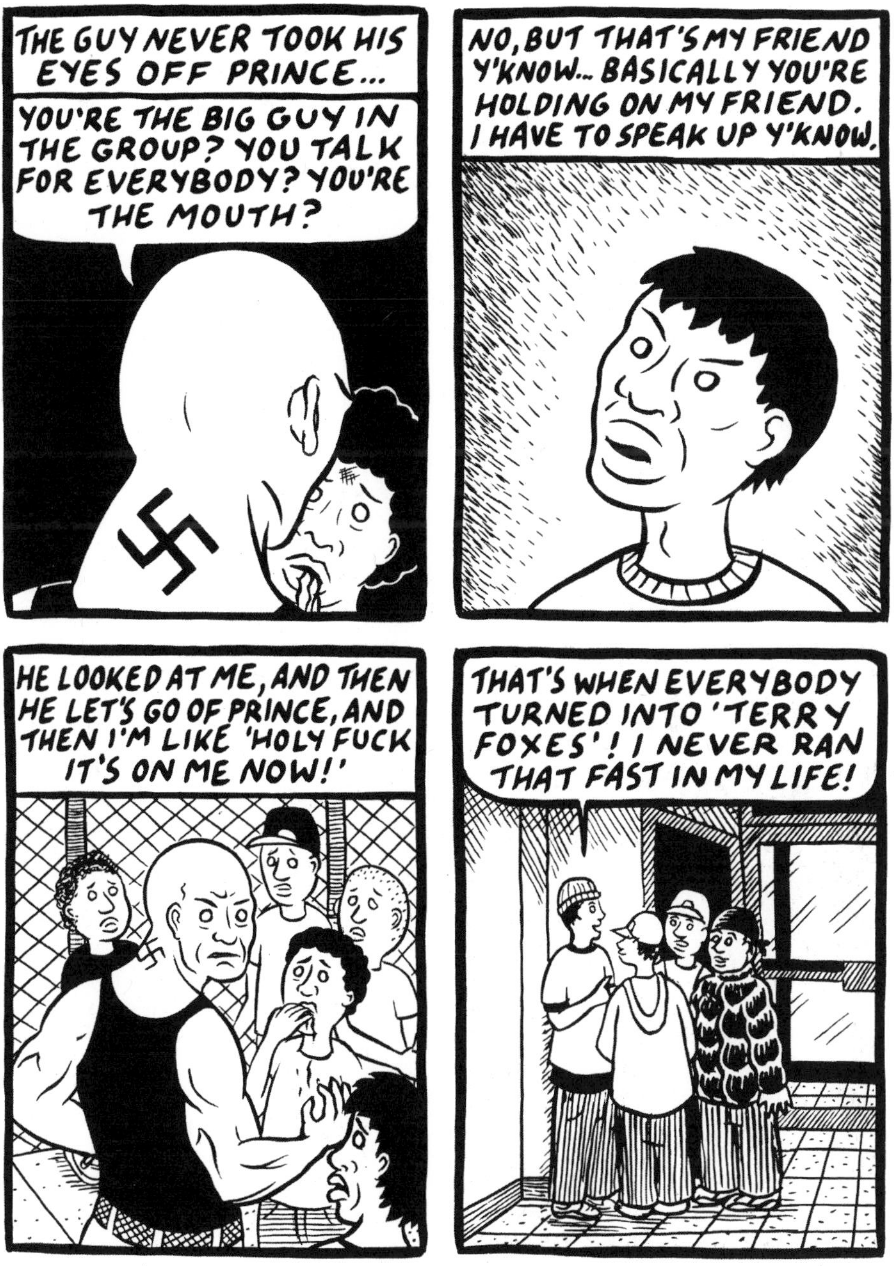
THE GUY NEVER TOOK HIS EYES OFF PRINCE...
YOU'RE THE BIG GUY IN THE GROUP? YOU TALK FOR EVERYBODY? YOU'RE THE MOUTH?
NO, BUT THAT'S MY FRIEND Y'KNOW... BASICALLY YOU'RE HOLDING ON MY FRIEND. I HAVE TO SPEAK UP Y'KNOW.
HE LOOKED AT ME, AND THEN HE LET'S GO OF PRINCE, AND THEN I'M LIKE 'HOLY FUCK IT'S ON ME NOW!'
THAT'S WHEN EVERYBODY TURNED INTO 'TERRY FOXES'! I NEVER RAN THAT FAST IN MY LIFE!

shot

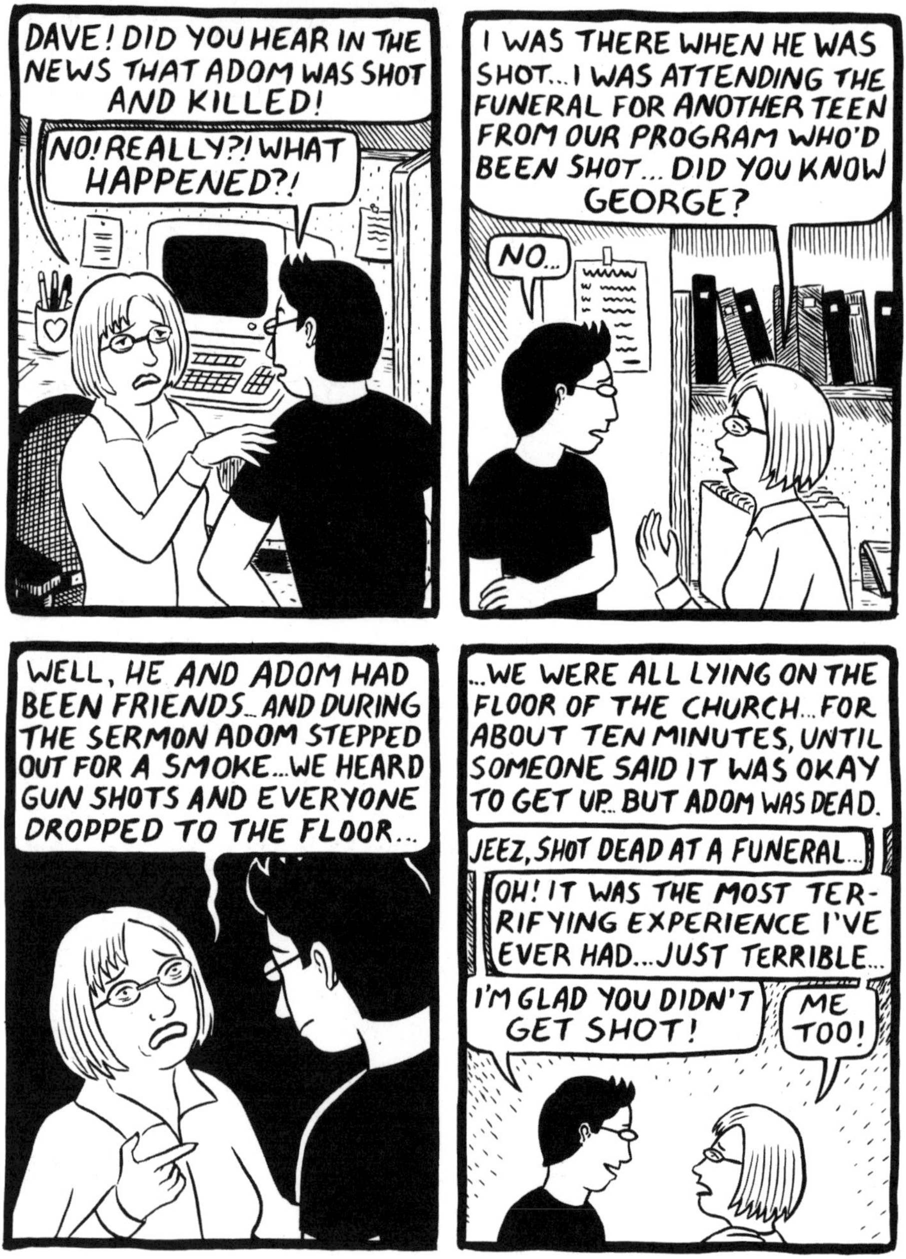
DAVE! DID YOU HEAR IN THE NEWS THAT ADOM WAS SHOT AND KILLED!
NO! REALLY?! WHAT HAPPENED?!
I WAS THERE WHEN HE WAS SHOT... I WAS ATTENDING THE FUNERAL FOR ANOTHER TEEN FROM OUR PROGRAM WHO'D BEEN SHOT... DID YOU KNOW GEORGE?
NO...
WELL, HE AND ADOM HAD BEEN FRIENDS... AND DURING THE SERMON ADOM STEPPED OUT FOR A SMOKE... WE HEARD GUN SHOTS AND EVERYONE DROPPED TO THE FLOOR...
...WE WERE ALL LYING ON THE FLOOR OF THE CHURCH... FOR ABOUT TEN MINUTES, UNTIL SOMEONE SAID IT WAS OKAY TO GET UP... BUT ADOM WAS DEAD.
JEEZ, SHOT DEAD AT A FUNERAL...
OH! IT WAS THE MOST TERRIFYING EXPERIENCE I'VE EVER HAD... JUST TERRIBLE...
I'M GLAD YOU DIDN'T GET SHOT!
ME TOO!

shot

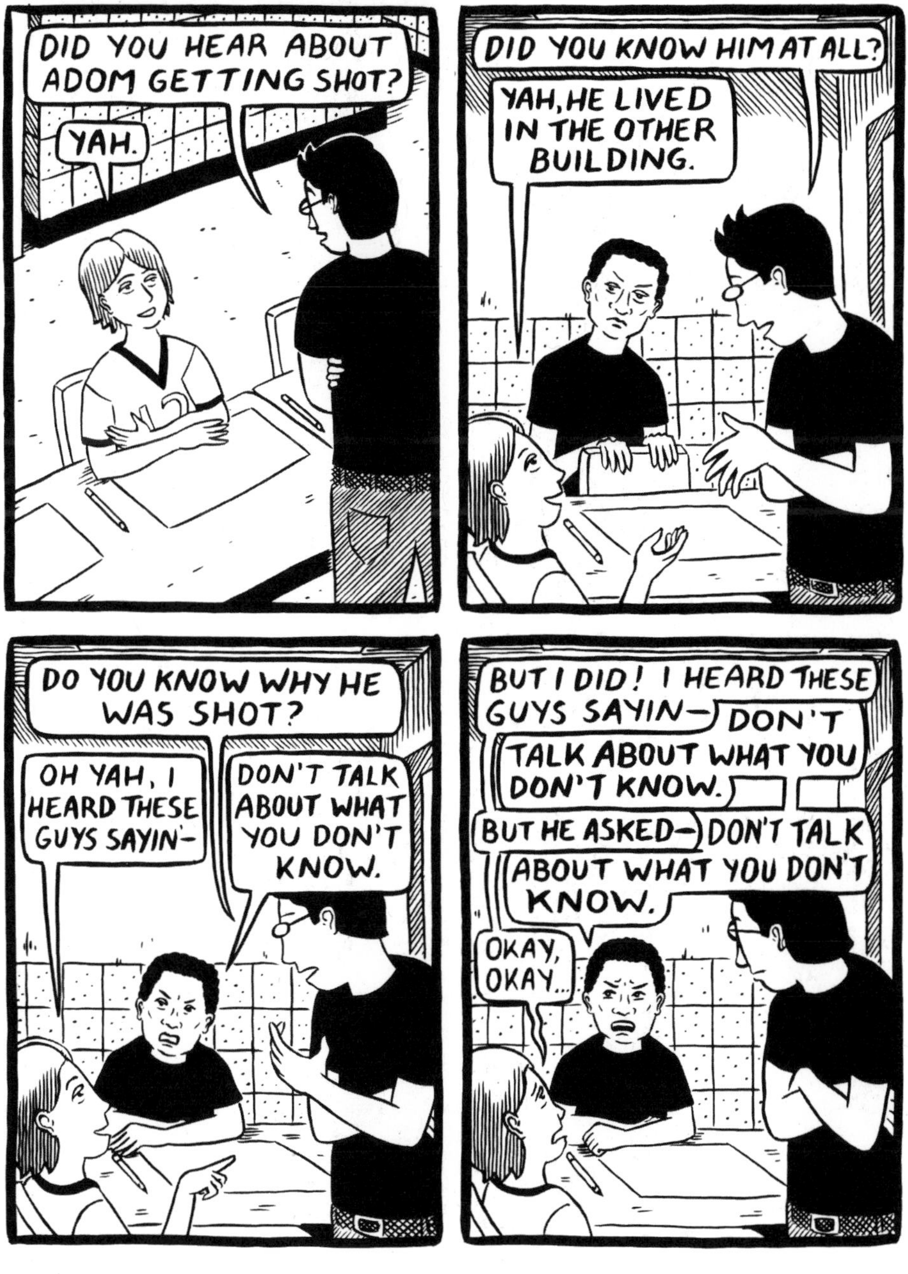
DID YOU HEAR ABOUT ADOM GETTING SHOT?
YAH.
DID YOU KNOW HIM AT ALL?
YAH, HE LIVED IN THE OTHER BUILDING.
DO YOU KNOW WHY HE WAS SHOT?
OH YAH, I HEARD THESE GUYS SAYIN'-
DON'T TALK ABOUT WHAT YOU DON'T KNOW.
BUT I DID! I HEARD THESE GUYS SAYIN-
DON'T TALK ABOUT WHAT YOU DON'T KNOW.
BUT HE ASKED-
DON'T TALK ABOUT WHAT YOU DON'T KNOW.
OKAY, OKAY...

shot

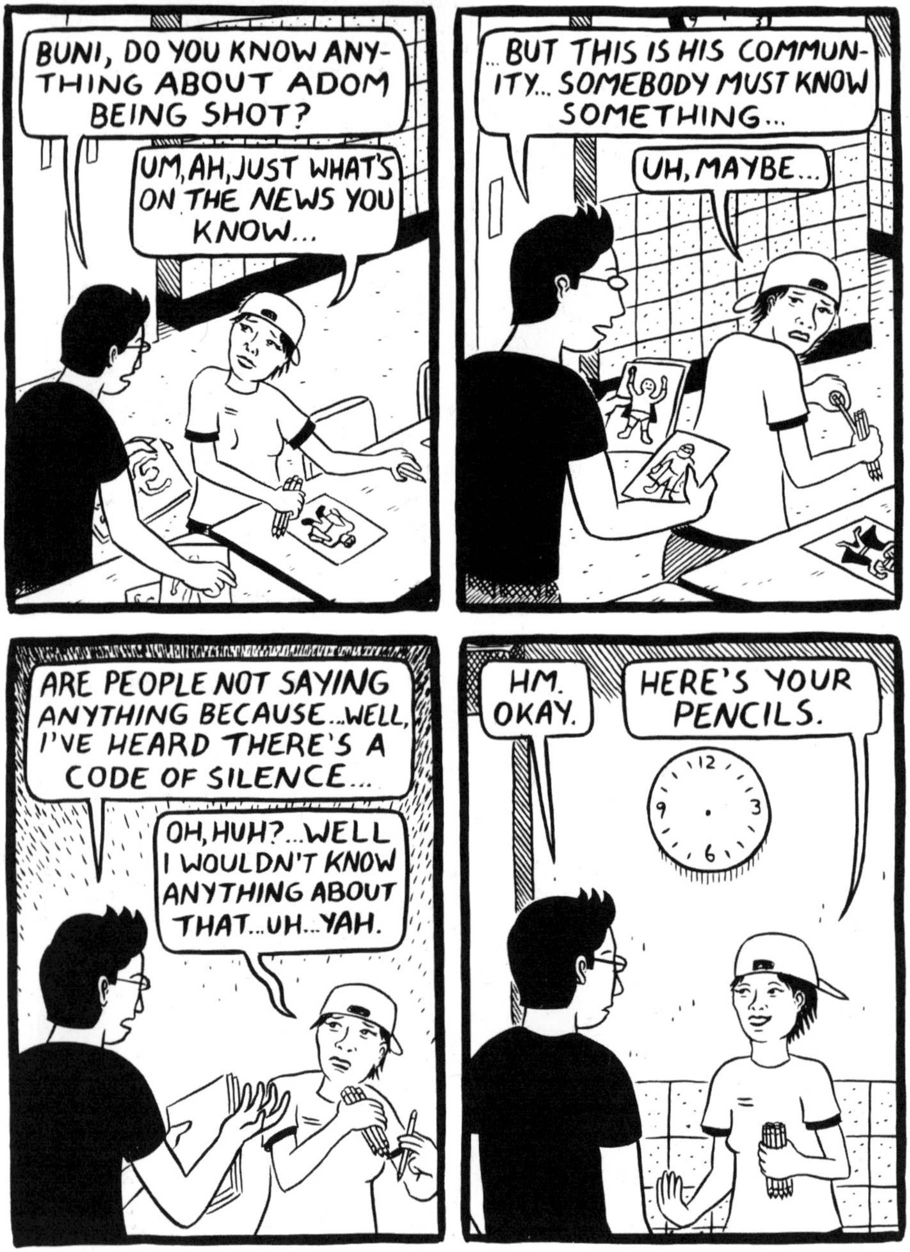
BUNI, DO YOU KNOW ANYTHING ABOUT ADOM BEING SHOT?
UM, AH, JUST WHAT'S ON THE NEWS YOU KNOW...
...BUT THIS IS HIS COMMUNITY... SOMEBODY MUST KNOW SOMETHING...
UH, MAYBE...
ARE PEOPLE NOT SAYING ANYTHING BECAUSE...WELL, I'VE HEARD THERE'S A CODE OF SILENCE...
OH, HUH?...WELL I WOULDN'T KNOW ANYTHING ABOUT THAT...UH...YAH.
HM. OKAY.
HERE'S YOUR PENCILS.

props

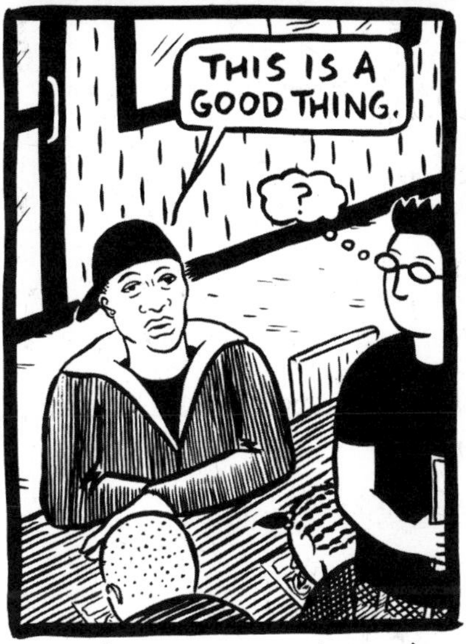
THIS IS A GOOD THING.
?

Jesus! This guy is huge!... never seen him before... uh oh he's speaking to me...

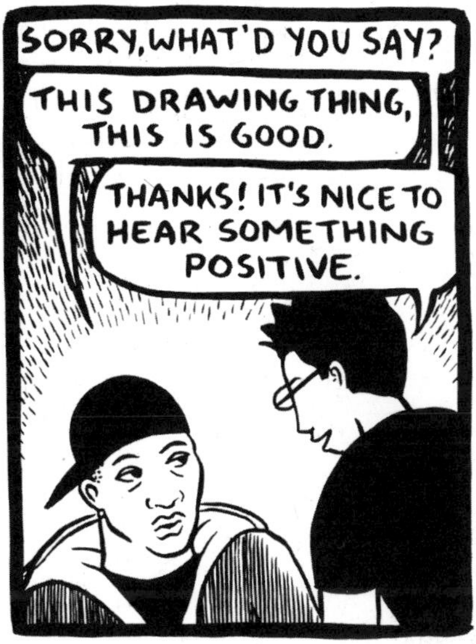
SORRY, WHAT'D YOU SAY?
THIS DRAWING THING, THIS IS GOOD.
THANKS! IT'S NICE TO HEAR SOMETHING POSITIVE.

I'm shocked! Everything is a fight here and this guy is being positive ...?! What's the catch?

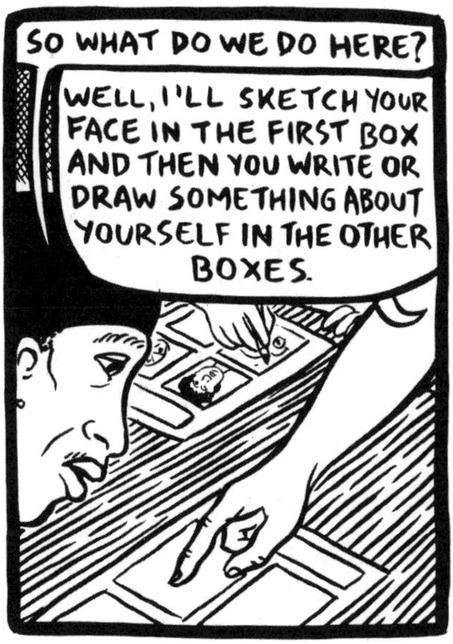
SO WHAT DO WE DO HERE?
WELL, I'LL SKETCH YOUR FACE IN THE FIRST BOX AND THEN YOU WRITE OR DRAW SOMETHING ABOUT YOURSELF IN THE OTHER BOXES.

Stick with the program... sigh... we'll see if he actually does anything...

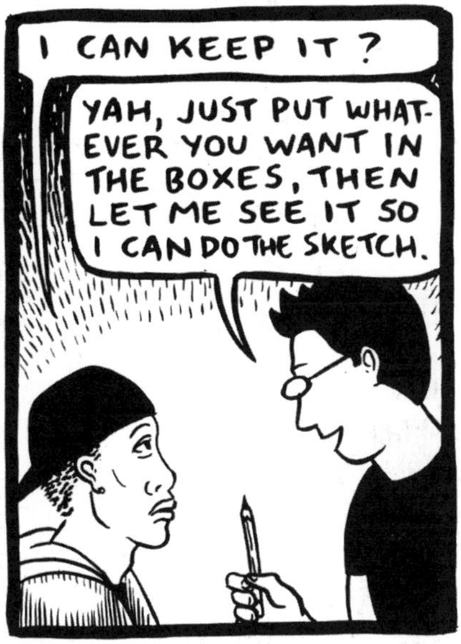
I CAN KEEP IT ?
YAH, JUST PUT WHATEVER YOU WANT IN THE BOXES, THEN LET ME SEE IT SO I CAN DO THE SKETCH.

He speaks without blinking or smiling... no affect... he makes me nervous...

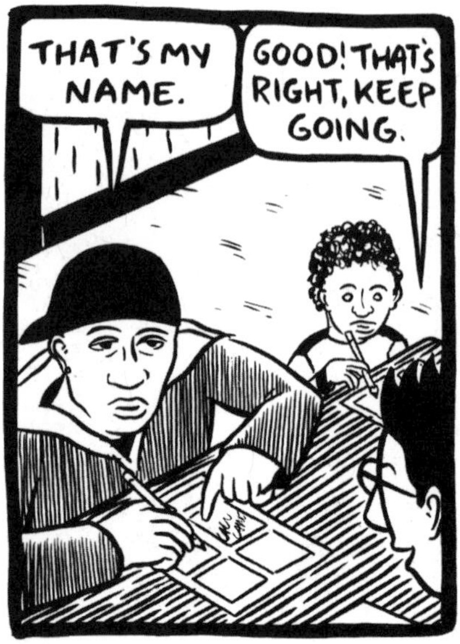
THAT'S MY NAME.
GOOD! THAT'S RIGHT, KEEP GOING.

He shows me his first panel, 'Cali-Caine'...

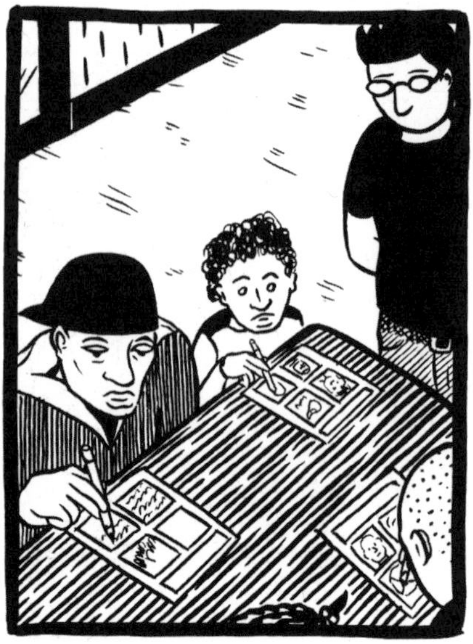

Lots of drawing is happening today and after seven months of this program, this is the best day so far!

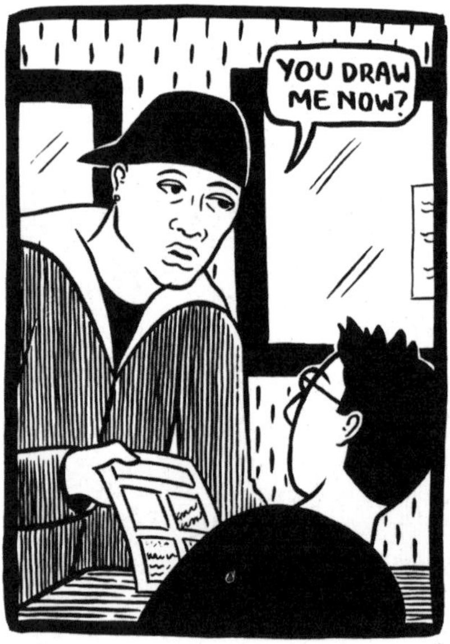
YOU DRAW ME NOW?

Cali-Caine has finished his page and he really wants me to do his sketch.

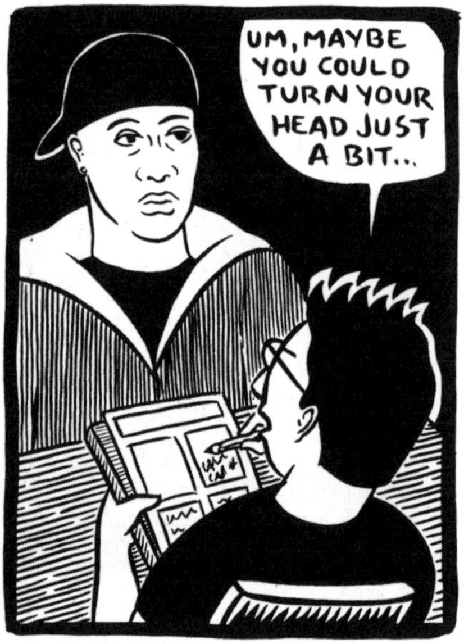
UM, MAYBE YOU COULD TURN YOUR HEAD JUST A BIT...

He sits across from me staring straight at me... unblinking... it's too much, so I try to get him to turn his head a bit...

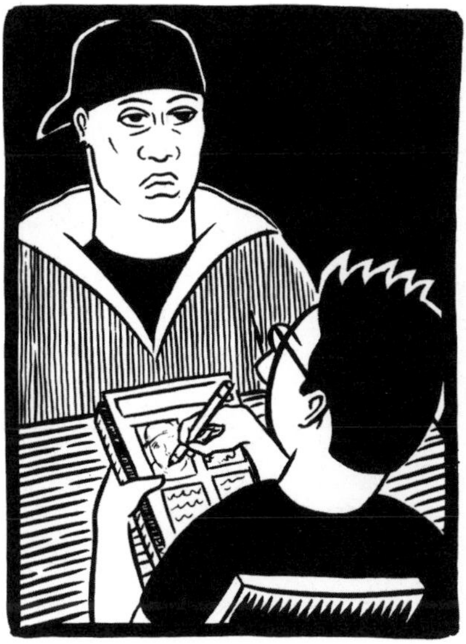

...he turns back and continues staring at me... he does not blink.

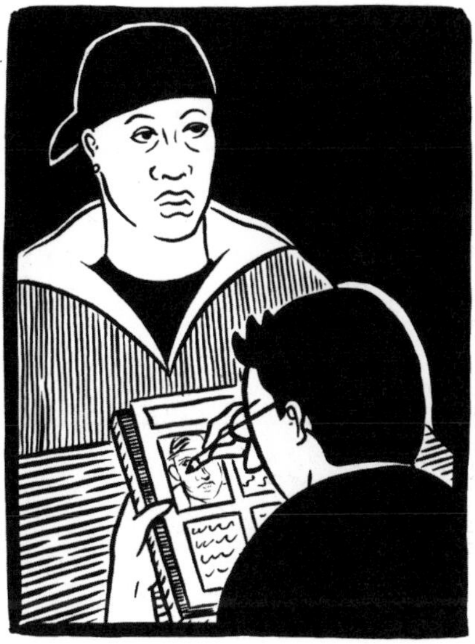

I feel extra pressure to draw well...he's so intense... if I do poorly...I can't let him down.

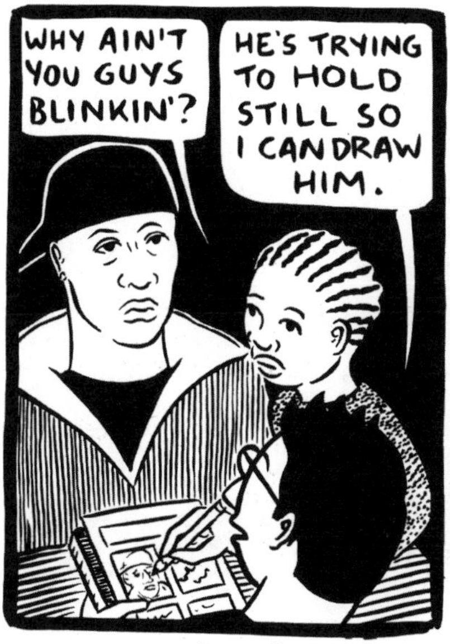
WHY AIN'T YOU GUYS BLINKIN'?
HE'S TRYING TO HOLD STILL SO I CAN DRAW HIM.

Breanna lightens the tension...

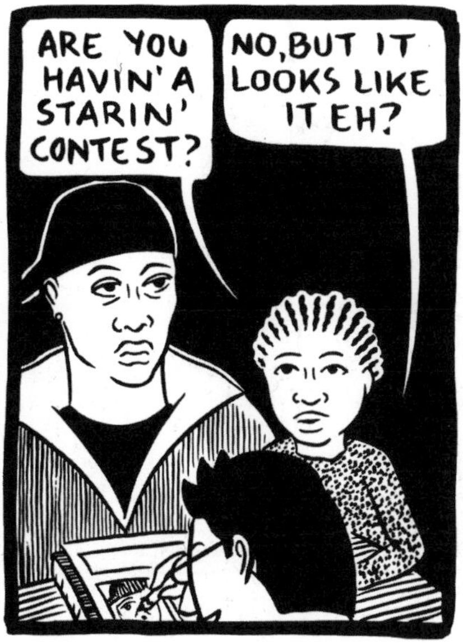
ARE YOU HAVIN' A STARIN' CONTEST?
NO, BUT IT LOOKS LIKE IT EH?

... I'm so worried I'll insult him with a bad drawing...

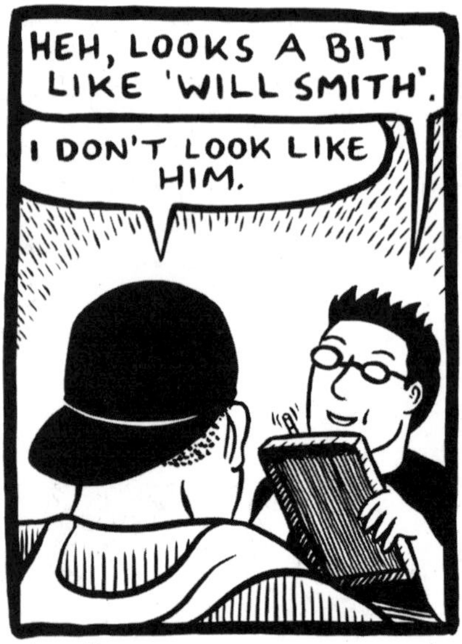
HEH, LOOKS A BIT LIKE 'WILL SMITH'.
I DON'T LOOK LIKE HIM.

I'm finishing the sketch and it's a good one ... I try to make a little comment...

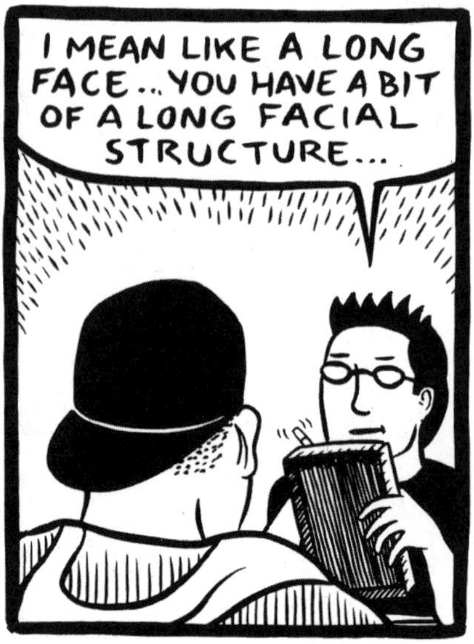
I MEAN LIKE A LONG FACE... YOU HAVE A BIT OF A LONG FACIAL STRUCTURE...

Whew mistake! Recover, recover!

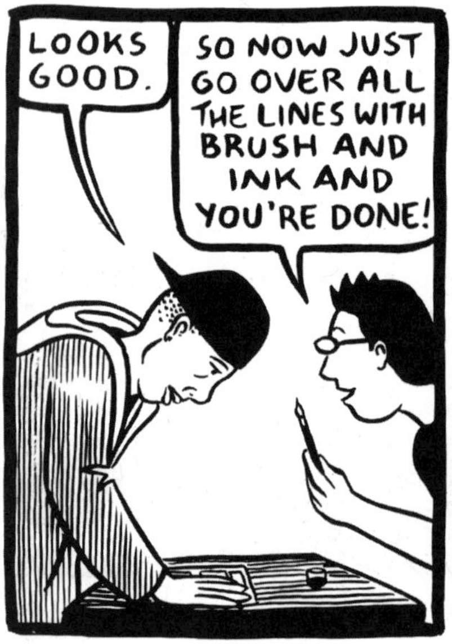
LOOKS GOOD.
SO NOW JUST GO OVER ALL THE LINES WITH BRUSH AND INK AND YOU'RE DONE!

So I show him some brush and ink techniques and let him go to it.

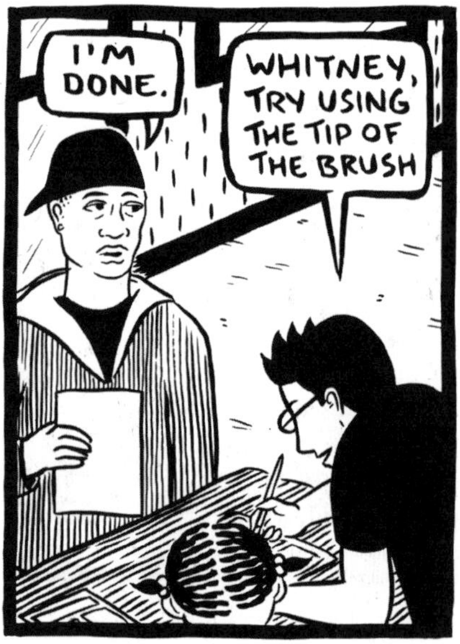
I'M DONE.
WHITNEY, TRY USING THE TIP OF THE BRUSH

I walk around the tables checking everybody's work...

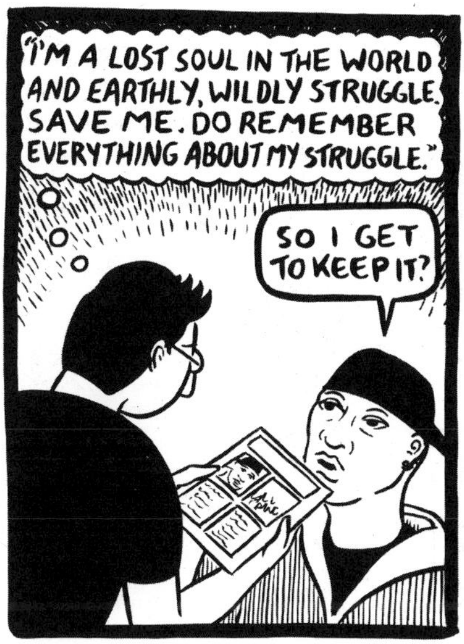
"I'M A LOST SOUL IN THE WORLD AND EARTHLY, WILDLY STRUGGLE. SAVE ME. DO REMEMBER EVERYTHING ABOUT MY STRUGGLE."
SO I GET TO KEEP IT?

God... Are these his real thoughts and feelings...? Are they song lyrics?

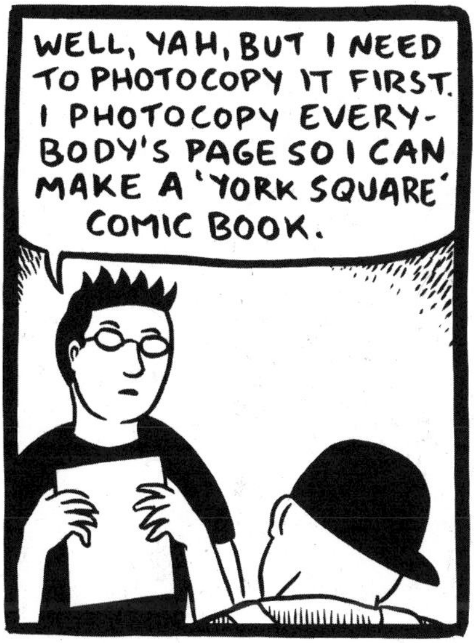
WELL, YAH, BUT I NEED TO PHOTOCOPY IT FIRST. I PHOTOCOPY EVERY-BODY'S PAGE SO I CAN MAKE A 'YORK SQUARE' COMIC BOOK.

He wants the art, but I must first use it to make a comic book for this place!

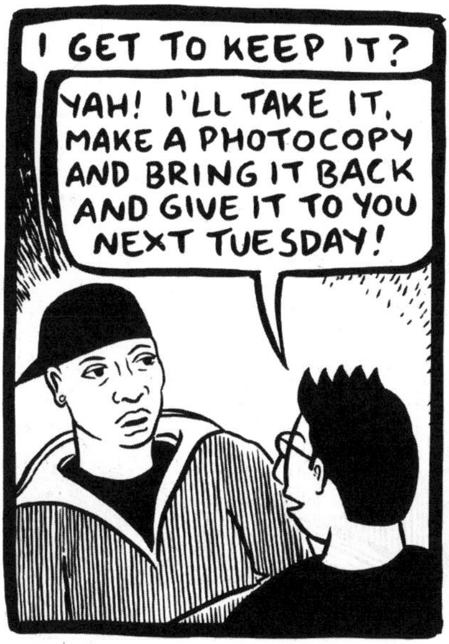
I GET TO KEEP IT?
YAH! I'LL TAKE IT, MAKE A PHOTOCOPY AND BRING IT BACK AND GIVE IT TO YOU NEXT TUESDAY!

He wants the page now... but I stand my ground. This page has got to be in the book...

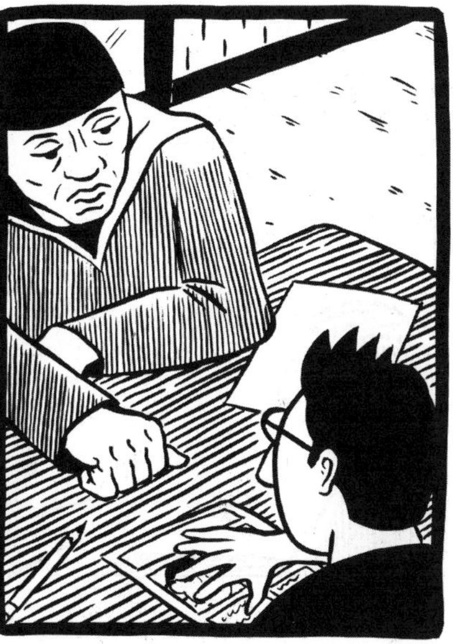

Cali-Caine extends his fist across the table toward me...

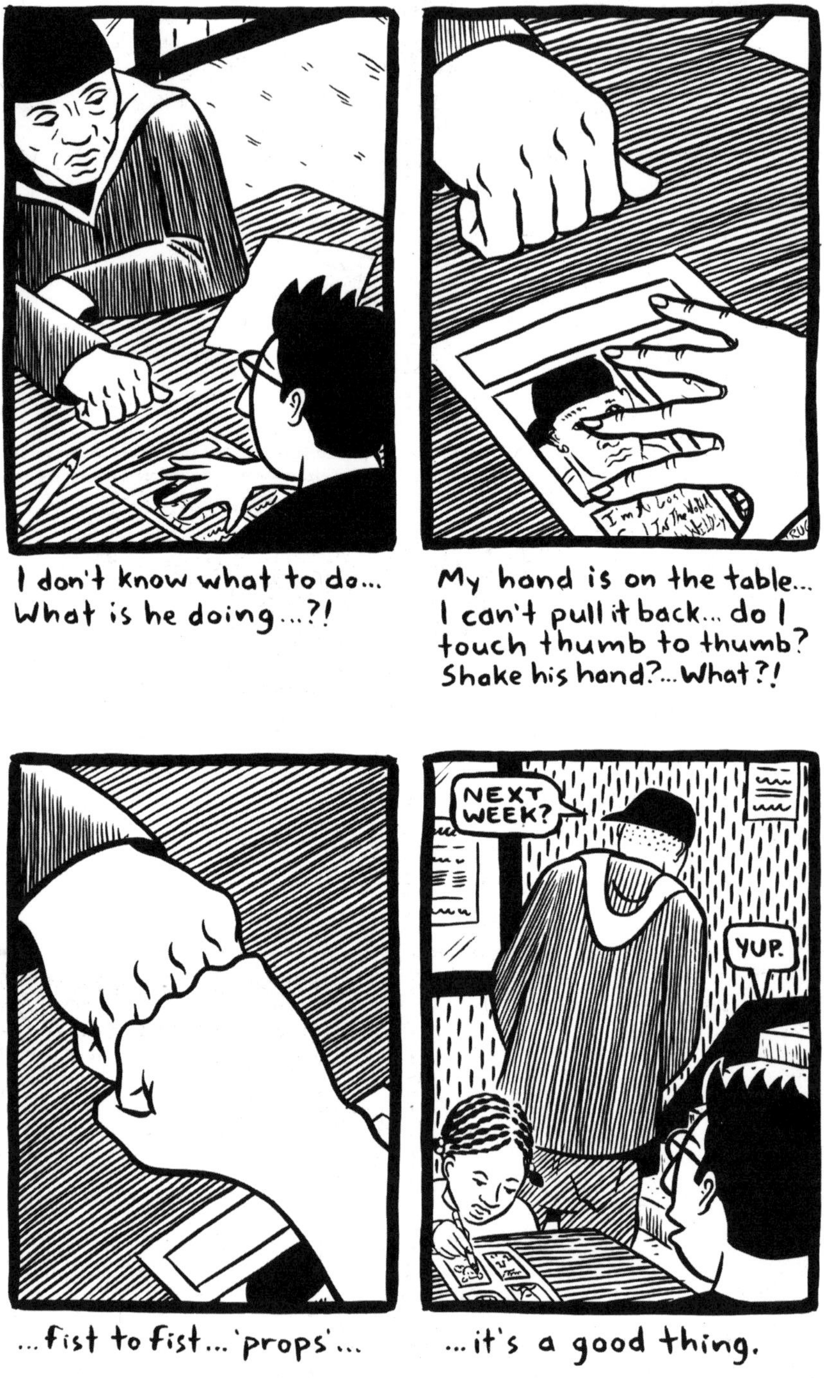
I don't know what to do... What is he doing...?!
My hand is on the table... I can't pull it back... do I touch thumb to thumb? Shake his hand?...What?!
...fist to fist... 'props'...
NEXT WEEK?
YUP.
...it's a good thing.